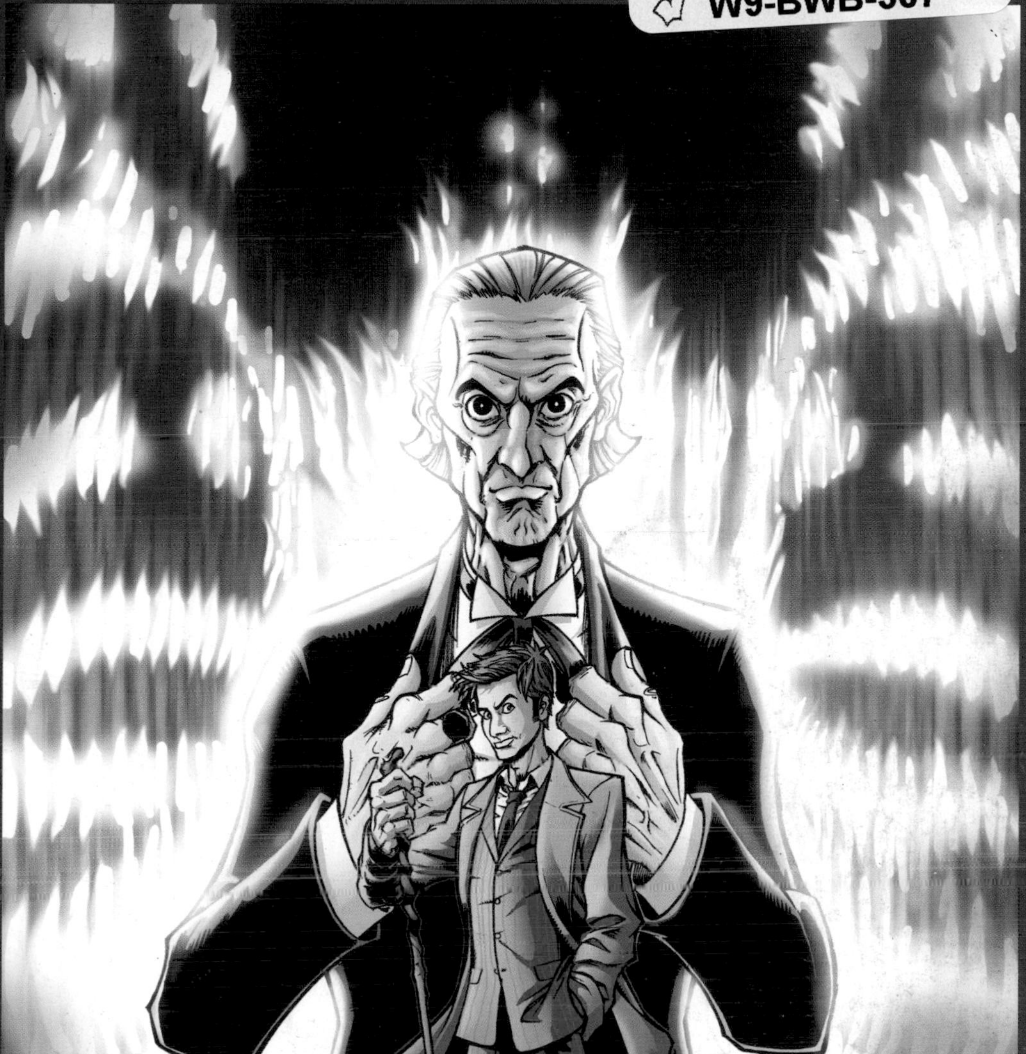
NICK 08-CK

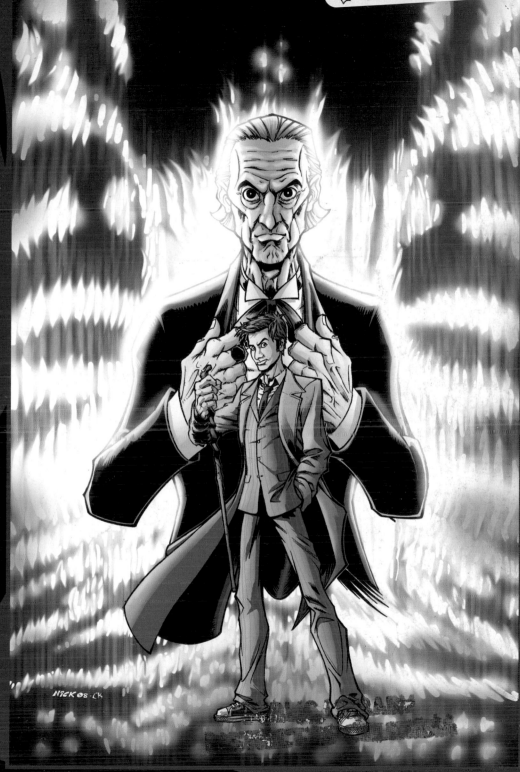

ART BY NICK ROCHE • COLOR BY CHARLIE KIRCHOFF

CHAPTER • ONE
AMPUTATION

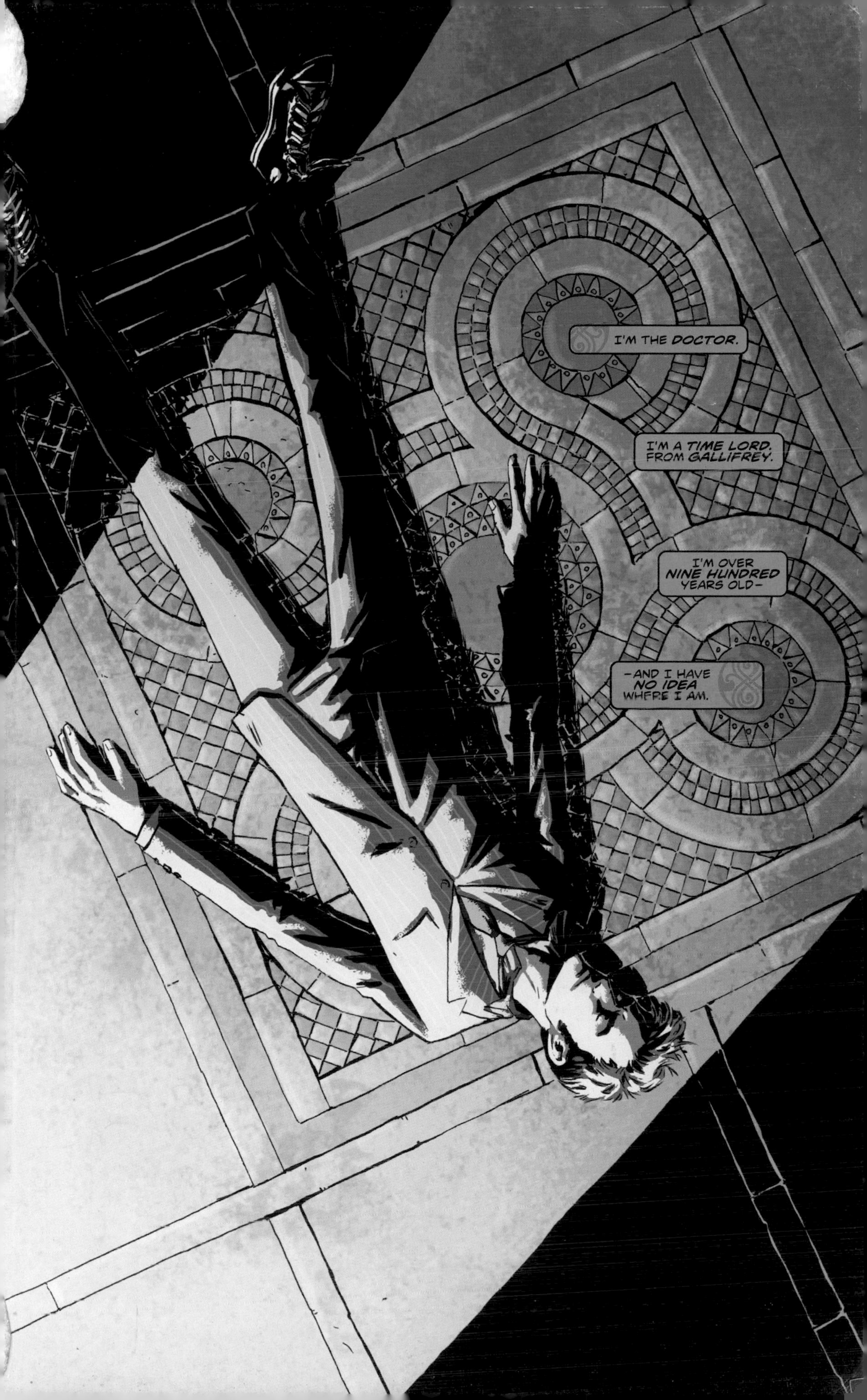
I'M THE DOCTOR.
I'M A TIME LORD. FROM GALLIFREY.
I'M OVER NINE HUNDRED YEARS OLD–
–AND I HAVE NO IDEA WHERE I AM.

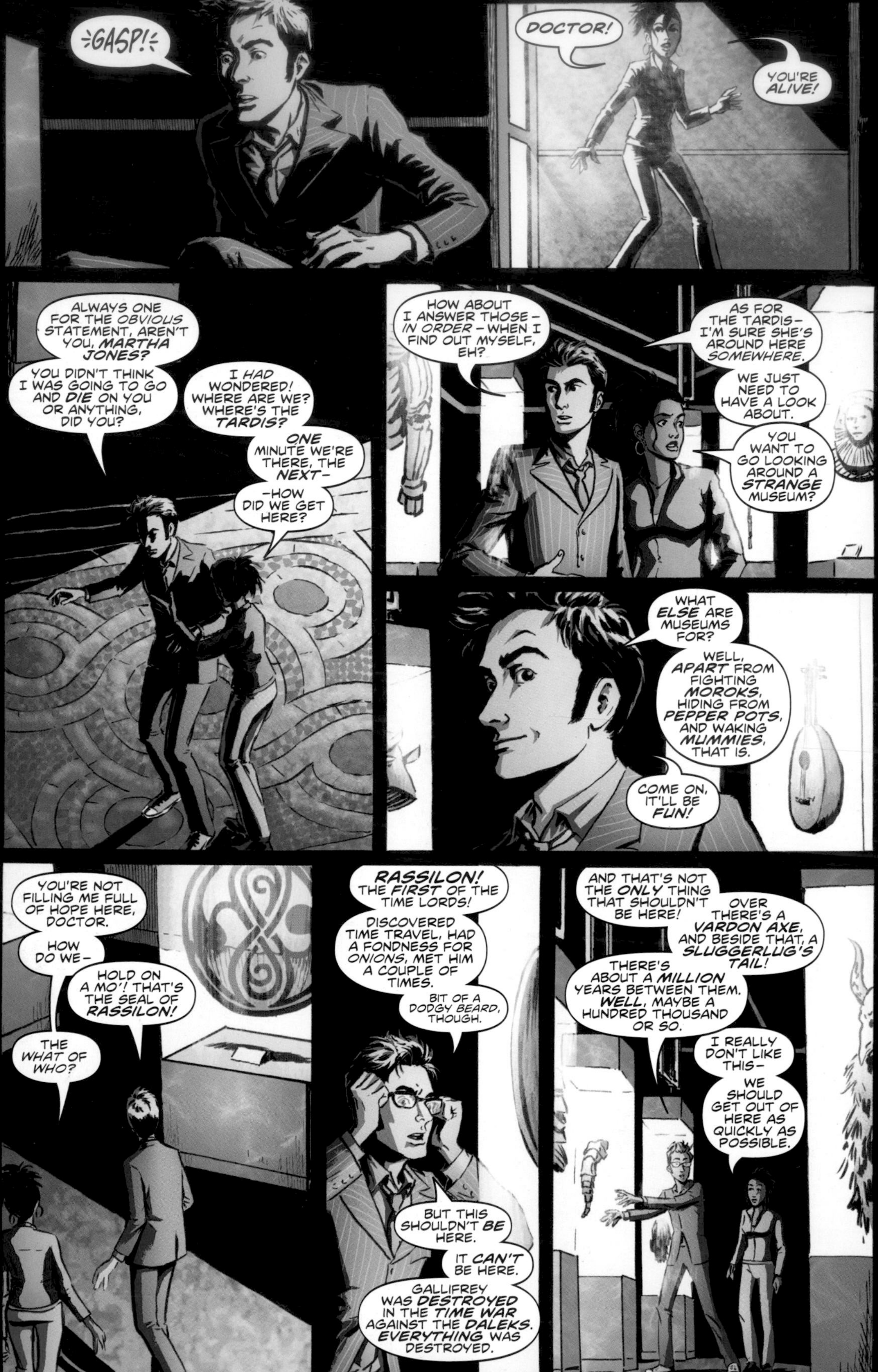
GASP!
DOCTOR!
YOU'RE ALIVE!
ALWAYS ONE FOR THE OBVIOUS STATEMENT, AREN'T YOU, MARTHA JONES?
YOU DIDN'T THINK I WAS GOING TO GO AND DIE ON YOU OR ANYTHING, DID YOU?
I HAD WONDERED! WHERE ARE WE? WHERE'S THE TARDIS?
ONE MINUTE WE'RE THERE, THE NEXT–
–HOW DID WE GET HERE?
HOW ABOUT I ANSWER THOSE– IN ORDER– WHEN I FIND OUT MYSELF, EH?
AS FOR THE TARDIS– I'M SURE SHE'S AROUND HERE SOMEWHERE.
WE JUST NEED TO HAVE A LOOK ABOUT.
YOU WANT TO GO LOOKING AROUND A STRANGE MUSEUM?
WHAT ELSE ARE MUSEUMS FOR?
WELL, APART FROM FIGHTING MOROKS, HIDING FROM PEPPER POTS, AND WAKING MUMMIES, THAT IS.
COME ON, IT'LL BE FUN!
YOU'RE NOT FILLING ME FULL OF HOPE HERE, DOCTOR.
HOW DO WE–
HOLD ON A MO'! THAT'S THE SEAL OF RASSILON!
THE WHAT OF WHO?
RASSILON! THE FIRST OF THE TIME LORDS!
DISCOVERED TIME TRAVEL, HAD A FONDNESS FOR ONIONS, MET HIM A COUPLE OF TIMES.
BIT OF A DODGY BEARD, THOUGH.
BUT THIS SHOULDN'T BE HERE.
IT CAN'T BE HERE.
GALLIFREY WAS DESTROYED IN THE TIME WAR AGAINST THE DALEKS. EVERYTHING WAS DESTROYED.
AND THAT'S NOT THE ONLY THING THAT SHOULDN'T BE HERE!
OVER THERE'S A VARDON AXE, AND BESIDE THAT, A SLUGGERLUG'S TAIL!
THERE'S ABOUT A MILLION YEARS BETWEEN THEM. WELL, MAYBE A HUNDRED THOUSAND OR SO.
I REALLY DON'T LIKE THIS–
WE SHOULD GET OUT OF HERE AS QUICKLY AS POSSIBLE.

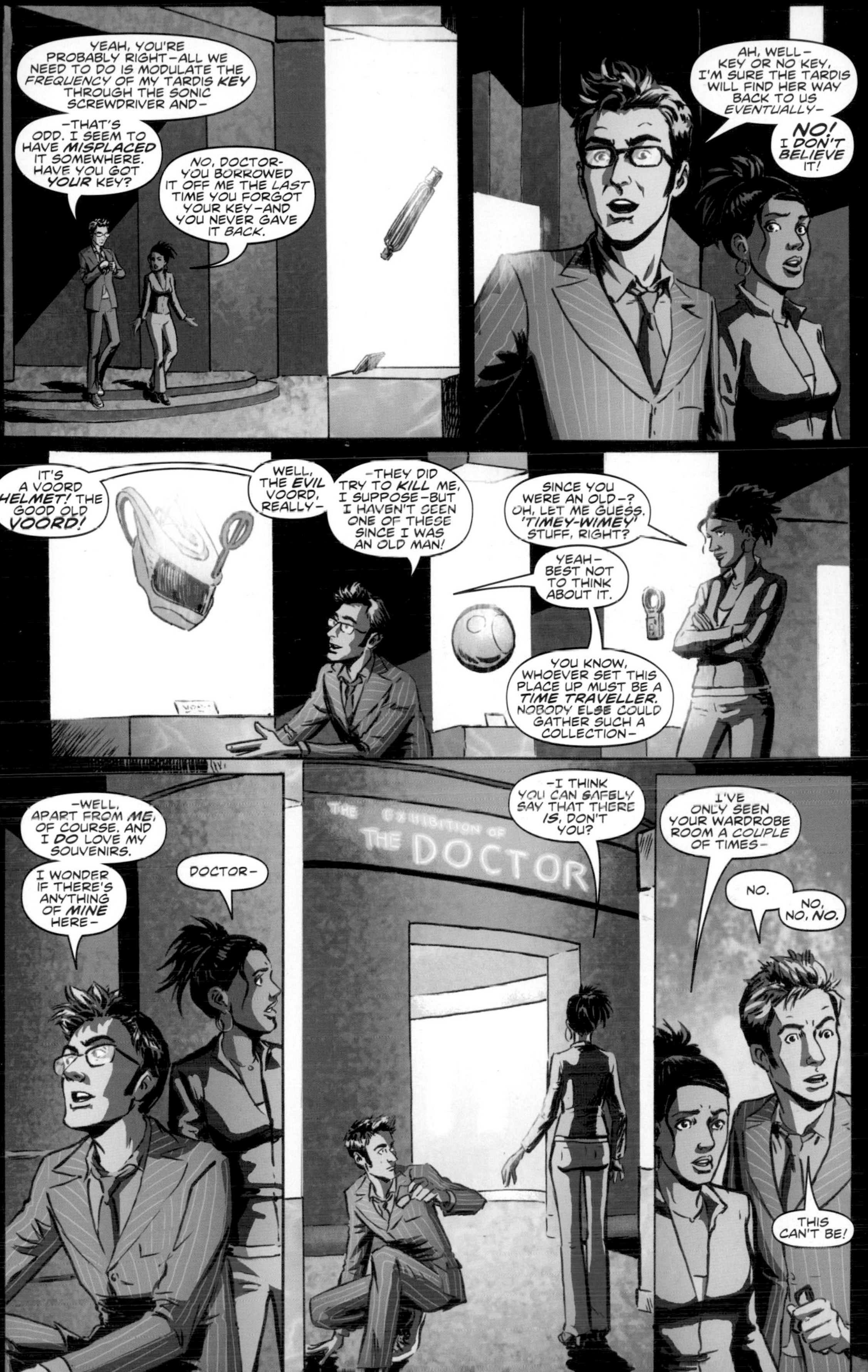
YEAH, YOU'RE PROBABLY RIGHT–ALL WE NEED TO DO IS MODULATE THE FREQUENCY OF MY TARDIS KEY THROUGH THE SONIC SCREWDRIVER AND–
–THAT'S ODD. I SEEM TO HAVE MISPLACED IT SOMEWHERE. HAVE YOU GOT YOUR KEY?
NO, DOCTOR– YOU BORROWED IT OFF ME THE LAST TIME YOU FORGOT YOUR KEY–AND YOU NEVER GAVE IT BACK.
AH, WELL– KEY OR NO KEY, I'M SURE THE TARDIS WILL FIND HER WAY BACK TO US EVENTUALLY–
NO! I DON'T BELIEVE IT!
IT'S A VOORD HELMET! THE GOOD OLD VOORD!
WELL, THE EVIL VOORD, REALLY–
–THEY DID TRY TO KILL ME, I SUPPOSE–BUT I HAVEN'T SEEN ONE OF THESE SINCE I WAS AN OLD MAN!
SINCE YOU WERE AN OLD–? OH, LET ME GUESS. 'TIMEY-WIMEY' STUFF, RIGHT?
YEAH– BEST NOT TO THINK ABOUT IT.
YOU KNOW, WHOEVER SET THIS PLACE UP MUST BE A TIME TRAVELLER. NOBODY ELSE COULD GATHER SUCH A COLLECTION–
–WELL, APART FROM ME, OF COURSE. AND I DO LOVE MY SOUVENIRS.
I WONDER IF THERE'S ANYTHING OF MINE HERE–
DOCTOR–
THE EXHIBITION OF THE DOCTOR
–I THINK YOU CAN SAFELY SAY THAT THERE IS, DON'T YOU?
I'VE ONLY SEEN YOUR WARDROBE ROOM A COUPLE OF TIMES–
NO.
NO, NO, NO.
THIS CAN'T BE!

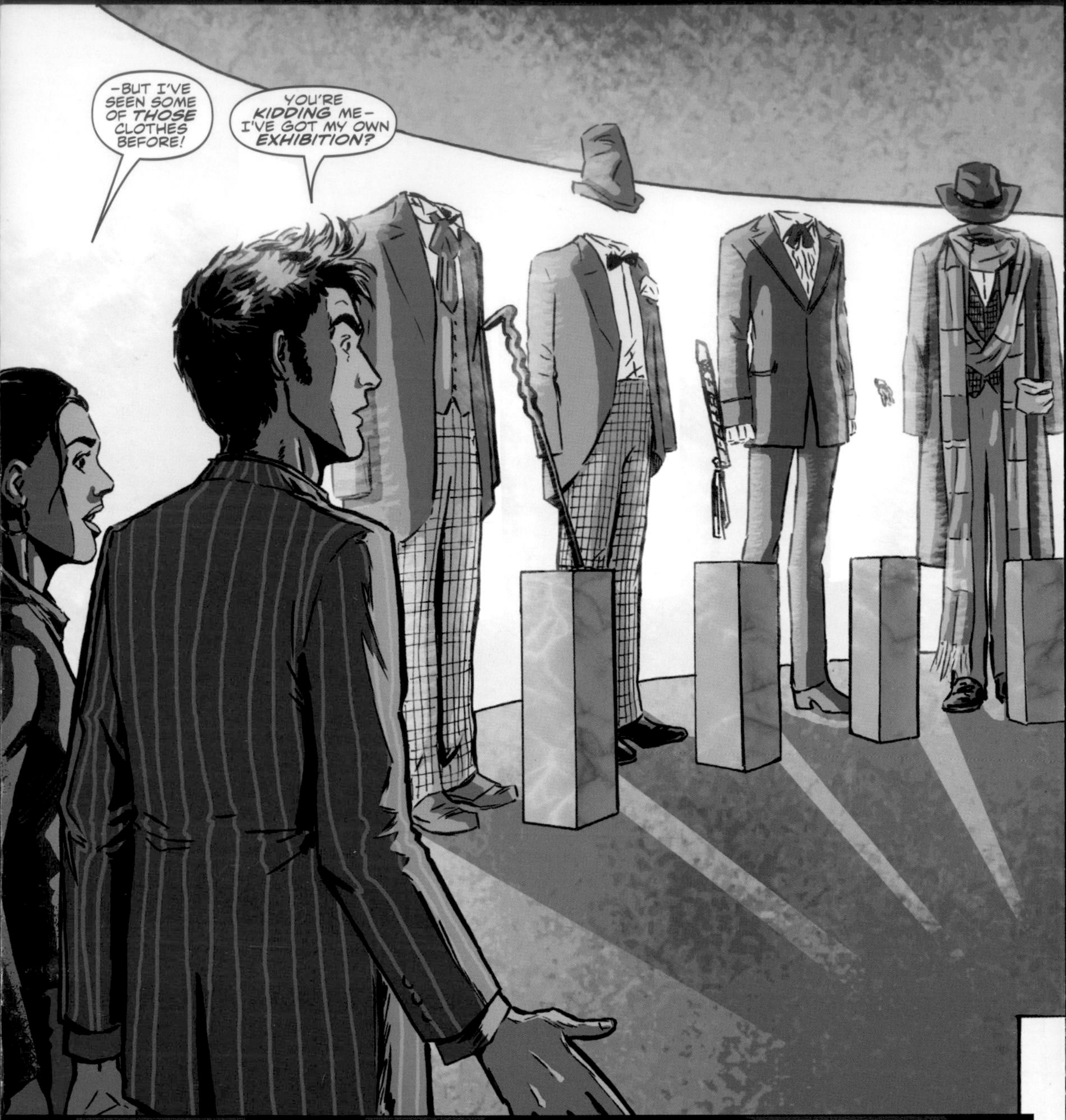
-BUT I'VE SEEN SOME OF THOSE CLOTHES BEFORE!
YOU'RE KIDDING ME-I'VE GOT MY OWN EXHIBITION?

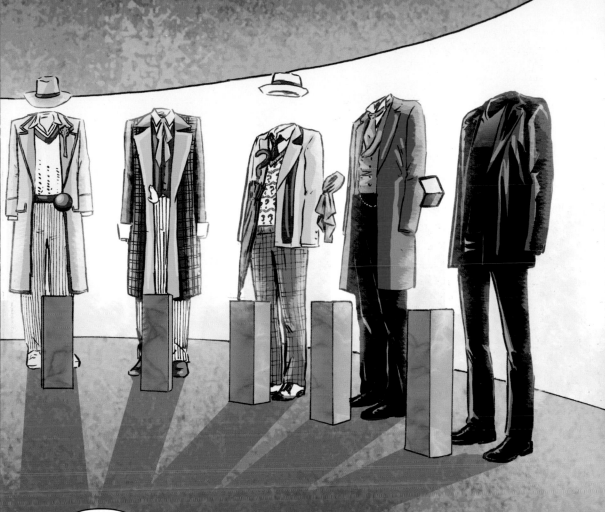

I'M *RIGHT*, AREN'T I?

YOU USED TO WEAR THESE! I MEAN, I THOUGHT TRAINERS AND A PIN STRIPE WAS A BIT WRONG –

– BUT LOOK AT *THAT* MULTI-COLORED *THING*! WERE YOU AUDITIONING FOR *JOSEPH* OR SOMETHING?

COME ON, MARTHA– EVERYONE HAS FASHION DISASTERS IN THEIR PAST. THEIR *SCARVES*, THEIR *HATS*, THEIR...

...VEGETATION.

BUT THERE'S NO *WAY* THAT SOMEONE COULD HAVE DONE THIS. NOBODY KNOWS ABOUT ALL *NINE*.

NOBODY STILL *ALIVE*, ANYWAY

THE TIME LORDS ARE *DEAD*. AND WITH THEM DIED SECRETS LIKE THIS.

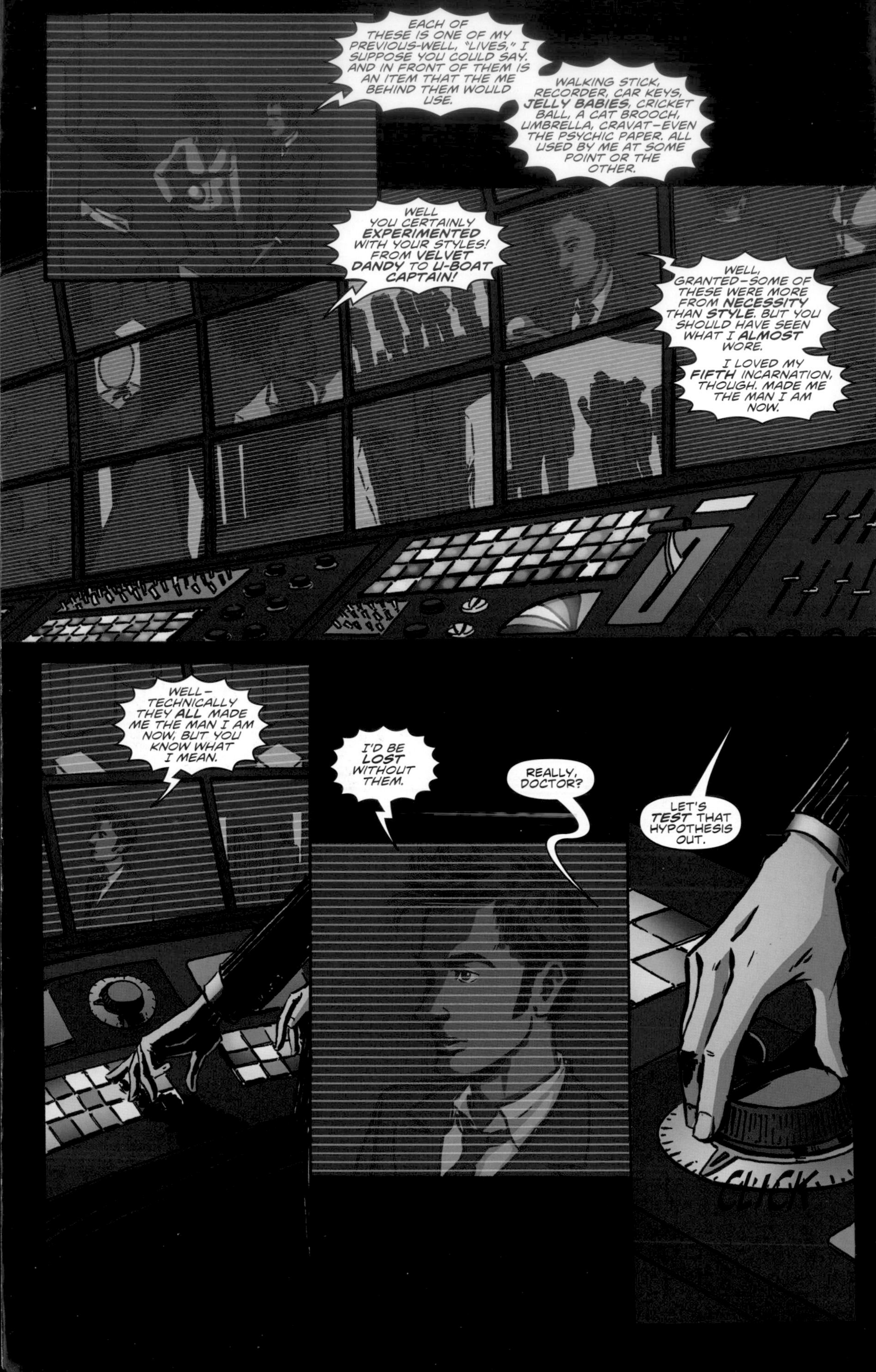

EACH OF THESE IS ONE OF MY PREVIOUS-WELL, "LIVES," I SUPPOSE YOU COULD SAY. AND IN FRONT OF THEM IS AN ITEM THAT THE ME BEHIND THEM WOULD USE.
WALKING STICK, RECORDER, CAR KEYS, JELLY BABIES, CRICKET BALL, A CAT BROOCH, UMBRELLA, CRAVAT–EVEN THE PSYCHIC PAPER. ALL USED BY ME AT SOME POINT OR THE OTHER.
WELL YOU CERTAINLY EXPERIMENTED WITH YOUR STYLES! FROM VELVET DANDY TO U-BOAT CAPTAIN!
WELL, GRANTED–SOME OF THESE WERE MORE FROM NECESSITY THAN STYLE. BUT YOU SHOULD HAVE SEEN WHAT I ALMOST WORE.
I LOVED MY FIFTH INCARNATION, THOUGH. MADE ME THE MAN I AM NOW.
WELL–TECHNICALLY THEY ALL MADE ME THE MAN I AM NOW, BUT YOU KNOW WHAT I MEAN.
I'D BE LOST WITHOUT THEM.
REALLY, DOCTOR?
LET'S TEST THAT HYPOTHESIS OUT.
CLICK

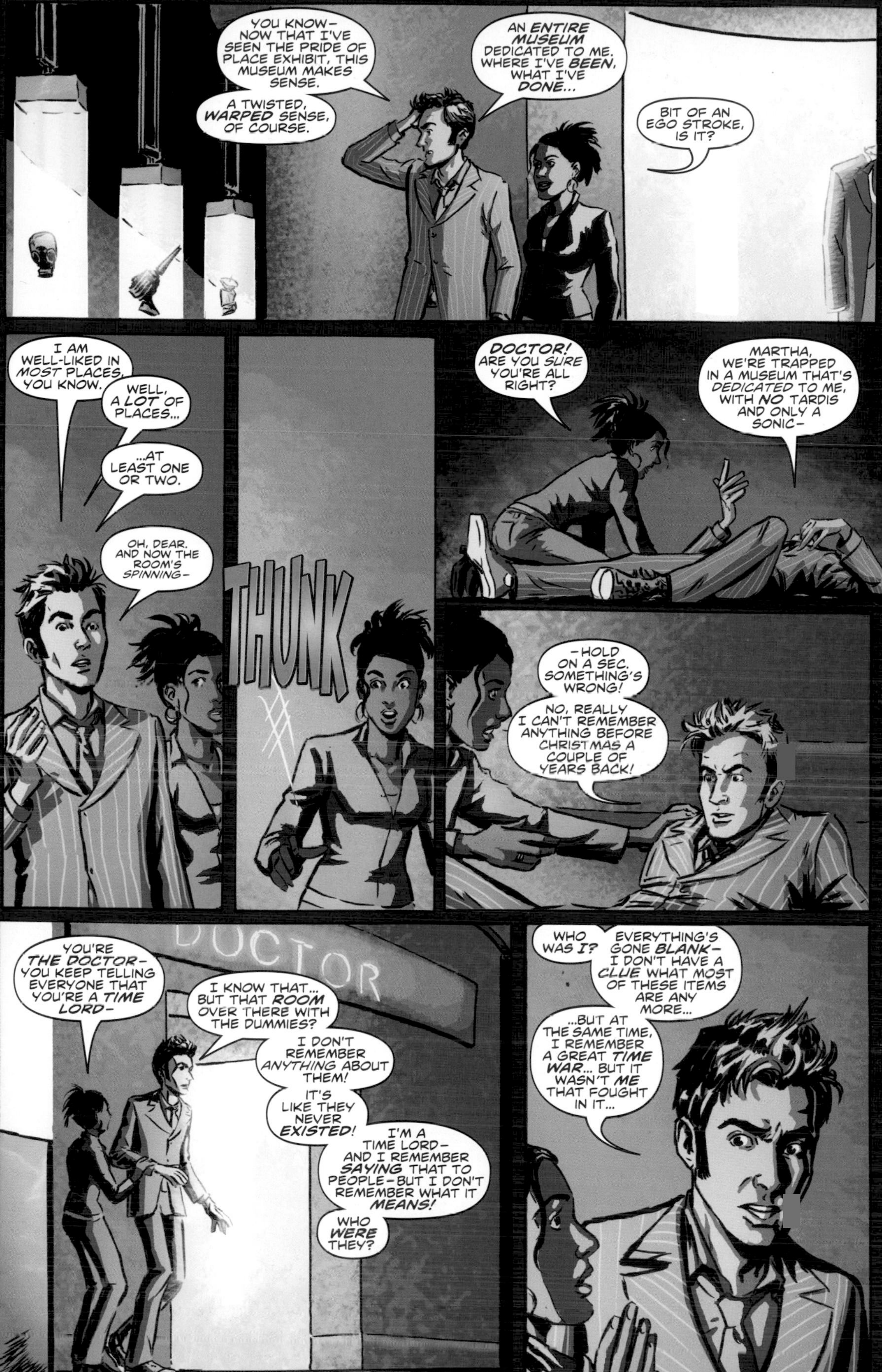
YOU KNOW–NOW THAT I'VE SEEN THE PRIDE OF PLACE EXHIBIT, THIS MUSEUM MAKES SENSE.
A TWISTED, WARPED SENSE, OF COURSE.
AN ENTIRE MUSEUM DEDICATED TO ME. WHERE I'VE BEEN, WHAT I'VE DONE...
BIT OF AN EGO STROKE, IS IT?
I AM WELL-LIKED IN MOST PLACES, YOU KNOW.
WELL, A LOT OF PLACES...
...AT LEAST ONE OR TWO.
OH, DEAR. AND NOW THE ROOM'S SPINNING–
THUNK
DOCTOR! ARE YOU SURE YOU'RE ALL RIGHT?
MARTHA, WE'RE TRAPPED IN A MUSEUM THAT'S DEDICATED TO ME, WITH NO TARDIS AND ONLY A SONIC–
–HOLD ON A SEC. SOMETHING'S WRONG!
NO, REALLY I CAN'T REMEMBER ANYTHING BEFORE CHRISTMAS A COUPLE OF YEARS BACK!
DOCTOR
YOU'RE THE DOCTOR–YOU KEEP TELLING EVERYONE THAT YOU'RE A TIME LORD–
I KNOW THAT... BUT THAT ROOM OVER THERE WITH THE DUMMIES?
I DON'T REMEMBER ANYTHING ABOUT THEM!
IT'S LIKE THEY NEVER EXISTED!
I'M A TIME LORD–AND I REMEMBER SAYING THAT TO PEOPLE–BUT I DON'T REMEMBER WHAT IT MEANS!
WHO WERE THEY?
WHO WAS I?
EVERYTHING'S GONE BLANK–I DON'T HAVE A CLUE WHAT MOST OF THESE ITEMS ARE ANY MORE...
...BUT AT THE SAME TIME, I REMEMBER A GREAT TIME WAR... BUT IT WASN'T ME THAT FOUGHT IN IT...

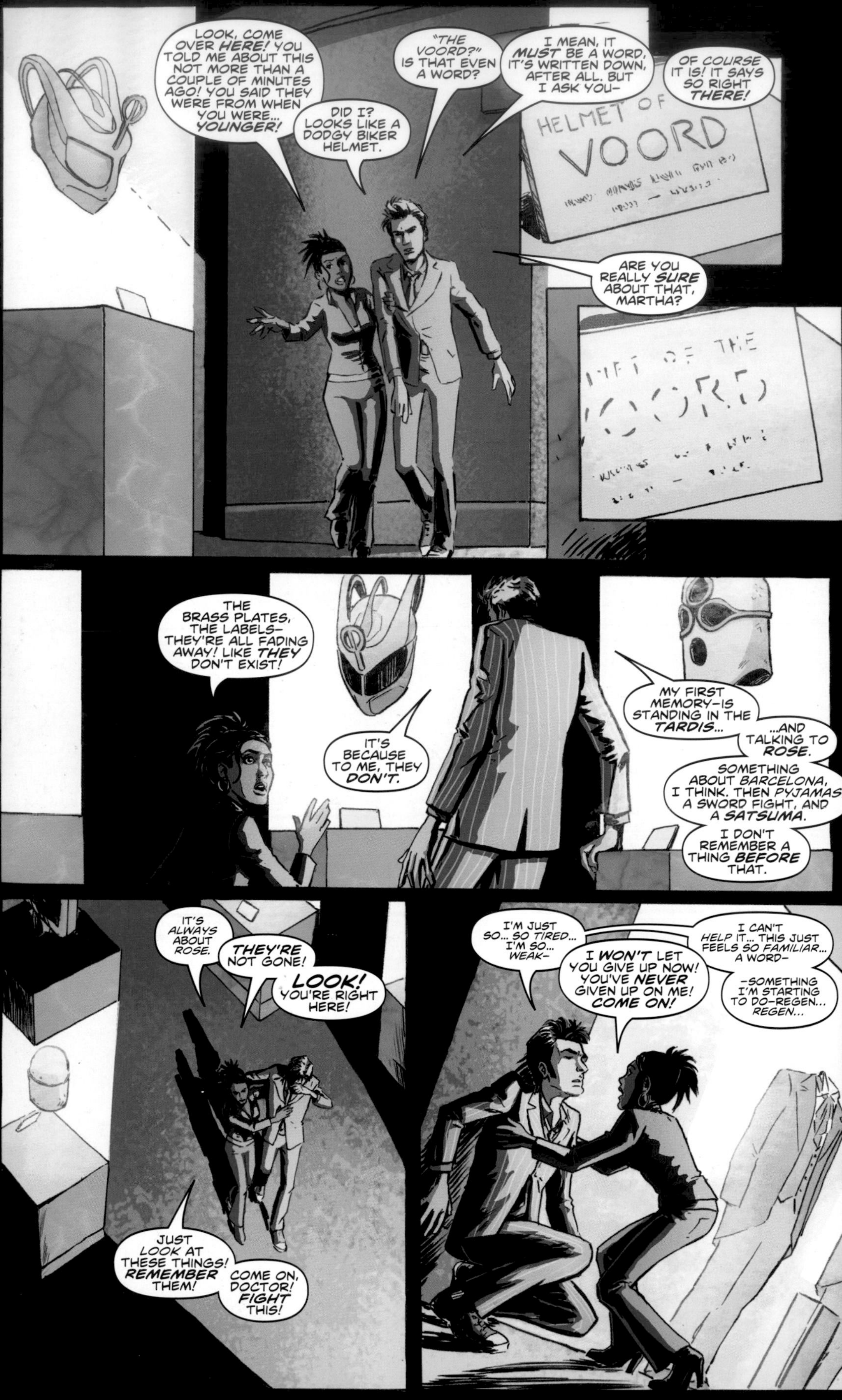

LOOK, COME OVER HERE! YOU TOLD ME ABOUT THIS NOT MORE THAN A COUPLE OF MINUTES AGO! YOU SAID THEY WERE FROM WHEN YOU WERE... YOUNGER!
DID I? LOOKS LIKE A DODGY BIKER HELMET.
"THE VOORD?" IS THAT EVEN A WORD?
I MEAN, IT MUST BE A WORD, IT'S WRITTEN DOWN, AFTER ALL. BUT I ASK YOU–
OF COURSE IT IS! IT SAYS SO RIGHT THERE!
HELMET OF VOORD
ARE YOU REALLY SURE ABOUT THAT, MARTHA?
THE BRASS PLATES, THE LABELS– THEY'RE ALL FADING AWAY! LIKE THEY DON'T EXIST!
IT'S BECAUSE TO ME, THEY DON'T.
MY FIRST MEMORY–IS STANDING IN THE TARDIS...
...AND TALKING TO ROSE.
SOMETHING ABOUT BARCELONA, I THINK. THEN PYJAMAS, A SWORD FIGHT, AND A SATSUMA.
I DON'T REMEMBER A THING BEFORE THAT.
IT'S ALWAYS ABOUT ROSE.
THEY'RE NOT GONE!
LOOK! YOU'RE RIGHT HERE!
JUST LOOK AT THESE THINGS! REMEMBER THEM!
COME ON, DOCTOR! FIGHT THIS!
I'M JUST SO... SO TIRED... I'M SO... WEAK–
I WON'T LET YOU GIVE UP NOW! YOU'VE NEVER GIVEN UP ON ME! COME ON!
I CAN'T HELP IT... THIS JUST FEELS SO FAMILIAR... A WORD–
–SOMETHING I'M STARTING TO DO–REGEN... REGEN...

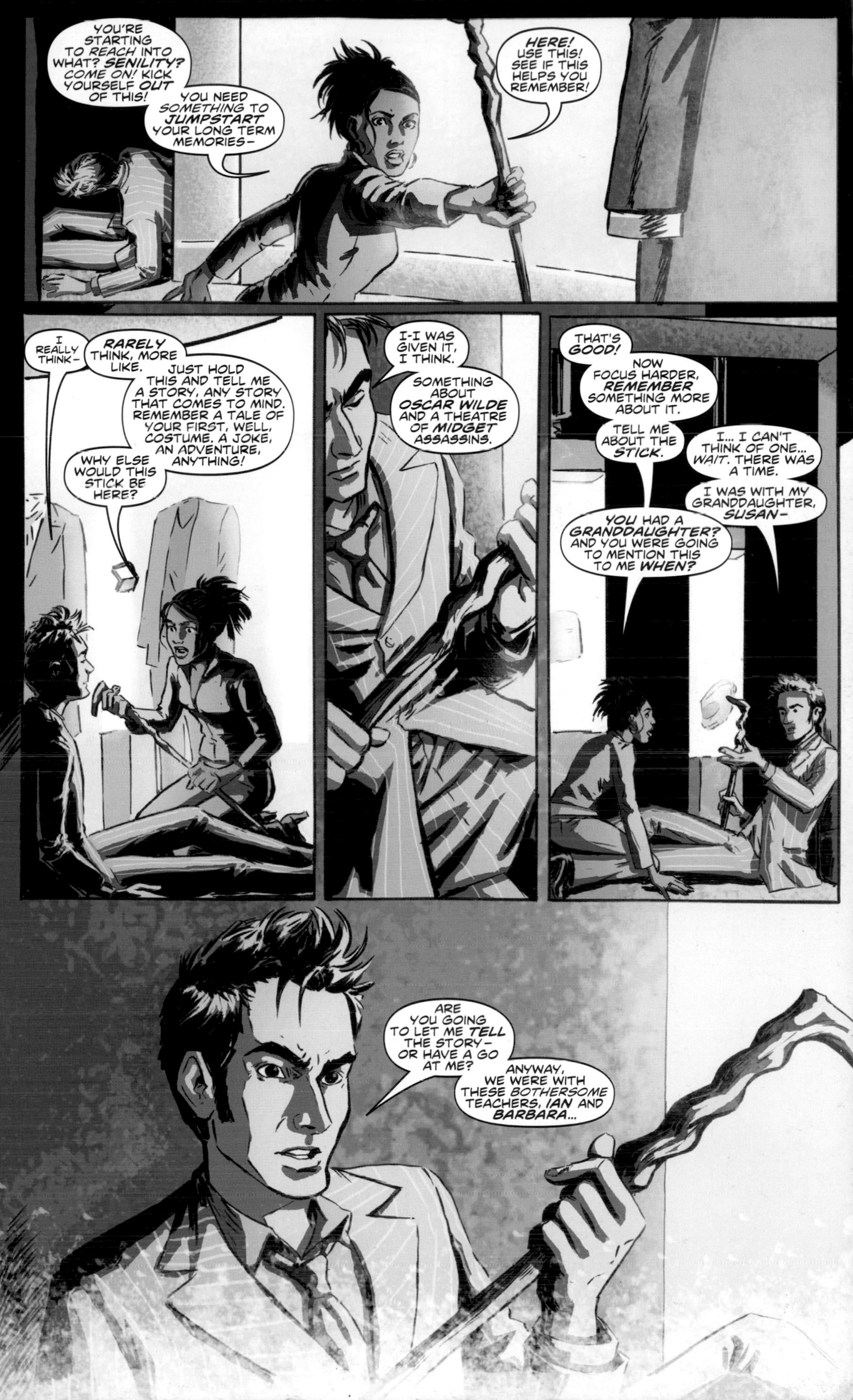
YOU'RE STARTING TO *REACH* INTO WHAT? ***SENILITY?*** COME ON! KICK YOURSELF ***OUT*** OF THIS!
YOU NEED SOMETHING TO ***JUMPSTART*** YOUR LONG TERM MEMORIES–
HERE! USE THIS! SEE IF THIS HELPS YOU REMEMBER!
I REALLY THINK–
RARELY THINK, MORE LIKE.
JUST HOLD THIS AND TELL ME A STORY, ANY STORY THAT COMES TO MIND. REMEMBER A TALE OF YOUR FIRST, WELL, COSTUME. A JOKE, AN ADVENTURE, ANYTHING!
WHY ELSE WOULD THIS STICK BE HERE?
I-I WAS GIVEN IT, I THINK.
SOMETHING ABOUT ***OSCAR WILDE*** AND A THEATRE OF ***MIDGET*** ASSASSINS.
THAT'S ***GOOD!***
NOW FOCUS HARDER, ***REMEMBER*** SOMETHING MORE ABOUT IT.
TELL ME ABOUT THE ***STICK.***
I... I CAN'T THINK OF ONE... *WAIT*. THERE WAS A TIME.
I WAS WITH MY GRANDDAUGHTER, ***SUSAN***–
YOU HAD A ***GRANDDAUGHTER?*** AND YOU WERE GOING TO MENTION THIS TO ME ***WHEN?***
ARE YOU GOING TO LET ME ***TELL*** THE STORY– OR HAVE A GO AT ME?
ANYWAY, WE WERE WITH THESE *BOTHERSOME* TEACHERS, ***IAN*** AND ***BARBARA***...

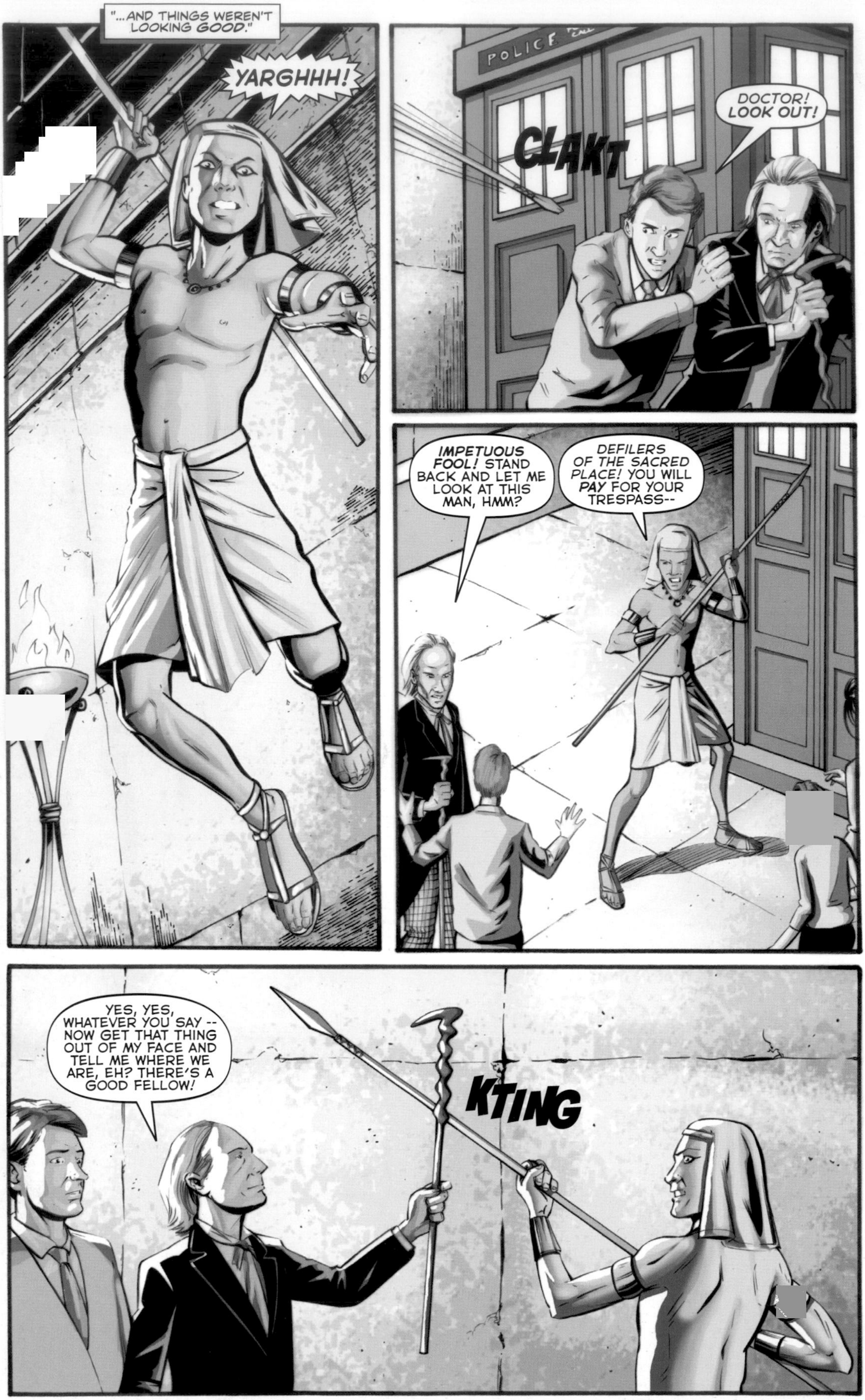
"...AND THINGS WEREN'T LOOKING GOOD."
YARGHHH!
CLAKT
DOCTOR! LOOK OUT!
DEFILERS OF THE SACRED PLACE! YOU WILL PAY FOR YOUR TRESPASS--
IMPETUOUS FOOL! STAND BACK AND LET ME LOOK AT THIS MAN, HMM?
YES, YES, WHATEVER YOU SAY -- NOW GET THAT THING OUT OF MY FACE AND TELL ME WHERE WE ARE, EH? THERE'S A GOOD FELLOW!
KTING

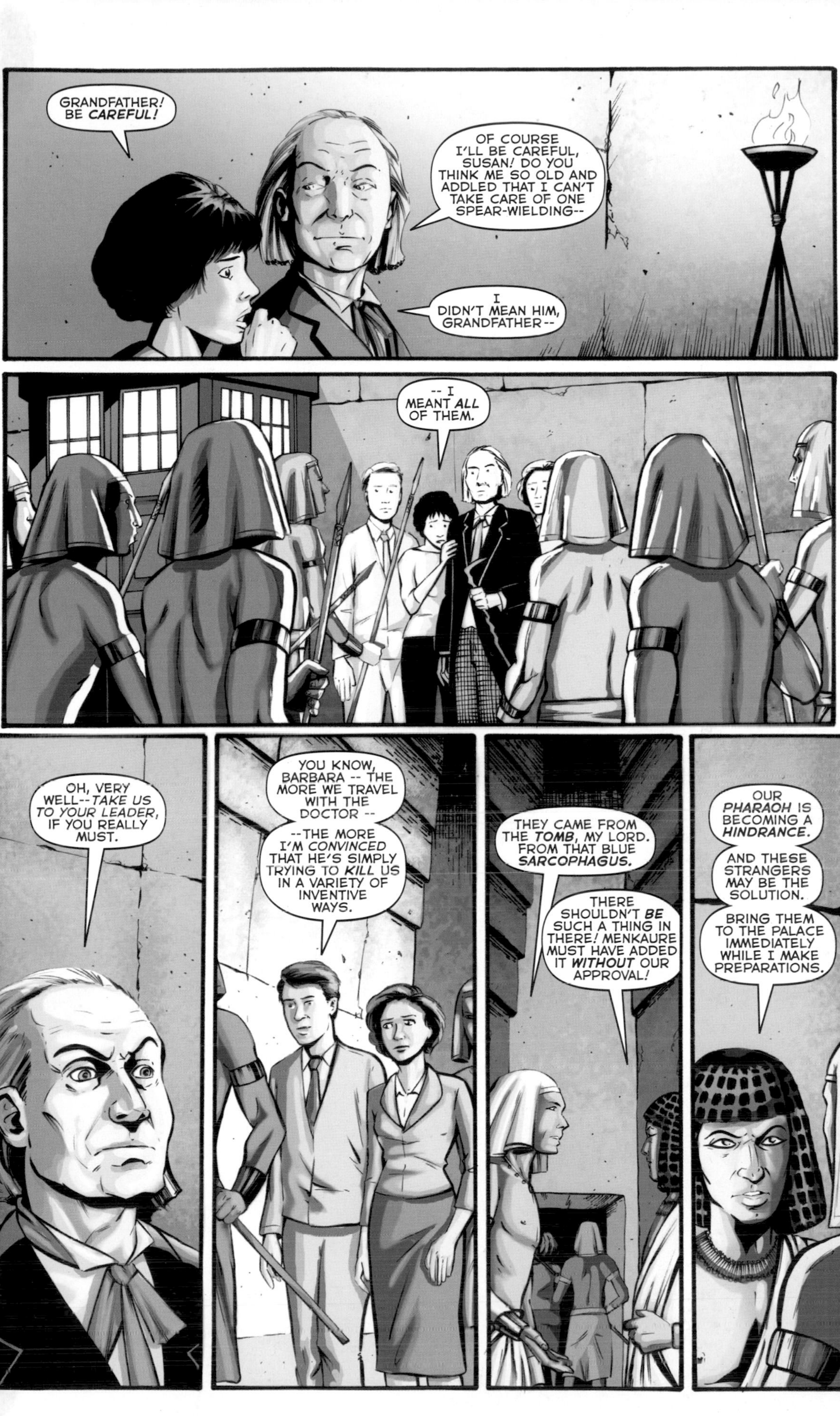
GRANDFATHER! BE CAREFUL!
OF COURSE I'LL BE CAREFUL, SUSAN! DO YOU THINK ME SO OLD AND ADDLED THAT I CAN'T TAKE CARE OF ONE SPEAR-WIELDING--
I DIDN'T MEAN HIM, GRANDFATHER--
-- I MEANT ALL OF THEM.
OH, VERY WELL--TAKE US TO YOUR LEADER, IF YOU REALLY MUST.
YOU KNOW, BARBARA -- THE MORE WE TRAVEL WITH THE DOCTOR --
--THE MORE I'M CONVINCED THAT HE'S SIMPLY TRYING TO KILL US IN A VARIETY OF INVENTIVE WAYS.
THEY CAME FROM THE TOMB, MY LORD. FROM THAT BLUE SARCOPHAGUS.
THERE SHOULDN'T BE SUCH A THING IN THERE! MENKAURE MUST HAVE ADDED IT WITHOUT OUR APPROVAL!
OUR PHARAOH IS BECOMING A HINDRANCE.
AND THESE STRANGERS MAY BE THE SOLUTION.
BRING THEM TO THE PALACE IMMEDIATELY WHILE I MAKE PREPARATIONS.

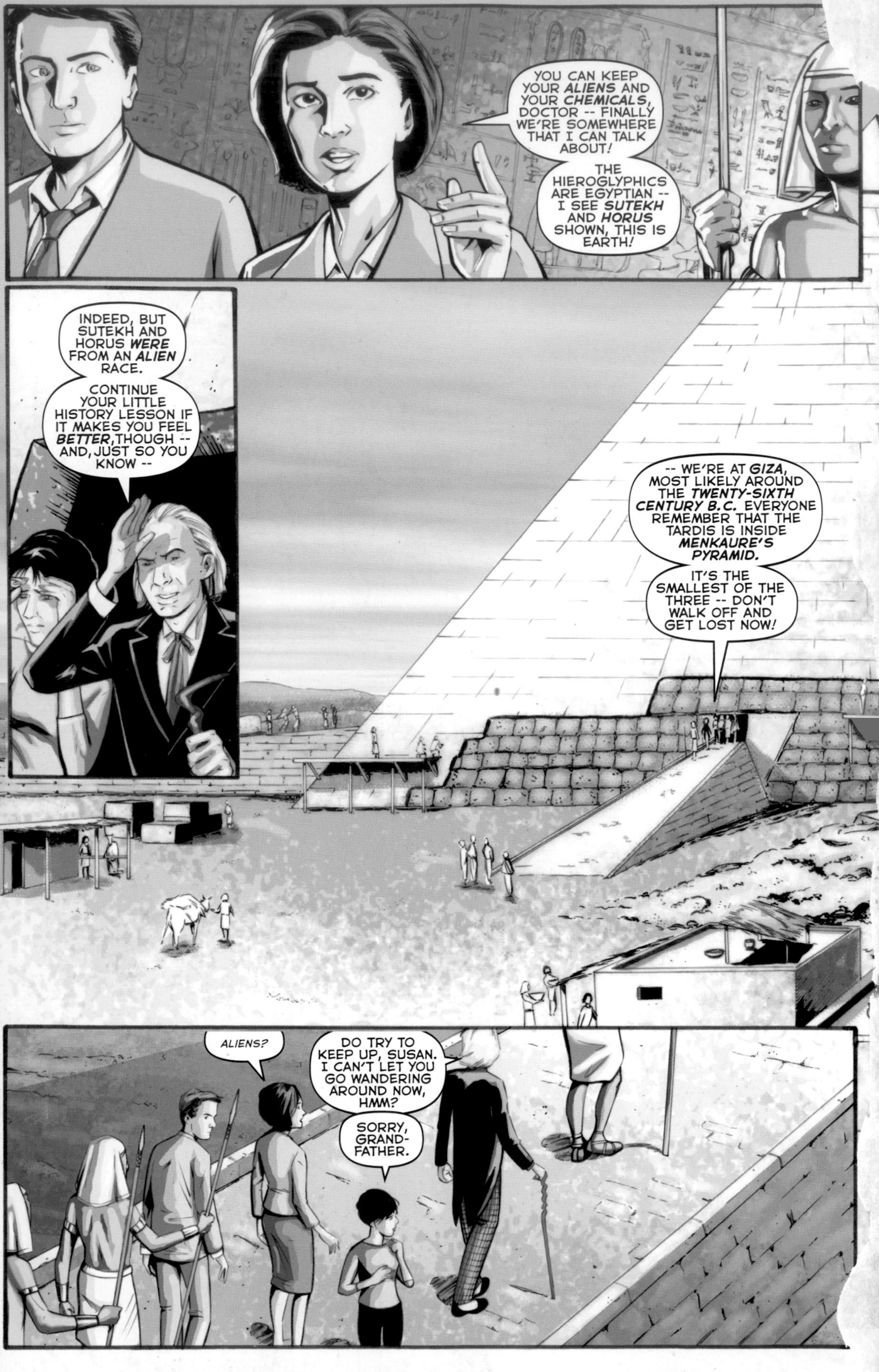
YOU CAN KEEP YOUR ALIENS AND YOUR CHEMICALS, DOCTOR -- FINALLY WE'RE SOMEWHERE THAT I CAN TALK ABOUT!
THE HIEROGLYPHICS ARE EGYPTIAN -- I SEE SUTEKH AND HORUS SHOWN, THIS IS EARTH!
INDEED, BUT SUTEKH AND HORUS WERE FROM AN ALIEN RACE.
CONTINUE YOUR LITTLE HISTORY LESSON IF IT MAKES YOU FEEL BETTER, THOUGH -- AND, JUST SO YOU KNOW --
-- WE'RE AT GIZA, MOST LIKELY AROUND THE TWENTY-SIXTH CENTURY B.C. EVERYONE REMEMBER THAT THE TARDIS IS INSIDE MENKAURE'S PYRAMID.
IT'S THE SMALLEST OF THE THREE -- DON'T WALK OFF AND GET LOST NOW!
ALIENS?
DO TRY TO KEEP UP, SUSAN. I CAN'T LET YOU GO WANDERING AROUND NOW, HMM?
SORRY, GRAND-FATHER.

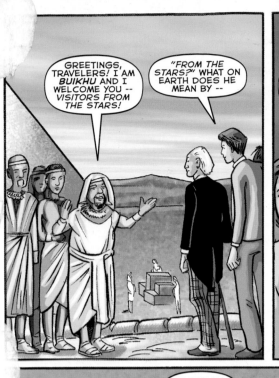

GREETINGS, TRAVELERS! I AM *BUIKHU* AND I WELCOME YOU -- *VISITORS FROM THE STARS!*

"FROM *THE STARS?*" WHAT ON EARTH DOES HE MEAN BY --

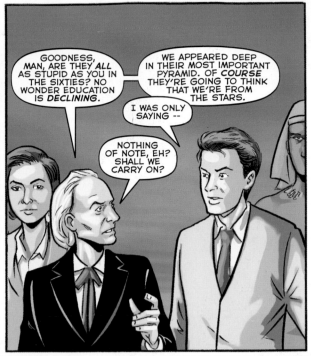

GOODNESS, MAN, ARE THEY *ALL* AS STUPID AS YOU IN THE SIXTIES? NO WONDER EDUCATION IS *DECLINING.*

WE APPEARED DEEP IN THEIR MOST IMPORTANT PYRAMID. OF *COURSE* THEY'RE GOING TO THINK THAT WE'RE FROM THE STARS.

I WAS ONLY SAYING --

NOTHING OF NOTE, EH? SHALL WE CARRY ON?

I REALLY HOPE THEY TURN *HIM* INTO A MUMMY.

WHY, SO HE'LL BE LESS SCARY?

NO -- SO THE *BANDAGES* COVER HIS *MOUTH.*

KEMNEBI -- I HAVE A *FAVOUR* TO ASK OF YOU. BRING YOUR BEST MAN TO THE PALACE WITH A BLOWPIPE AND DARTS.

WE HAVE AN OPPORTUNITY HERE TO *KILL* MENKAURE, AND BLAME THESE STRANGERS IN THE PROCESS.

AND HOW WOULD WE DO THAT, ITENNU?

POISON DARTS LEAVE NO VISIBLE WOUND. THE ONLY POSSIBLE ANSWER WILL BE THAT THESE "*VISITORS FROM THE STARS*" USED *MAGICS* TO KILL HIM.

AND ONCE WE CONVINCE THE POPULACE OF THIS, WE KILL *THEM.*

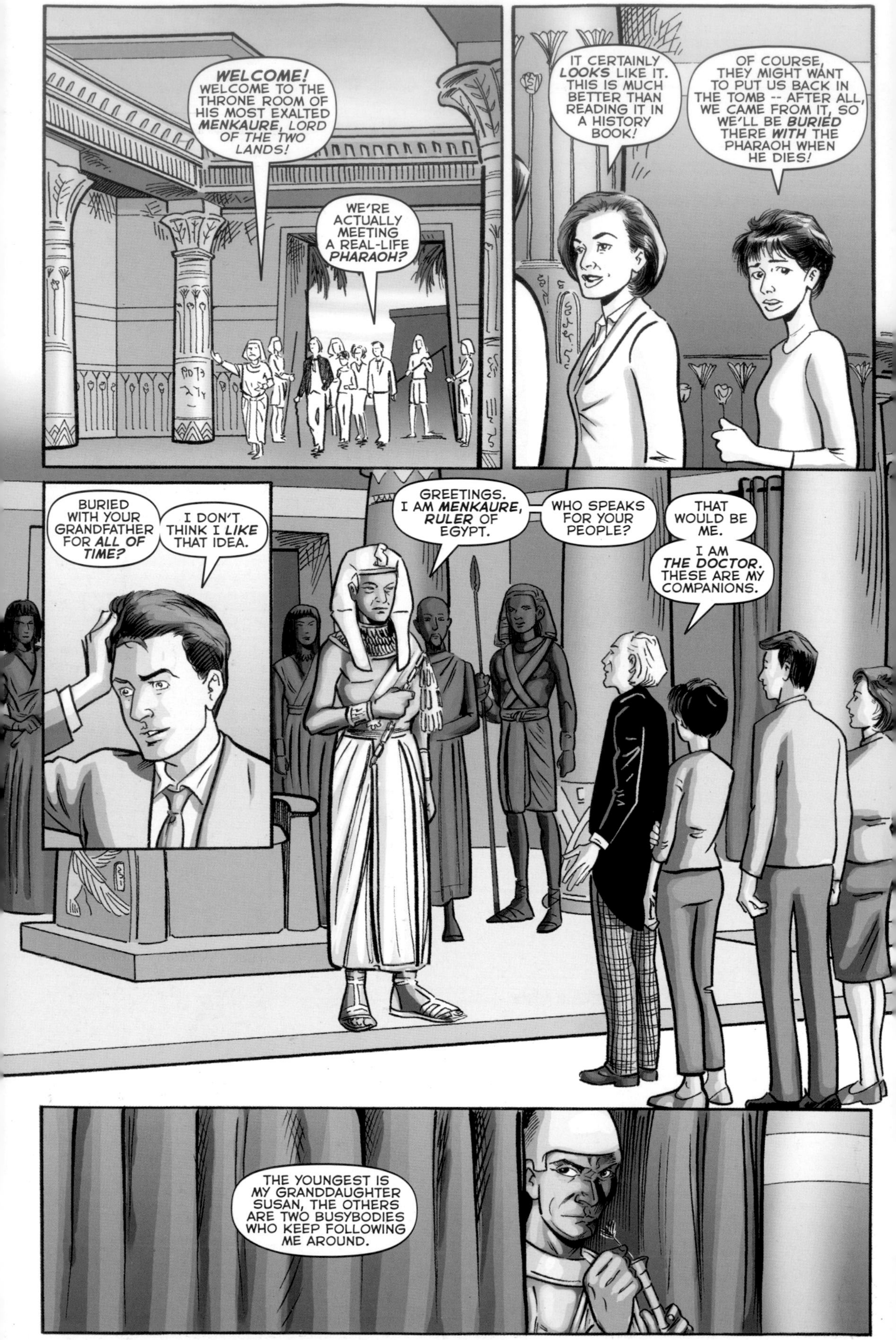
WELCOME! WELCOME TO THE THRONE ROOM OF HIS MOST EXALTED MENKAURE, LORD OF THE TWO LANDS!
WE'RE ACTUALLY MEETING A REAL-LIFE PHARAOH?
IT CERTAINLY LOOKS LIKE IT. THIS IS MUCH BETTER THAN READING IT IN A HISTORY BOOK!
OF COURSE, THEY MIGHT WANT TO PUT US BACK IN THE TOMB -- AFTER ALL, WE CAME FROM IT, SO WE'LL BE BURIED THERE WITH THE PHARAOH WHEN HE DIES!
BURIED WITH YOUR GRANDFATHER FOR ALL OF TIME?
I DON'T THINK I LIKE THAT IDEA.
GREETINGS. I AM MENKAURE, RULER OF EGYPT.
WHO SPEAKS FOR YOUR PEOPLE?
THAT WOULD BE ME.
I AM THE DOCTOR. THESE ARE MY COMPANIONS.
THE YOUNGEST IS MY GRANDDAUGHTER SUSAN, THE OTHERS ARE TWO BUSYBODIES WHO KEEP FOLLOWING ME AROUND.

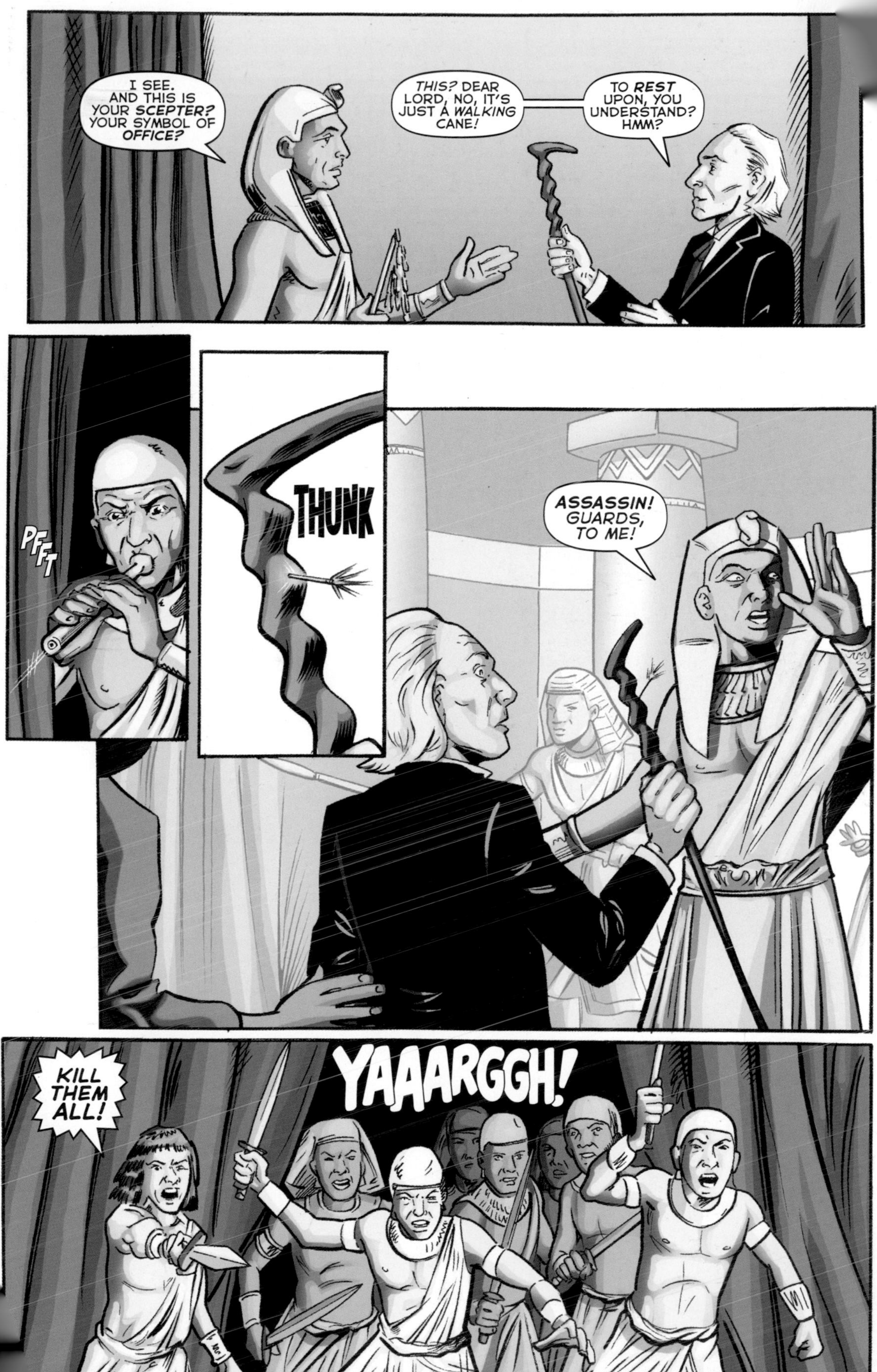
I SEE. AND THIS IS YOUR *SCEPTER?* YOUR SYMBOL OF *OFFICE?*
THIS? DEAR LORD, NO, IT'S JUST A *WALKING* CANE!
TO *REST* UPON, YOU UNDERSTAND? HMM?
PFFT
THUNK
ASSASSIN! GUARDS, TO ME!
KILL THEM ALL!
YAAARGGH!

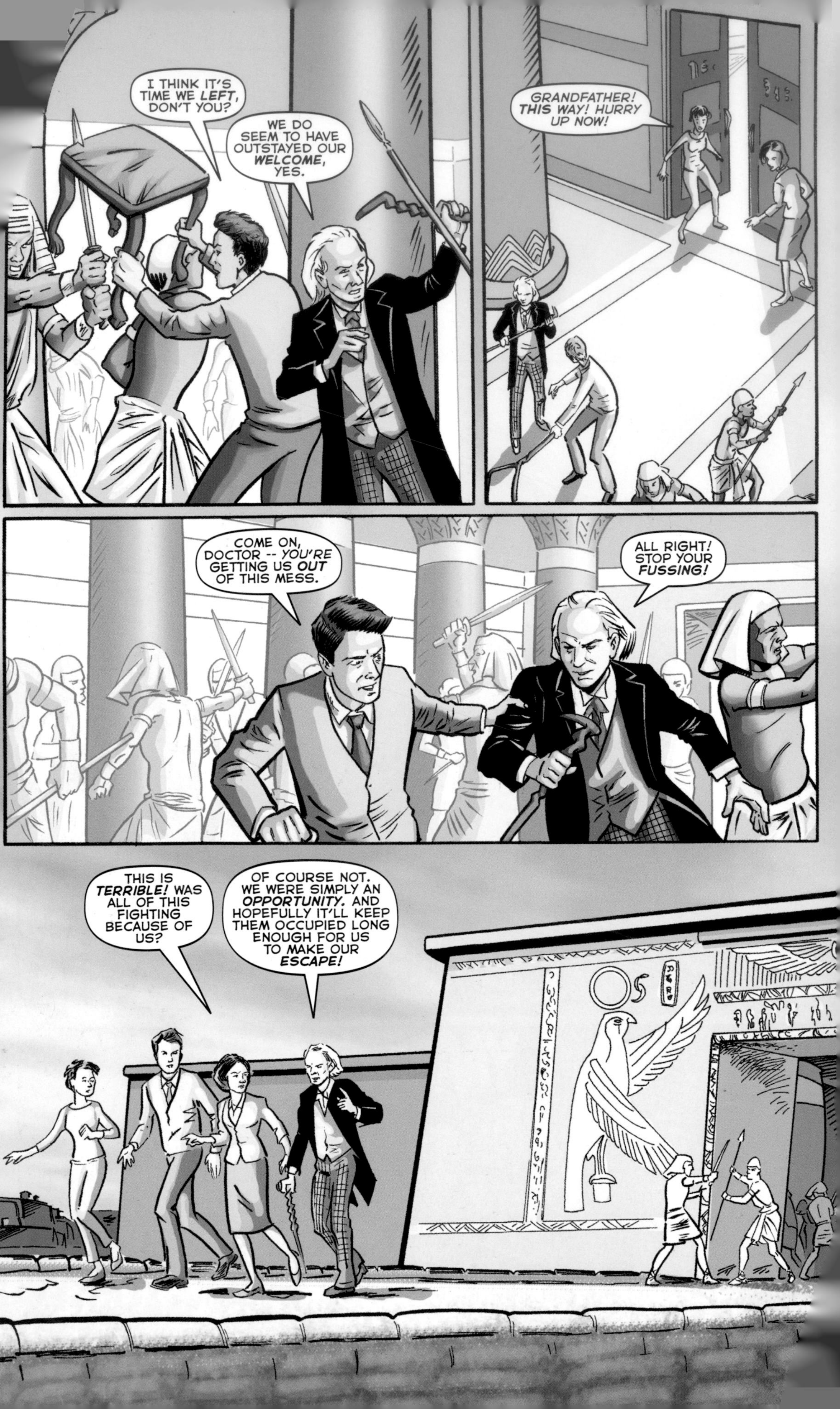
I THINK IT'S TIME WE *LEFT*, DON'T YOU?
WE DO SEEM TO HAVE OUTSTAYED OUR *WELCOME*, YES.
GRANDFATHER! *THIS WAY!* HURRY UP NOW!
COME ON, DOCTOR -- *YOU'RE* GETTING US *OUT* OF THIS MESS.
ALL RIGHT! STOP YOUR *FUSSING!*
THIS IS *TERRIBLE!* WAS ALL OF THIS FIGHTING BECAUSE OF US?
OF COURSE NOT. WE WERE SIMPLY AN *OPPORTUNITY.* AND HOPEFULLY IT'LL KEEP THEM OCCUPIED LONG ENOUGH FOR US TO MAKE OUR *ESCAPE!*

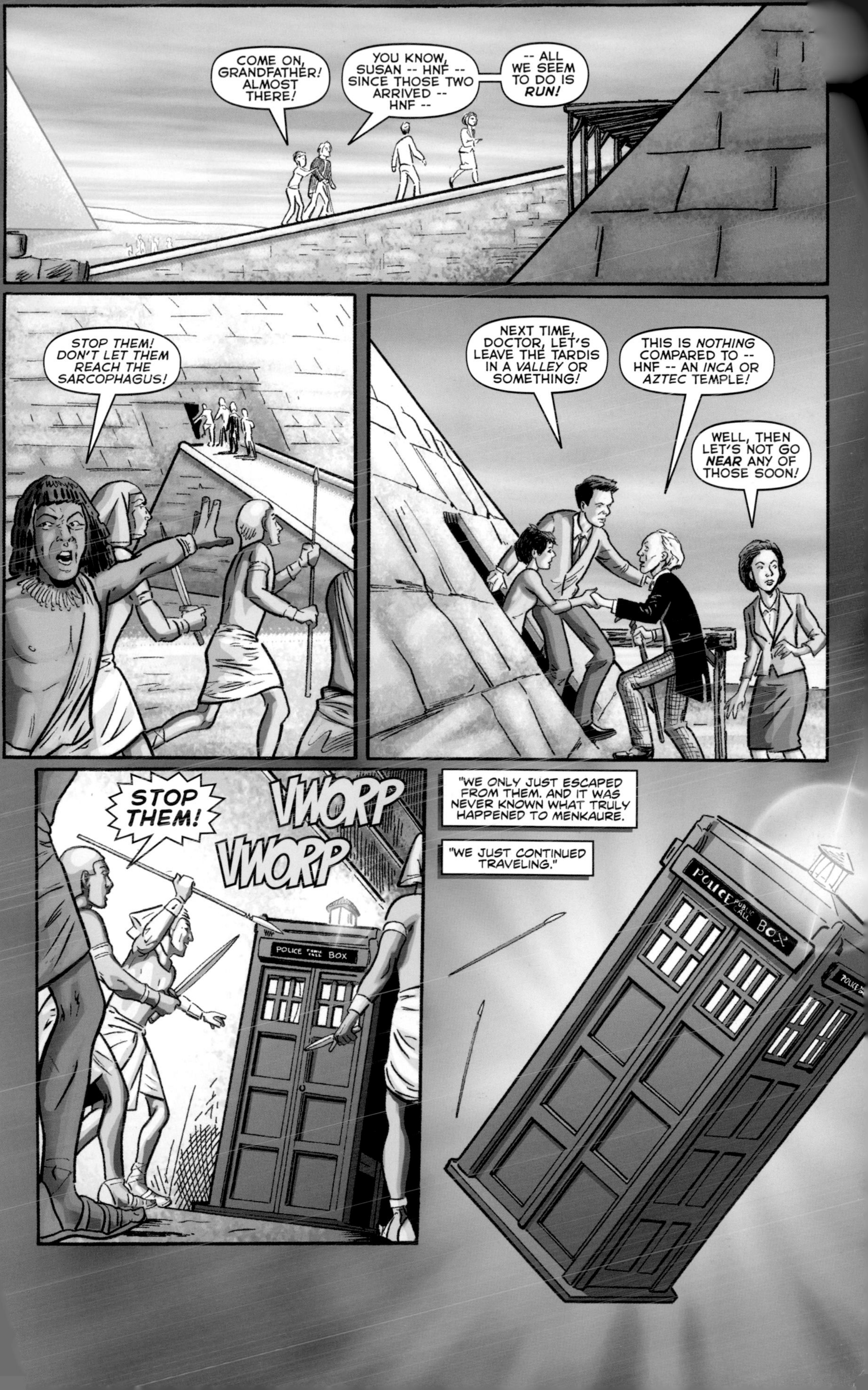
COME ON, GRANDFATHER! ALMOST THERE!
YOU KNOW, SUSAN -- HNF -- SINCE THOSE TWO ARRIVED -- HNF --
-- ALL WE SEEM TO DO IS RUN!
STOP THEM! DON'T LET THEM REACH THE SARCOPHAGUS!
NEXT TIME, DOCTOR, LET'S LEAVE THE TARDIS IN A VALLEY OR SOMETHING!
THIS IS NOTHING COMPARED TO -- HNF -- AN INCA OR AZTEC TEMPLE!
WELL, THEN LET'S NOT GO NEAR ANY OF THOSE SOON!
STOP THEM!
VWORP
VWORP
POLICE PUBLIC CALL BOX
"WE ONLY JUST ESCAPED FROM THEM. AND IT WAS NEVER KNOWN WHAT TRULY HAPPENED TO MENKAURE.
"WE JUST CONTINUED TRAVELING."
POLICE PUBLIC CALL BOX

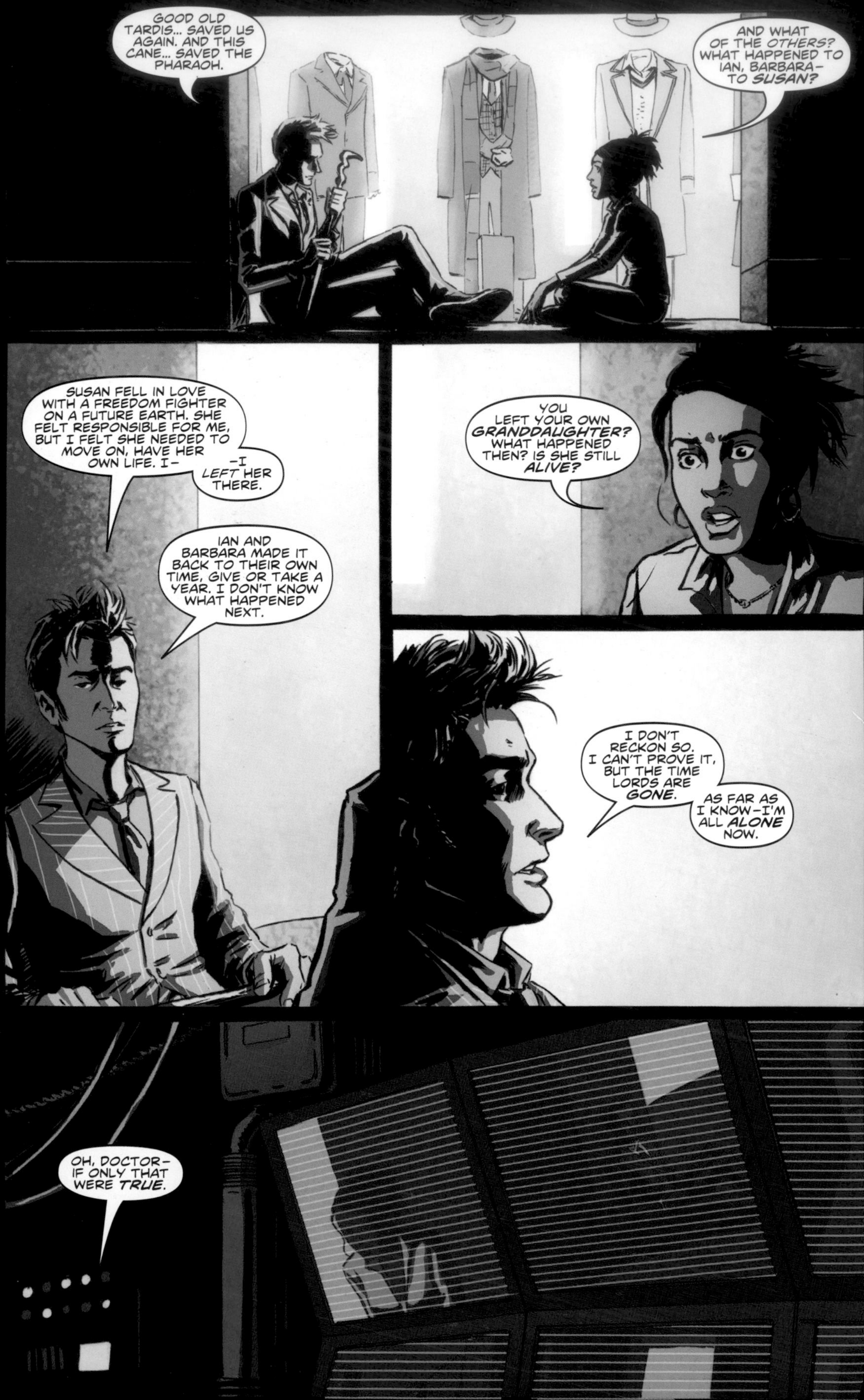
GOOD OLD TARDIS... SAVED US AGAIN. AND THIS CANE... SAVED THE PHARAOH.
AND WHAT OF THE OTHERS? WHAT HAPPENED TO IAN, BARBARA– TO SUSAN?
SUSAN FELL IN LOVE WITH A FREEDOM FIGHTER ON A FUTURE EARTH. SHE FELT RESPONSIBLE FOR ME, BUT I FELT SHE NEEDED TO MOVE ON, HAVE HER OWN LIFE. I–
–I LEFT HER THERE.
IAN AND BARBARA MADE IT BACK TO THEIR OWN TIME, GIVE OR TAKE A YEAR. I DON'T KNOW WHAT HAPPENED NEXT.
YOU LEFT YOUR OWN GRANDDAUGHTER? WHAT HAPPENED THEN? IS SHE STILL ALIVE?
I DON'T RECKON SO. I CAN'T PROVE IT, BUT THE TIME LORDS ARE GONE.
AS FAR AS I KNOW–I'M ALL ALONE NOW.
OH, DOCTOR– IF ONLY THAT WERE TRUE.

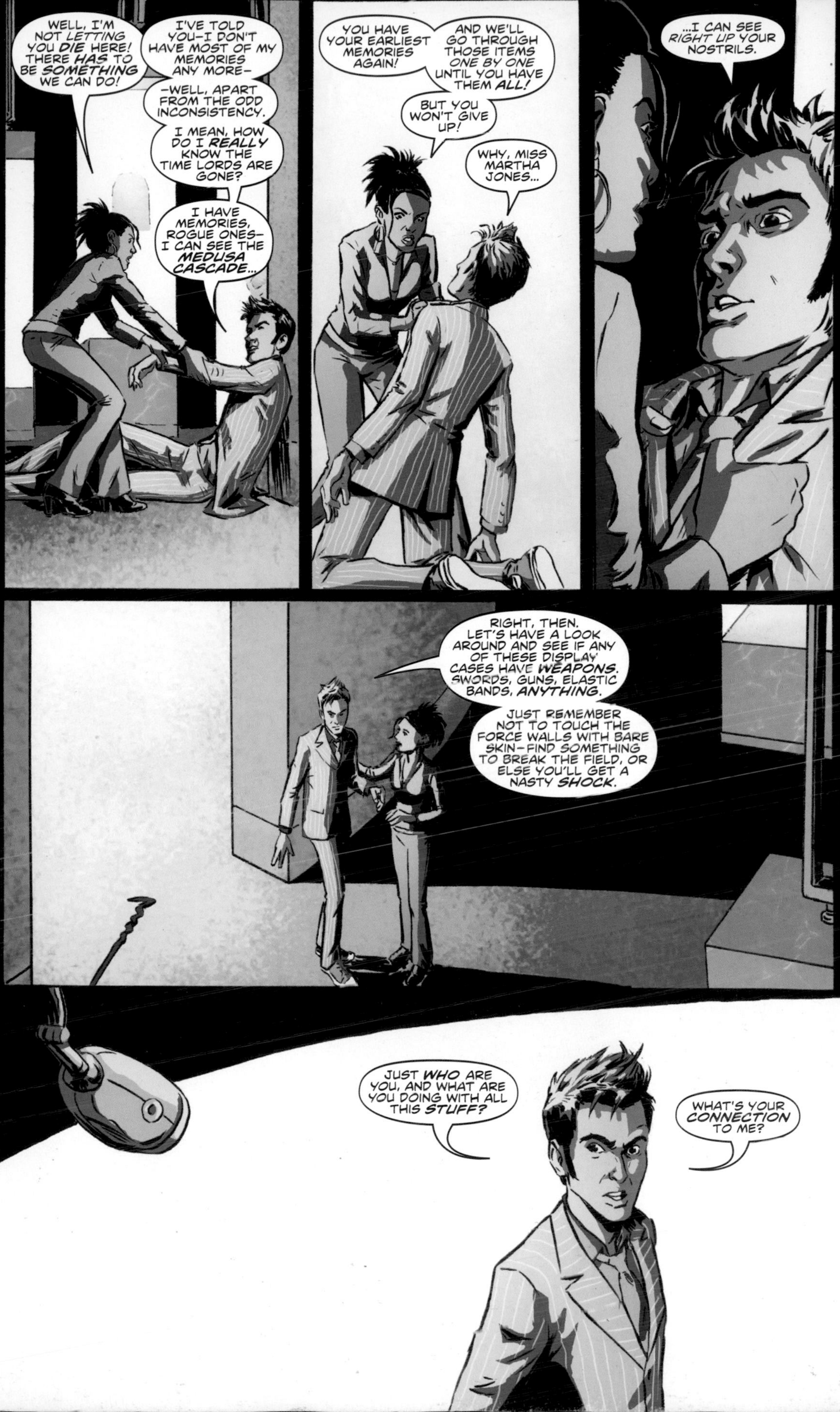
WELL, I'M NOT LETTING YOU DIE HERE! THERE HAS TO BE SOMETHING WE CAN DO!
I'VE TOLD YOU–I DON'T HAVE MOST OF MY MEMORIES ANY MORE–
–WELL, APART FROM THE ODD INCONSISTENCY.
I MEAN, HOW DO I REALLY KNOW THE TIME LORDS ARE GONE?
I HAVE MEMORIES, ROGUE ONES– I CAN SEE THE MEDUSA CASCADE...
YOU HAVE YOUR EARLIEST MEMORIES AGAIN!
AND WE'LL GO THROUGH THOSE ITEMS ONE BY ONE UNTIL YOU HAVE THEM ALL!
BUT YOU WON'T GIVE UP!
WHY, MISS MARTHA JONES...
...I CAN SEE RIGHT UP YOUR NOSTRILS.
RIGHT, THEN. LET'S HAVE A LOOK AROUND AND SEE IF ANY OF THESE DISPLAY CASES HAVE WEAPONS. SWORDS, GUNS, ELASTIC BANDS, ANYTHING.
JUST REMEMBER NOT TO TOUCH THE FORCE WALLS WITH BARE SKIN–FIND SOMETHING TO BREAK THE FIELD, OR ELSE YOU'LL GET A NASTY SHOCK.
JUST WHO ARE YOU, AND WHAT ARE YOU DOING WITH ALL THIS STUFF?
WHAT'S YOUR CONNECTION TO ME?

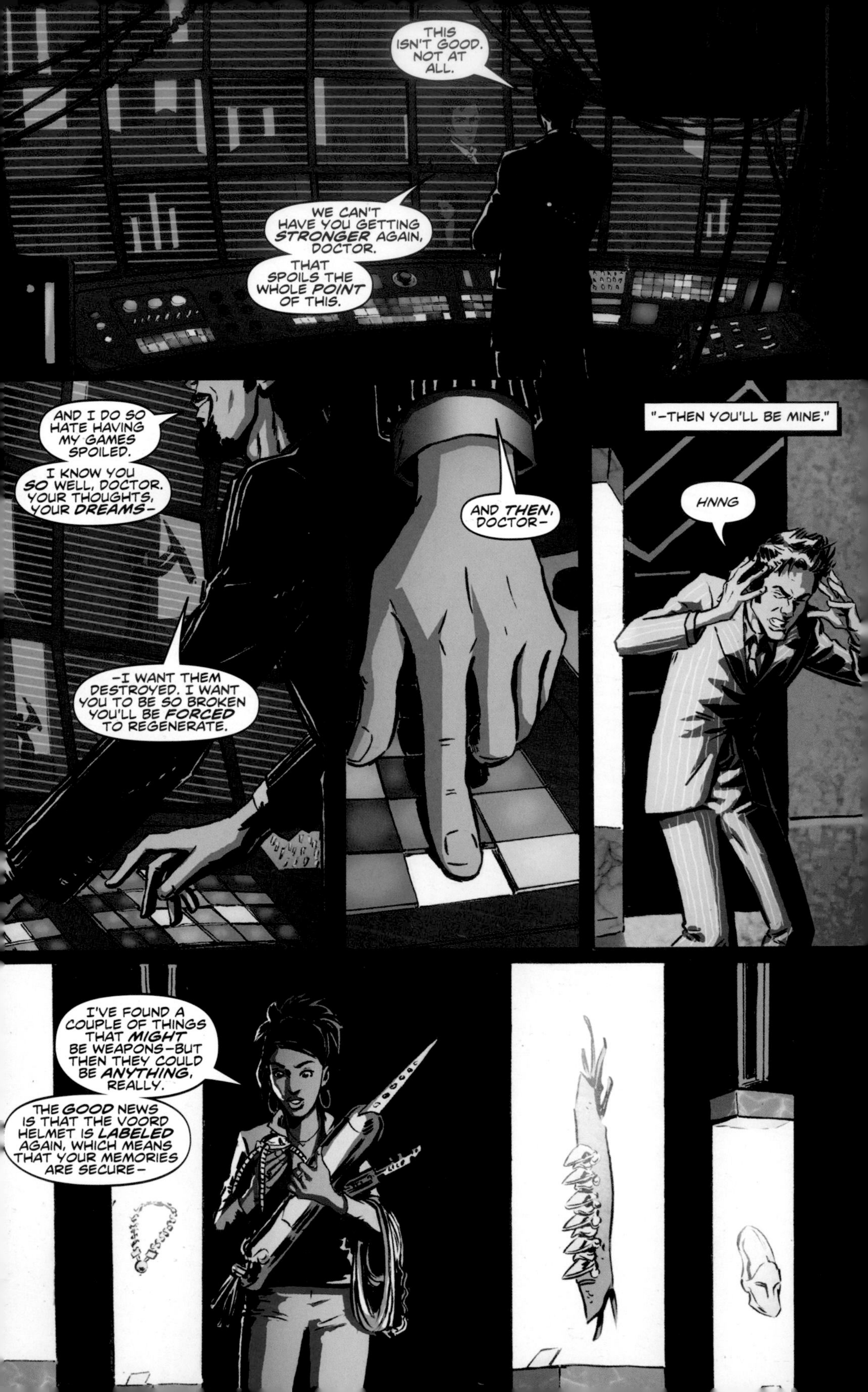
THIS ISN'T GOOD. NOT AT ALL.
WE CAN'T HAVE YOU GETTING STRONGER AGAIN, DOCTOR.
THAT SPOILS THE WHOLE POINT OF THIS.
AND I DO SO HATE HAVING MY GAMES SPOILED.
I KNOW YOU SO WELL, DOCTOR. YOUR THOUGHTS, YOUR DREAMS–
–I WANT THEM DESTROYED. I WANT YOU TO BE SO BROKEN YOU'LL BE FORCED TO REGENERATE.
AND THEN, DOCTOR–
"–THEN YOU'LL BE MINE."
HNNG
I'VE FOUND A COUPLE OF THINGS THAT MIGHT BE WEAPONS–BUT THEN THEY COULD BE ANYTHING, REALLY.
THE GOOD NEWS IS THAT THE VOORD HELMET IS LABELED AGAIN, WHICH MEANS THAT YOUR MEMORIES ARE SECURE–

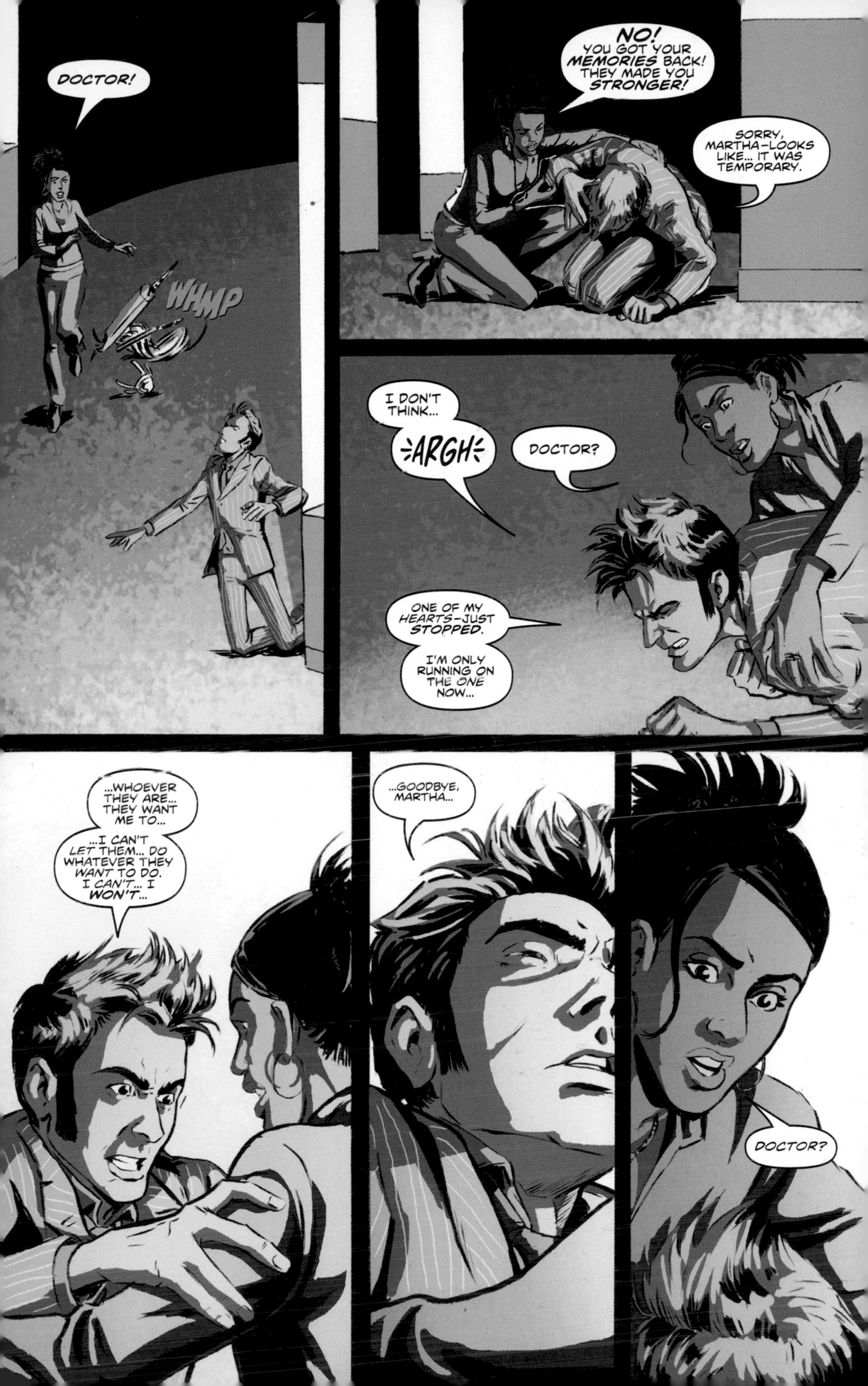
DOCTOR!
WHMP
NO! YOU GOT YOUR MEMORIES BACK! THEY MADE YOU STRONGER!
SORRY, MARTHA–LOOKS LIKE... IT WAS TEMPORARY.
I DON'T THINK...
ARGH
DOCTOR?
ONE OF MY HEARTS–JUST STOPPED.
I'M ONLY RUNNING ON THE ONE NOW...
...WHOEVER THEY ARE... THEY WANT ME TO...
...I CAN'T LET THEM... DO WHATEVER THEY WANT TO DO. I CAN'T... I WON'T...
...GOODBYE, MARTHA...
DOCTOR?

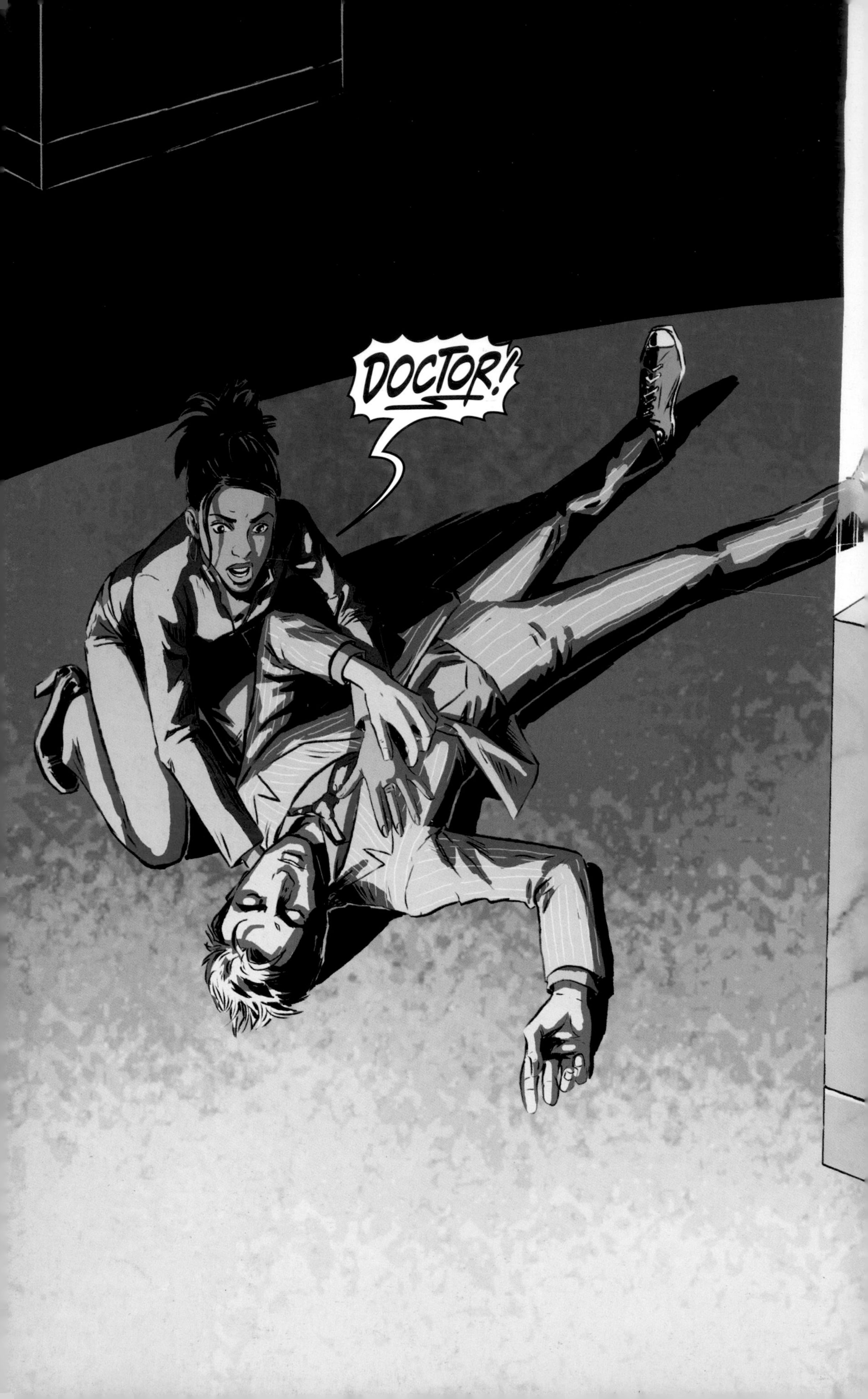
DOCTOR!

CHAPTER • TWO
RENEWAL

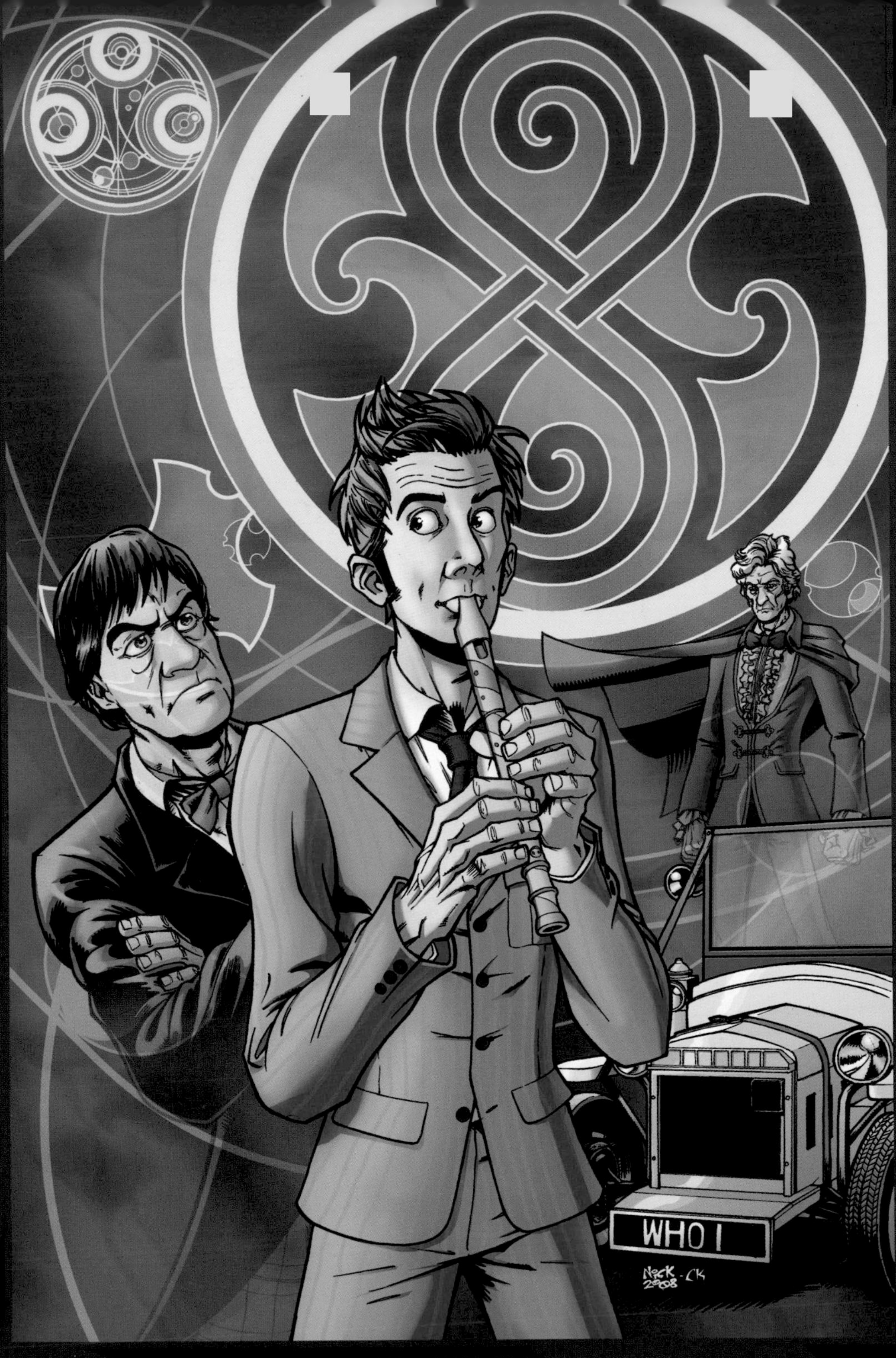
WHO 1
NICK 2008 - CK

ART BY NICK ROCHE • COLOR BY CHARLIE KIRCHOFF

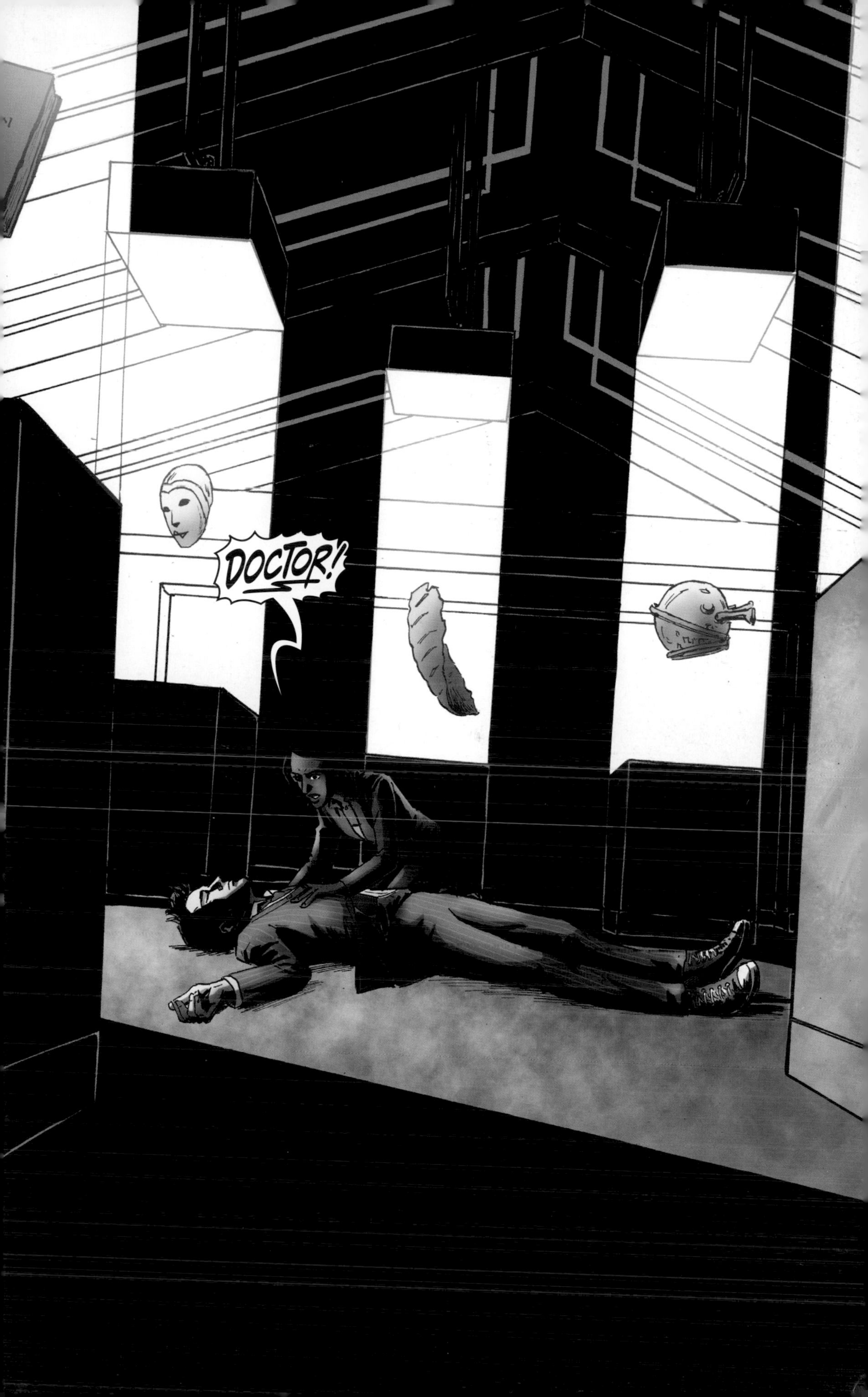
DOCTOR!

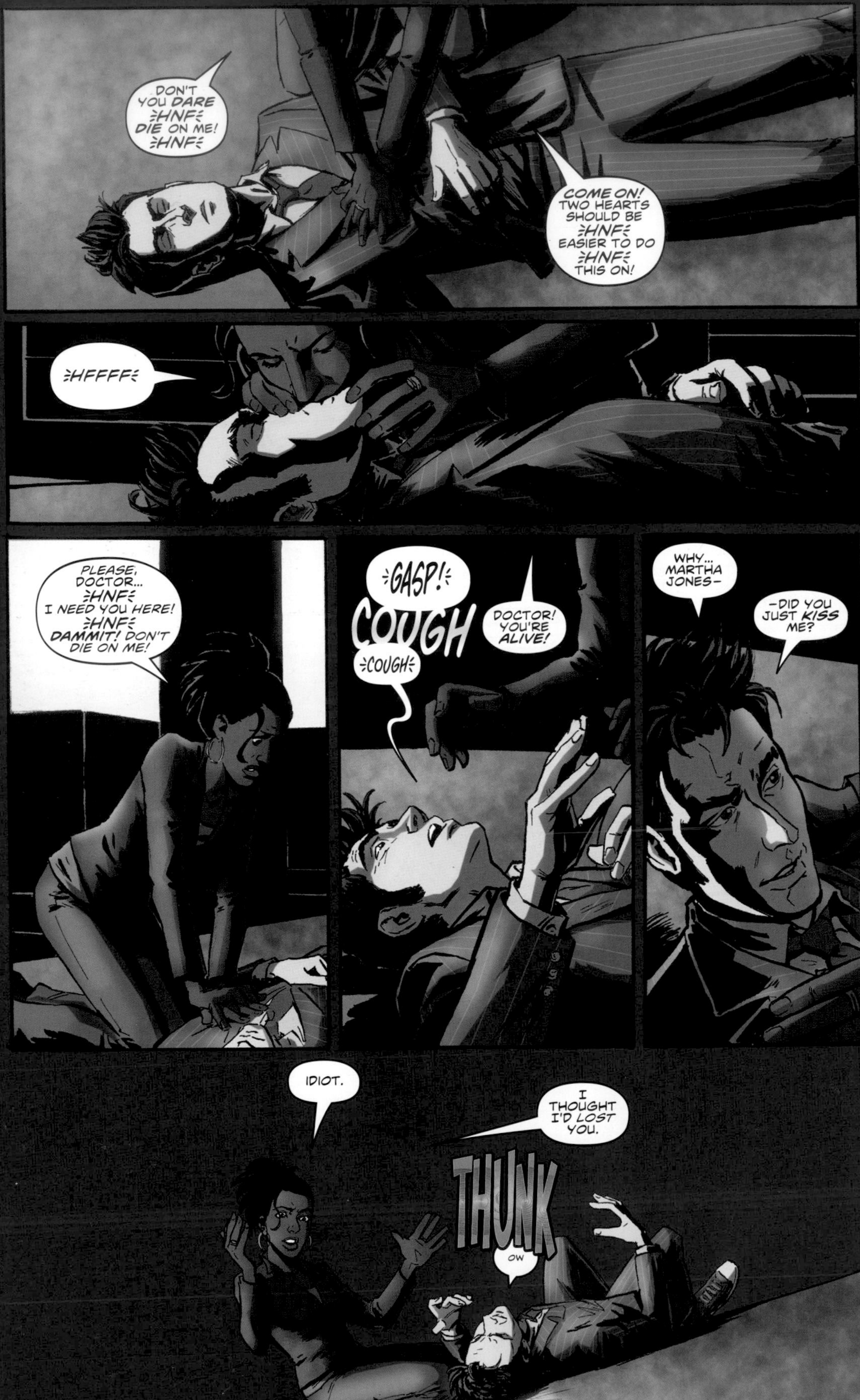
DON'T YOU DARE HNF DIE ON ME! HNF
COME ON! TWO HEARTS SHOULD BE HNF EASIER TO DO HNF THIS ON!
HFFFF
PLEASE, DOCTOR... HNF I NEED YOU HERE! HNF DAMMIT! DON'T DIE ON ME!
GASP!
COUGH
COUGH
DOCTOR! YOU'RE ALIVE!
WHY... MARTHA JONES—
—DID YOU JUST KISS ME?
IDIOT.
I THOUGHT I'D LOST YOU.
THUNK
OW

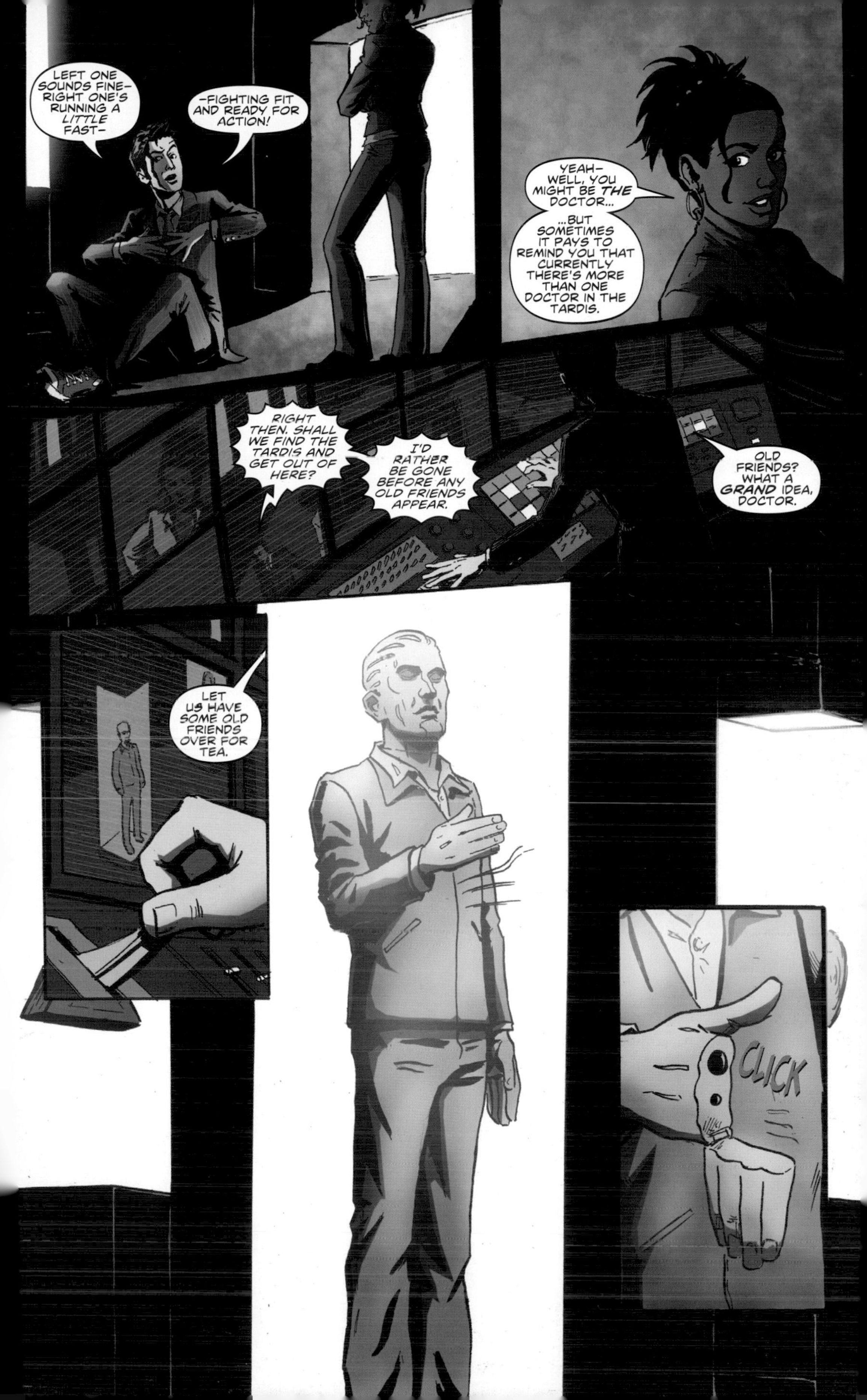
LEFT ONE SOUNDS FINE– RIGHT ONE'S RUNNING A *LITTLE* FAST–
–FIGHTING FIT AND READY FOR ACTION!
YEAH– WELL, YOU MIGHT BE *THE* DOCTOR...
...BUT SOMETIMES IT PAYS TO REMIND YOU THAT CURRENTLY THERE'S MORE THAN ONE DOCTOR IN THE TARDIS.
RIGHT THEN. SHALL WE FIND THE TARDIS AND GET OUT OF HERE?
I'D RATHER BE GONE BEFORE ANY OLD FRIENDS APPEAR.
OLD FRIENDS? WHAT A ***GRAND*** IDEA, DOCTOR.
LET US HAVE SOME OLD FRIENDS OVER FOR TEA.
CLICK

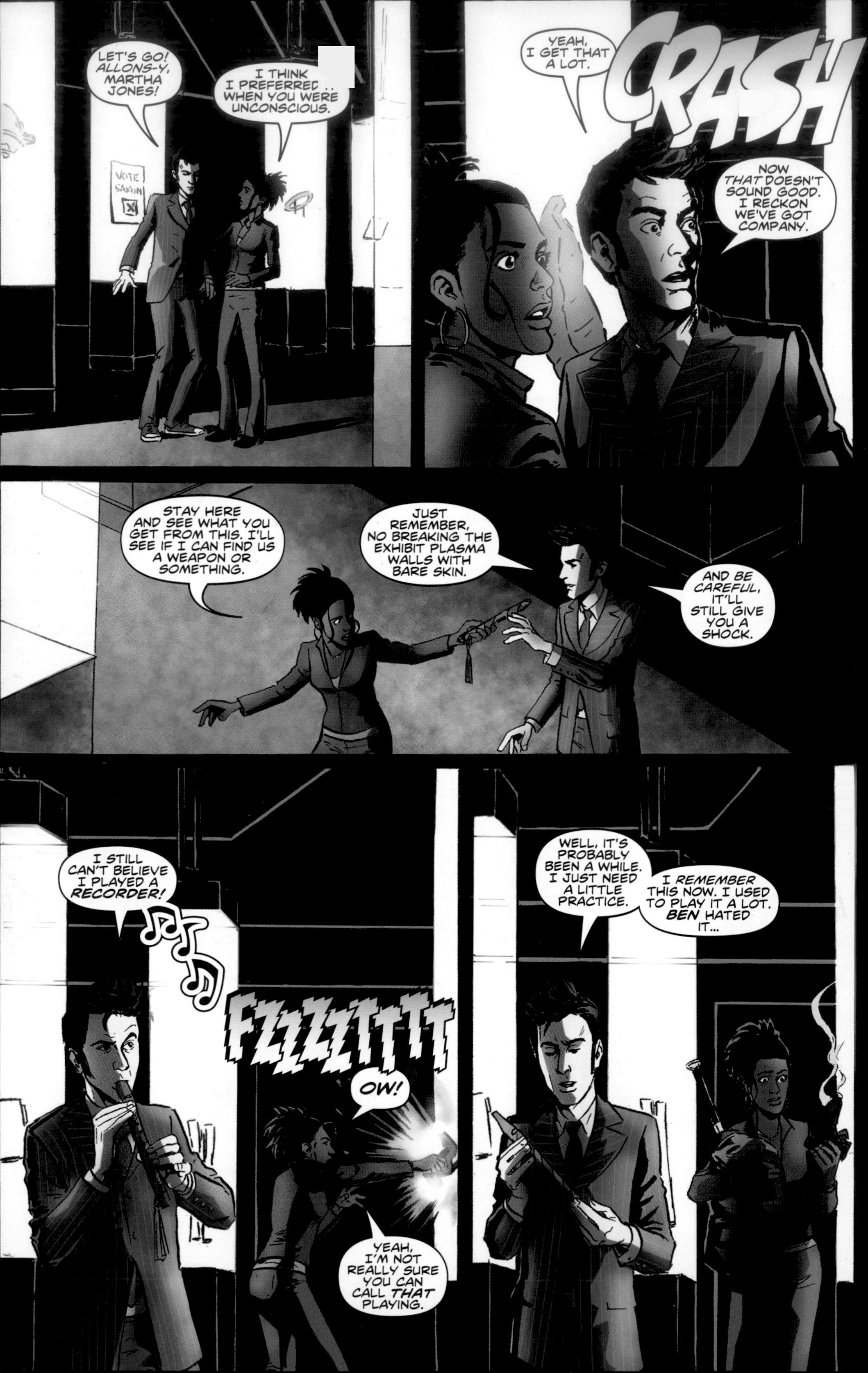
LET'S GO! ALLONS-Y, MARTHA JONES!
VOTE SAXON
I THINK I PREFERRED WHEN YOU WERE UNCONSCIOUS.
YEAH, I GET THAT A LOT.
CRASH
NOW *THAT* DOESN'T SOUND GOOD. I RECKON WE'VE GOT COMPANY.
STAY HERE AND SEE WHAT YOU GET FROM THIS. I'LL SEE IF I CAN FIND US A WEAPON OR SOMETHING.
JUST REMEMBER, NO BREAKING THE EXHIBIT PLASMA WALLS WITH BARE SKIN.
AND BE *CAREFUL*, IT'LL STILL GIVE YOU A SHOCK.
I STILL CAN'T BELIEVE I PLAYED A *RECORDER!*
FZZZZTTTT
OW!
YEAH, I'M NOT REALLY SURE YOU CAN CALL *THAT* PLAYING.
WELL, IT'S PROBABLY BEEN A WHILE. I JUST NEED A LITTLE PRACTICE.
I *REMEMBER* THIS NOW. I USED TO PLAY IT A LOT. ***BEN*** HATED IT...

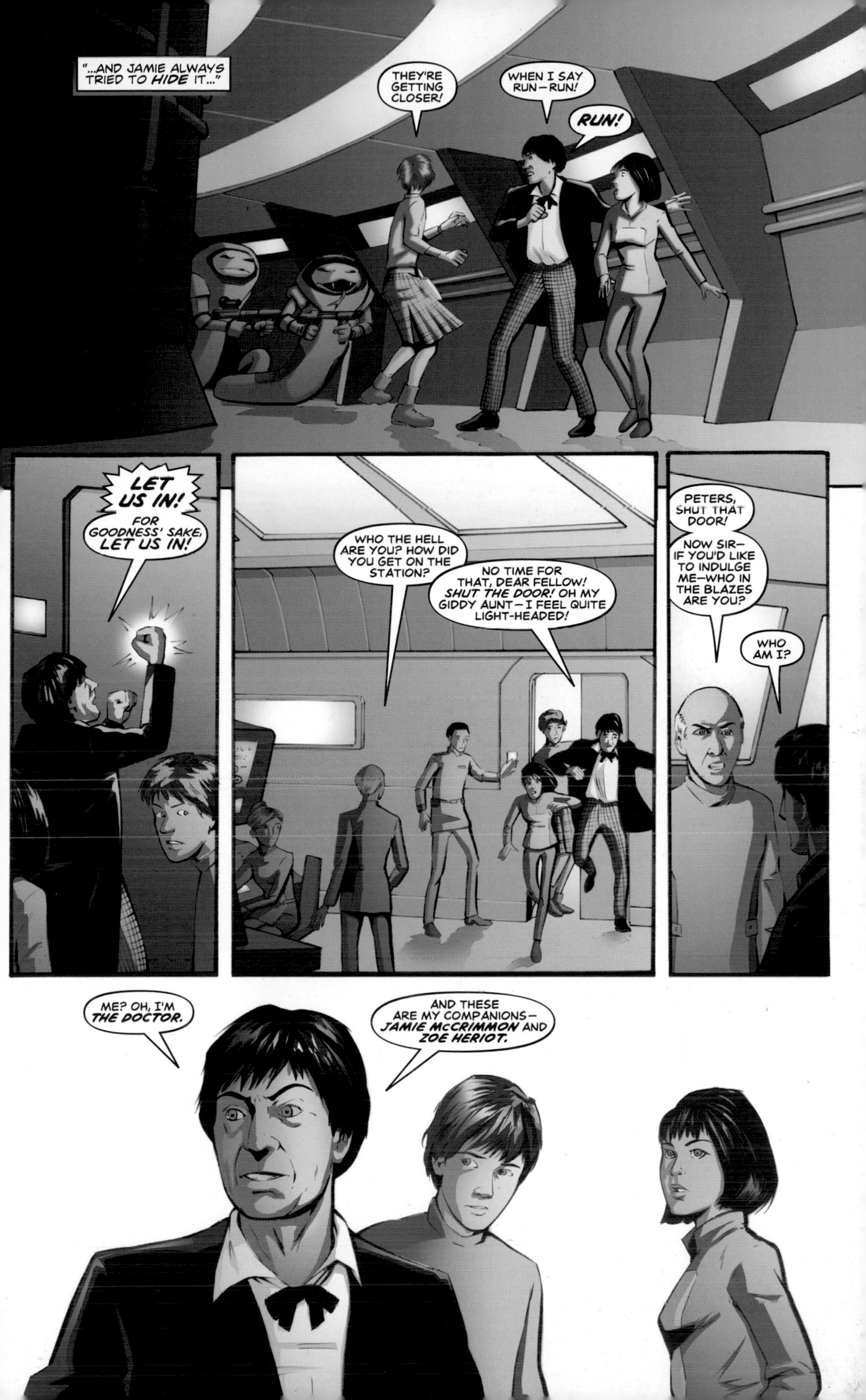
"...AND JAMIE ALWAYS TRIED TO HIDE IT..."
THEY'RE GETTING CLOSER!
WHEN I SAY RUN—RUN!
RUN!
LET US IN!
FOR GOODNESS' SAKE, LET US IN!
WHO THE HELL ARE YOU? HOW DID YOU GET ON THE STATION?
NO TIME FOR THAT, DEAR FELLOW! SHUT THE DOOR! OH MY GIDDY AUNT—I FEEL QUITE LIGHT-HEADED!
PETERS, SHUT THAT DOOR!
NOW SIR—IF YOU'D LIKE TO INDULGE ME—WHO IN THE BLAZES ARE YOU?
WHO AM I?
ME? OH, I'M THE DOCTOR.
AND THESE ARE MY COMPANIONS—JAMIE McCRIMMON AND ZOE HERIOT.

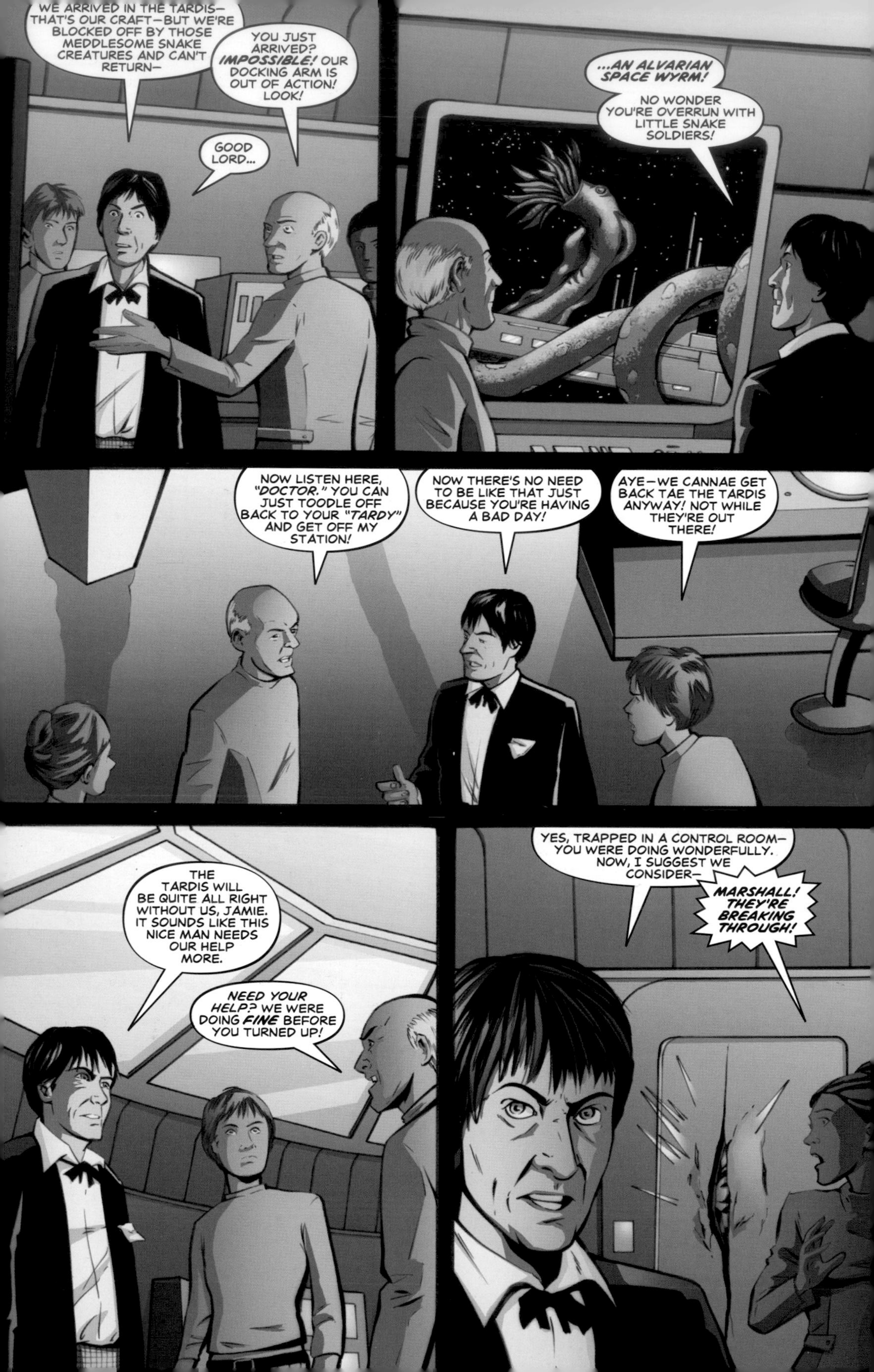
WE ARRIVED IN THE TARDIS—THAT'S OUR CRAFT—BUT WE'RE BLOCKED OFF BY THOSE MEDDLESOME SNAKE CREATURES AND CAN'T RETURN—
YOU JUST ARRIVED? IMPOSSIBLE! OUR DOCKING ARM IS OUT OF ACTION! LOOK!
GOOD LORD...
...AN ALVARIAN SPACE WYRM!
NO WONDER YOU'RE OVERRUN WITH LITTLE SNAKE SOLDIERS!
NOW LISTEN HERE, "DOCTOR." YOU CAN JUST TOODLE OFF BACK TO YOUR "TARDY" AND GET OFF MY STATION!
NOW THERE'S NO NEED TO BE LIKE THAT JUST BECAUSE YOU'RE HAVING A BAD DAY!
AYE—WE CANNAE GET BACK TAE THE TARDIS ANYWAY! NOT WHILE THEY'RE OUT THERE!
THE TARDIS WILL BE QUITE ALL RIGHT WITHOUT US, JAMIE. IT SOUNDS LIKE THIS NICE MAN NEEDS OUR HELP MORE.
NEED YOUR HELP? WE WERE DOING FINE BEFORE YOU TURNED UP!
YES, TRAPPED IN A CONTROL ROOM—YOU WERE DOING WONDERFULLY. NOW, I SUGGEST WE CONSIDER—
MARSHALL! THEY'RE BREAKING THROUGH!

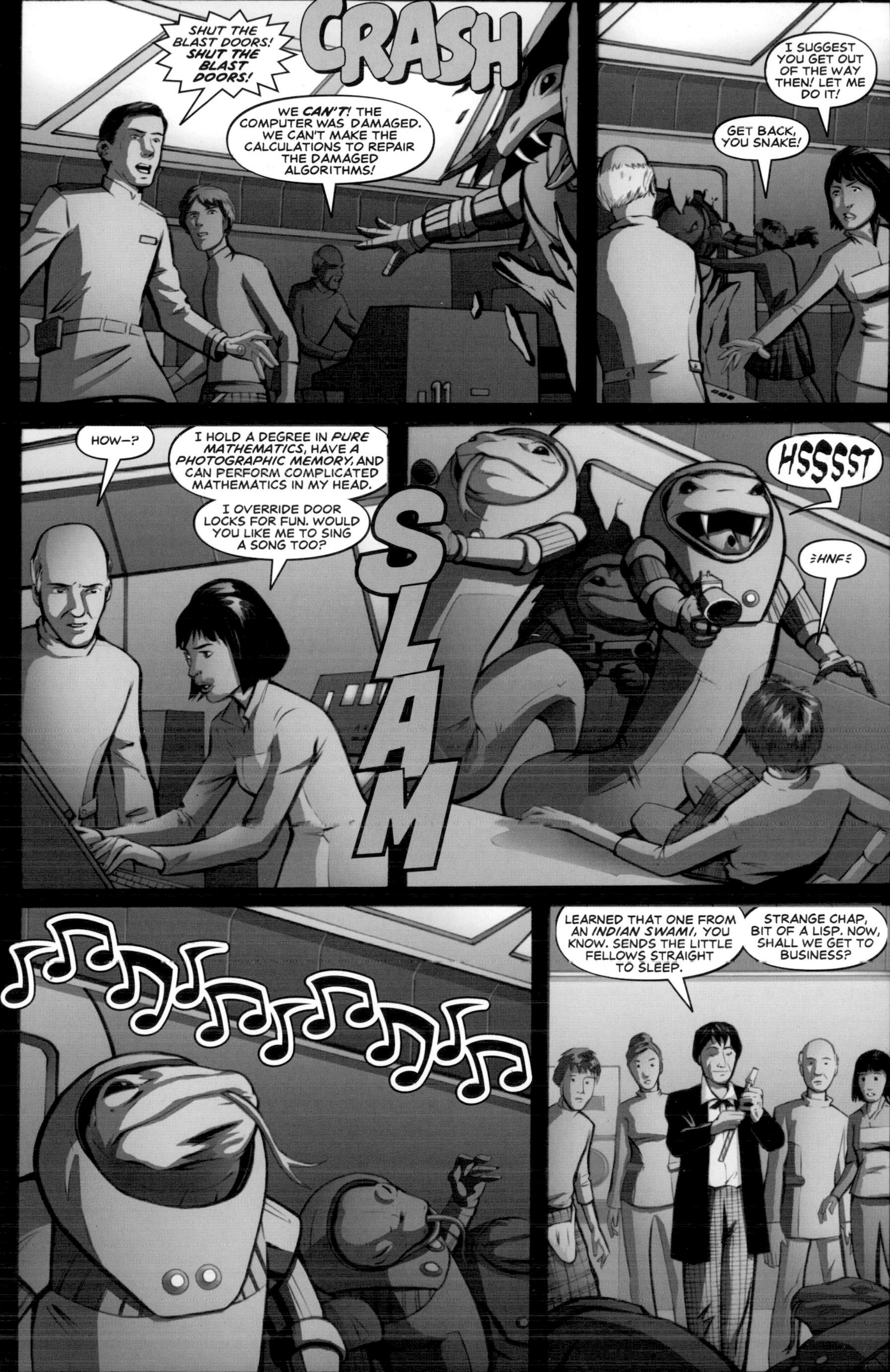
SHUT THE BLAST DOORS! SHUT THE BLAST DOORS!
CRASH
WE CAN'T! THE COMPUTER WAS DAMAGED. WE CAN'T MAKE THE CALCULATIONS TO REPAIR THE DAMAGED ALGORITHMS!
I SUGGEST YOU GET OUT OF THE WAY THEN! LET ME DO IT!
GET BACK, YOU SNAKE!
HOW—?
I HOLD A DEGREE IN PURE MATHEMATICS, HAVE A PHOTOGRAPHIC MEMORY, AND CAN PERFORM COMPLICATED MATHEMATICS IN MY HEAD.
I OVERRIDE DOOR LOCKS FOR FUN. WOULD YOU LIKE ME TO SING A SONG TOO?
SLAM
HSSSST
HNF
LEARNED THAT ONE FROM AN INDIAN SWAMI, YOU KNOW. SENDS THE LITTLE FELLOWS STRAIGHT TO SLEEP.
STRANGE CHAP, BIT OF A LISP. NOW, SHALL WE GET TO BUSINESS?

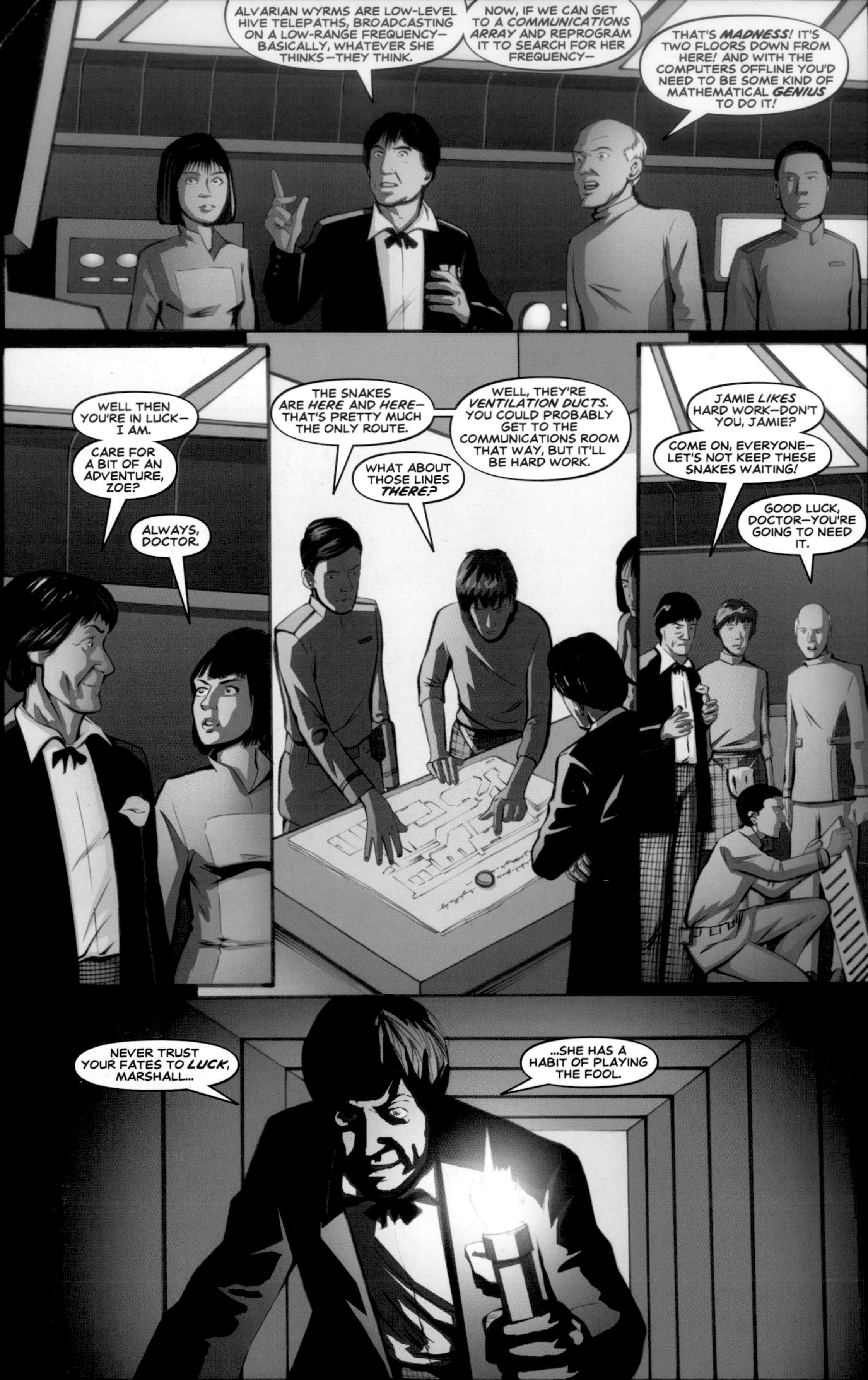
ALVARIAN WYRMS ARE LOW-LEVEL HIVE TELEPATHS, BROADCASTING ON A LOW-RANGE FREQUENCY—BASICALLY, WHATEVER SHE THINKS—THEY THINK.
NOW, IF WE CAN GET TO A COMMUNICATIONS ARRAY AND REPROGRAM IT TO SEARCH FOR HER FREQUENCY—
THAT'S MADNESS! IT'S TWO FLOORS DOWN FROM HERE! AND WITH THE COMPUTERS OFFLINE YOU'D NEED TO BE SOME KIND OF MATHEMATICAL GENIUS TO DO IT!
WELL THEN YOU'RE IN LUCK—I AM.
CARE FOR A BIT OF AN ADVENTURE, ZOE?
ALWAYS, DOCTOR.
THE SNAKES ARE HERE AND HERE—THAT'S PRETTY MUCH THE ONLY ROUTE.
WHAT ABOUT THOSE LINES THERE?
WELL, THEY'RE VENTILATION DUCTS. YOU COULD PROBABLY GET TO THE COMMUNICATIONS ROOM THAT WAY, BUT IT'LL BE HARD WORK.
JAMIE LIKES HARD WORK—DON'T YOU, JAMIE?
COME ON, EVERYONE—LET'S NOT KEEP THESE SNAKES WAITING!
GOOD LUCK, DOCTOR—YOU'RE GOING TO NEED IT.
NEVER TRUST YOUR FATES TO LUCK, MARSHALL...
...SHE HAS A HABIT OF PLAYING THE FOOL.

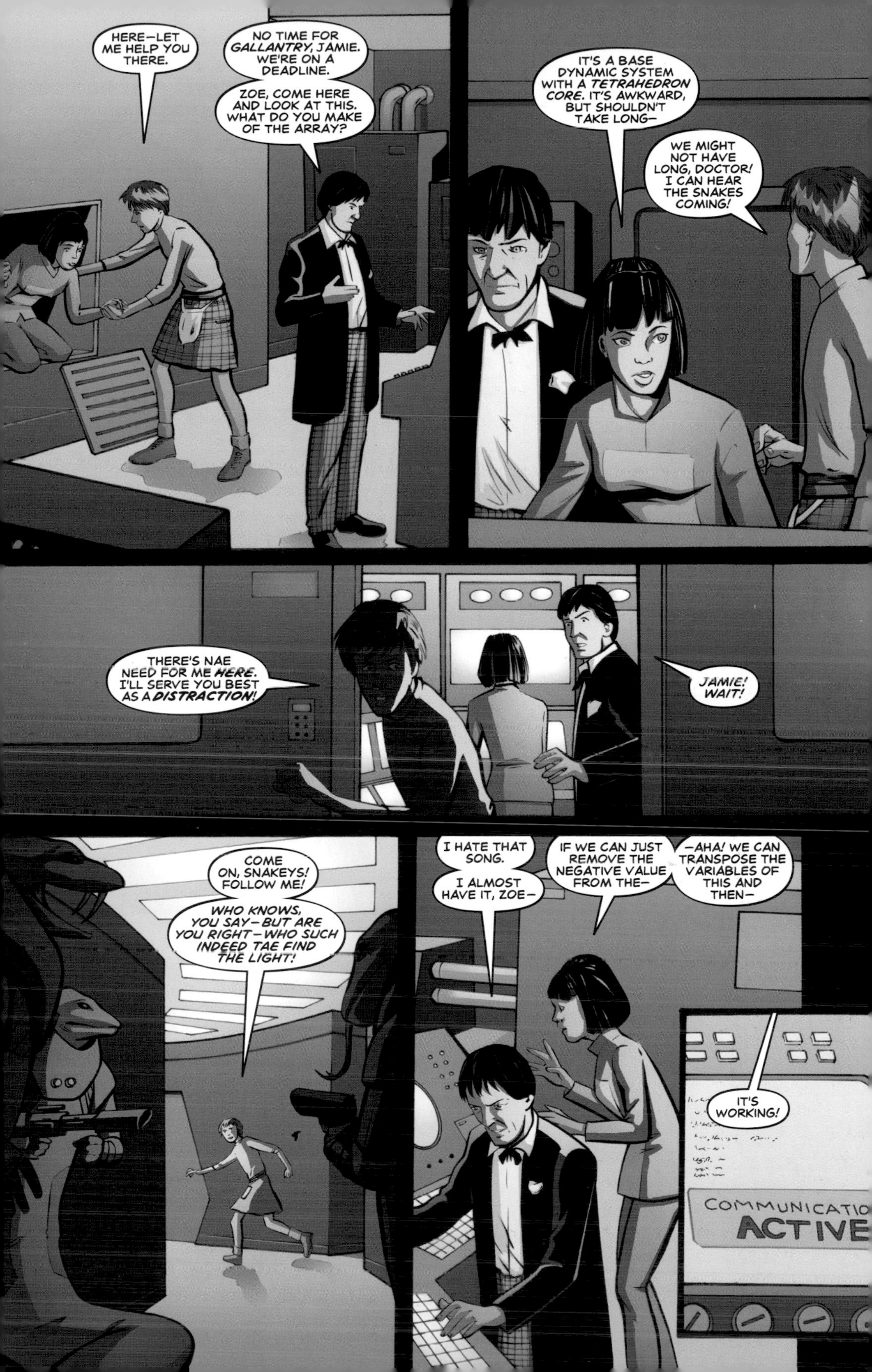
HERE—LET ME HELP YOU THERE.
NO TIME FOR GALLANTRY, JAMIE. WE'RE ON A DEADLINE.
ZOE, COME HERE AND LOOK AT THIS. WHAT DO YOU MAKE OF THE ARRAY?
IT'S A BASE DYNAMIC SYSTEM WITH A TETRAHEDRON CORE. IT'S AWKWARD, BUT SHOULDN'T TAKE LONG—
WE MIGHT NOT HAVE LONG, DOCTOR! I CAN HEAR THE SNAKES COMING!
THERE'S NAE NEED FOR ME HERE. I'LL SERVE YOU BEST AS A DISTRACTION!
JAMIE! WAIT!
COME ON, SNAKEYS! FOLLOW ME!
WHO KNOWS, YOU SAY—BUT ARE YOU RIGHT—WHO SUCH INDEED TAE FIND THE LIGHT!
I HATE THAT SONG.
I ALMOST HAVE IT, ZOE—
IF WE CAN JUST REMOVE THE NEGATIVE VALUE FROM THE—
—AHA! WE CAN TRANSPOSE THE VARIABLES OF THIS AND THEN—
IT'S WORKING!
COMMUNICATIO
ACTIVE

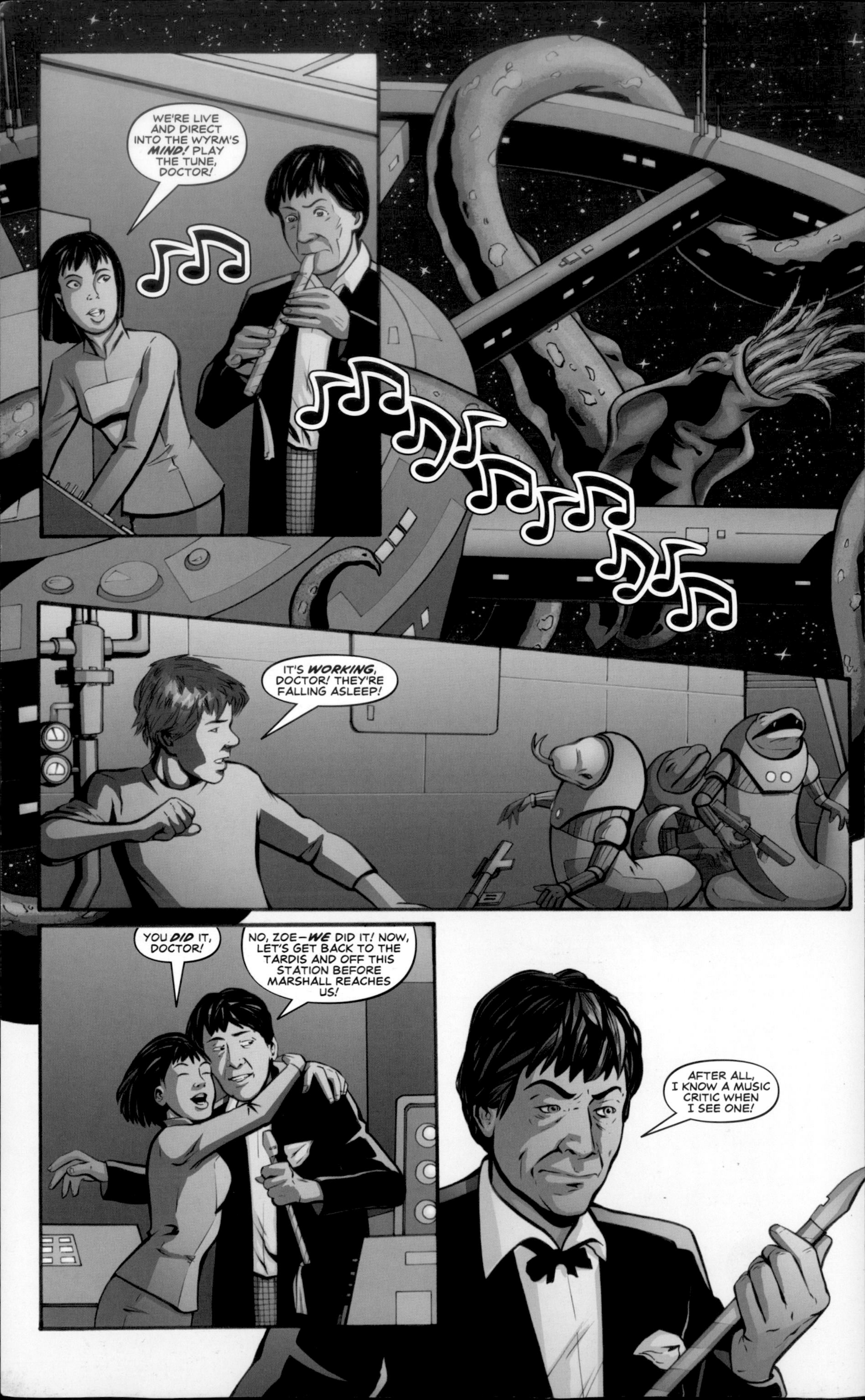
WE'RE LIVE AND DIRECT INTO THE WYRM'S *MIND!* PLAY THE TUNE, DOCTOR!
IT'S *WORKING*, DOCTOR! THEY'RE FALLING ASLEEP!
YOU *DID* IT, DOCTOR!
NO, ZOE—*WE* DID IT! NOW, LET'S GET BACK TO THE TARDIS AND OFF THIS STATION BEFORE MARSHALL REACHES US!
AFTER ALL, I KNOW A MUSIC CRITIC WHEN I SEE ONE!

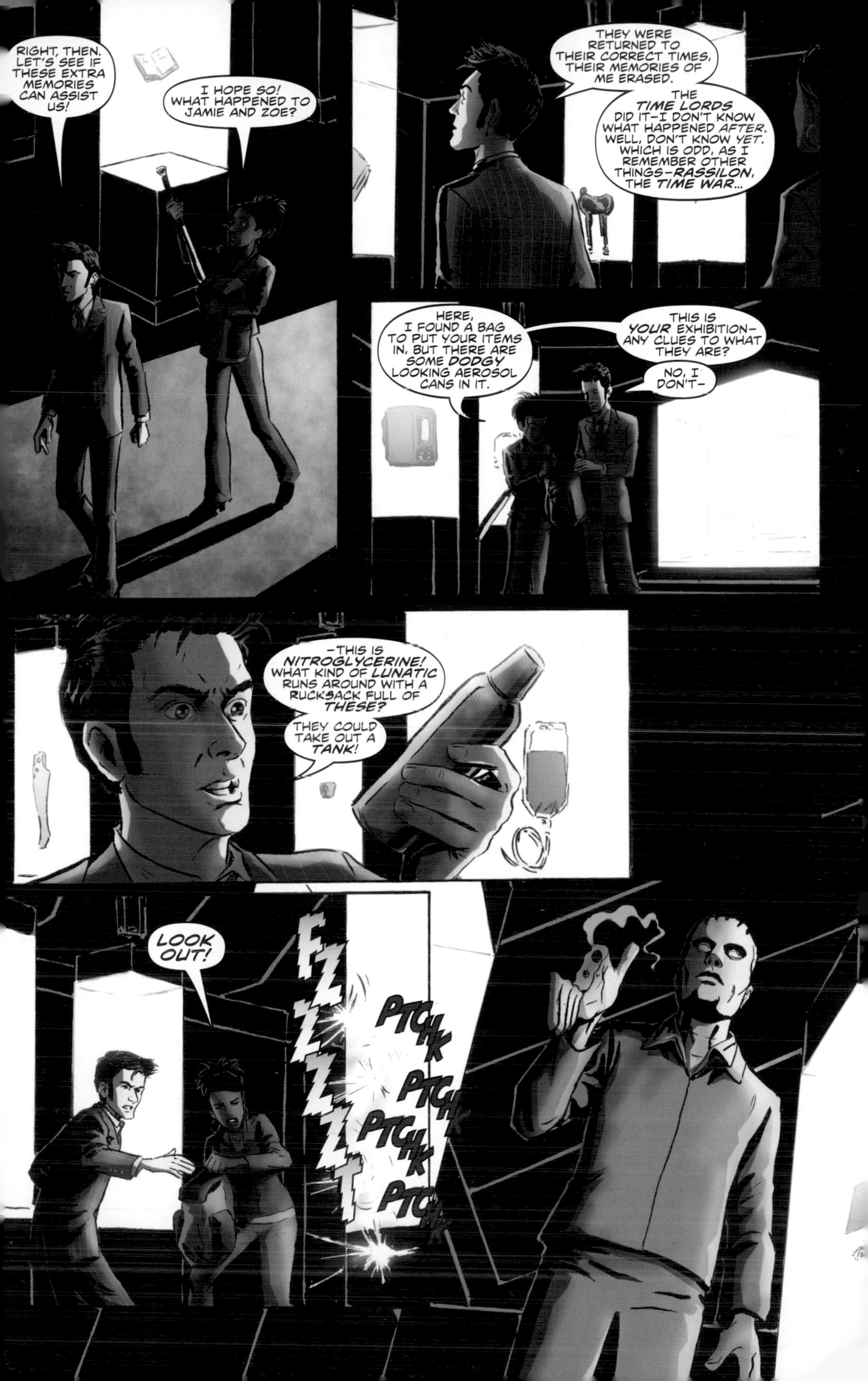
RIGHT, THEN. LET'S SEE IF THESE EXTRA MEMORIES CAN ASSIST US!
I HOPE SO! WHAT HAPPENED TO JAMIE AND ZOE?
THEY WERE RETURNED TO THEIR CORRECT TIMES, THEIR MEMORIES OF ME ERASED.
THE TIME LORDS DID IT—I DON'T KNOW WHAT HAPPENED AFTER. WELL, DON'T KNOW YET. WHICH IS ODD, AS I REMEMBER OTHER THINGS—RASSILON, THE TIME WAR...
HERE, I FOUND A BAG TO PUT YOUR ITEMS IN, BUT THERE ARE SOME DODGY LOOKING AEROSOL CANS IN IT.
THIS IS YOUR EXHIBITION—ANY CLUES TO WHAT THEY ARE?
NO, I DON'T—
—THIS IS NITROGLYCERINE! WHAT KIND OF LUNATIC RUNS AROUND WITH A RUCKSACK FULL OF THESE?
THEY COULD TAKE OUT A TANK!
LOOK OUT!
FZZZZZZZT
PTCHK
PTCHK
PTCHK
PTCHK

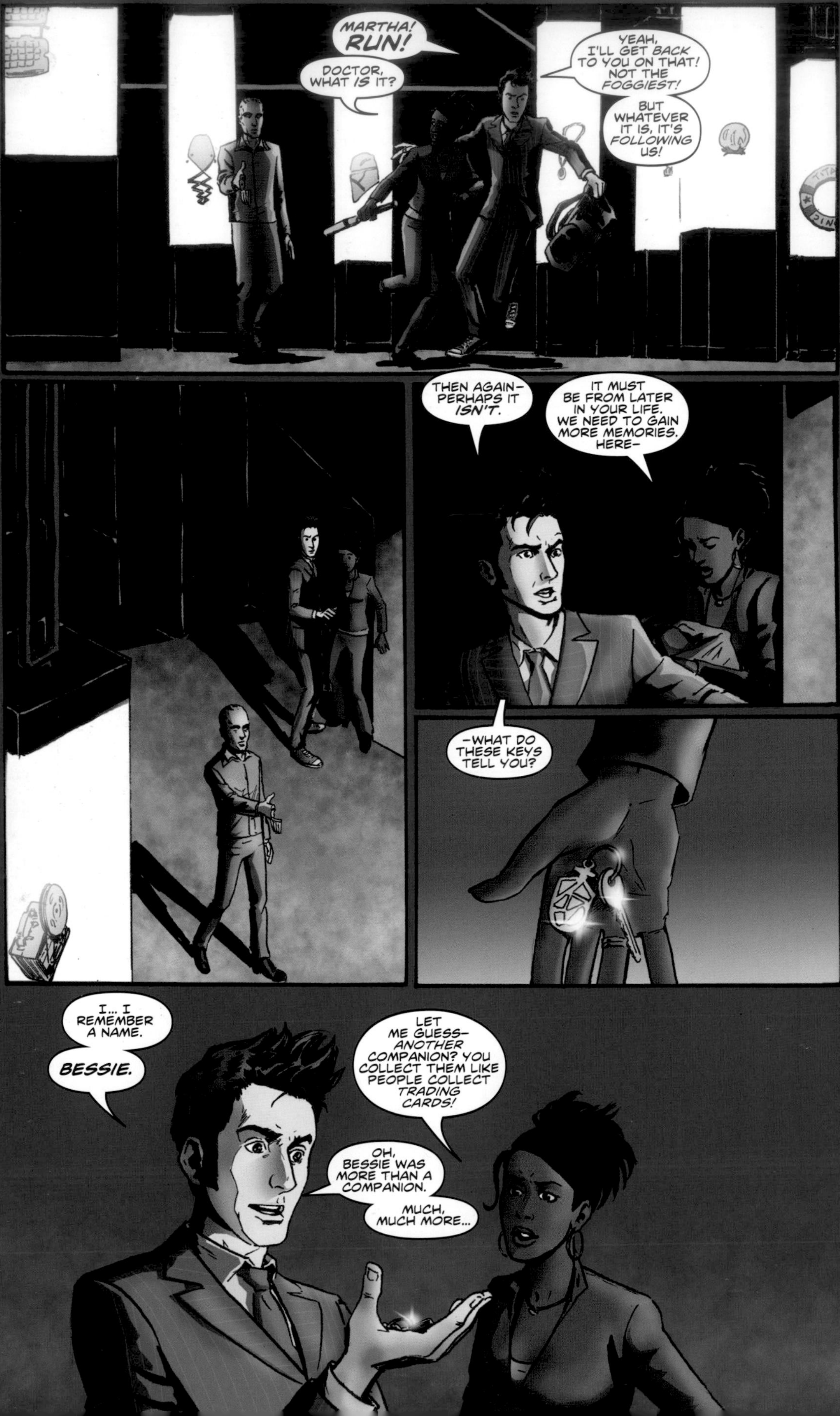
MARTHA! RUN!
DOCTOR, WHAT IS IT?
YEAH, I'LL GET BACK TO YOU ON THAT! NOT THE FOGGIEST!
BUT WHATEVER IT IS, IT'S FOLLOWING US!
THEN AGAIN– PERHAPS IT ISN'T.
IT MUST BE FROM LATER IN YOUR LIFE. WE NEED TO GAIN MORE MEMORIES. HERE–
–WHAT DO THESE KEYS TELL YOU?
I... I REMEMBER A NAME.
BESSIE.
LET ME GUESS– ANOTHER COMPANION? YOU COLLECT THEM LIKE PEOPLE COLLECT TRADING CARDS!
OH, BESSIE WAS MORE THAN A COMPANION.
MUCH, MUCH MORE...

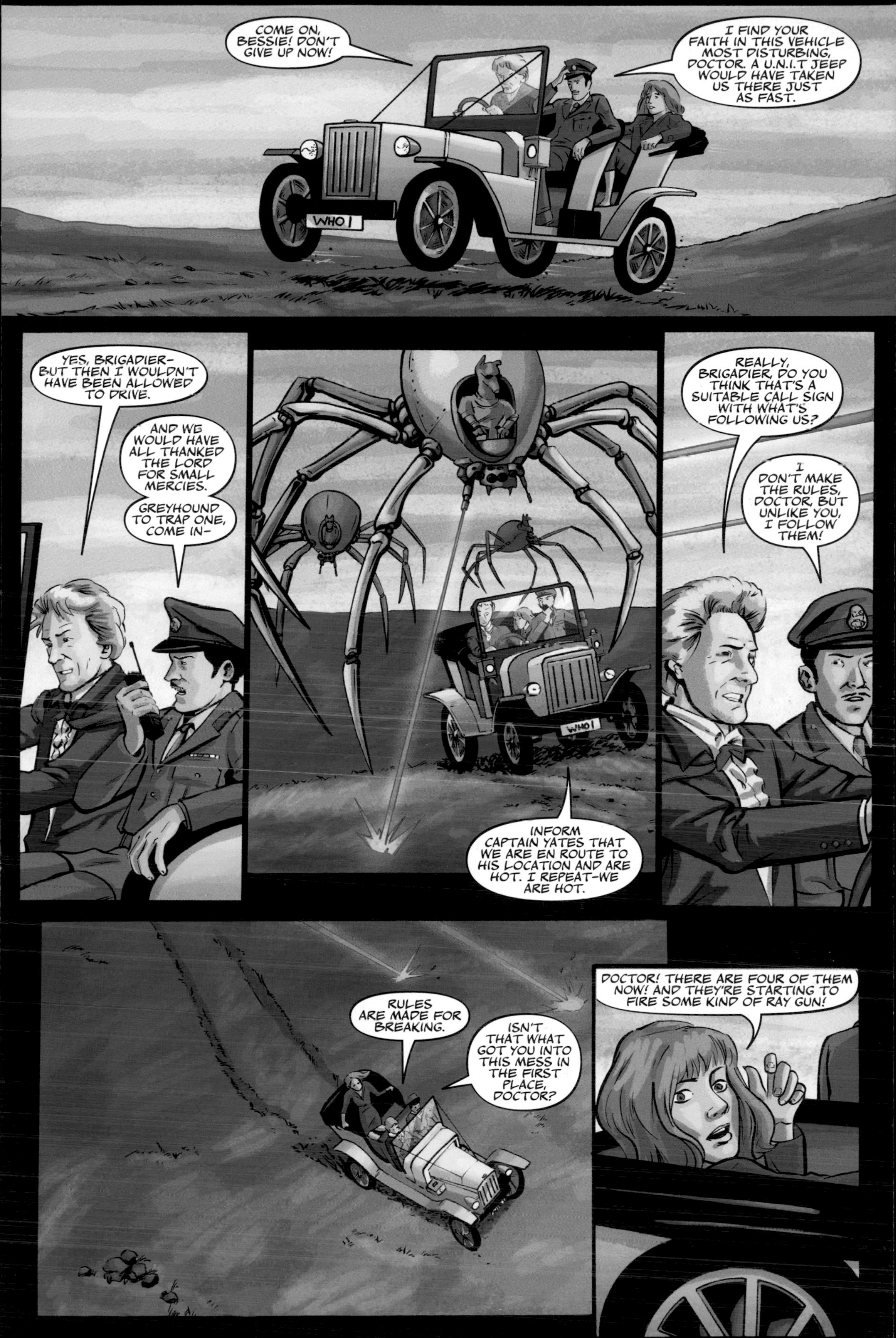
COME ON, BESSIE! DON'T GIVE UP NOW!
I FIND YOUR FAITH IN THIS VEHICLE MOST DISTURBING, DOCTOR. A U.N.I.T JEEP WOULD HAVE TAKEN US THERE JUST AS FAST.
WHO 1
YES, BRIGADIER-BUT THEN I WOULDN'T HAVE BEEN ALLOWED TO DRIVE.
AND WE WOULD HAVE ALL THANKED THE LORD FOR SMALL MERCIES.
GREYHOUND TO TRAP ONE, COME IN-
WHO 1
INFORM CAPTAIN YATES THAT WE ARE EN ROUTE TO HIS LOCATION AND ARE HOT. I REPEAT-WE ARE HOT.
REALLY, BRIGADIER, DO YOU THINK THAT'S A SUITABLE CALL SIGN WITH WHAT'S FOLLOWING US?
I DON'T MAKE THE RULES, DOCTOR, BUT UNLIKE YOU, I FOLLOW THEM!
RULES ARE MADE FOR BREAKING.
ISN'T THAT WHAT GOT YOU INTO THIS MESS IN THE FIRST PLACE, DOCTOR?
DOCTOR! THERE ARE FOUR OF THEM NOW! AND THEY'RE STARTING TO FIRE SOME KIND OF RAY GUN!

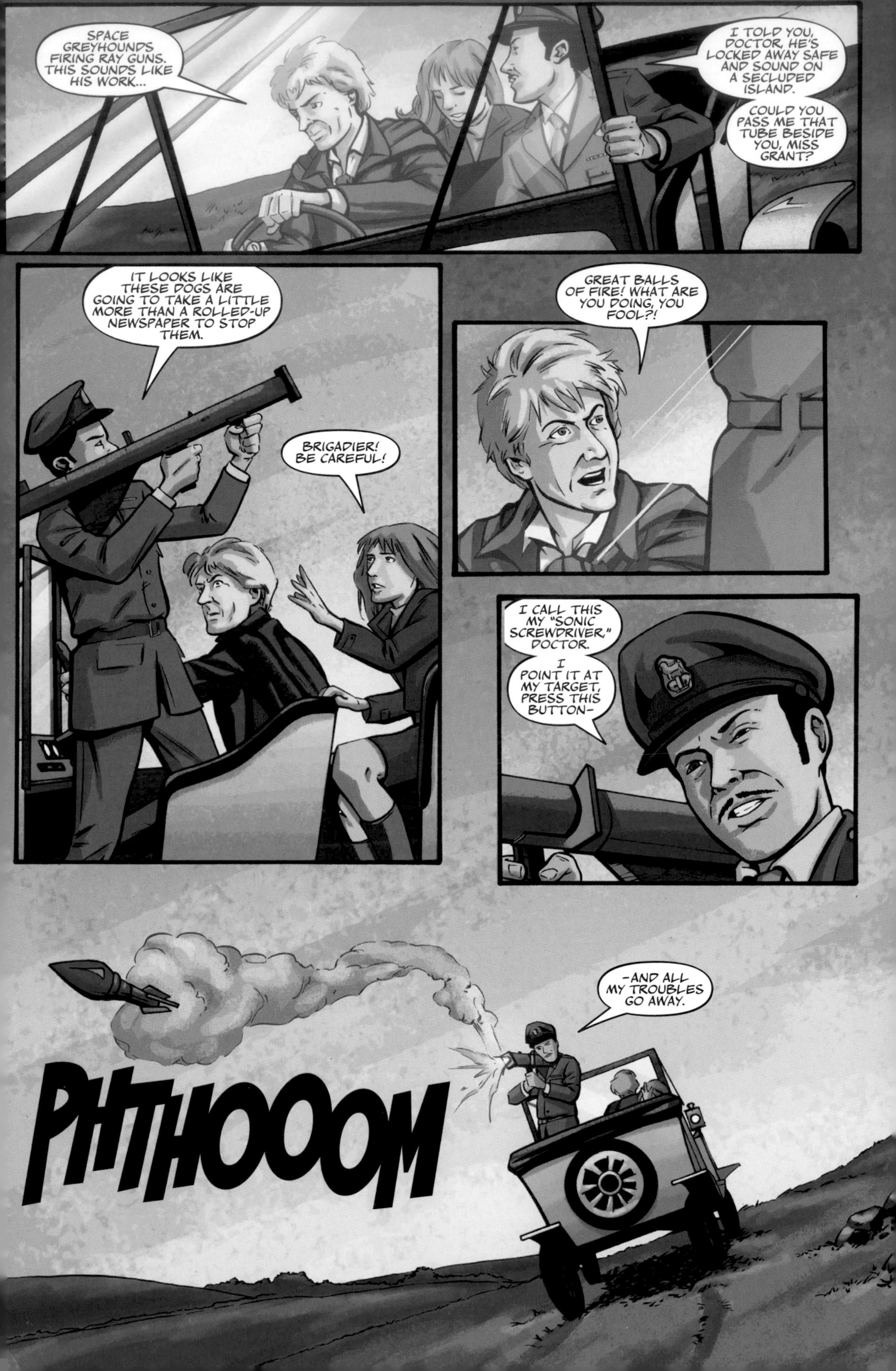
SPACE GREYHOUNDS FIRING RAY GUNS. THIS SOUNDS LIKE HIS WORK...
I TOLD YOU, DOCTOR, HE'S LOCKED AWAY SAFE AND SOUND ON A SECLUDED ISLAND.
COULD YOU PASS ME THAT TUBE BESIDE YOU, MISS GRANT?
IT LOOKS LIKE THESE DOGS ARE GOING TO TAKE A LITTLE MORE THAN A ROLLED-UP NEWSPAPER TO STOP THEM.
BRIGADIER! BE CAREFUL!
GREAT BALLS OF FIRE! WHAT ARE YOU DOING, YOU FOOL?!
I CALL THIS MY "SONIC SCREWDRIVER," DOCTOR.
I POINT IT AT MY TARGET, PRESS THIS BUTTON-
-AND ALL MY TROUBLES GO AWAY.
PHTHOOOM

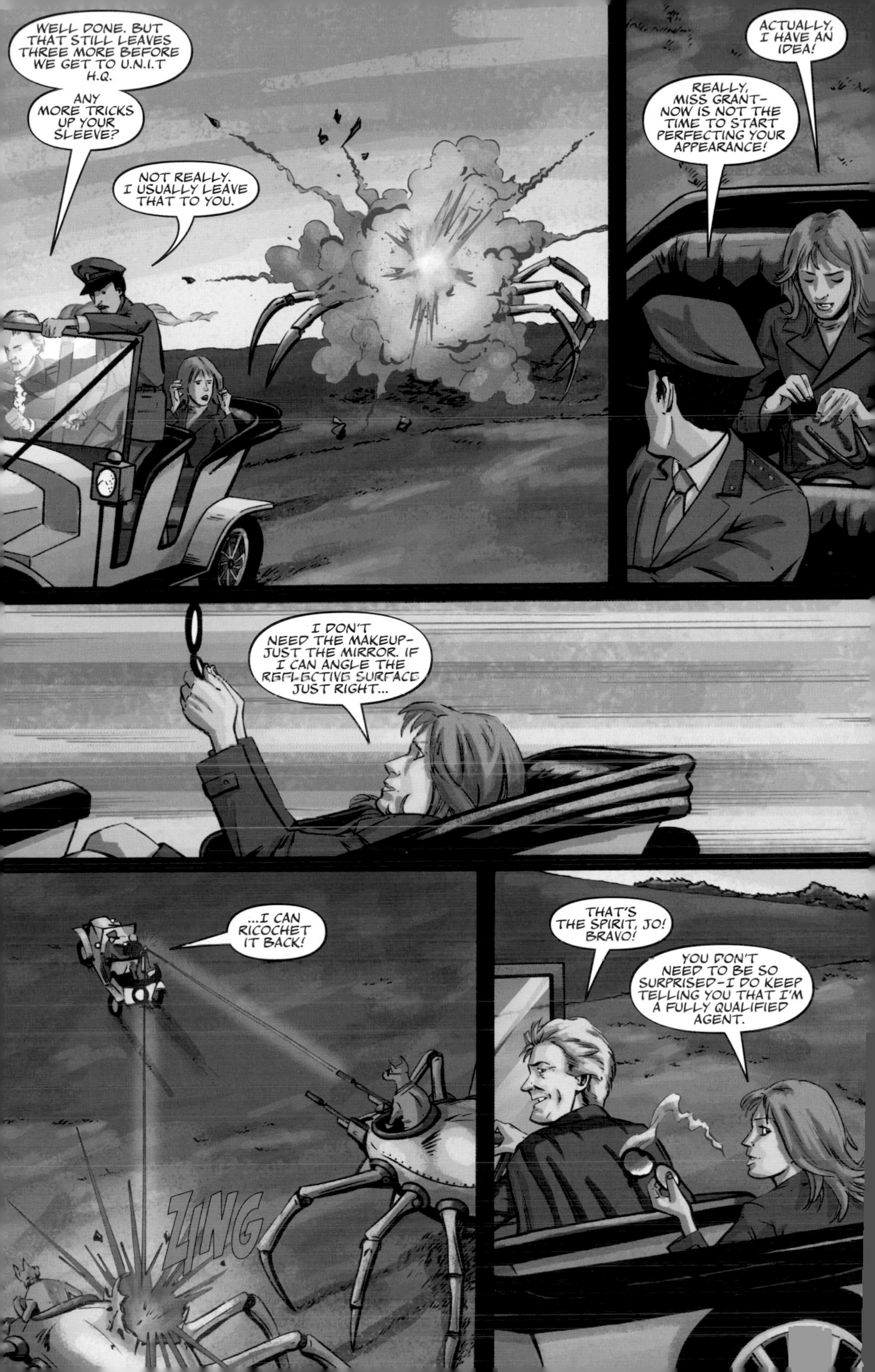
WELL DONE. BUT THAT STILL LEAVES THREE MORE BEFORE WE GET TO U.N.I.T H.Q.
ANY MORE TRICKS UP YOUR SLEEVE?
NOT REALLY. I USUALLY LEAVE THAT TO YOU.
ACTUALLY, I HAVE AN IDEA!
REALLY, MISS GRANT-NOW IS NOT THE TIME TO START PERFECTING YOUR APPEARANCE!
I DON'T NEED THE MAKEUP-JUST THE MIRROR. IF I CAN ANGLE THE REFLECTIVE SURFACE JUST RIGHT...
...I CAN RICOCHET IT BACK!
ZING
THAT'S THE SPIRIT, JO! BRAVO!
YOU DON'T NEED TO BE SO SURPRISED-I DO KEEP TELLING YOU THAT I'M A FULLY QUALIFIED AGENT.

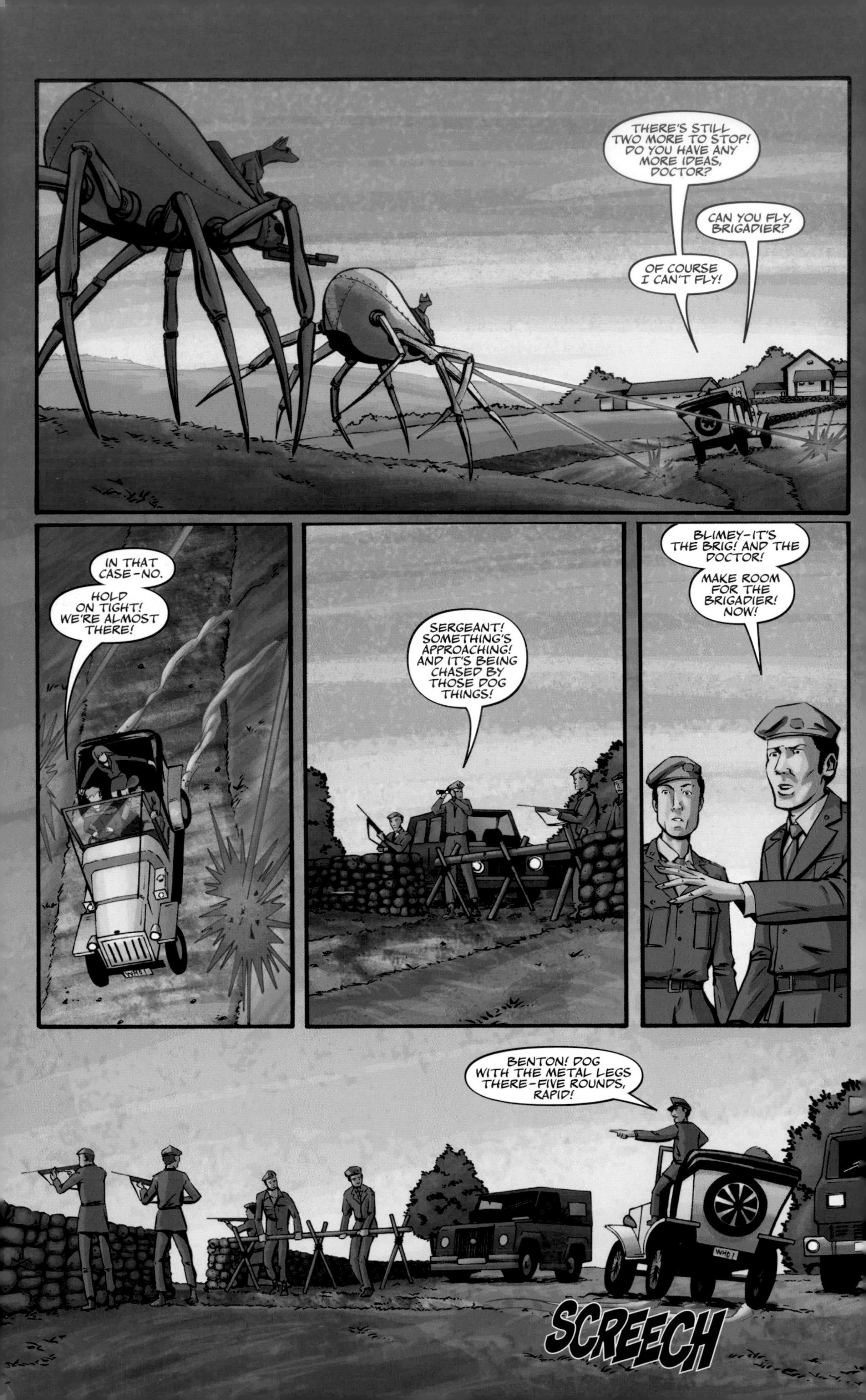
THERE'S STILL TWO MORE TO STOP! DO YOU HAVE ANY MORE IDEAS, DOCTOR?
CAN YOU FLY, BRIGADIER?
OF COURSE I CAN'T FLY!
IN THAT CASE-NO.
HOLD ON TIGHT! WE'RE ALMOST THERE!
SERGEANT! SOMETHING'S APPROACHING! AND IT'S BEING CHASED BY THOSE DOG THINGS!
BLIMEY-IT'S THE BRIG! AND THE DOCTOR!
MAKE ROOM FOR THE BRIGADIER! NOW!
BENTON! DOG WITH THE METAL LEGS THERE-FIVE ROUNDS, RAPID!
SCREECH

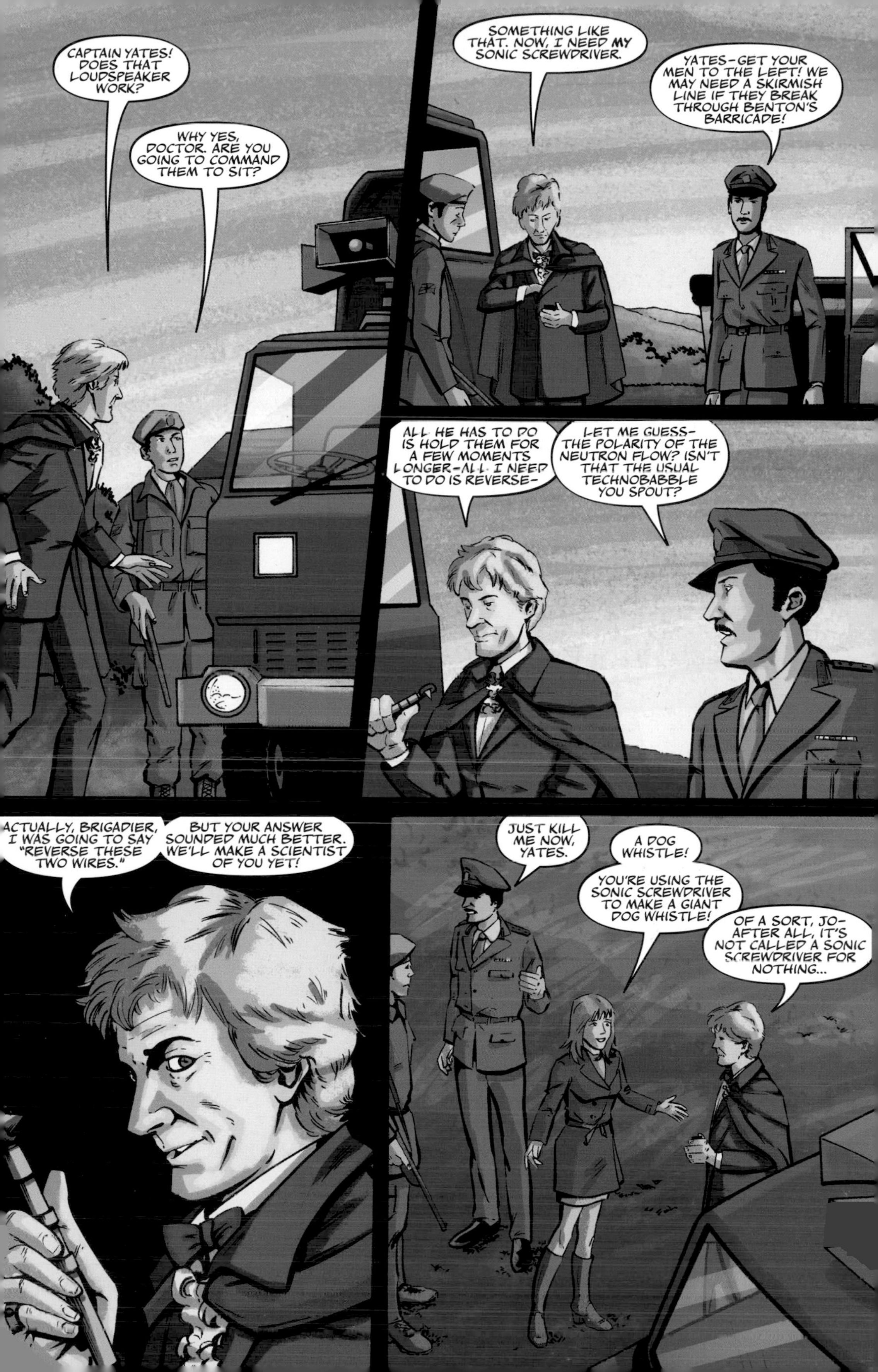
CAPTAIN YATES! DOES THAT LOUDSPEAKER WORK?
WHY YES, DOCTOR. ARE YOU GOING TO COMMAND THEM TO SIT?
SOMETHING LIKE THAT. NOW, I NEED MY SONIC SCREWDRIVER.
YATES—GET YOUR MEN TO THE LEFT! WE MAY NEED A SKIRMISH LINE IF THEY BREAK THROUGH BENTON'S BARRICADE!
ALL HE HAS TO DO IS HOLD THEM FOR A FEW MOMENTS LONGER—ALL I NEED TO DO IS REVERSE-
LET ME GUESS—THE POLARITY OF THE NEUTRON FLOW? ISN'T THAT THE USUAL TECHNOBABBLE YOU SPOUT?
ACTUALLY, BRIGADIER, I WAS GOING TO SAY "REVERSE THESE TWO WIRES."
BUT YOUR ANSWER SOUNDED MUCH BETTER. WE'LL MAKE A SCIENTIST OF YOU YET!
JUST KILL ME NOW, YATES.
A DOG WHISTLE!
YOU'RE USING THE SONIC SCREWDRIVER TO MAKE A GIANT DOG WHISTLE!
OF A SORT, JO—AFTER ALL, IT'S NOT CALLED A SONIC SCREWDRIVER FOR NOTHING...

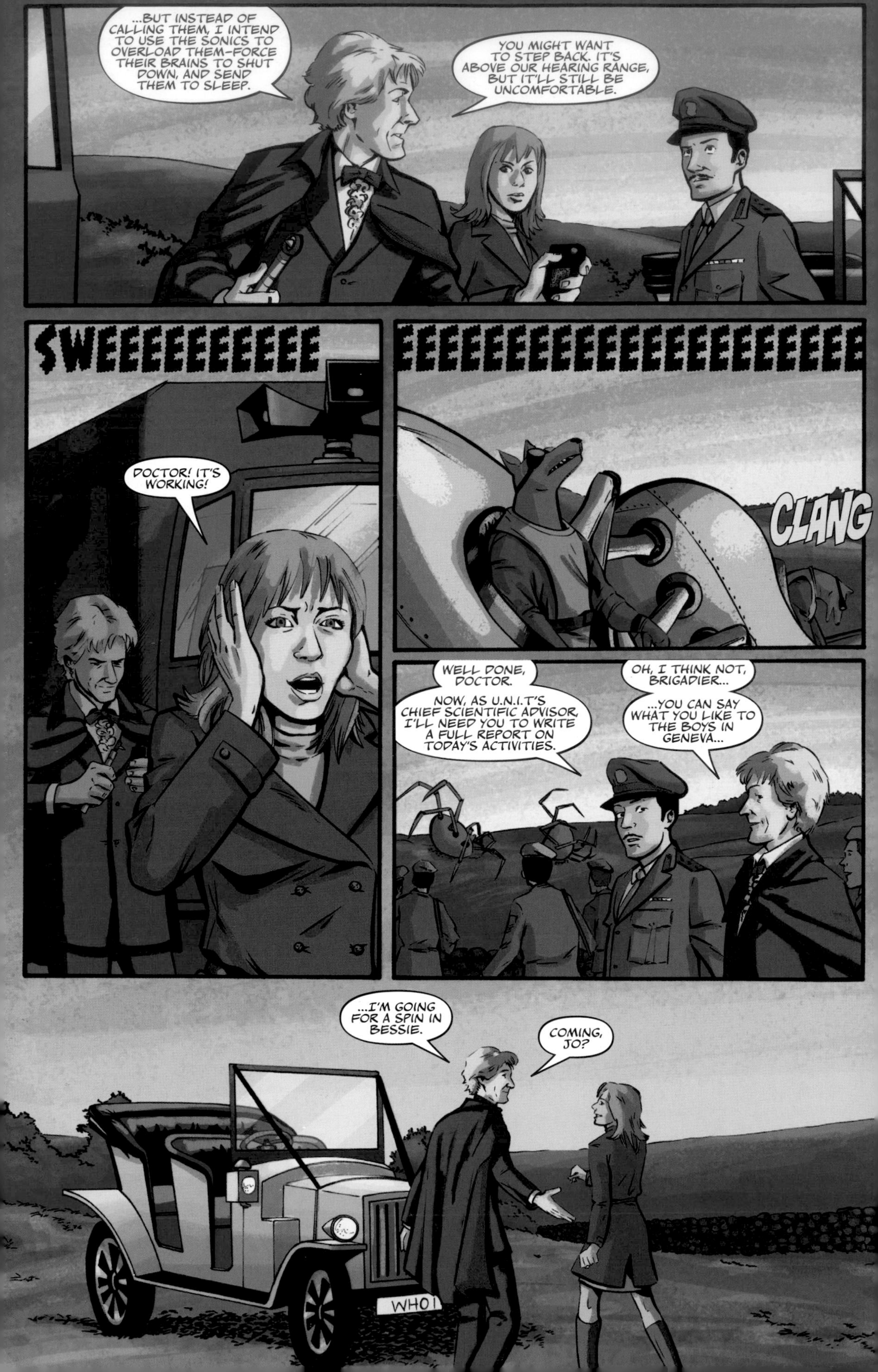
...BUT INSTEAD OF CALLING THEM, I INTEND TO USE THE SONICS TO OVERLOAD THEM—FORCE THEIR BRAINS TO SHUT DOWN, AND SEND THEM TO SLEEP.
YOU MIGHT WANT TO STEP BACK. IT'S ABOVE OUR HEARING RANGE, BUT IT'LL STILL BE UNCOMFORTABLE.
SWEEEEEEEEEE
DOCTOR! IT'S WORKING!
EEEEEEEEEEEEEEEEEEEEEEE
CLANG
WELL DONE, DOCTOR.
NOW, AS U.N.I.T.'S CHIEF SCIENTIFIC ADVISOR, I'LL NEED YOU TO WRITE A FULL REPORT ON TODAY'S ACTIVITIES.
OH, I THINK NOT, BRIGADIER...
...YOU CAN SAY WHAT YOU LIKE TO THE BOYS IN GENEVA...
...I'M GOING FOR A SPIN IN BESSIE.
COMING, JO?
WHO 1

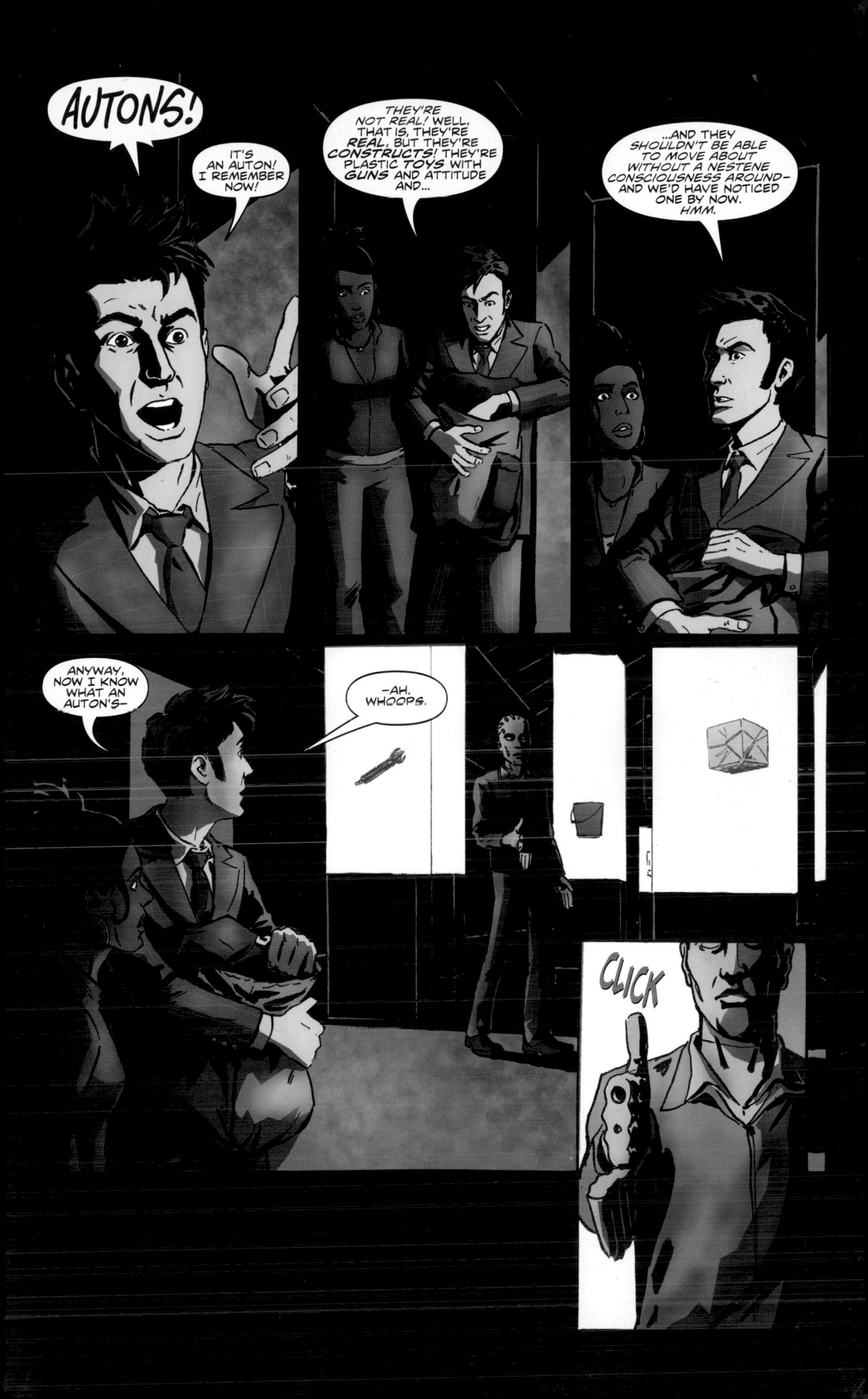
AUTONS!
IT'S AN AUTON! I REMEMBER NOW!
THEY'RE NOT REAL! WELL, THAT IS, THEY'RE REAL, BUT THEY'RE CONSTRUCTS! THEY'RE PLASTIC TOYS WITH GUNS AND ATTITUDE AND...
...AND THEY SHOULDN'T BE ABLE TO MOVE ABOUT WITHOUT A NESTENE CONSCIOUSNESS AROUND-AND WE'D HAVE NOTICED ONE BY NOW. HMM.
ANYWAY, NOW I KNOW WHAT AN AUTON'S-
-AH. WHOOPS.
CLICK

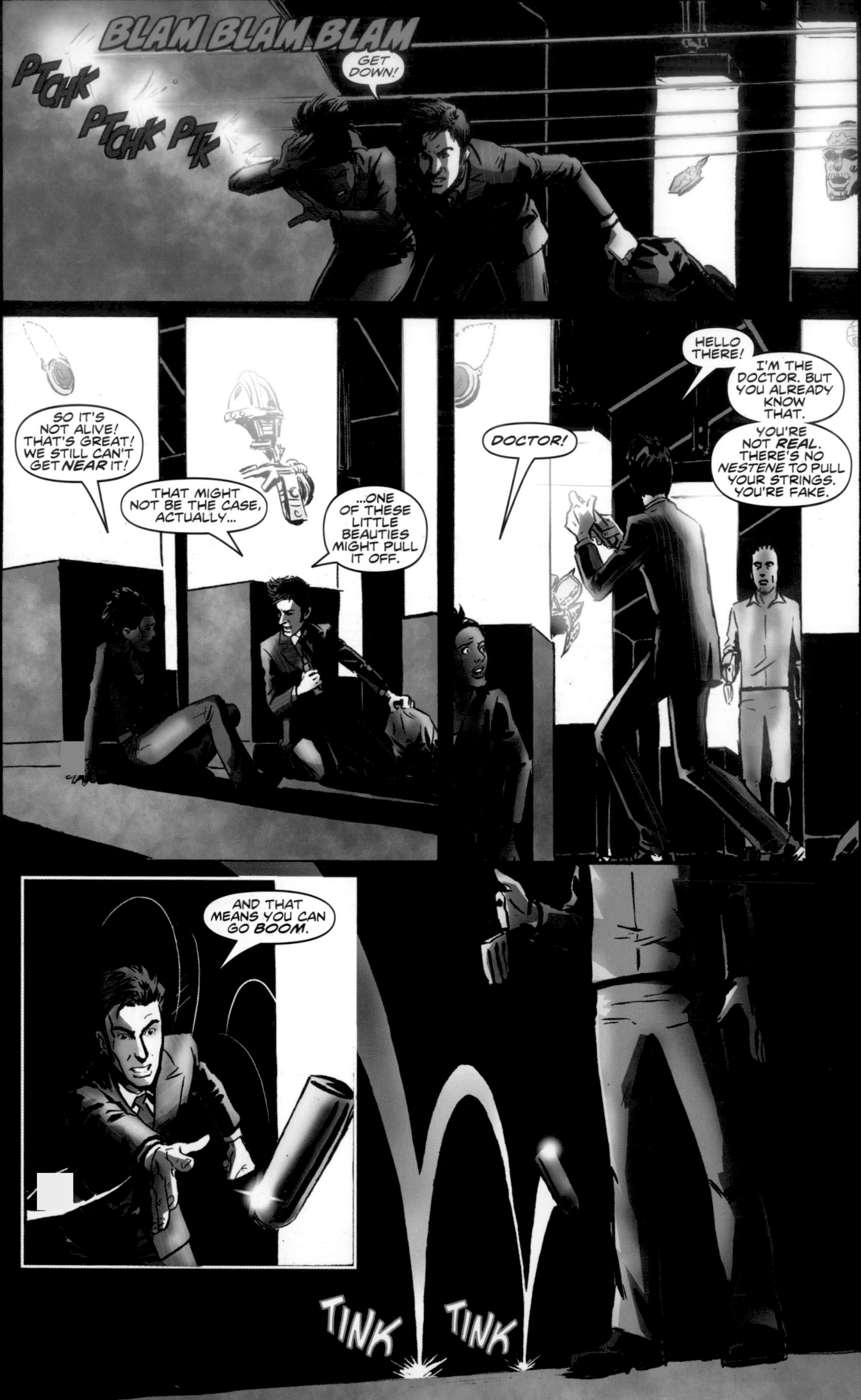
BLAM BLAM BLAM
PTCHK PTCHK PTK
GET DOWN!
SO IT'S NOT ALIVE! THAT'S GREAT! WE STILL CAN'T GET NEAR IT!
THAT MIGHT NOT BE THE CASE, ACTUALLY...
...ONE OF THESE LITTLE BEAUTIES MIGHT PULL IT OFF.
DOCTOR!
HELLO THERE!
I'M THE DOCTOR. BUT YOU ALREADY KNOW THAT.
YOU'RE NOT REAL. THERE'S NO NESTENE TO PULL YOUR STRINGS. YOU'RE FAKE.
AND THAT MEANS YOU CAN GO BOOM.
TINK TINK

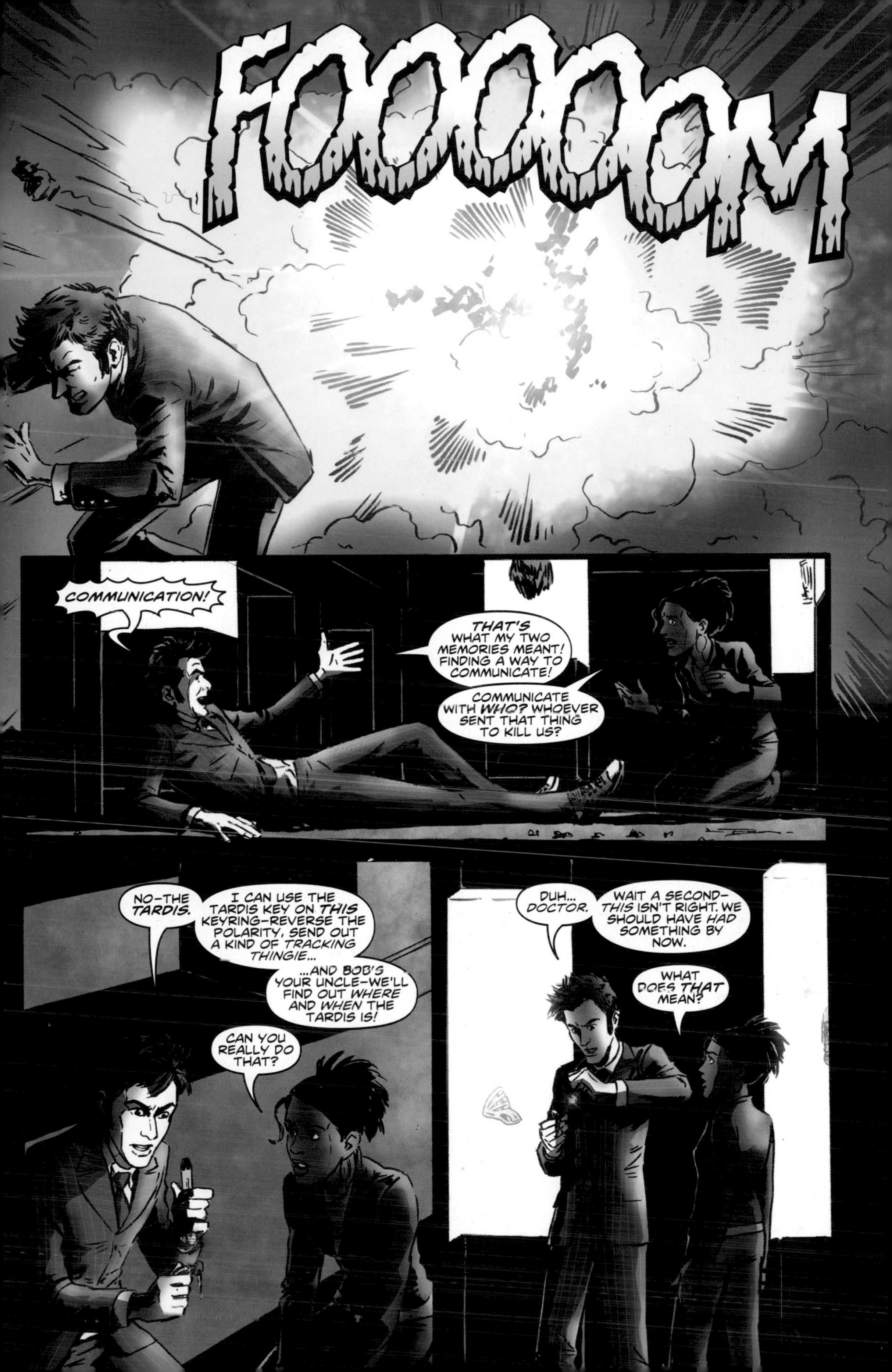
FOOOOOM
COMMUNICATION!
THAT'S WHAT MY TWO MEMORIES MEANT! FINDING A WAY TO COMMUNICATE!
COMMUNICATE WITH WHO? WHOEVER SENT THAT THING TO KILL US?
NO–THE TARDIS.
I CAN USE THE TARDIS KEY ON THIS KEYRING–REVERSE THE POLARITY, SEND OUT A KIND OF TRACKING THINGIE...
...AND BOB'S YOUR UNCLE–WE'LL FIND OUT WHERE AND WHEN THE TARDIS IS!
CAN YOU REALLY DO THAT?
DUH... DOCTOR.
WAIT A SECOND– THIS ISN'T RIGHT. WE SHOULD HAVE HAD SOMETHING BY NOW.
WHAT DOES THAT MEAN?

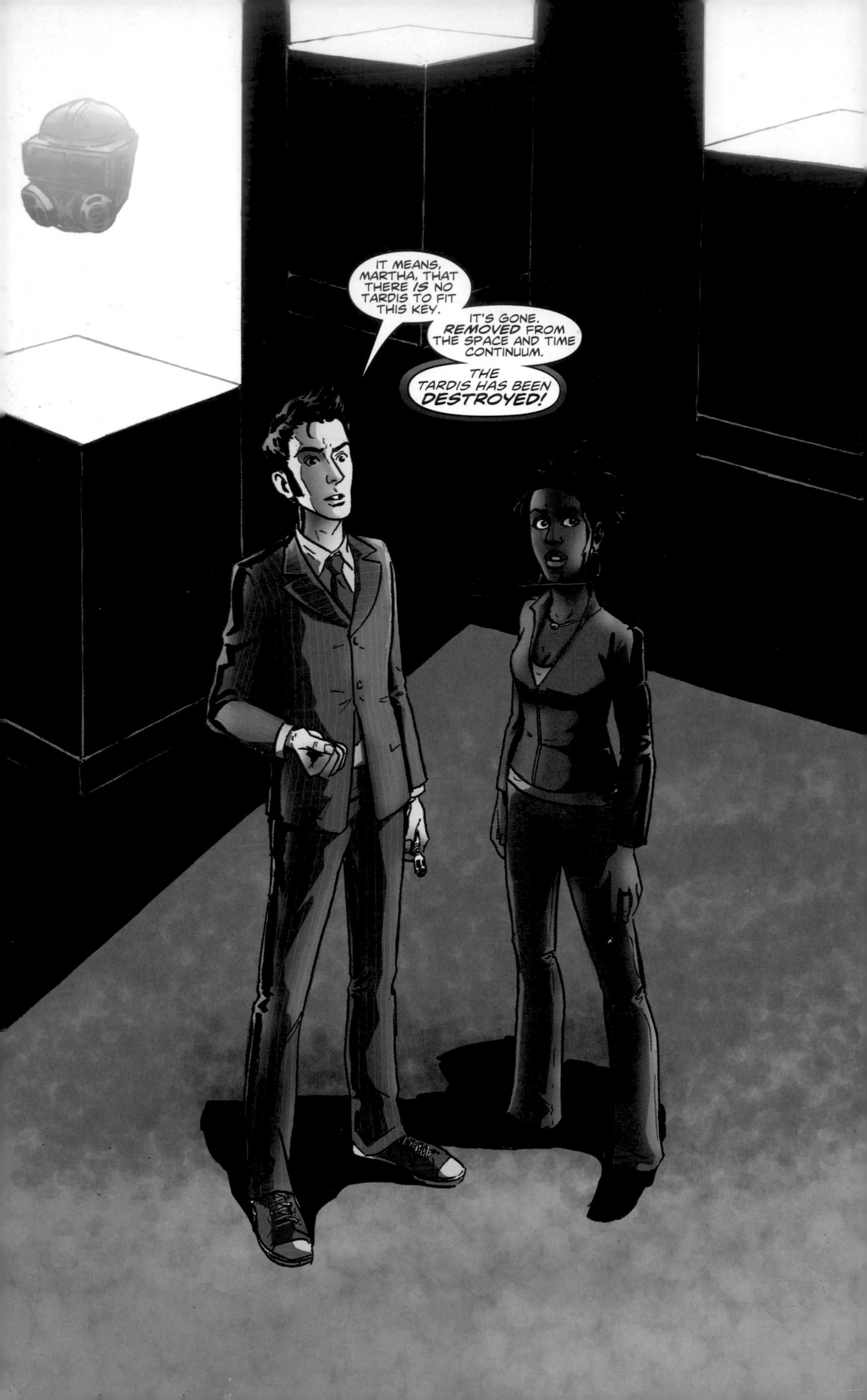
IT MEANS, MARTHA, THAT THERE *IS* NO TARDIS TO FIT THIS KEY.
IT'S GONE. **REMOVED** FROM THE SPACE AND TIME CONTINUUM.
THE TARDIS HAS BEEN **DESTROYED!**

CHAPTER · THREE
MISDIRECTION

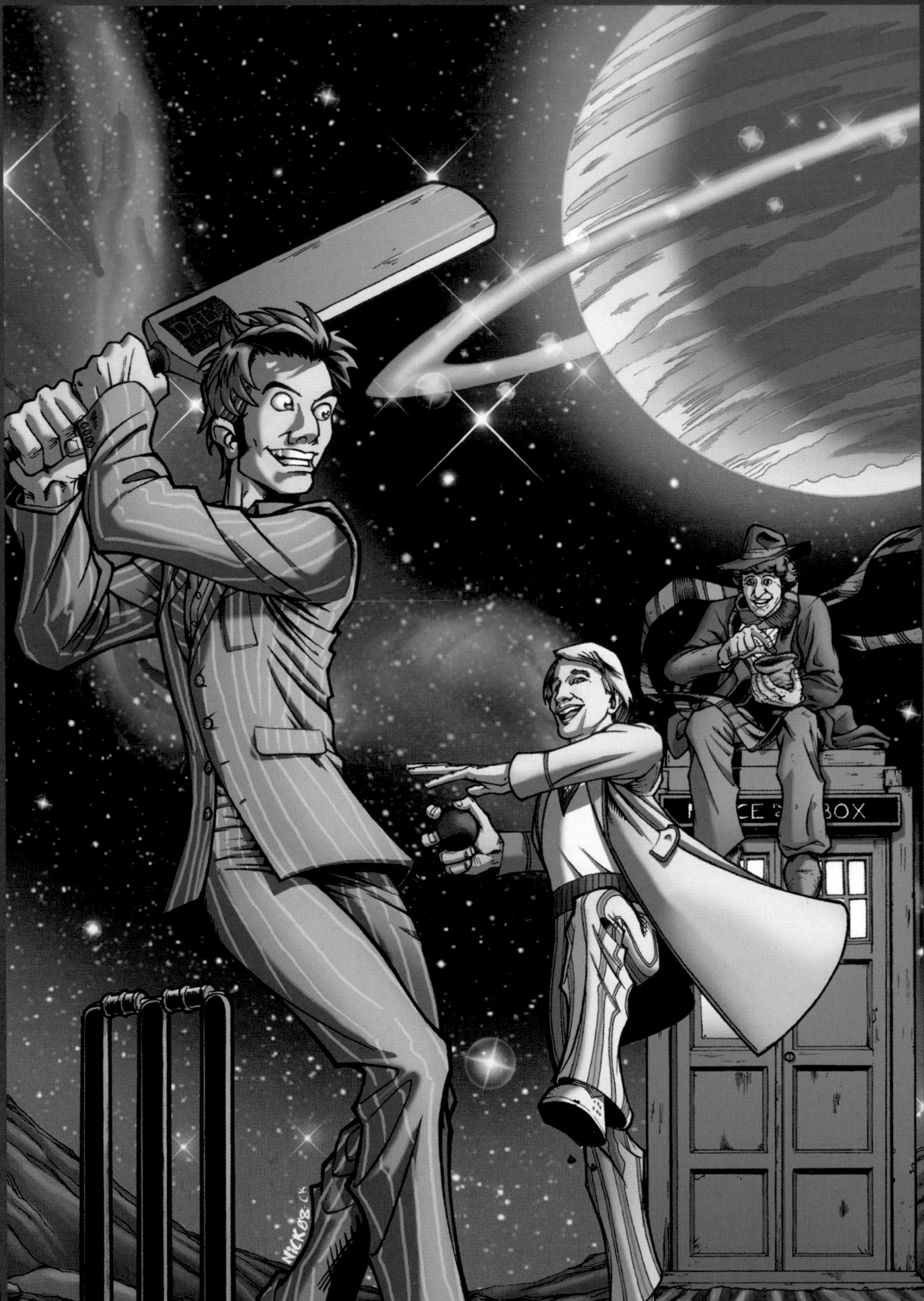
DAILY
POLICE BOX

ART BY NICK ROCHE • COLOR BY CHARLIE KIRCHOFF

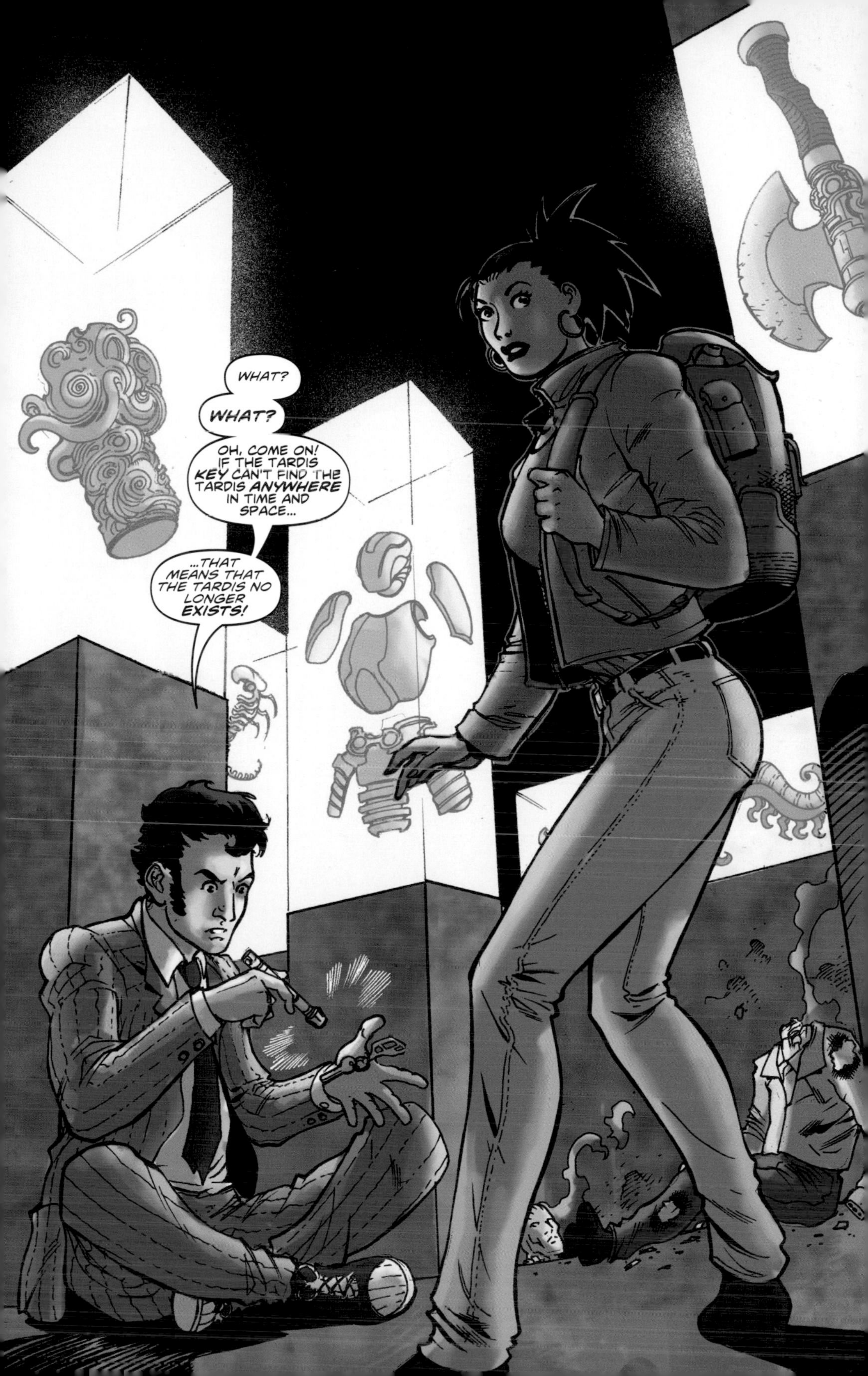
WHAT?
WHAT?
OH, COME ON! IF THE TARDIS KEY CAN'T FIND THE TARDIS ANYWHERE IN TIME AND SPACE...
...THAT MEANS THAT THE TARDIS NO LONGER EXISTS!

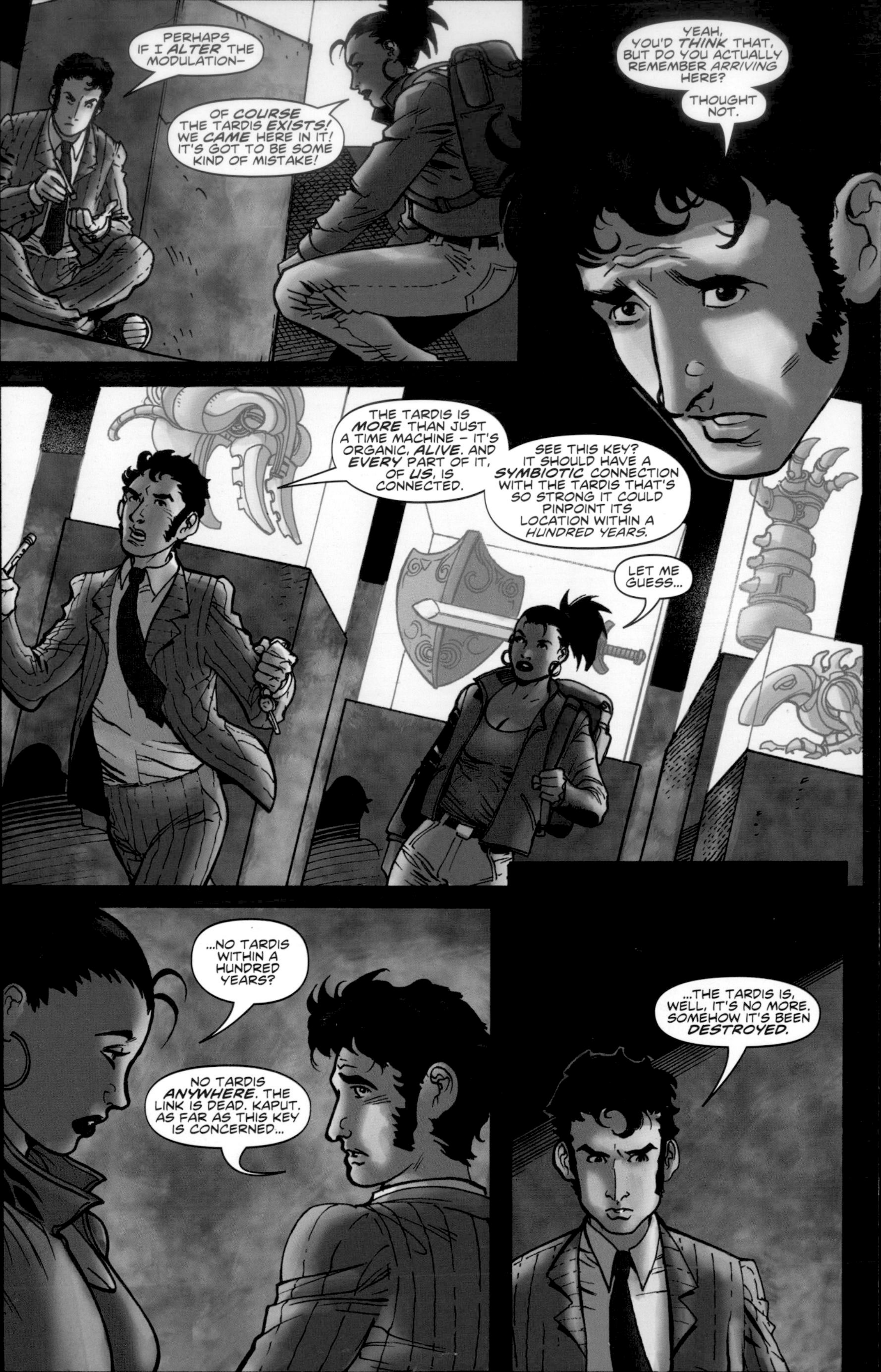
PERHAPS IF I ALTER THE MODULATION–
OF COURSE THE TARDIS EXISTS! WE CAME HERE IN IT! IT'S GOT TO BE SOME KIND OF MISTAKE!
YEAH, YOU'D THINK THAT, BUT DO YOU ACTUALLY REMEMBER ARRIVING HERE?
THOUGHT NOT.
THE TARDIS IS MORE THAN JUST A TIME MACHINE – IT'S ORGANIC, ALIVE. AND EVERY PART OF IT, OF US, IS CONNECTED.
SEE THIS KEY? IT SHOULD HAVE A SYMBIOTIC CONNECTION WITH THE TARDIS THAT'S SO STRONG IT COULD PINPOINT ITS LOCATION WITHIN A HUNDRED YEARS.
LET ME GUESS...
...NO TARDIS WITHIN A HUNDRED YEARS?
NO TARDIS ANYWHERE. THE LINK IS DEAD. KAPUT. AS FAR AS THIS KEY IS CONCERNED...
...THE TARDIS IS, WELL, IT'S NO MORE. SOMEHOW IT'S BEEN DESTROYED.

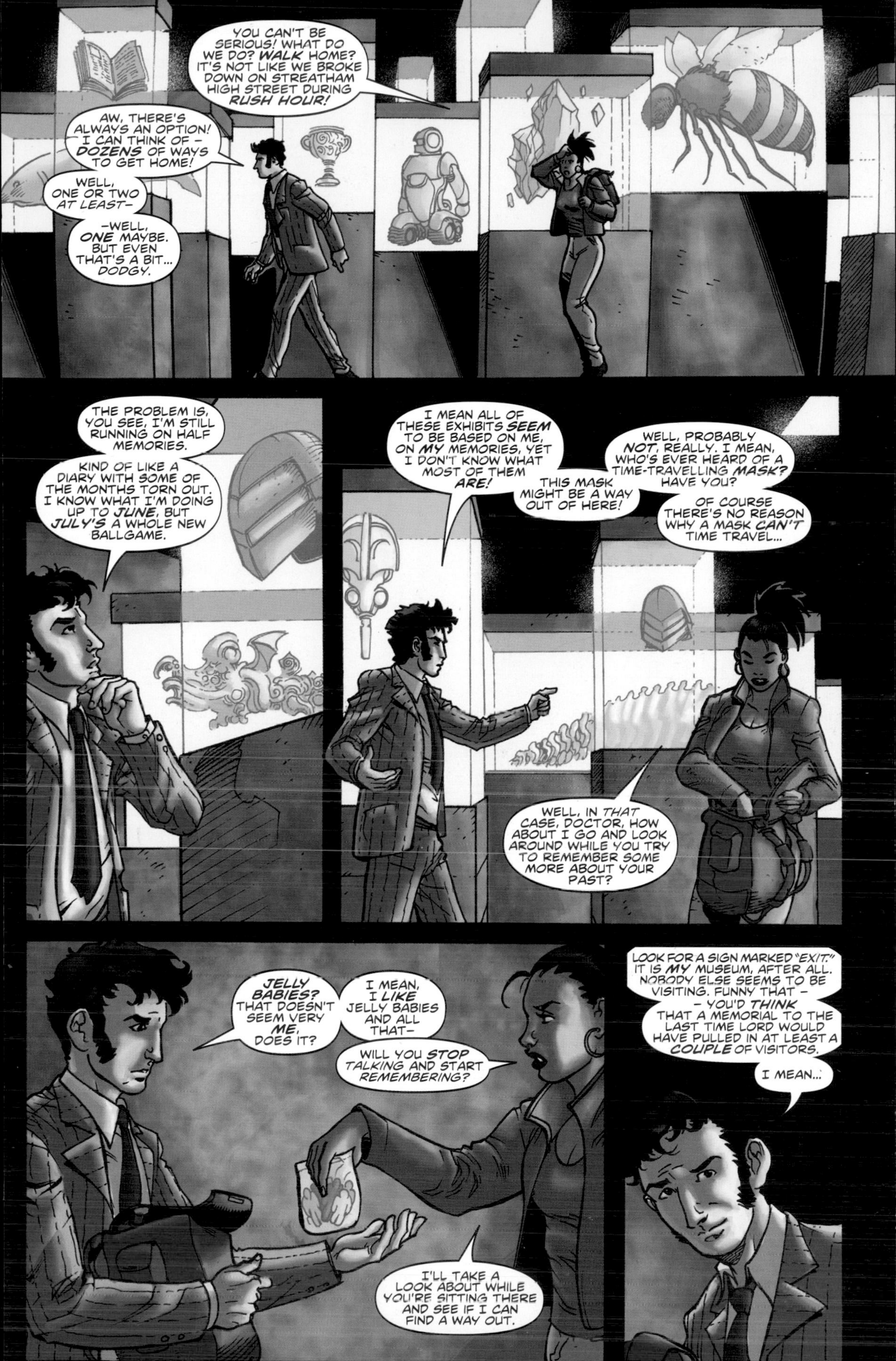

YOU CAN'T BE SERIOUS! WHAT DO WE DO? WALK HOME? IT'S NOT LIKE WE BROKE DOWN ON STREATHAM HIGH STREET DURING RUSH HOUR!
AW, THERE'S ALWAYS AN OPTION! I CAN THINK OF -- DOZENS OF WAYS TO GET HOME!
WELL, ONE OR TWO AT LEAST--
--WELL, ONE MAYBE. BUT EVEN THAT'S A BIT... DODGY.
THE PROBLEM IS, YOU SEE, I'M STILL RUNNING ON HALF MEMORIES.
KIND OF LIKE A DIARY WITH SOME OF THE MONTHS TORN OUT. I KNOW WHAT I'M DOING UP TO JUNE, BUT JULY'S A WHOLE NEW BALLGAME.
I MEAN ALL OF THESE EXHIBITS SEEM TO BE BASED ON ME, ON MY MEMORIES, YET I DON'T KNOW WHAT MOST OF THEM ARE!
THIS MASK MIGHT BE A WAY OUT OF HERE!
WELL, PROBABLY NOT, REALLY. I MEAN, WHO'S EVER HEARD OF A TIME-TRAVELLING MASK? HAVE YOU?
OF COURSE THERE'S NO REASON WHY A MASK CAN'T TIME TRAVEL...
WELL, IN THAT CASE, DOCTOR, HOW ABOUT I GO AND LOOK AROUND WHILE YOU TRY TO REMEMBER SOME MORE ABOUT YOUR PAST?
JELLY BABIES? THAT DOESN'T SEEM VERY ME, DOES IT?
I MEAN, I LIKE JELLY BABIES AND ALL THAT--
WILL YOU STOP TALKING AND START REMEMBERING?
I'LL TAKE A LOOK ABOUT WHILE YOU'RE SITTING THERE AND SEE IF I CAN FIND A WAY OUT.
LOOK FOR A SIGN MARKED "EXIT." IT IS MY MUSEUM, AFTER ALL. NOBODY ELSE SEEMS TO BE VISITING. FUNNY THAT --
-- YOU'D THINK THAT A MEMORIAL TO THE LAST TIME LORD WOULD HAVE PULLED IN AT LEAST A COUPLE OF VISITORS.
I MEAN...

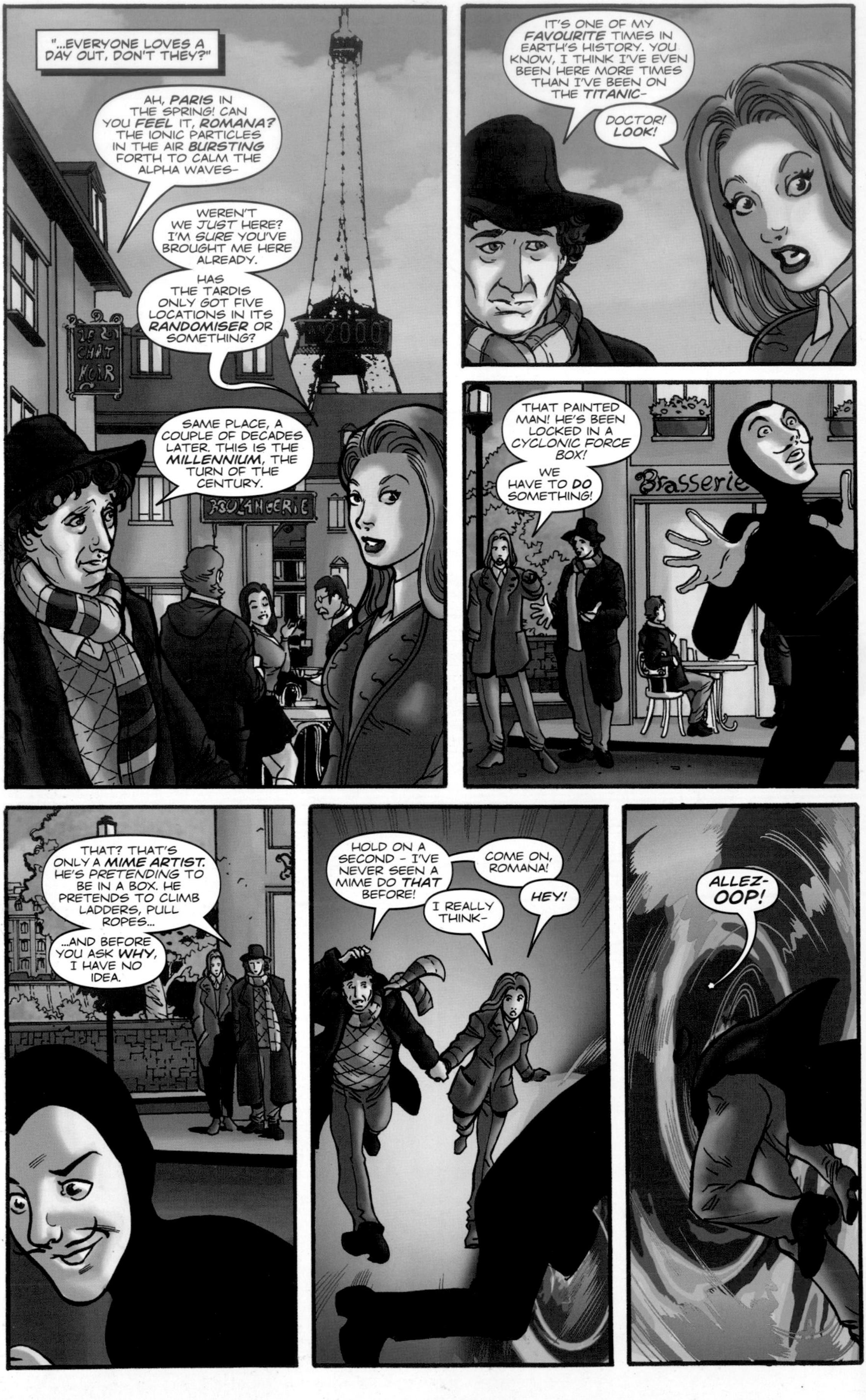
"...EVERYONE LOVES A DAY OUT, DON'T THEY?"
AH, PARIS IN THE SPRING! CAN YOU FEEL IT, ROMANA? THE IONIC PARTICLES IN THE AIR BURSTING FORTH TO CALM THE ALPHA WAVES-
WEREN'T WE JUST HERE? I'M SURE YOU'VE BROUGHT ME HERE ALREADY.
HAS THE TARDIS ONLY GOT FIVE LOCATIONS IN ITS RANDOMISER OR SOMETHING?
CHAT NOIR
2000
SAME PLACE, A COUPLE OF DECADES LATER. THIS IS THE MILLENNIUM, THE TURN OF THE CENTURY.
BOULANGERIE
IT'S ONE OF MY FAVOURITE TIMES IN EARTH'S HISTORY. YOU KNOW, I THINK I'VE EVEN BEEN HERE MORE TIMES THAN I'VE BEEN ON THE TITANIC-
DOCTOR! LOOK!
THAT PAINTED MAN! HE'S BEEN LOCKED IN A CYCLONIC FORCE BOX!
WE HAVE TO DO SOMETHING!
Brasserie
THAT? THAT'S ONLY A MIME ARTIST. HE'S PRETENDING TO BE IN A BOX. HE PRETENDS TO CLIMB LADDERS, PULL ROPES...
...AND BEFORE YOU ASK WHY, I HAVE NO IDEA.
HOLD ON A SECOND - I'VE NEVER SEEN A MIME DO THAT BEFORE!
COME ON, ROMANA!
I REALLY THINK-
HEY!
ALLEZ-OOP!

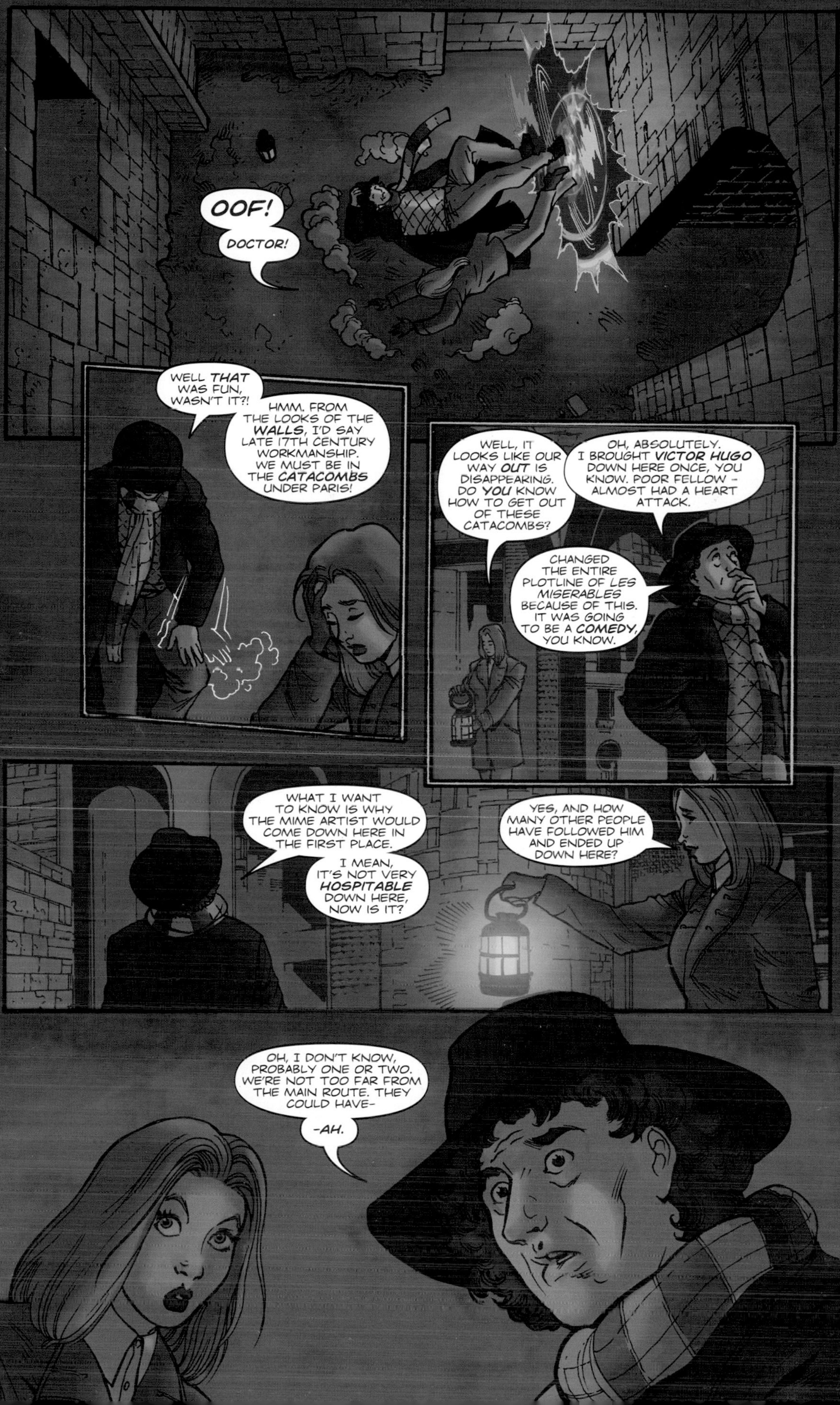

OOF!
DOCTOR!
WELL THAT WAS FUN, WASN'T IT?!
HMM. FROM THE LOOKS OF THE WALLS, I'D SAY LATE 17TH CENTURY WORKMANSHIP. WE MUST BE IN THE CATACOMBS UNDER PARIS!
WELL, IT LOOKS LIKE OUR WAY OUT IS DISAPPEARING. DO YOU KNOW HOW TO GET OUT OF THESE CATACOMBS?
OH, ABSOLUTELY. I BROUGHT VICTOR HUGO DOWN HERE ONCE, YOU KNOW. POOR FELLOW – ALMOST HAD A HEART ATTACK.
CHANGED THE ENTIRE PLOTLINE OF LES MISERABLES BECAUSE OF THIS. IT WAS GOING TO BE A COMEDY, YOU KNOW.
WHAT I WANT TO KNOW IS WHY THE MIME ARTIST WOULD COME DOWN HERE IN THE FIRST PLACE.
I MEAN, IT'S NOT VERY HOSPITABLE DOWN HERE, NOW IS IT?
YES, AND HOW MANY OTHER PEOPLE HAVE FOLLOWED HIM AND ENDED UP DOWN HERE?
OH, I DON'T KNOW, PROBABLY ONE OR TWO. WE'RE NOT TOO FAR FROM THE MAIN ROUTE. THEY COULD HAVE–
–AH.

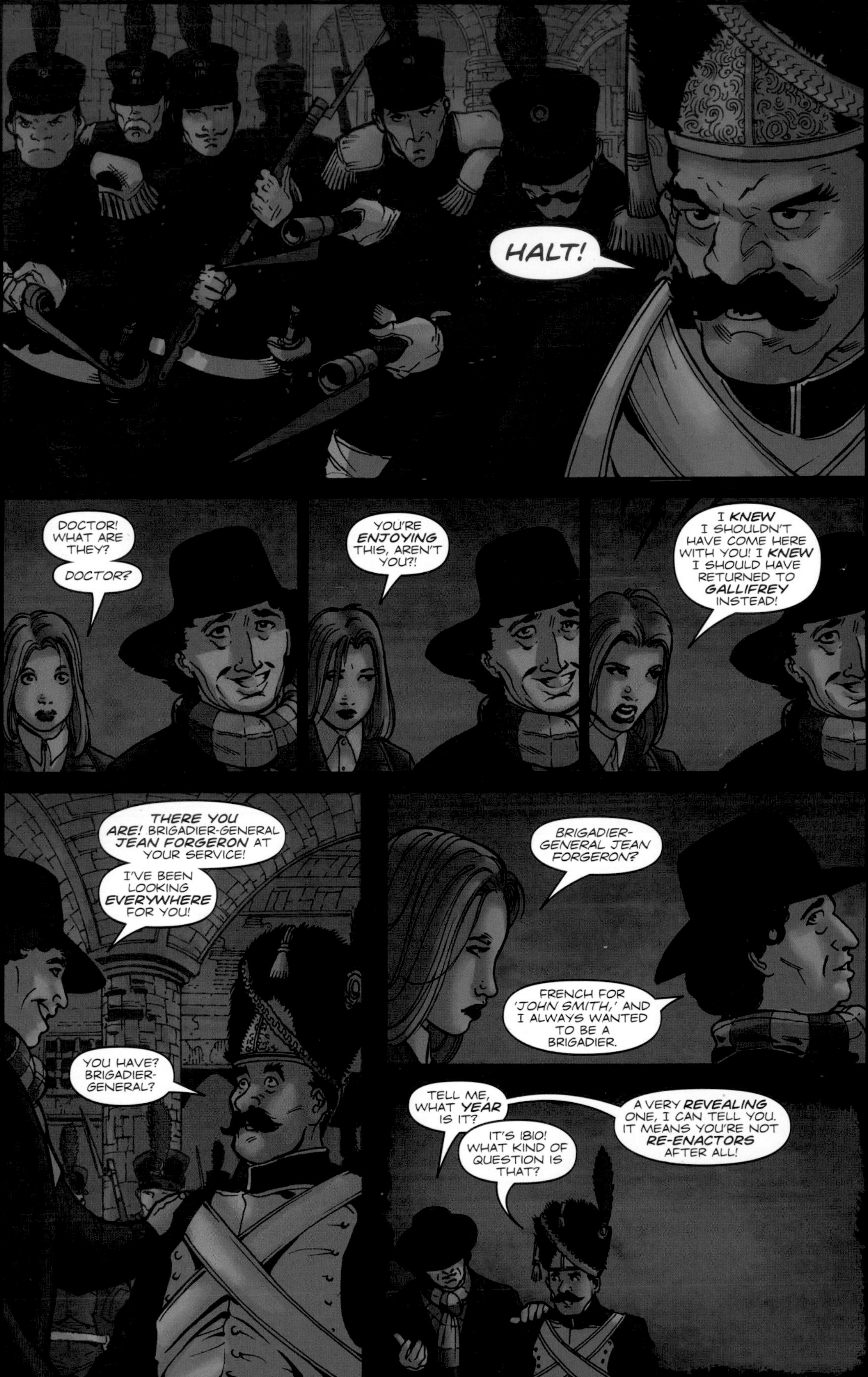
HALT!
DOCTOR! WHAT ARE THEY?
DOCTOR?
YOU'RE ENJOYING THIS, AREN'T YOU?!
I KNEW I SHOULDN'T HAVE COME HERE WITH YOU! I KNEW I SHOULD HAVE RETURNED TO GALLIFREY INSTEAD!
THERE YOU ARE! BRIGADIER-GENERAL JEAN FORGERON AT YOUR SERVICE!
I'VE BEEN LOOKING EVERYWHERE FOR YOU!
YOU HAVE? BRIGADIER-GENERAL?
BRIGADIER-GENERAL JEAN FORGERON?
FRENCH FOR 'JOHN SMITH,' AND I ALWAYS WANTED TO BE A BRIGADIER.
TELL ME, WHAT YEAR IS IT?
IT'S 1810! WHAT KIND OF QUESTION IS THAT?
A VERY REVEALING ONE, I CAN TELL YOU. IT MEANS YOU'RE NOT RE-ENACTORS AFTER ALL!

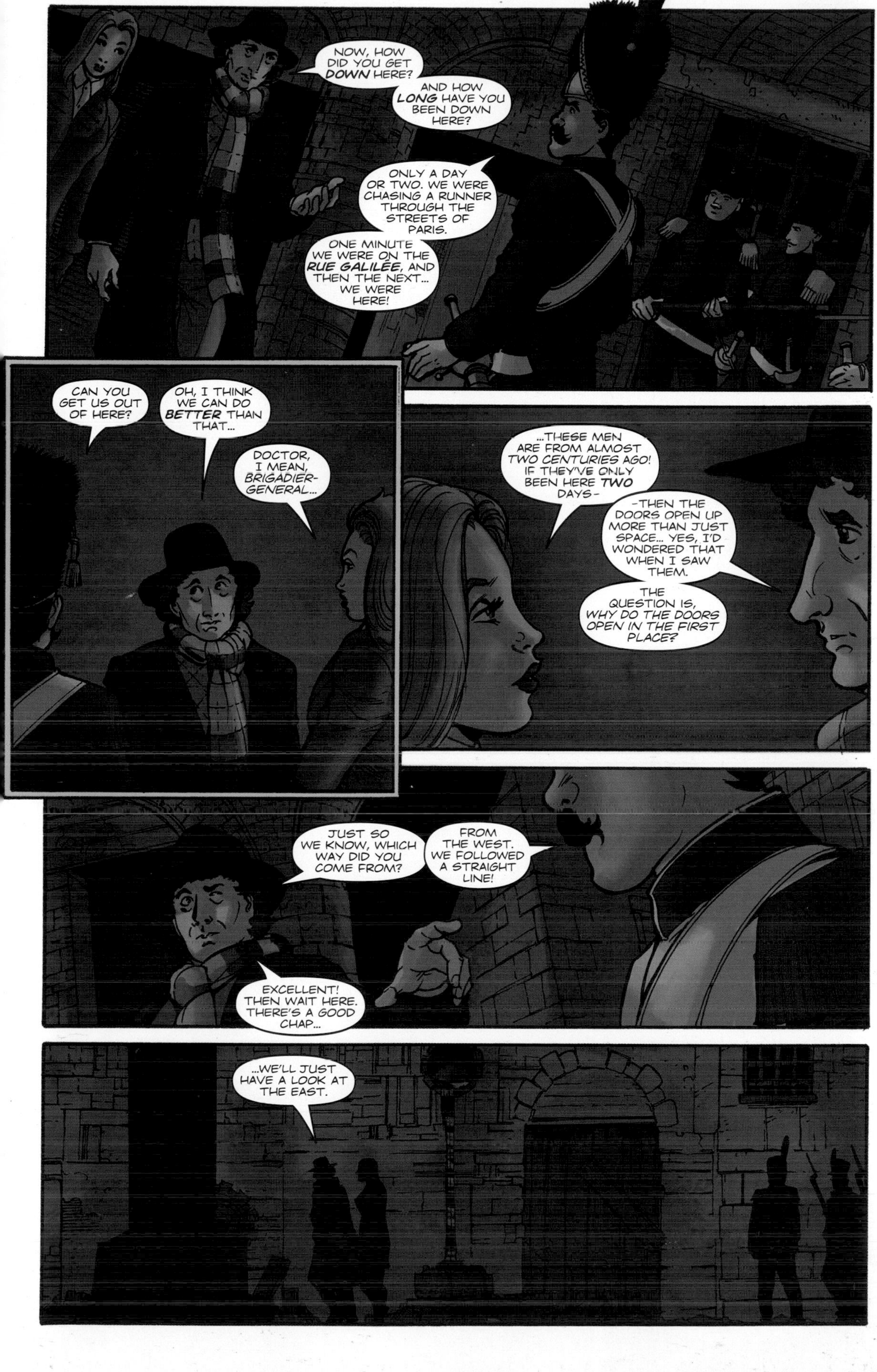
NOW, HOW DID YOU GET DOWN HERE?
AND HOW LONG HAVE YOU BEEN DOWN HERE?
ONLY A DAY OR TWO. WE WERE CHASING A RUNNER THROUGH THE STREETS OF PARIS.
ONE MINUTE WE WERE ON THE RUE GALILÉE, AND THEN THE NEXT... WE WERE HERE!
CAN YOU GET US OUT OF HERE?
OH, I THINK WE CAN DO BETTER THAN THAT...
DOCTOR, I MEAN, BRIGADIER-GENERAL...
...THESE MEN ARE FROM ALMOST TWO CENTURIES AGO! IF THEY'VE ONLY BEEN HERE TWO DAYS-
-THEN THE DOORS OPEN UP MORE THAN JUST SPACE... YES, I'D WONDERED THAT WHEN I SAW THEM.
THE QUESTION IS, WHY DO THE DOORS OPEN IN THE FIRST PLACE?
JUST SO WE KNOW, WHICH WAY DID YOU COME FROM?
FROM THE WEST. WE FOLLOWED A STRAIGHT LINE!
EXCELLENT! THEN WAIT HERE. THERE'S A GOOD CHAP...
...WE'LL JUST HAVE A LOOK AT THE EAST.

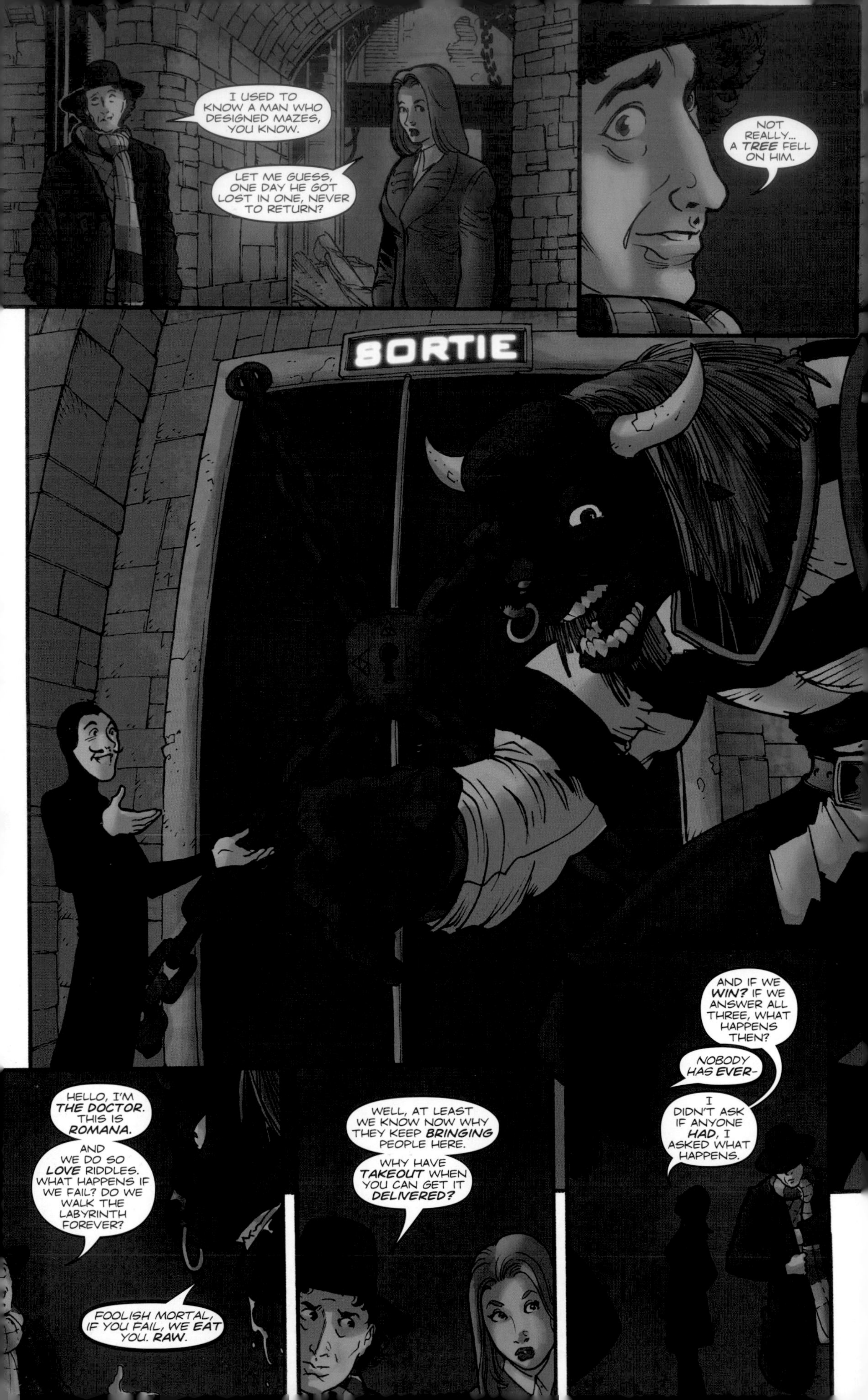

I USED TO KNOW A MAN WHO DESIGNED MAZES, YOU KNOW.
LET ME GUESS, ONE DAY HE GOT LOST IN ONE, NEVER TO RETURN?
NOT REALLY... A **TREE** FELL ON HIM.
SORTIE
AND IF WE **WIN?** IF WE ANSWER ALL THREE, WHAT HAPPENS THEN?
HELLO, I'M **THE DOCTOR**. THIS IS **ROMANA.**
AND WE DO SO **LOVE** RIDDLES. WHAT HAPPENS IF WE FAIL? DO WE WALK THE LABYRINTH FOREVER?
FOOLISH MORTAL, IF YOU FAIL, WE **EAT** YOU. **RAW**.
WELL, AT LEAST WE KNOW NOW WHY THEY KEEP **BRINGING** PEOPLE HERE.
WHY HAVE **TAKEOUT** WHEN YOU CAN GET IT **DELIVERED?**
NOBODY HAS **EVER**-
I DIDN'T ASK IF ANYONE **HAD**, I ASKED WHAT HAPPENS.

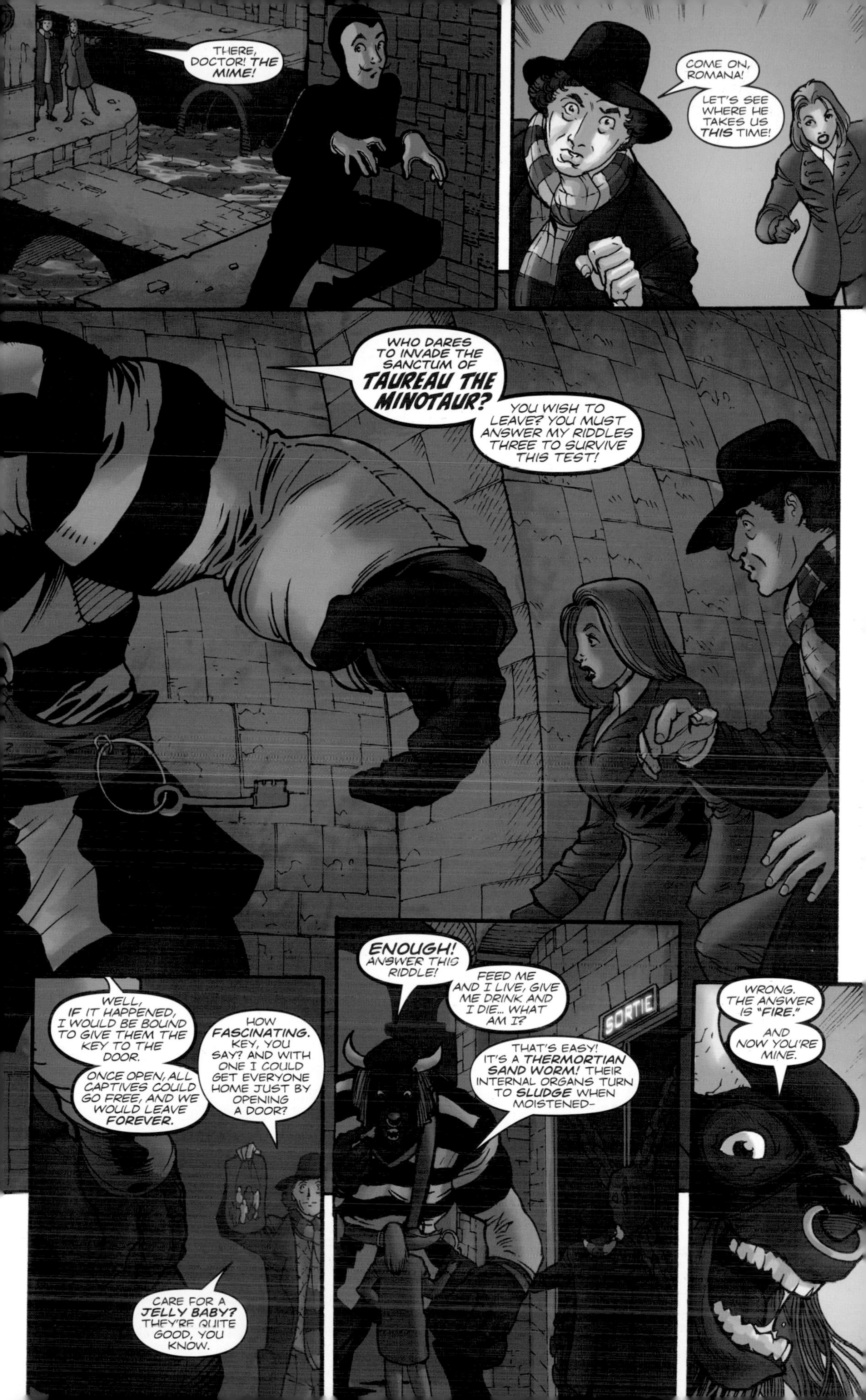
THERE, DOCTOR! THE MIME!
COME ON, ROMANA!
LET'S SEE WHERE HE TAKES US THIS TIME!
WHO DARES TO INVADE THE SANCTUM OF TAUREAU THE MINOTAUR?
YOU WISH TO LEAVE? YOU MUST ANSWER MY RIDDLES THREE TO SURVIVE THIS TEST!
WELL, IF IT HAPPENED, I WOULD BE BOUND TO GIVE THEM THE KEY TO THE DOOR.
ONCE OPEN, ALL CAPTIVES COULD GO FREE, AND WE WOULD LEAVE FOREVER.
HOW FASCINATING. KEY, YOU SAY? AND WITH ONE I COULD GET EVERYONE HOME JUST BY OPENING A DOOR?
CARE FOR A JELLY BABY? THEY'RE QUITE GOOD, YOU KNOW.
ENOUGH! ANSWER THIS RIDDLE!
FEED ME AND I LIVE, GIVE ME DRINK AND I DIE... WHAT AM I?
SORTIE
THAT'S EASY! IT'S A THERMORTIAN SAND WORM! THEIR INTERNAL ORGANS TURN TO SLUDGE WHEN MOISTENED–
WRONG. THE ANSWER IS "FIRE."
AND NOW YOU'RE MINE.

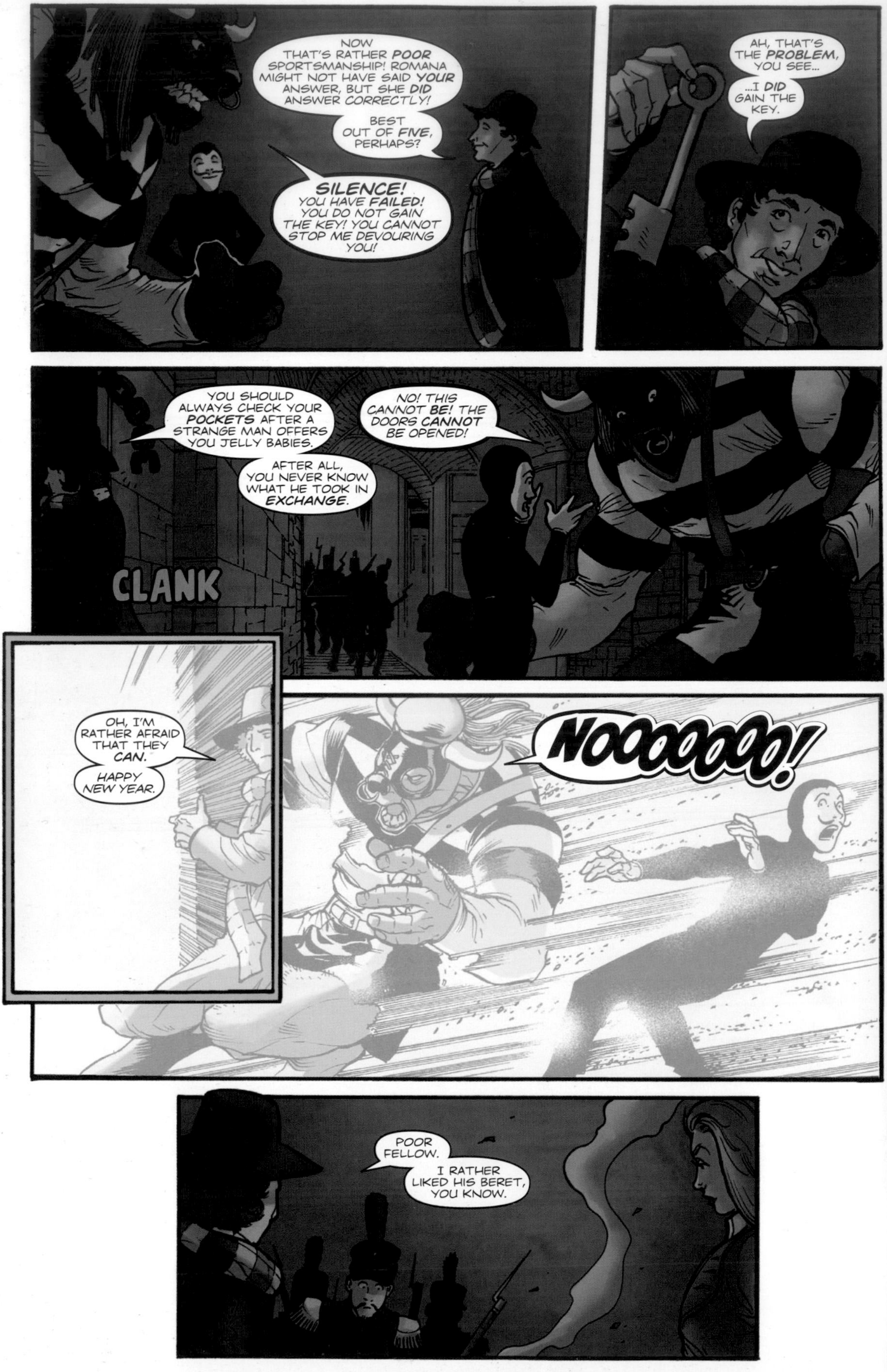
NOW THAT'S RATHER POOR SPORTSMANSHIP! ROMANA MIGHT NOT HAVE SAID YOUR ANSWER, BUT SHE DID ANSWER CORRECTLY!
BEST OUT OF FIVE, PERHAPS?
SILENCE! YOU HAVE FAILED! YOU DO NOT GAIN THE KEY! YOU CANNOT STOP ME DEVOURING YOU!
AH, THAT'S THE PROBLEM, YOU SEE...
...I DID GAIN THE KEY.
YOU SHOULD ALWAYS CHECK YOUR POCKETS AFTER A STRANGE MAN OFFERS YOU JELLY BABIES.
AFTER ALL, YOU NEVER KNOW WHAT HE TOOK IN EXCHANGE.
NO! THIS CANNOT BE! THE DOORS CANNOT BE OPENED!
CLANK
OH, I'M RATHER AFRAID THAT THEY CAN.
HAPPY NEW YEAR.
NOOOOOOO!
POOR FELLOW.
I RATHER LIKED HIS BERET, YOU KNOW.

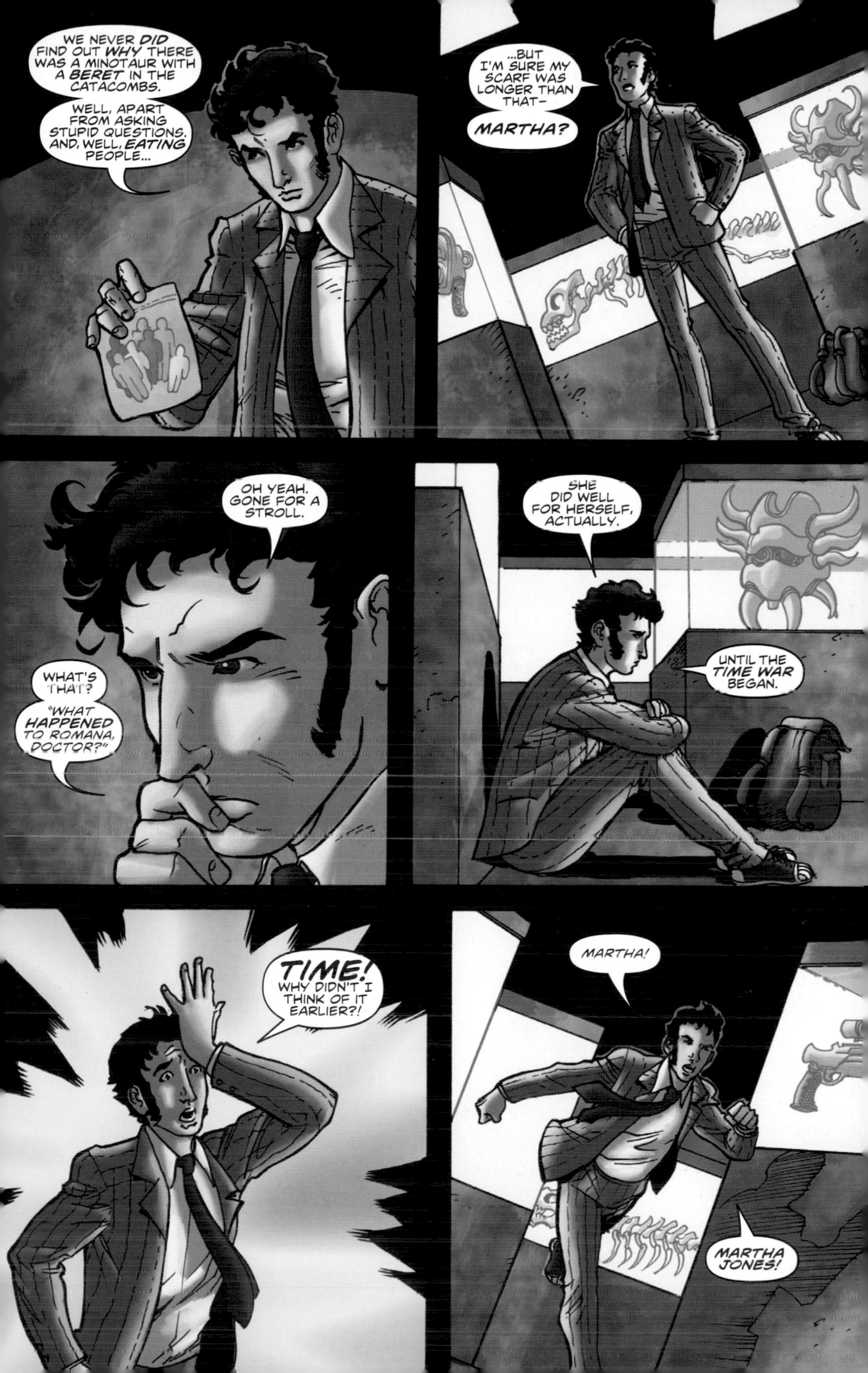
WE NEVER DID FIND OUT WHY THERE WAS A MINOTAUR WITH A BERET IN THE CATACOMBS.
WELL, APART FROM ASKING STUPID QUESTIONS. AND, WELL, EATING PEOPLE...
...BUT I'M SURE MY SCARF WAS LONGER THAN THAT–
MARTHA?
OH YEAH. GONE FOR A STROLL.
WHAT'S THAT?
"WHAT HAPPENED TO ROMANA, DOCTOR?"
SHE DID WELL FOR HERSELF, ACTUALLY.
UNTIL THE TIME WAR BEGAN.
TIME! WHY DIDN'T I THINK OF IT EARLIER?!
MARTHA!
MARTHA JONES!

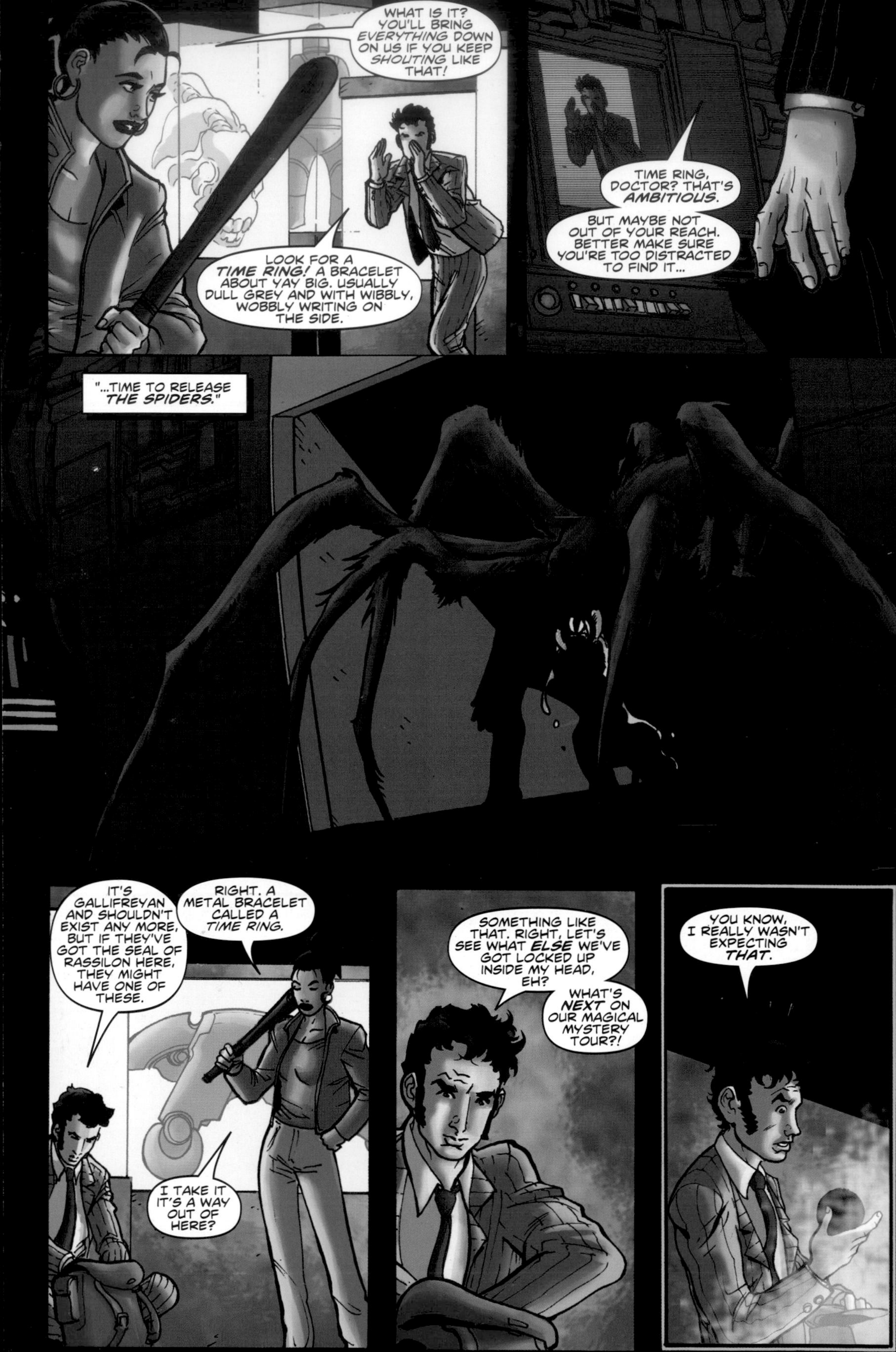
WHAT IS IT? YOU'LL BRING EVERYTHING DOWN ON US IF YOU KEEP SHOUTING LIKE THAT!
LOOK FOR A TIME RING! A BRACELET ABOUT YAY BIG. USUALLY DULL GREY AND WITH WIBBLY, WOBBLY WRITING ON THE SIDE.
TIME RING, DOCTOR? THAT'S AMBITIOUS.
BUT MAYBE NOT OUT OF YOUR REACH. BETTER MAKE SURE YOU'RE TOO DISTRACTED TO FIND IT...
"...TIME TO RELEASE THE SPIDERS."
IT'S GALLIFREYAN AND SHOULDN'T EXIST ANY MORE, BUT IF THEY'VE GOT THE SEAL OF RASSILON HERE, THEY MIGHT HAVE ONE OF THESE.
RIGHT. A METAL BRACELET CALLED A TIME RING.
I TAKE IT IT'S A WAY OUT OF HERE?
SOMETHING LIKE THAT. RIGHT, LET'S SEE WHAT ELSE WE'VE GOT LOCKED UP INSIDE MY HEAD, EH?
WHAT'S NEXT ON OUR MAGICAL MYSTERY TOUR?!
YOU KNOW, I REALLY WASN'T EXPECTING THAT.

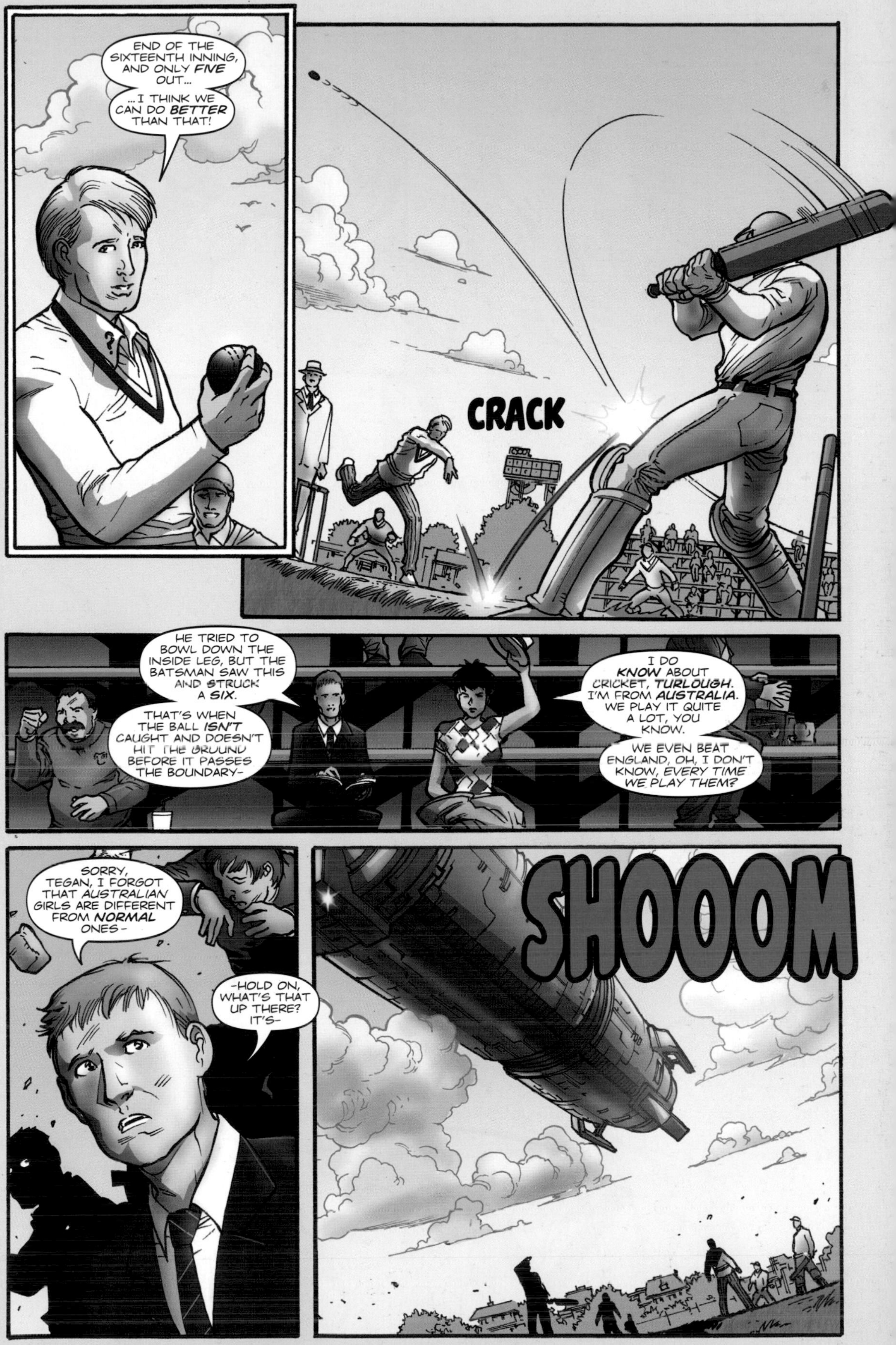
END OF THE SIXTEENTH INNING, AND ONLY FIVE OUT...
...I THINK WE CAN DO BETTER THAN THAT!
CRACK
HE TRIED TO BOWL DOWN THE INSIDE LEG, BUT THE BATSMAN SAW THIS AND STRUCK A SIX.
THAT'S WHEN THE BALL ISN'T CAUGHT AND DOESN'T HIT THE GROUND BEFORE IT PASSES THE BOUNDARY-
I DO KNOW ABOUT CRICKET, TURLOUGH. I'M FROM AUSTRALIA. WE PLAY IT QUITE A LOT, YOU KNOW.
WE EVEN BEAT ENGLAND, OH, I DON'T KNOW, EVERY TIME WE PLAY THEM?
SORRY, TEGAN, I FORGOT THAT AUSTRALIAN GIRLS ARE DIFFERENT FROM NORMAL ONES-
-HOLD ON, WHAT'S THAT UP THERE? IT'S-
SHOOOM

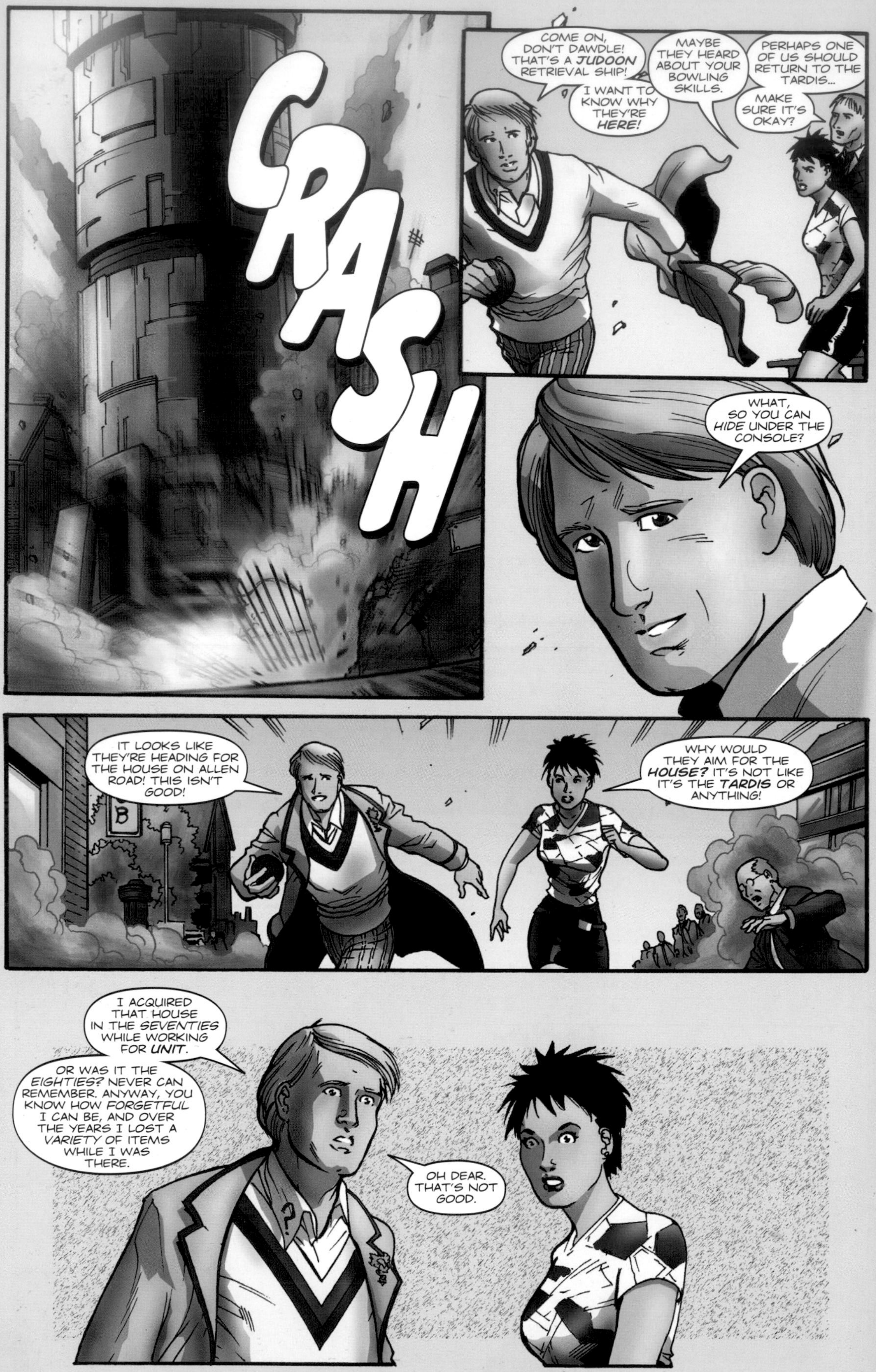
CRASH
COME ON, DON'T DAWDLE! THAT'S A JUDOON RETRIEVAL SHIP!
I WANT TO KNOW WHY THEY'RE HERE!
MAYBE THEY HEARD ABOUT YOUR BOWLING SKILLS.
PERHAPS ONE OF US SHOULD RETURN TO THE TARDIS...
MAKE SURE IT'S OKAY?
WHAT, SO YOU CAN HIDE UNDER THE CONSOLE?
IT LOOKS LIKE THEY'RE HEADING FOR THE HOUSE ON ALLEN ROAD! THIS ISN'T GOOD!
WHY WOULD THEY AIM FOR THE HOUSE? IT'S NOT LIKE IT'S THE TARDIS OR ANYTHING!
I ACQUIRED THAT HOUSE IN THE SEVENTIES WHILE WORKING FOR UNIT.
OR WAS IT THE EIGHTIES? NEVER CAN REMEMBER. ANYWAY, YOU KNOW HOW FORGETFUL I CAN BE, AND OVER THE YEARS I LOST A VARIETY OF ITEMS WHILE I WAS THERE.
OH DEAR. THAT'S NOT GOOD.

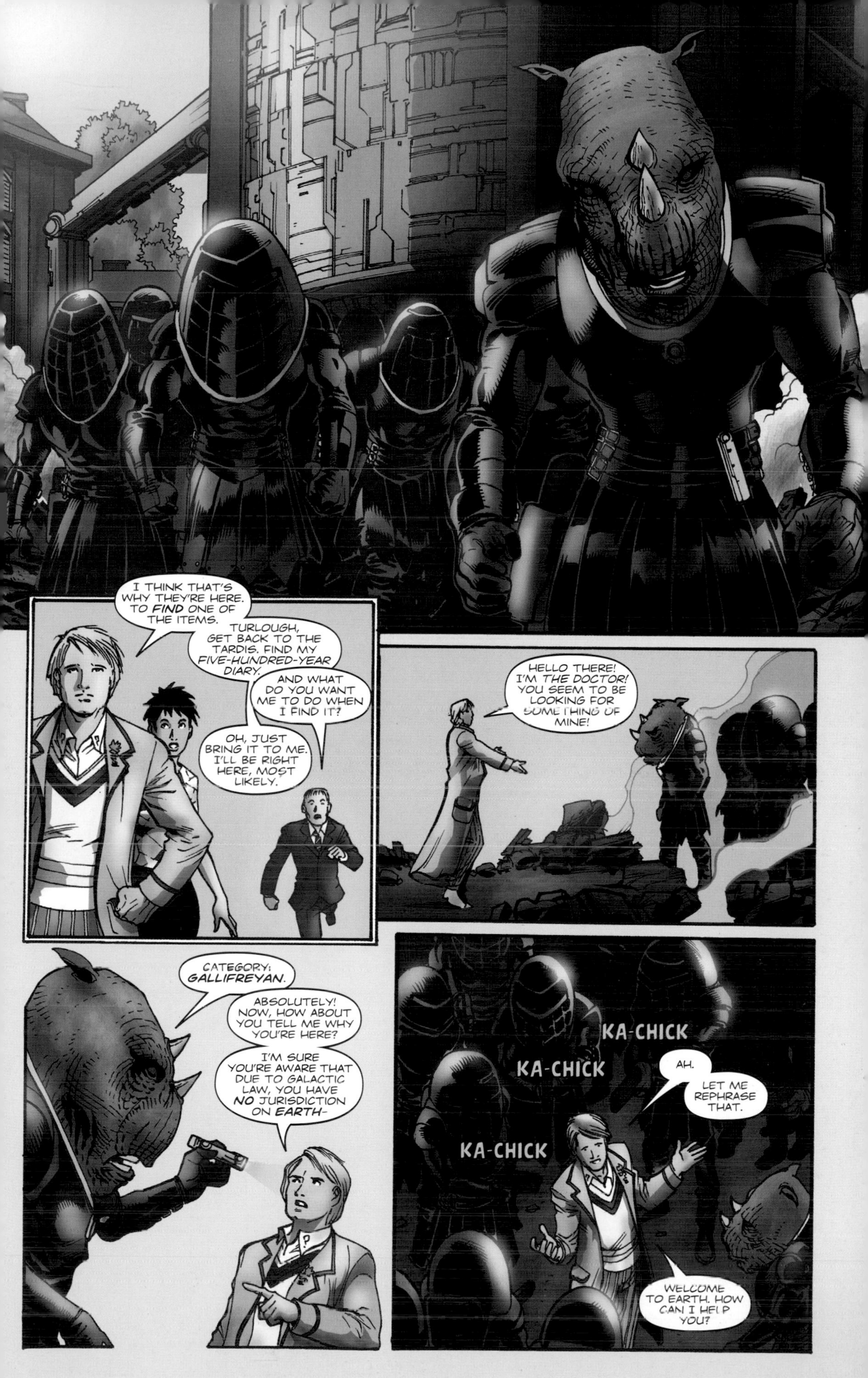
I THINK THAT'S WHY THEY'RE HERE. TO FIND ONE OF THE ITEMS.
TURLOUGH, GET BACK TO THE TARDIS. FIND MY FIVE-HUNDRED-YEAR DIARY.
AND WHAT DO YOU WANT ME TO DO WHEN I FIND IT?
OH, JUST BRING IT TO ME. I'LL BE RIGHT HERE, MOST LIKELY.
HELLO THERE! I'M THE DOCTOR! YOU SEEM TO BE LOOKING FOR SOMETHING OF MINE!
CATEGORY: GALLIFREYAN.
ABSOLUTELY! NOW, HOW ABOUT YOU TELL ME WHY YOU'RE HERE?
I'M SURE YOU'RE AWARE THAT DUE TO GALACTIC LAW, YOU HAVE NO JURISDICTION ON EARTH-
KA-CHICK
KA-CHICK
KA-CHICK
AH.
LET ME REPHRASE THAT.
WELCOME TO EARTH. HOW CAN I HELP YOU?

DIARY, DIARY... ...WHERE DID HE PUT THE DIARY?

THERE YOU ARE!

SOMEONE REMIND ME WHY I'M DOING THIS AGAIN? I MEAN, THE TARDIS IS WARM, SAFE... AND NOT FULL OF *KILLER* ALIENS.

WELL, NOT *THIS* WEEK ANYWAY.

DOCTOR! I'VE *GOT* IT!

EXCELLENT! YOU SEE, I *TOLD* YOU I COULD FIND OUT FOR YOU!

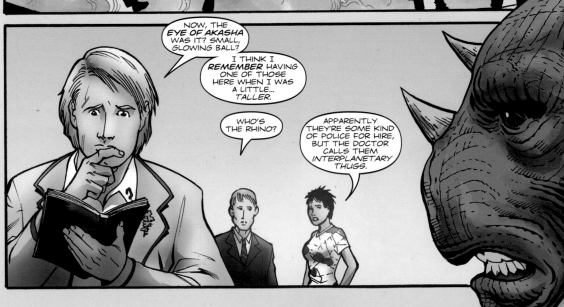

NOW, THE *EYE OF AKASHA* WAS IT? SMALL, GLOWING BALL?

I THINK I *REMEMBER* HAVING ONE OF THOSE HERE WHEN I WAS A LITTLE... TALLER.

WHO'S THE RHINO?

APPARENTLY THEY'RE SOME KIND OF POLICE FOR HIRE, BUT THE DOCTOR CALLS THEM INTERPLANETARY THUGS.

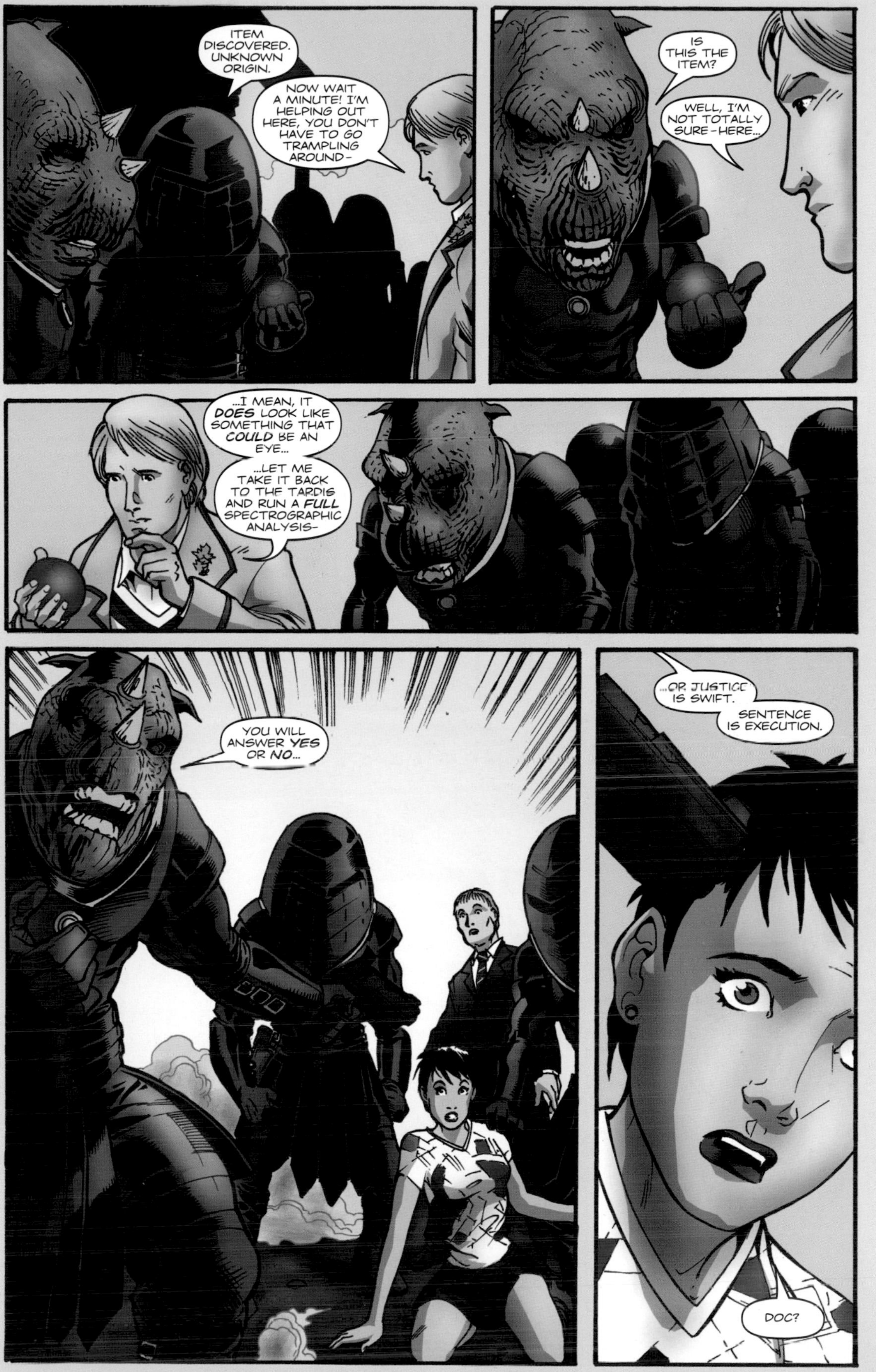
ITEM DISCOVERED. UNKNOWN ORIGIN.
NOW WAIT A MINUTE! I'M HELPING OUT HERE, YOU DON'T HAVE TO GO TRAMPLING AROUND-
IS THIS THE ITEM?
WELL, I'M NOT TOTALLY SURE-HERE...
...I MEAN, IT **DOES** LOOK LIKE SOMETHING THAT **COULD** BE AN EYE...
...LET ME TAKE IT BACK TO THE TARDIS AND RUN A **FULL** SPECTROGRAPHIC ANALYSIS-
YOU WILL ANSWER **YES** OR **NO**...
...OR JUSTICE IS SWIFT.
SENTENCE IS EXECUTION.
DOC?

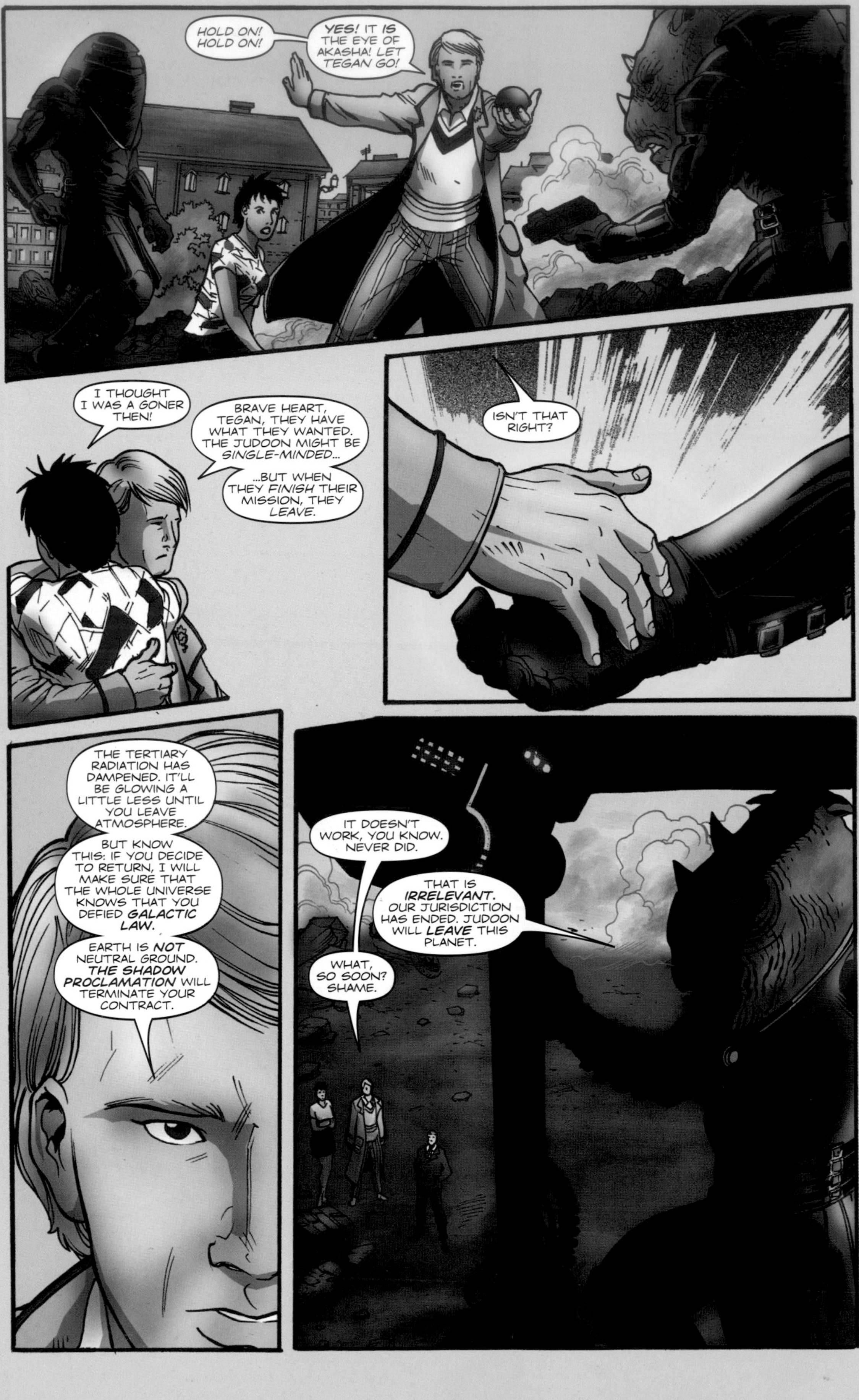
HOLD ON! HOLD ON!
YES! IT IS THE EYE OF AKASHA! LET TEGAN GO!
I THOUGHT I WAS A GONER THEN!
BRAVE HEART, TEGAN, THEY HAVE WHAT THEY WANTED. THE JUDOON MIGHT BE SINGLE-MINDED...
...BUT WHEN THEY FINISH THEIR MISSION, THEY LEAVE.
ISN'T THAT RIGHT?
THE TERTIARY RADIATION HAS DAMPENED. IT'LL BE GLOWING A LITTLE LESS UNTIL YOU LEAVE ATMOSPHERE.
BUT KNOW THIS: IF YOU DECIDE TO RETURN, I WILL MAKE SURE THAT THE WHOLE UNIVERSE KNOWS THAT YOU DEFIED GALACTIC LAW.
EARTH IS NOT NEUTRAL GROUND. THE SHADOW PROCLAMATION WILL TERMINATE YOUR CONTRACT.
IT DOESN'T WORK, YOU KNOW. NEVER DID.
THAT IS IRRELEVANT. OUR JURISDICTION HAS ENDED. JUDOON WILL LEAVE THIS PLANET.
WHAT, SO SOON? SHAME.

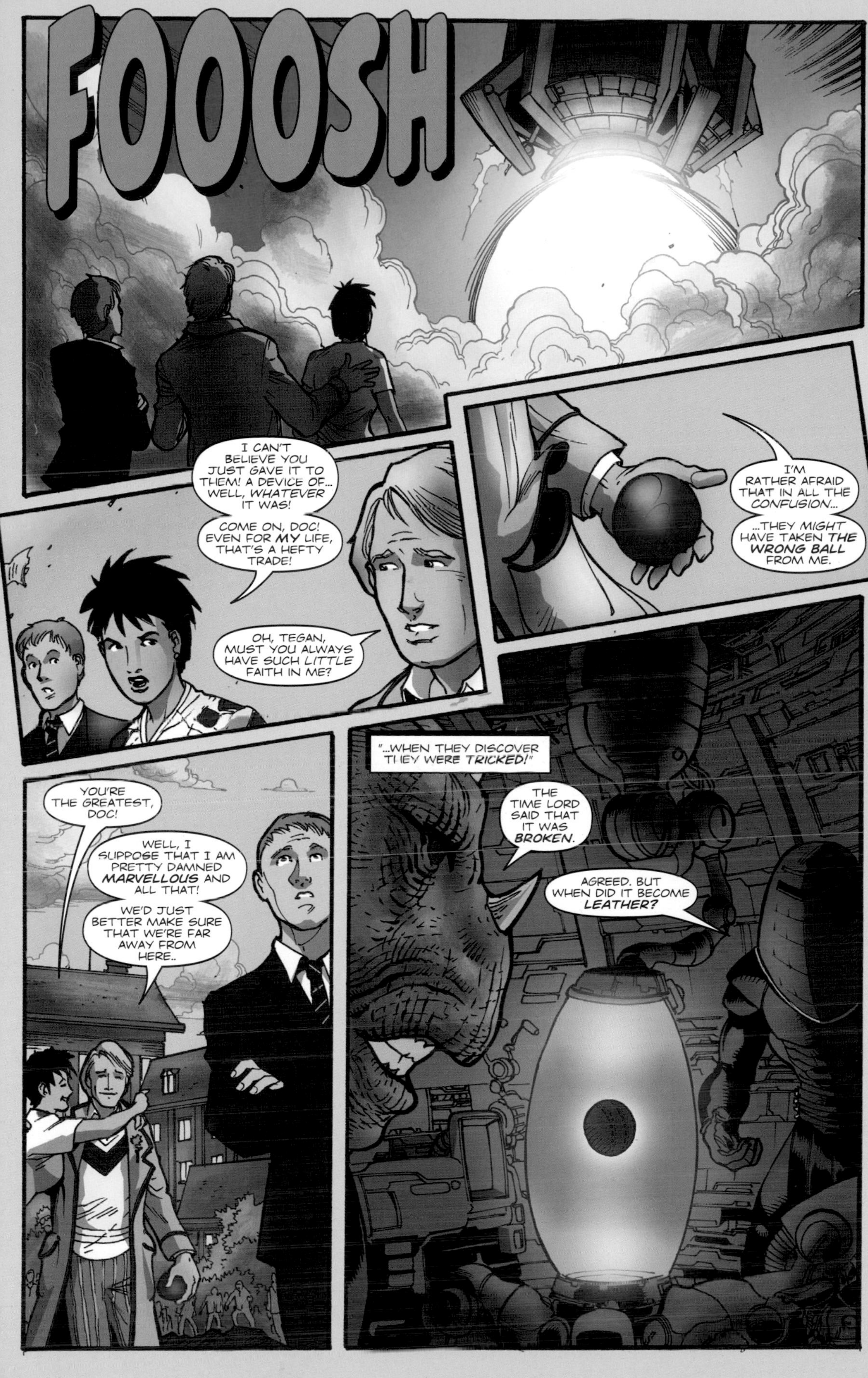
FOOOSH
I CAN'T BELIEVE YOU JUST GAVE IT TO THEM! A DEVICE OF... WELL, WHATEVER IT WAS!
COME ON, DOC! EVEN FOR MY LIFE, THAT'S A HEFTY TRADE!
OH, TEGAN, MUST YOU ALWAYS HAVE SUCH LITTLE FAITH IN ME?
I'M RATHER AFRAID THAT IN ALL THE CONFUSION...
...THEY MIGHT HAVE TAKEN THE WRONG BALL FROM ME.
YOU'RE THE GREATEST, DOC!
WELL, I SUPPOSE THAT I AM PRETTY DAMNED MARVELLOUS AND ALL THAT!
WE'D JUST BETTER MAKE SURE THAT WE'RE FAR AWAY FROM HERE..
"...WHEN THEY DISCOVER THEY WERE TRICKED!"
THE TIME LORD SAID THAT IT WAS BROKEN.
AGREED. BUT WHEN DID IT BECOME LEATHER?

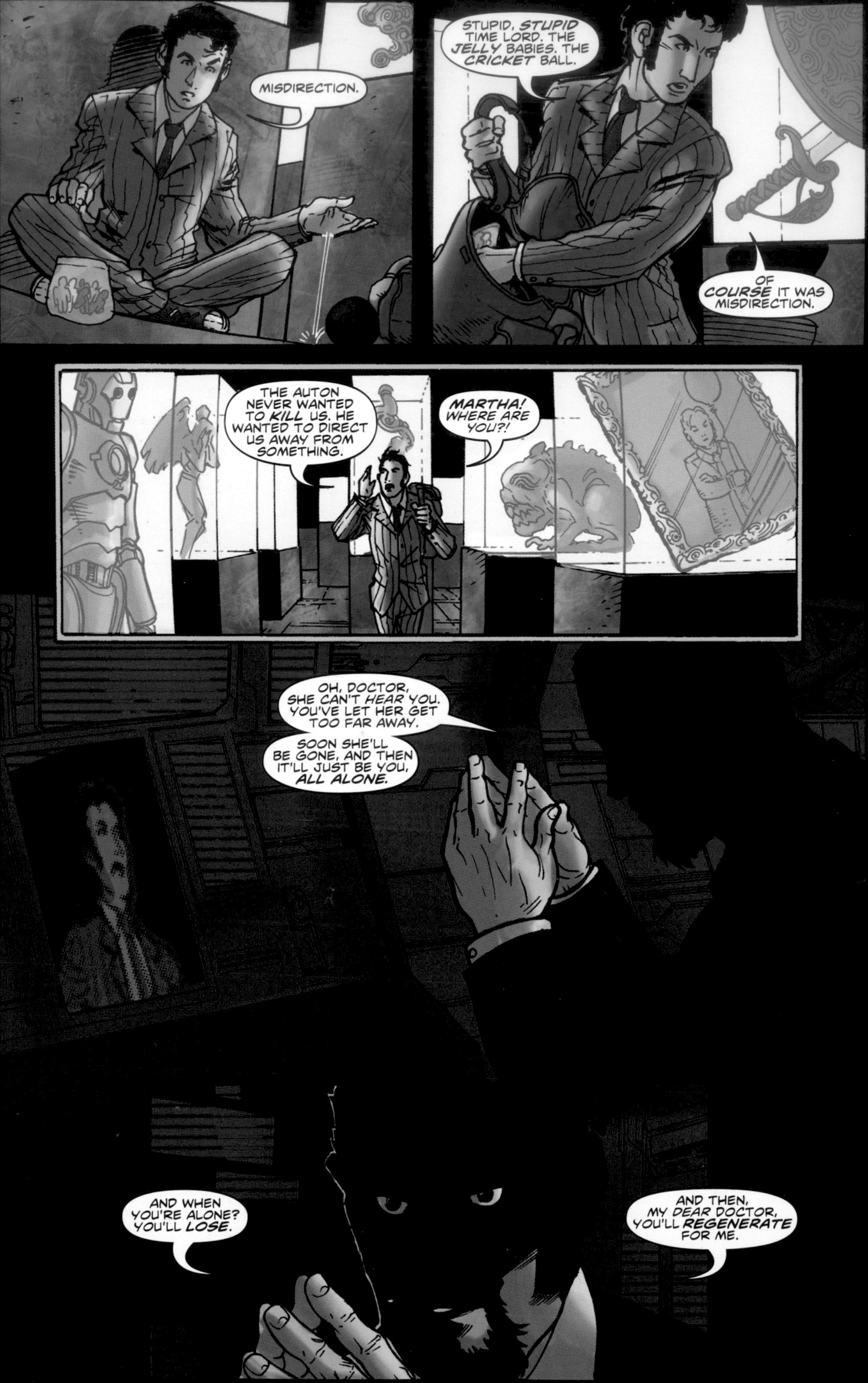
MISDIRECTION.
STUPID, STUPID TIME LORD. THE JELLY BABIES. THE CRICKET BALL.
OF COURSE IT WAS MISDIRECTION.
THE AUTON NEVER WANTED TO KILL US. HE WANTED TO DIRECT US AWAY FROM SOMETHING.
MARTHA! WHERE ARE YOU?!
OH, DOCTOR, SHE CAN'T HEAR YOU. YOU'VE LET HER GET TOO FAR AWAY.
SOON SHE'LL BE GONE, AND THEN IT'LL JUST BE YOU, ALL ALONE.
AND WHEN YOU'RE ALONE? YOU'LL LOSE.
AND THEN, MY DEAR DOCTOR, YOU'LL REGENERATE FOR ME.

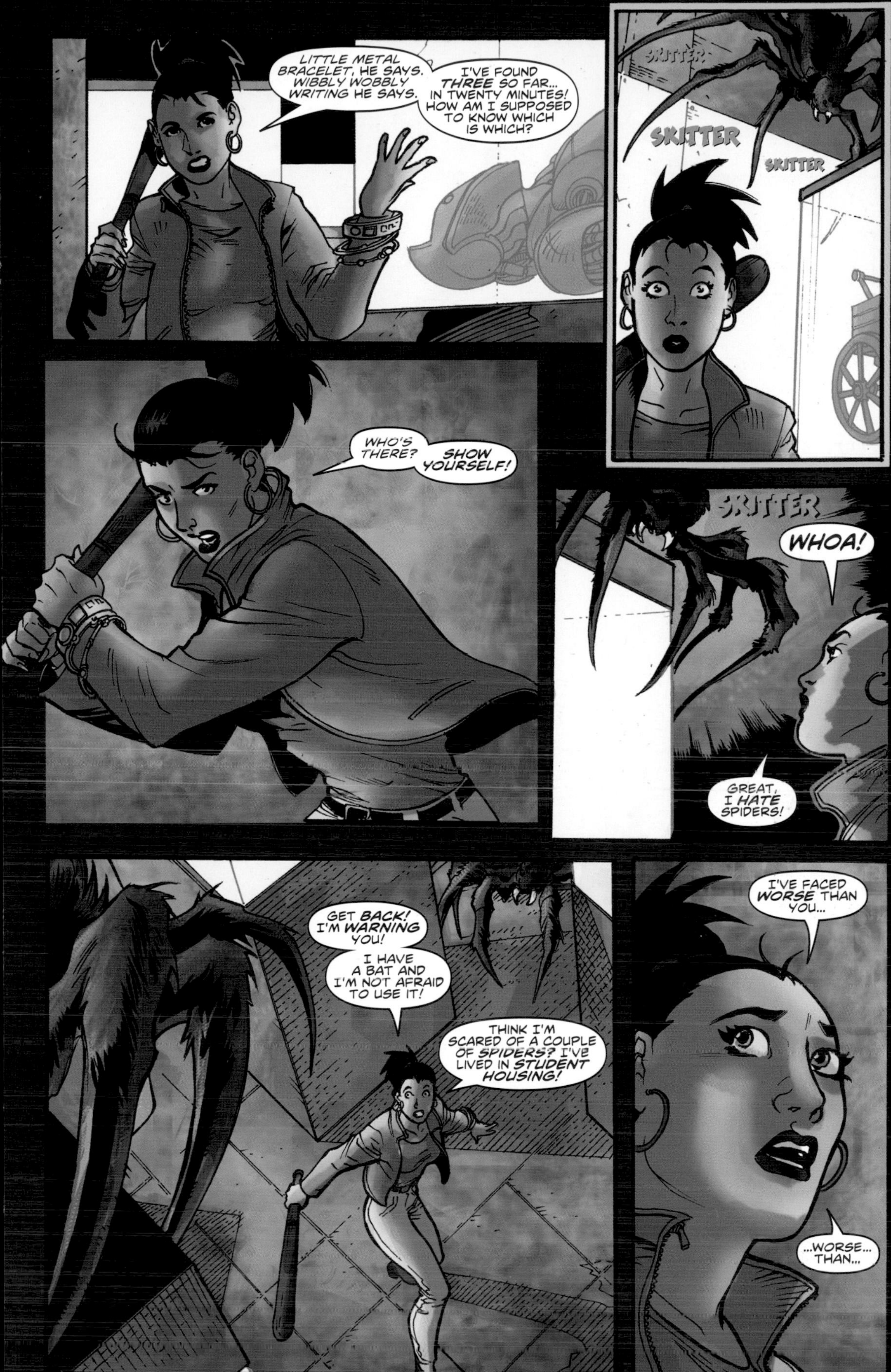

LITTLE METAL BRACELET, HE SAYS. WIBBLY WOBBLY WRITING HE SAYS.
I'VE FOUND THREE SO FAR... IN TWENTY MINUTES! HOW AM I SUPPOSED TO KNOW WHICH IS WHICH?
SKITTER
SKITTER
SKITTER
WHO'S THERE? SHOW YOURSELF!
SKITTER
WHOA!
GREAT, I HATE SPIDERS!
GET BACK! I'M WARNING YOU!
I HAVE A BAT AND I'M NOT AFRAID TO USE IT!
THINK I'M SCARED OF A COUPLE OF SPIDERS? I'VE LIVED IN STUDENT HOUSING!
I'VE FACED WORSE THAN YOU...
...WORSE... THAN...

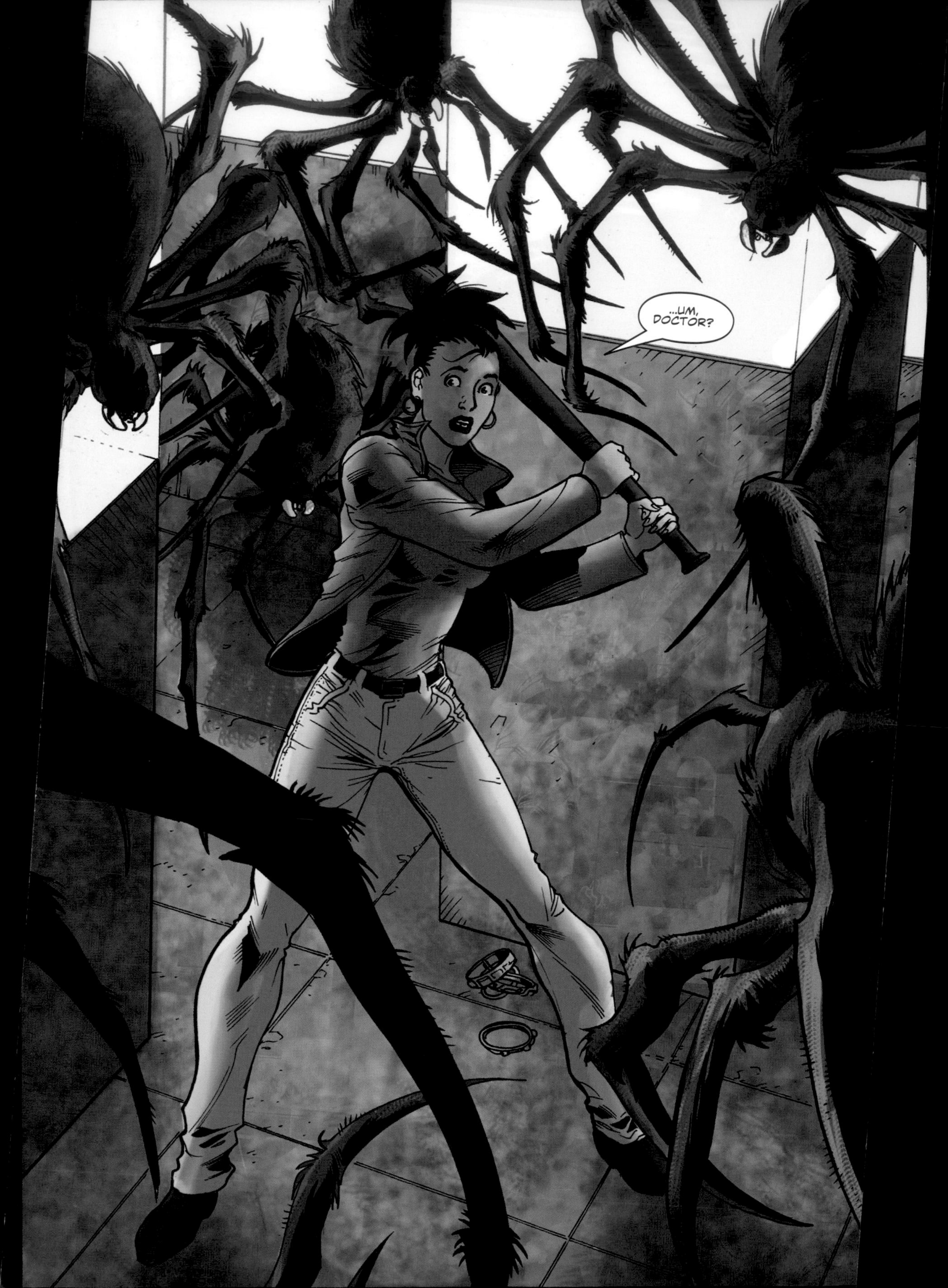
...UM, DOCTOR?

CHAPTER • FOUR
SURVIVAL

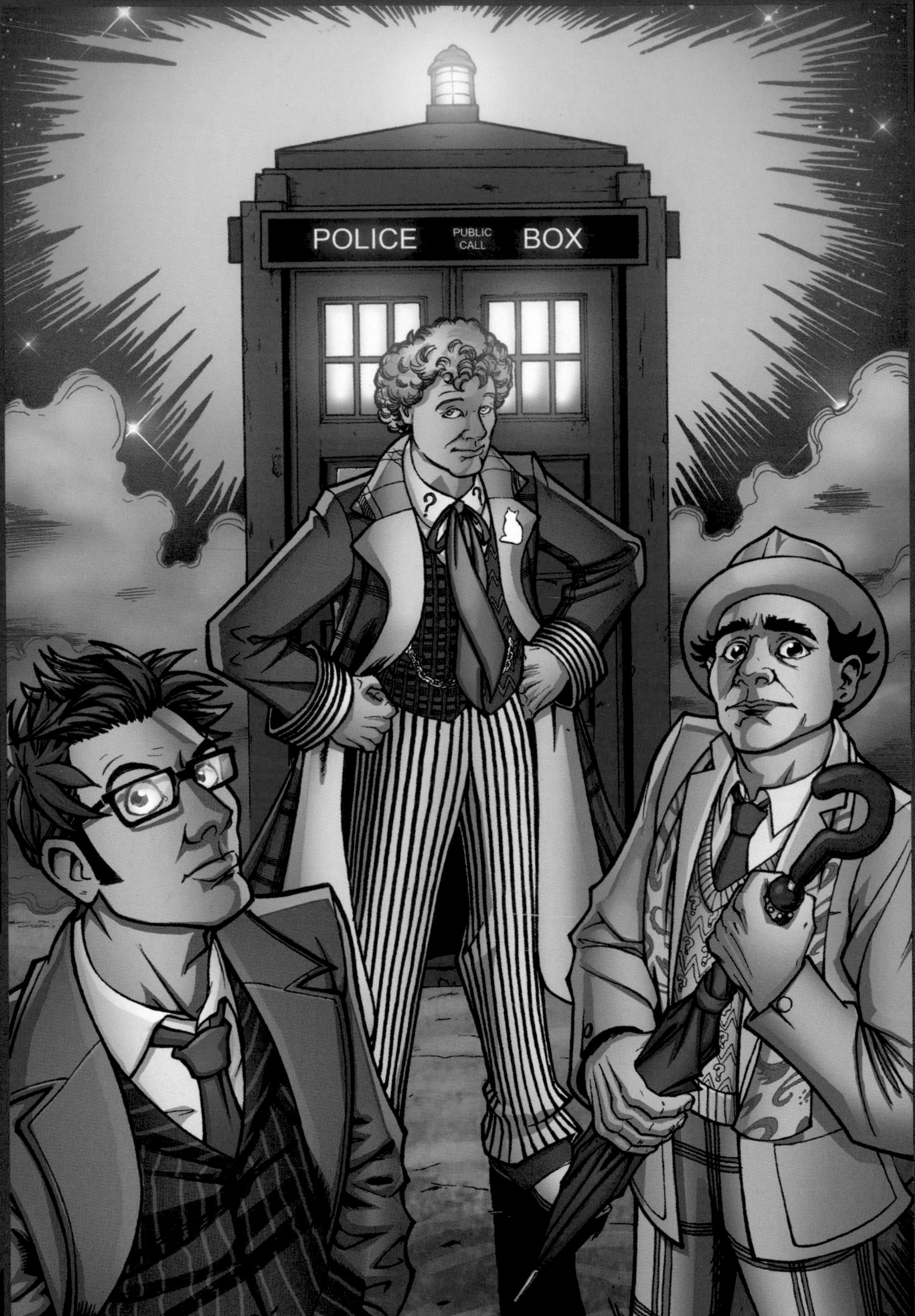
POLICE
PUBLIC CALL
BOX
NICK CK 2008

ART BY NICK ROCHE • COLOR BY CHARLIE KIRCHOFF

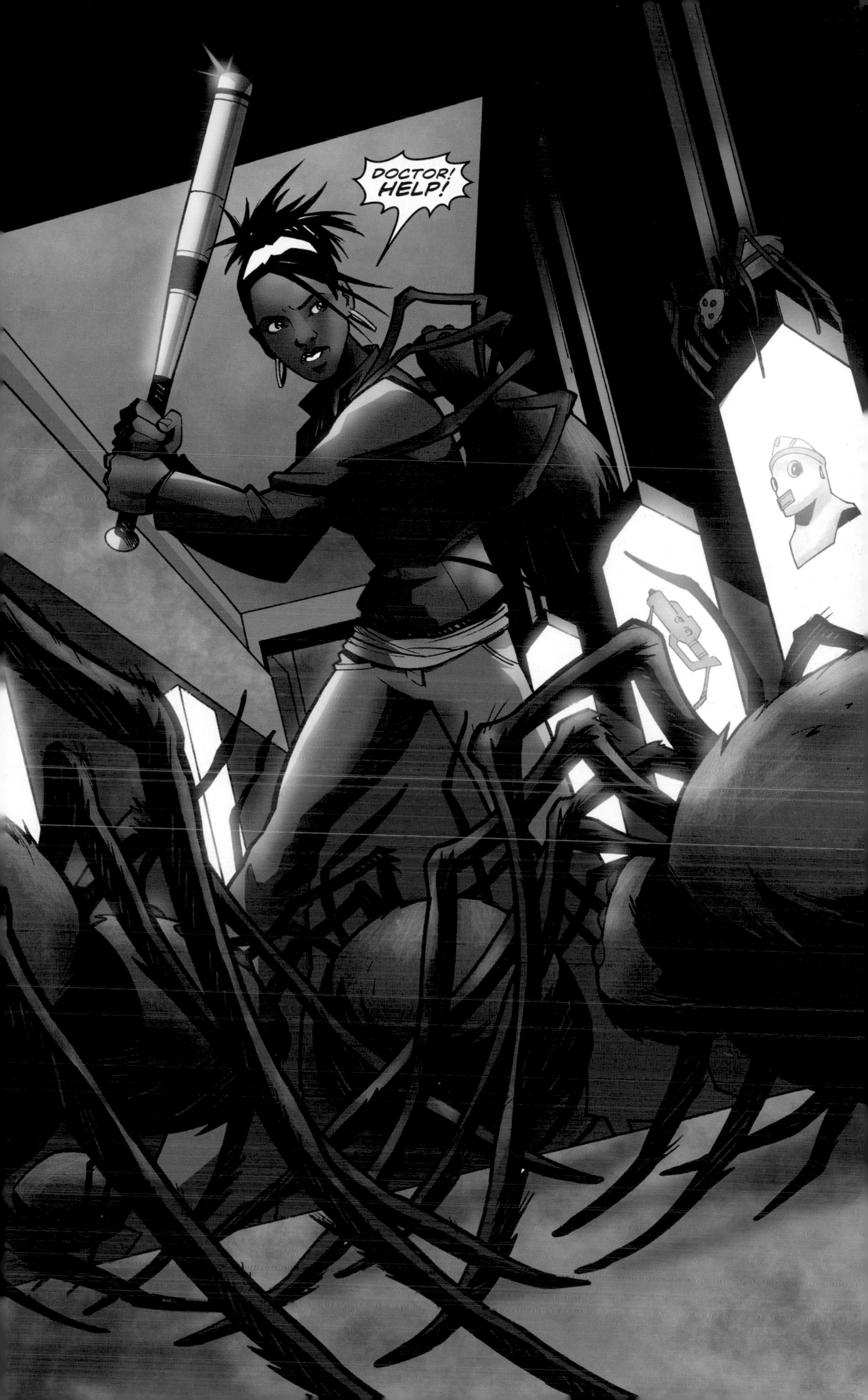
DOCTOR! HELP!

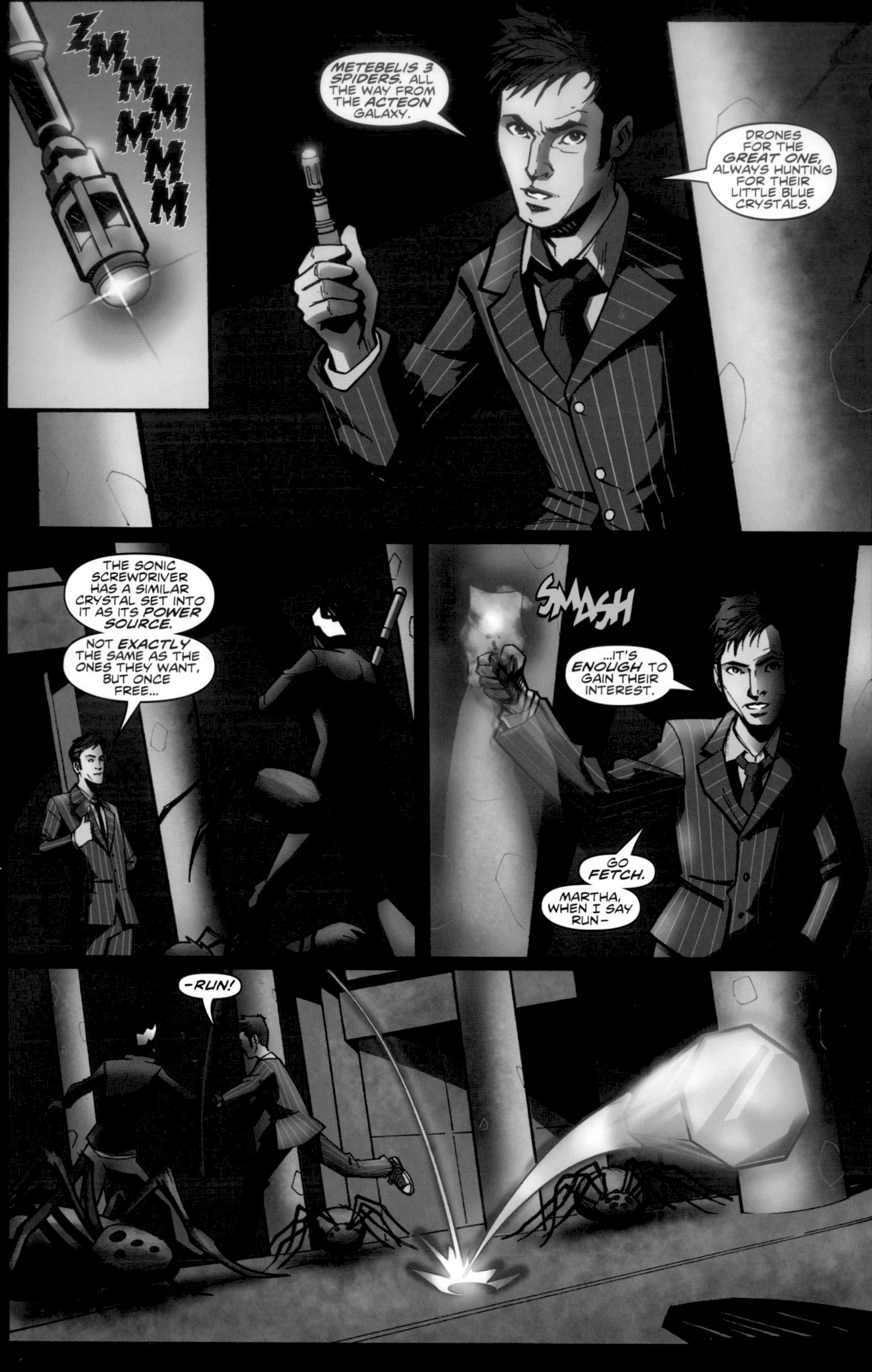
ZMMMMMMMMM
METEBELIS 3 SPIDERS. ALL THE WAY FROM THE ACTEON GALAXY.
DRONES FOR THE GREAT ONE, ALWAYS HUNTING FOR THEIR LITTLE BLUE CRYSTALS.
THE SONIC SCREWDRIVER HAS A SIMILAR CRYSTAL SET INTO IT AS ITS POWER SOURCE.
NOT EXACTLY THE SAME AS THE ONES THEY WANT, BUT ONCE FREE...
SMASH
...IT'S ENOUGH TO GAIN THEIR INTEREST.
GO FETCH.
MARTHA, WHEN I SAY RUN–
–RUN!

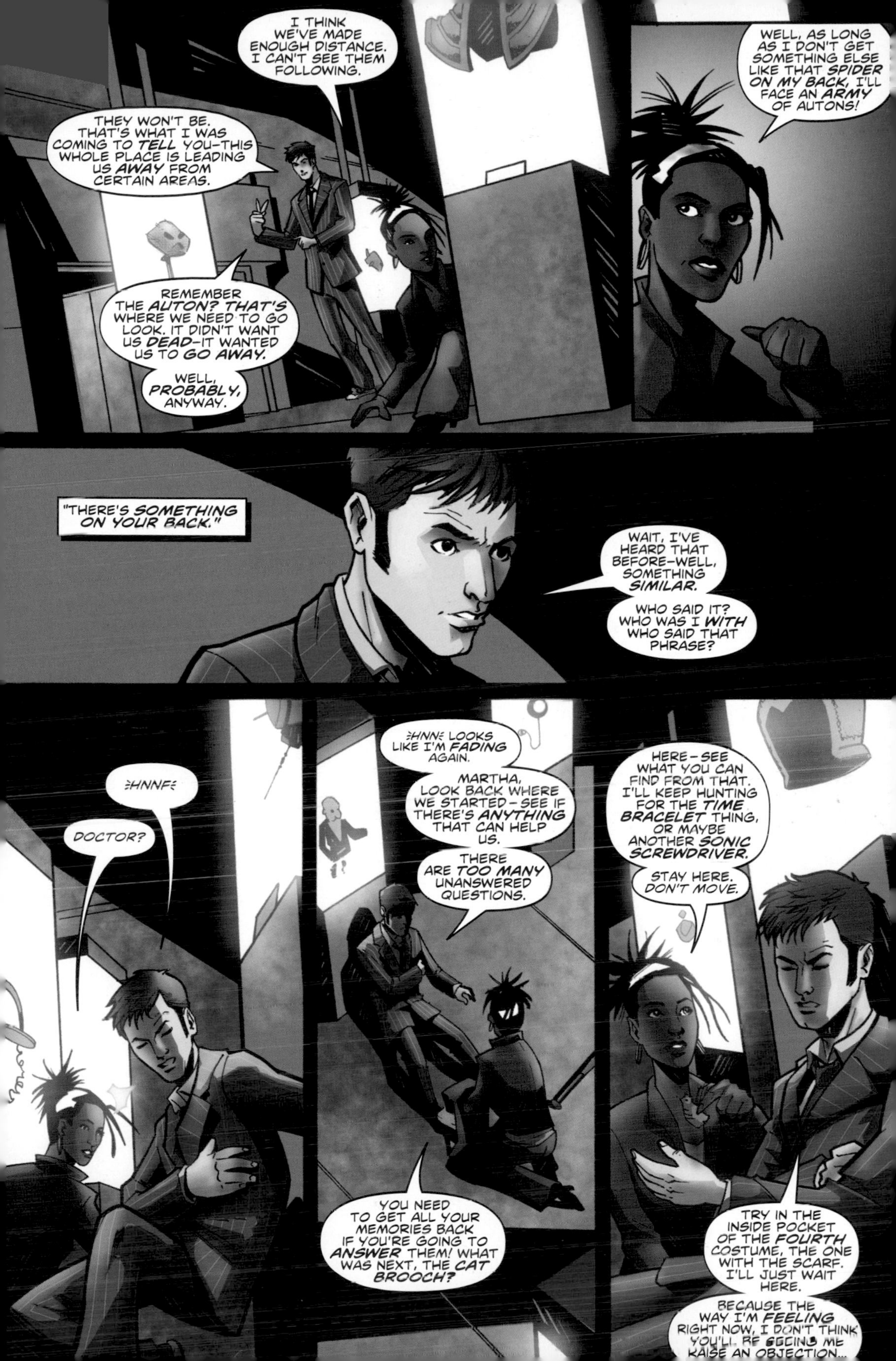
I THINK WE'VE MADE ENOUGH DISTANCE. I CAN'T SEE THEM FOLLOWING.
THEY WON'T BE. THAT'S WHAT I WAS COMING TO TELL YOU–THIS WHOLE PLACE IS LEADING US AWAY FROM CERTAIN AREAS.
REMEMBER THE AUTON? THAT'S WHERE WE NEED TO GO LOOK. IT DIDN'T WANT US DEAD–IT WANTED US TO GO AWAY.
WELL, PROBABLY, ANYWAY.
WELL, AS LONG AS I DON'T GET SOMETHING ELSE LIKE THAT SPIDER ON MY BACK, I'LL FACE AN ARMY OF AUTONS!
"THERE'S SOMETHING ON YOUR BACK."
WAIT, I'VE HEARD THAT BEFORE–WELL, SOMETHING SIMILAR.
WHO SAID IT? WHO WAS I WITH WHO SAID THAT PHRASE?
HNNF
DOCTOR?
HNN LOOKS LIKE I'M FADING AGAIN.
MARTHA, LOOK BACK WHERE WE STARTED–SEE IF THERE'S ANYTHING THAT CAN HELP US.
THERE ARE TOO MANY UNANSWERED QUESTIONS.
YOU NEED TO GET ALL YOUR MEMORIES BACK IF YOU'RE GOING TO ANSWER THEM! WHAT WAS NEXT, THE CAT BROOCH?
HERE–SEE WHAT YOU CAN FIND FROM THAT. I'LL KEEP HUNTING FOR THE TIME BRACELET THING, OR MAYBE ANOTHER SONIC SCREWDRIVER.
STAY HERE. DON'T MOVE.
TRY IN THE INSIDE POCKET OF THE FOURTH COSTUME, THE ONE WITH THE SCARF. I'LL JUST WAIT HERE.
BECAUSE THE WAY I'M FEELING RIGHT NOW, I DON'T THINK YOU'LL BE SEEING ME RAISE AN OBJECTION...

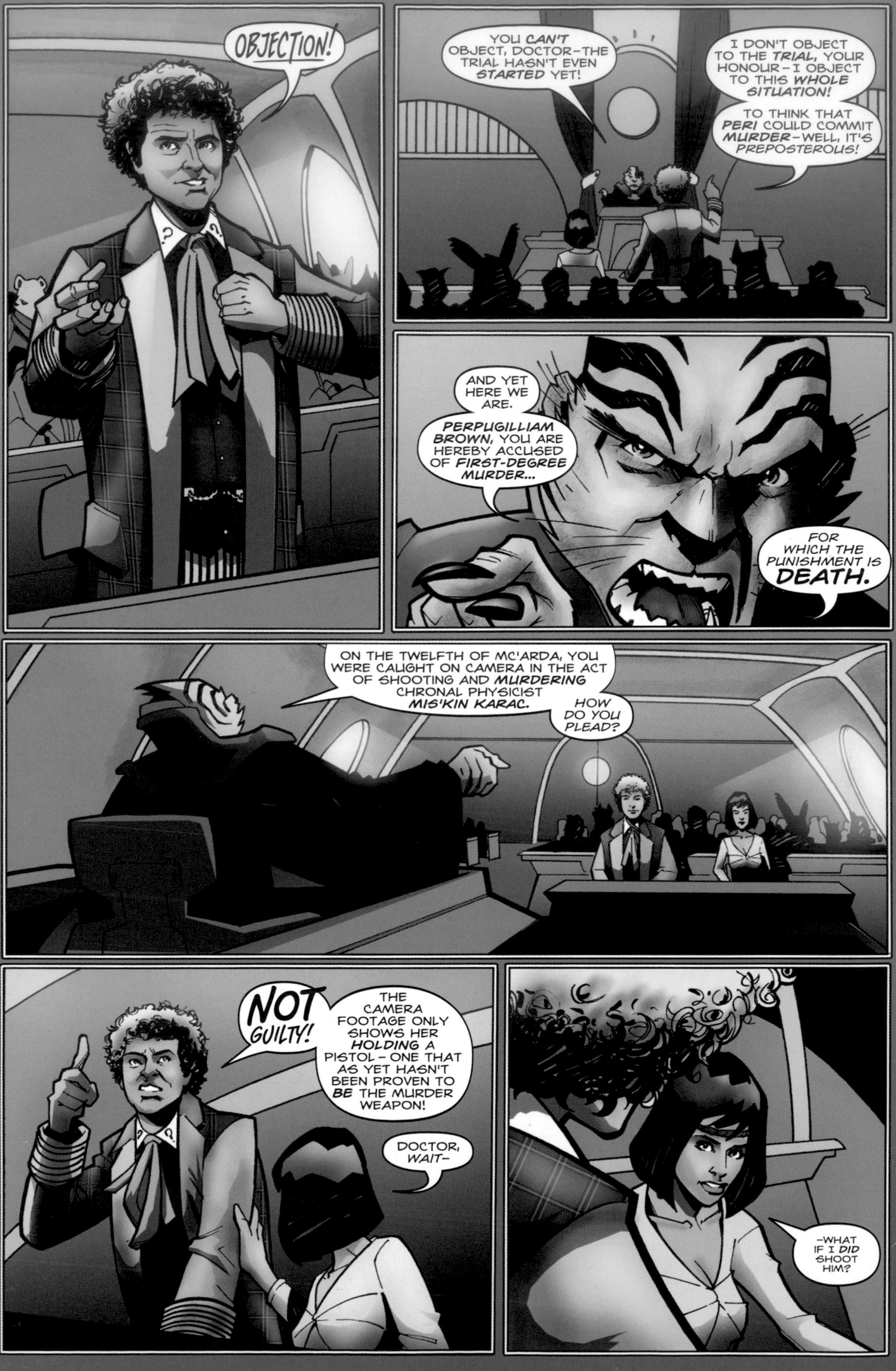
OBJECTION!
YOU CAN'T OBJECT, DOCTOR–THE TRIAL HASN'T EVEN STARTED YET!
I DON'T OBJECT TO THE TRIAL, YOUR HONOUR–I OBJECT TO THIS WHOLE SITUATION!
TO THINK THAT PERI COULD COMMIT MURDER–WELL, IT'S PREPOSTEROUS!
AND YET HERE WE ARE.
PERPUGILLIAM BROWN, YOU ARE HEREBY ACCUSED OF FIRST-DEGREE MURDER...
FOR WHICH THE PUNISHMENT IS DEATH.
ON THE TWELFTH OF MC'ARDA, YOU WERE CAUGHT ON CAMERA IN THE ACT OF SHOOTING AND MURDERING CHRONAL PHYSICIST MIS'KIN KARAC.
HOW DO YOU PLEAD?
NOT GUILTY!
THE CAMERA FOOTAGE ONLY SHOWS HER HOLDING A PISTOL–ONE THAT AS YET HASN'T BEEN PROVEN TO BE THE MURDER WEAPON!
DOCTOR, WAIT–
–WHAT IF I DID SHOOT HIM?

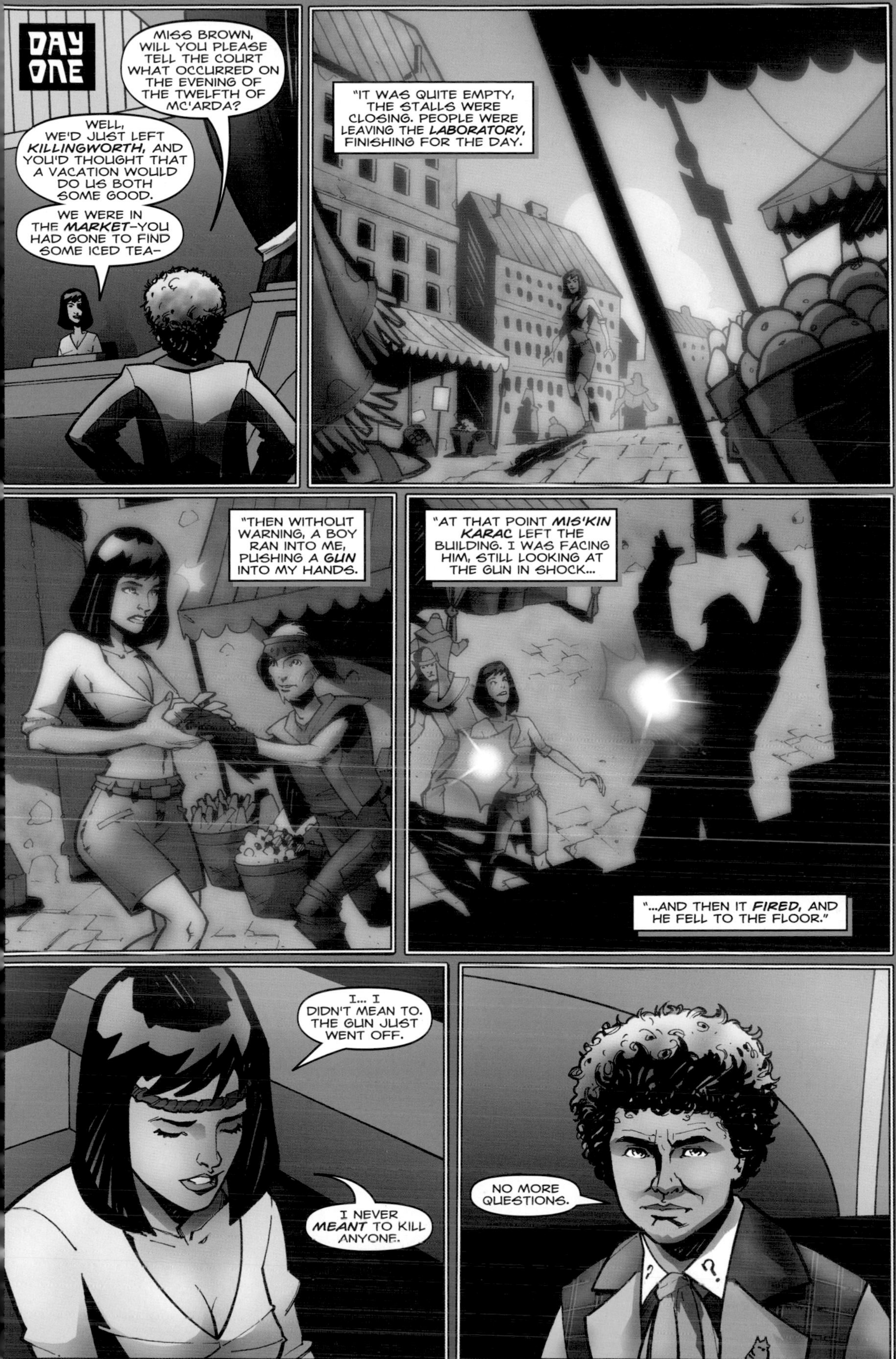
DAY ONE
MISS BROWN, WILL YOU PLEASE TELL THE COURT WHAT OCCURRED ON THE EVENING OF THE TWELFTH OF MC'ARDA?
WELL, WE'D JUST LEFT KILLINGWORTH, AND YOU'D THOUGHT THAT A VACATION WOULD DO US BOTH SOME GOOD.
WE WERE IN THE MARKET–YOU HAD GONE TO FIND SOME ICED TEA–
"IT WAS QUITE EMPTY, THE STALLS WERE CLOSING. PEOPLE WERE LEAVING THE LABORATORY, FINISHING FOR THE DAY.
"THEN WITHOUT WARNING, A BOY RAN INTO ME, PUSHING A GUN INTO MY HANDS.
"AT THAT POINT MIS'KIN KARAC LEFT THE BUILDING. I WAS FACING HIM, STILL LOOKING AT THE GUN IN SHOCK...
"...AND THEN IT FIRED, AND HE FELL TO THE FLOOR."
I... I DIDN'T MEAN TO. THE GUN JUST WENT OFF.
I NEVER MEANT TO KILL ANYONE.
NO MORE QUESTIONS.

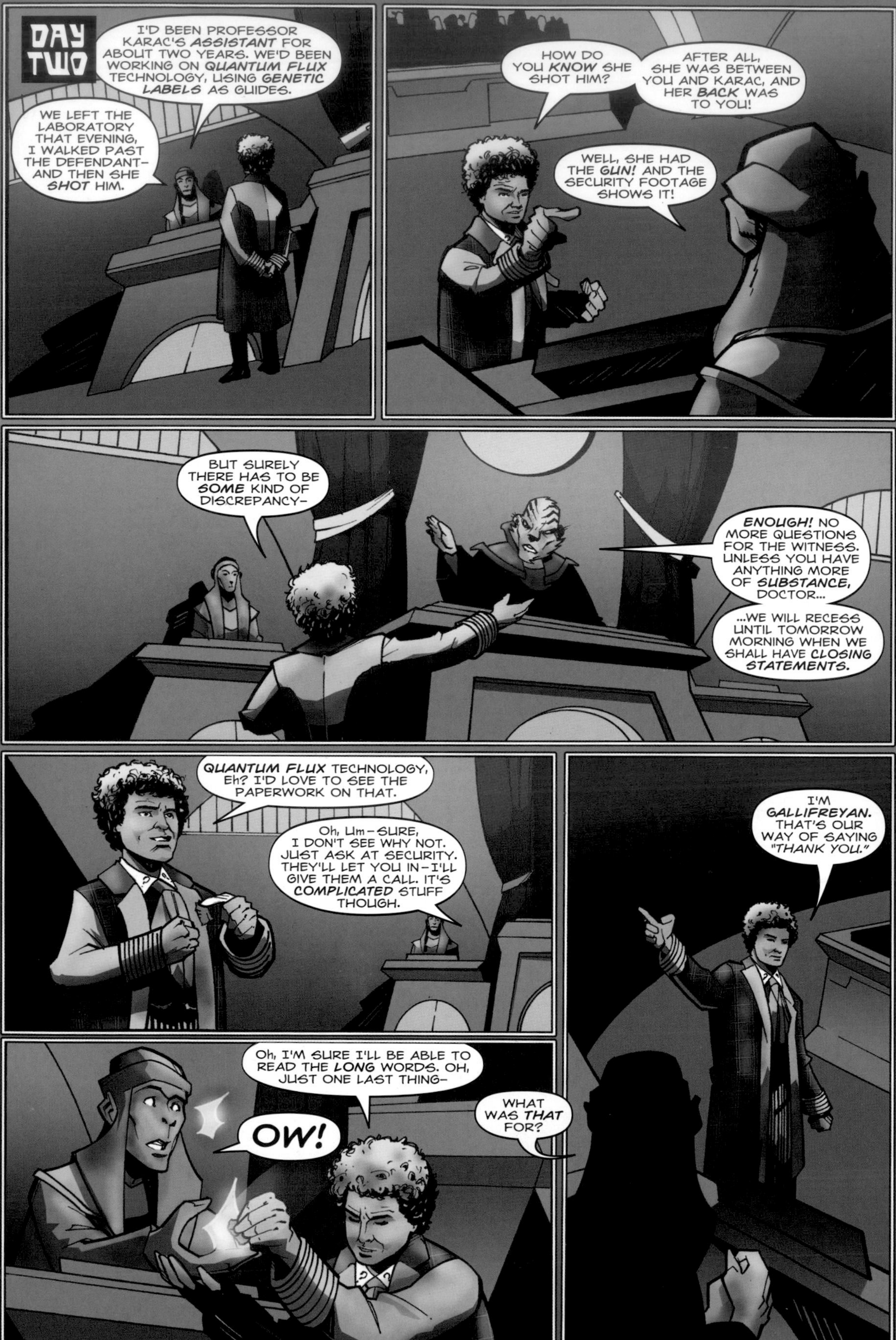
DAY TWO
I'D BEEN PROFESSOR KARAC'S ASSISTANT FOR ABOUT TWO YEARS. WE'D BEEN WORKING ON QUANTUM FLUX TECHNOLOGY, USING GENETIC LABELS AS GUIDES.
WE LEFT THE LABORATORY THAT EVENING, I WALKED PAST THE DEFENDANT– AND THEN SHE SHOT HIM.
HOW DO YOU KNOW SHE SHOT HIM?
AFTER ALL, SHE WAS BETWEEN YOU AND KARAC, AND HER BACK WAS TO YOU!
WELL, SHE HAD THE GUN! AND THE SECURITY FOOTAGE SHOWS IT!
BUT SURELY THERE HAS TO BE SOME KIND OF DISCREPANCY–
ENOUGH! NO MORE QUESTIONS FOR THE WITNESS. UNLESS YOU HAVE ANYTHING MORE OF SUBSTANCE, DOCTOR...
...WE WILL RECESS UNTIL TOMORROW MORNING WHEN WE SHALL HAVE CLOSING STATEMENTS.
QUANTUM FLUX TECHNOLOGY, EH? I'D LOVE TO SEE THE PAPERWORK ON THAT.
OH, UM–SURE, I DON'T SEE WHY NOT. JUST ASK AT SECURITY. THEY'LL LET YOU IN–I'LL GIVE THEM A CALL. IT'S COMPLICATED STUFF THOUGH.
OH, I'M SURE I'LL BE ABLE TO READ THE LONG WORDS. OH, JUST ONE LAST THING–
OW!
WHAT WAS THAT FOR?
I'M GALLIFREYAN. THAT'S OUR WAY OF SAYING "THANK YOU."

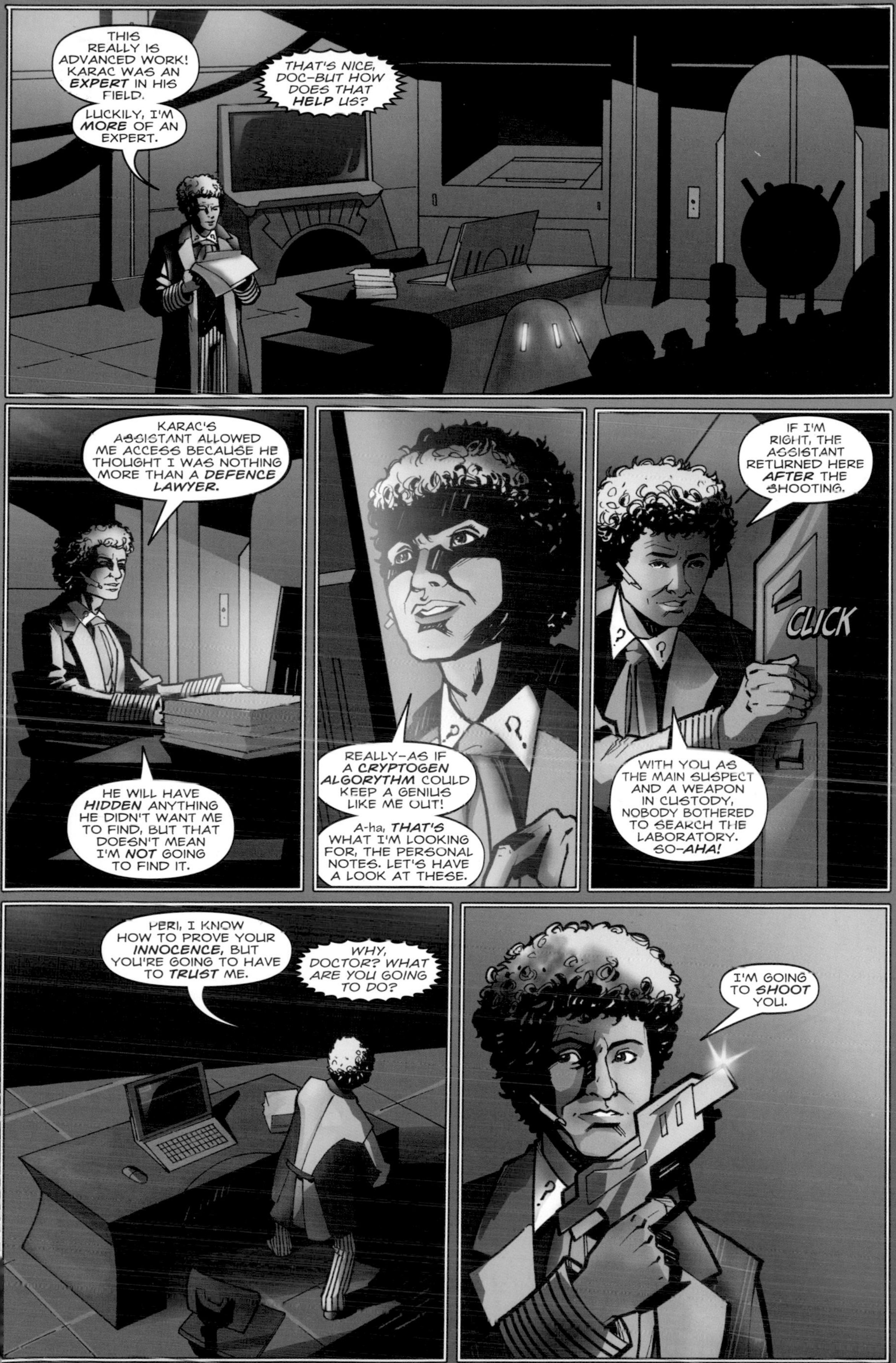

THIS REALLY IS ADVANCED WORK! KARAC WAS AN EXPERT IN HIS FIELD.
LUCKILY, I'M MORE OF AN EXPERT.
THAT'S NICE, DOC–BUT HOW DOES THAT HELP US?
KARAC'S ASSISTANT ALLOWED ME ACCESS BECAUSE HE THOUGHT I WAS NOTHING MORE THAN A DEFENCE LAWYER.
HE WILL HAVE HIDDEN ANYTHING HE DIDN'T WANT ME TO FIND, BUT THAT DOESN'T MEAN I'M NOT GOING TO FIND IT.
REALLY–AS IF A CRYPTOGEN ALGORYTHM COULD KEEP A GENIUS LIKE ME OUT!
A-ha, THAT'S WHAT I'M LOOKING FOR, THE PERSONAL NOTES. LET'S HAVE A LOOK AT THESE.
IF I'M RIGHT, THE ASSISTANT RETURNED HERE AFTER THE SHOOTING.
CLICK
WITH YOU AS THE MAIN SUSPECT AND A WEAPON IN CUSTODY, NOBODY BOTHERED TO SEARCH THE LABORATORY. SO–AHA!
PERI, I KNOW HOW TO PROVE YOUR INNOCENCE, BUT YOU'RE GOING TO HAVE TO TRUST ME.
WHY, DOCTOR? WHAT ARE YOU GOING TO DO?
I'M GOING TO SHOOT YOU.

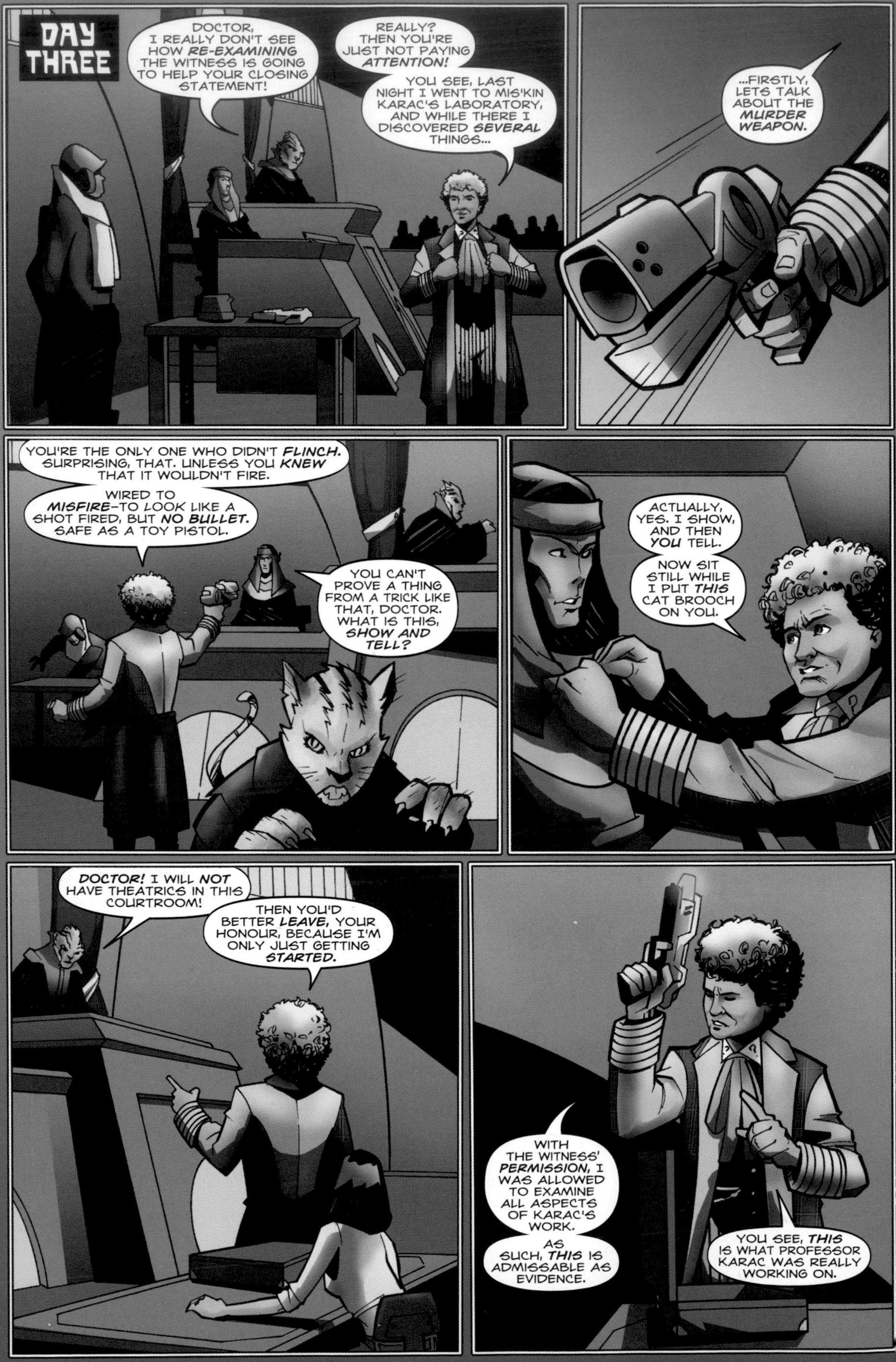
DAY THREE
DOCTOR, I REALLY DON'T SEE HOW RE-EXAMINING THE WITNESS IS GOING TO HELP YOUR CLOSING STATEMENT!
REALLY? THEN YOU'RE JUST NOT PAYING ATTENTION!
YOU SEE, LAST NIGHT I WENT TO MIS'KIN KARAC'S LABORATORY, AND WHILE THERE I DISCOVERED SEVERAL THINGS...
...FIRSTLY, LETS TALK ABOUT THE MURDER WEAPON.
YOU'RE THE ONLY ONE WHO DIDN'T FLINCH. SURPRISING, THAT. UNLESS YOU KNEW THAT IT WOULDN'T FIRE.
WIRED TO MISFIRE—TO LOOK LIKE A SHOT FIRED, BUT NO BULLET. SAFE AS A TOY PISTOL.
YOU CAN'T PROVE A THING FROM A TRICK LIKE THAT, DOCTOR. WHAT IS THIS, SHOW AND TELL?
ACTUALLY, YES. I SHOW, AND THEN YOU TELL.
NOW SIT STILL WHILE I PUT THIS CAT BROOCH ON YOU.
DOCTOR! I WILL NOT HAVE THEATRICS IN THIS COURTROOM!
THEN YOU'D BETTER LEAVE, YOUR HONOUR, BECAUSE I'M ONLY JUST GETTING STARTED.
WITH THE WITNESS' PERMISSION, I WAS ALLOWED TO EXAMINE ALL ASPECTS OF KARAC'S WORK.
AS SUCH, THIS IS ADMISSABLE AS EVIDENCE.
YOU SEE, THIS IS WHAT PROFESSOR KARAC WAS REALLY WORKING ON.

QUANTUM FLUX TECHNOLOGY IS THE ABILITY TO MAKE SOMETHING *INTANGIBLE* UNTIL IT'S NEEDED.

THIS GUN IS SATURATED IN *CHRONAL ENERGY.* SO WAS PROFESSOR KARAC'S *I.D. PASS,* WHICH THE BULLET HIT, DEAD CENTER.

Um, DOCTOR?

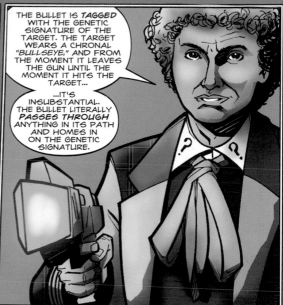

THE BULLET IS *TAGGED* WITH THE GENETIC SIGNATURE OF THE TARGET. THE TARGET WEARS A CHRONAL *"BULLSEYE,"* AND FROM THE MOMENT IT LEAVES THE GUN UNTIL THE MOMENT IT HITS THE TARGET...

...IT'S INSUBSTANTIAL. THE BULLET LITERALLY *PASSES THROUGH* ANYTHING IN ITS PATH AND HOMES IN ON THE GENETIC SIGNATURE.

THAT IS WHY YOU WERE *DIRECTLY BEHIND* PERI. YOU DIDN'T NEED A *CLEAR VIEW* – AND THE PATHOLOGISTS WOULD BELIEVE THAT THE ANGLE OF THE SHOT MATCHED HER GUN...

...A GUN THAT *YOU* GAVE HER.

THIS IS *INSANE!* WHAT YOU SUGGEST IS IN THE WORLD OF FANTASY! *NOBODY* CAN DO SUCH A THING!

IF YOU FIRE THAT GUN, ALL YOU DO IS *KILL YOUR FRIEND!*

REALLY? LET'S TEST THAT. YOU SEE THAT *CAT BROOCH* YOU WEAR? *DRENCHED* IN CHRONAL ENERGY, YOU KNOW.

AND ON IT? A DROP OF *BLOOD* THAT I TOOK FROM YOU YESTERDAY WHEN I PRICKED YOU. THE SAME GENETIC TAG THAT THIS BULLET HAS BEEN PRIMED TO *SEARCH* FOR.

BUT WHY WOULD YOU *CARE?* THIS ISN'T GOING TO WORK. I'LL JUST KILL *PERI,* AND THE COURT WAS GOING TO DO THAT ANYWAY.

SO... *THREE, TWO*–

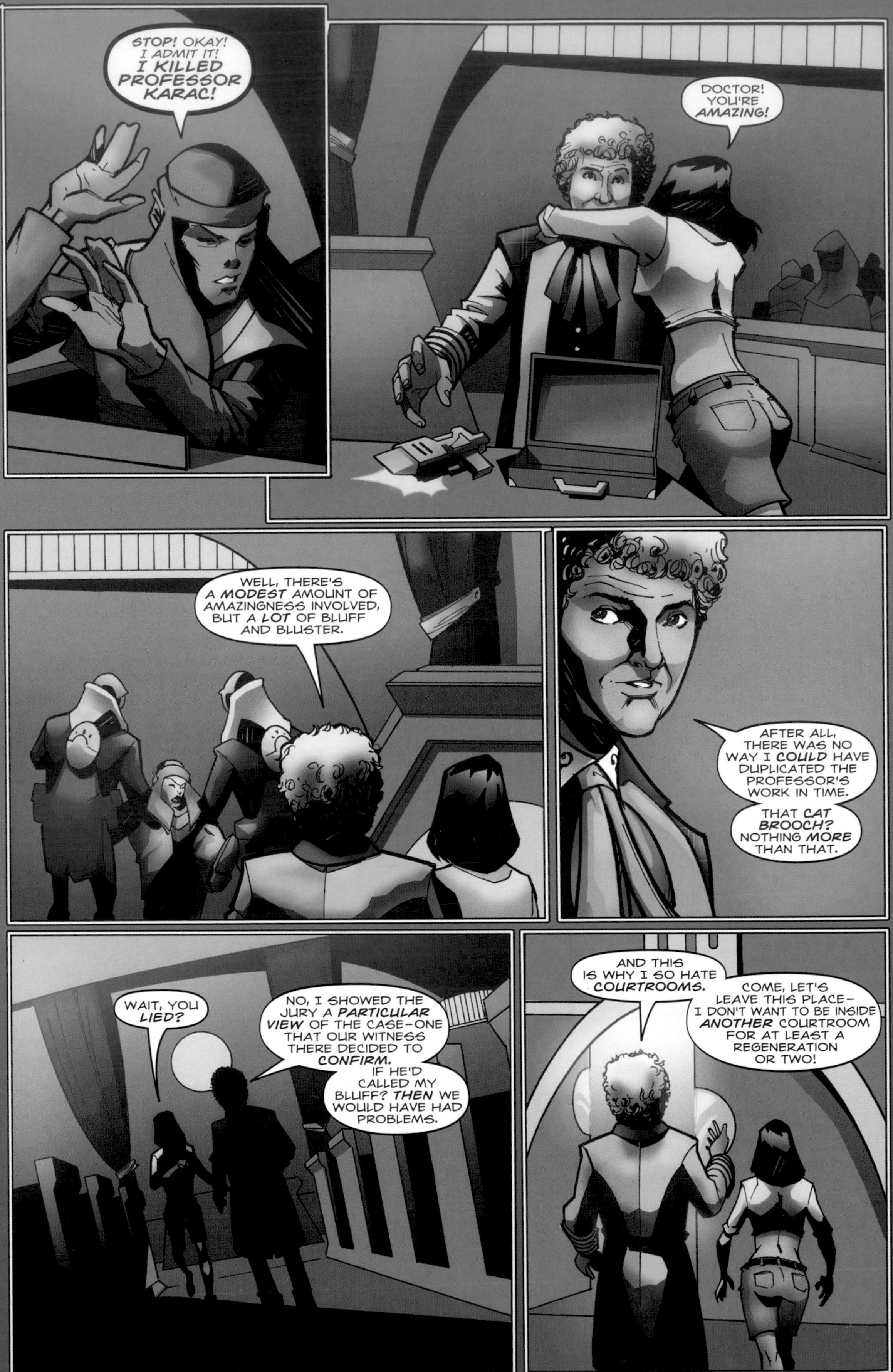
STOP! OKAY! I ADMIT IT! I KILLED PROFESSOR KARAC!
DOCTOR! YOU'RE AMAZING!
WELL, THERE'S A MODEST AMOUNT OF AMAZINGNESS INVOLVED, BUT A LOT OF BLUFF AND BLUSTER.
AFTER ALL, THERE WAS NO WAY I COULD HAVE DUPLICATED THE PROFESSOR'S WORK IN TIME.
THAT CAT BROOCH? NOTHING MORE THAN THAT.
WAIT, YOU LIED?
NO, I SHOWED THE JURY A PARTICULAR VIEW OF THE CASE–ONE THAT OUR WITNESS THERE DECIDED TO CONFIRM.
IF HE'D CALLED MY BLUFF? THEN WE WOULD HAVE HAD PROBLEMS.
AND THIS IS WHY I SO HATE COURTROOMS.
COME, LET'S LEAVE THIS PLACE– I DON'T WANT TO BE INSIDE ANOTHER COURTROOM FOR AT LEAST A REGENERATION OR TWO!

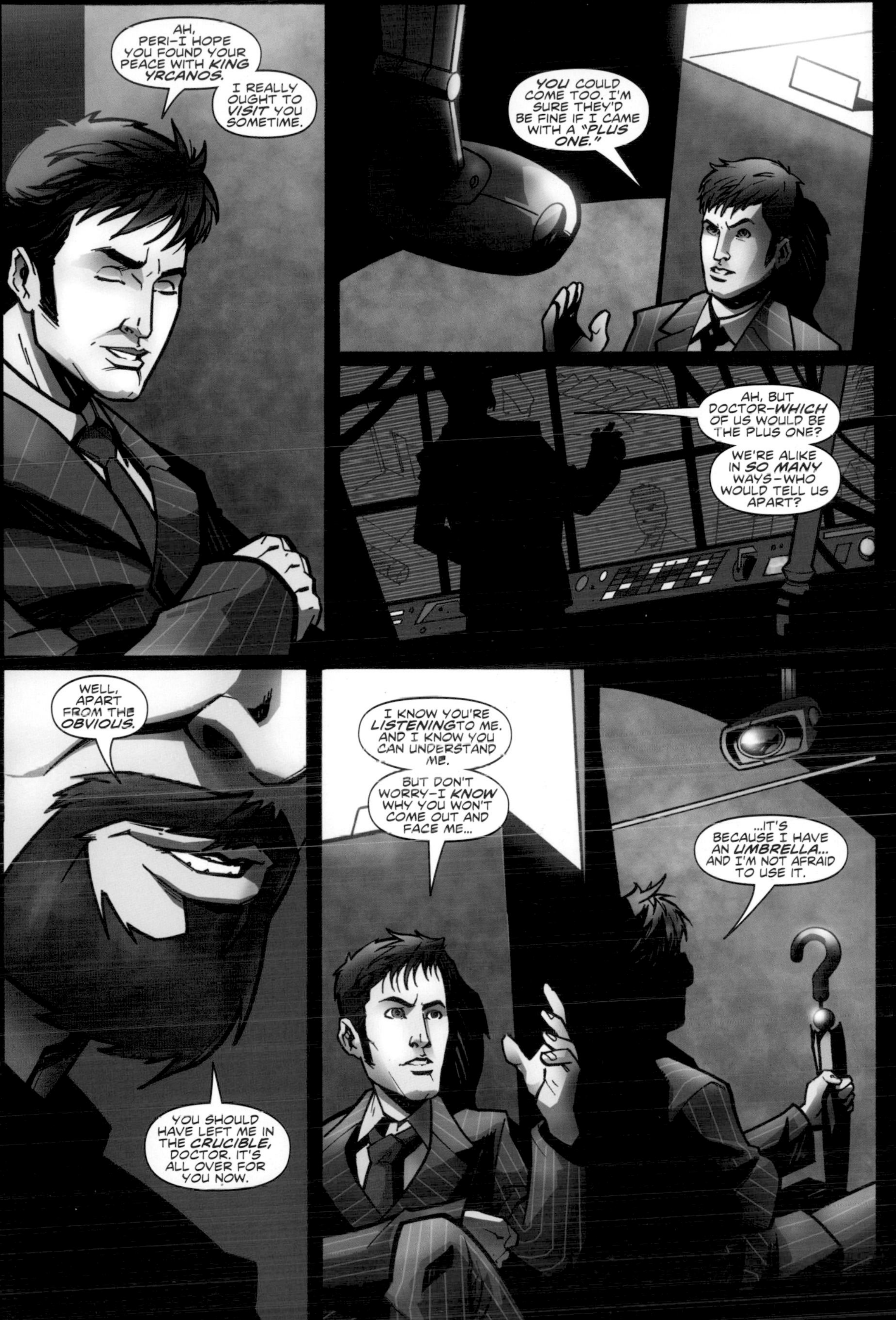
AH, PERI–I HOPE YOU FOUND YOUR PEACE WITH KING YRCANOS.
I REALLY OUGHT TO VISIT YOU SOMETIME.
YOU COULD COME TOO. I'M SURE THEY'D BE FINE IF I CAME WITH A "PLUS ONE."
AH, BUT DOCTOR–WHICH OF US WOULD BE THE PLUS ONE?
WE'RE ALIKE IN SO MANY WAYS–WHO WOULD TELL US APART?
WELL, APART FROM THE OBVIOUS.
YOU SHOULD HAVE LEFT ME IN THE CRUCIBLE, DOCTOR. IT'S ALL OVER FOR YOU NOW.
I KNOW YOU'RE LISTENING TO ME. AND I KNOW YOU CAN UNDERSTAND ME.
BUT DON'T WORRY–I KNOW WHY YOU WON'T COME OUT AND FACE ME...
...IT'S BECAUSE I HAVE AN UMBRELLA... AND I'M NOT AFRAID TO USE IT.

COME ON, ACE—*HURRY!*

I'M RUNNING AS FAST AS I CAN, *PROFESSOR!* THIS BACKPACK IS HEAVY!

WELL, I *DID* TELL YOU TO TRAVEL LIGHT.

AT LEAST YOU DON'T HAVE THAT AWFUL *TAPE PLAYER.*

HEY! THAT'S *CUTTING-EDGE* TECHNOLOGY!

ANYWAY, I THOUGHT IT MIGHT *STAND OUT* A LITTLE.

LOOK, ARE YOU *SURE* THAT WE COULDN'T HAVE LANDED THE TARDIS A LITTLE *CLOSER?*

THE WAR OF *AGROVAN SEVEN* HAS LASTED FOR *FIFTEEN HUNDRED* YEARS. THE TIME LORDS HAVE DECREED IT A NON-INTERVENTION SITE.

WHICH *OBVIOUSLY* MEANS THAT YOU'RE GOING TO *IGNORE* THEM.

THE *DOCTOR,* AT YOUR SERVICE. ANYWAY, IF I'D LANDED *CLOSER,* THEY'D HAVE SEEN IT.

I MAY KEEP TELLING THEM I'M *PRESIDENT-ELECT,* BUT THAT ISN'T A *"GET OUT OF JAIL FREE"* CARD.

THE PROBLEM WITH NON-INTERVENTION IS THAT SOMEONE *ALWAYS* IGNORES IT.

THE *STRYKES* AND THE *MARATS* HAVE BEEN EQUALLY MATCHED FOR GENERATIONS. THEIR ENTIRE STRUCTURE IS *BUILT* ON THIS.

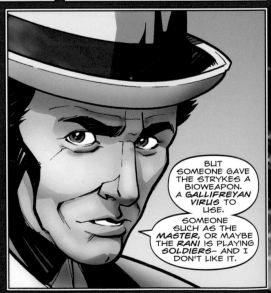

BUT SOMEONE GAVE THE STRYKES A BIOWEAPON. A *GALLIFREYAN VIRUS* TO USE.

SOMEONE SUCH AS THE *MASTER,* OR MAYBE THE *RANI* IS PLAYING SOLDIERS— AND I DON'T LIKE IT.

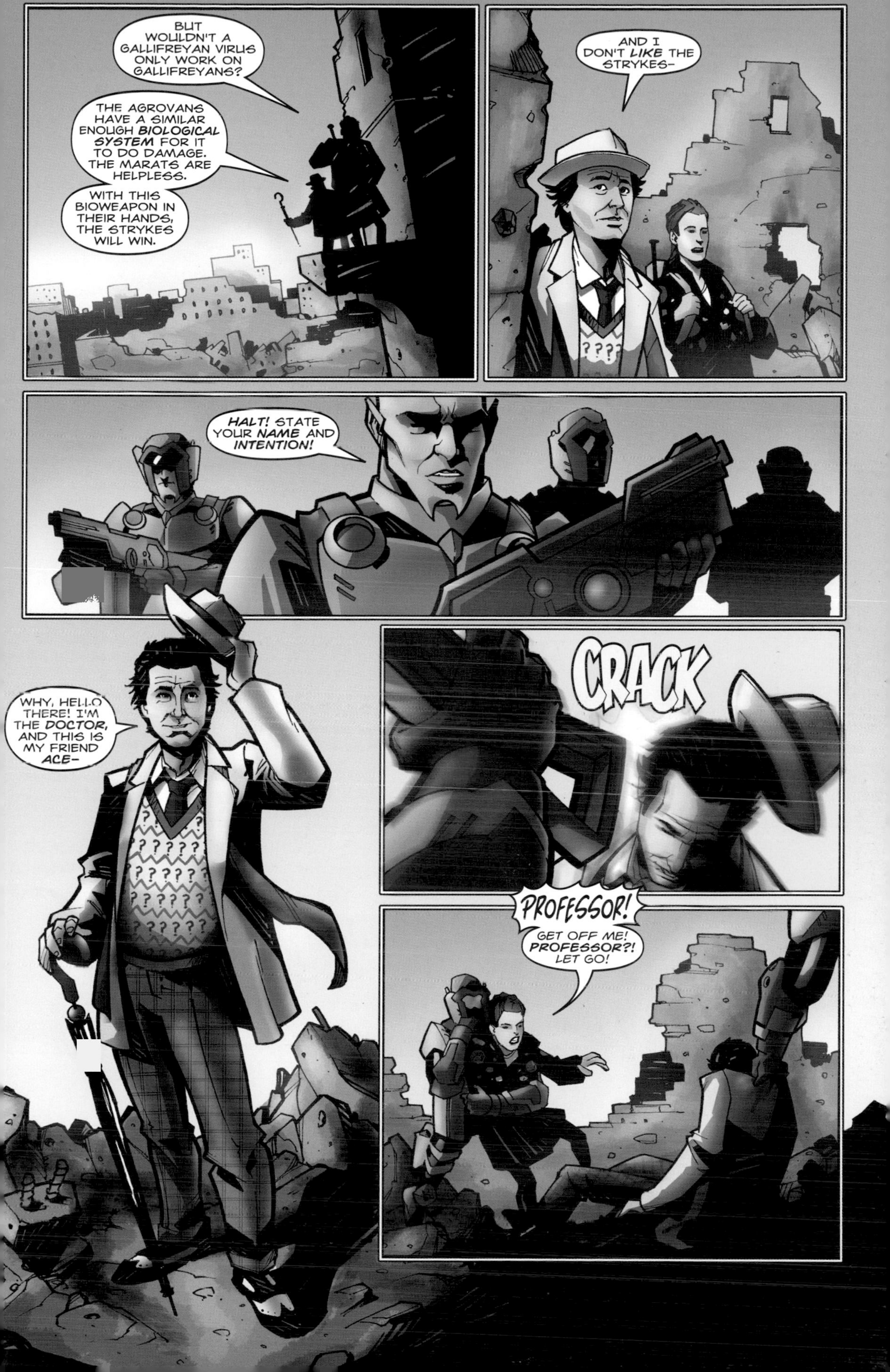
BUT WOULDN'T A GALLIFREYAN VIRUS ONLY WORK ON GALLIFREYANS?
THE AGROVANS HAVE A SIMILAR ENOUGH BIOLOGICAL SYSTEM FOR IT TO DO DAMAGE. THE MARATS ARE HELPLESS.
WITH THIS BIOWEAPON IN THEIR HANDS, THE STRYKES WILL WIN.
AND I DON'T LIKE THE STRYKES–
HALT! STATE YOUR NAME AND INTENTION!
WHY, HELLO THERE! I'M THE DOCTOR, AND THIS IS MY FRIEND ACE–
CRACK
PROFESSOR!
GET OFF ME! PROFESSOR?! LET GO!

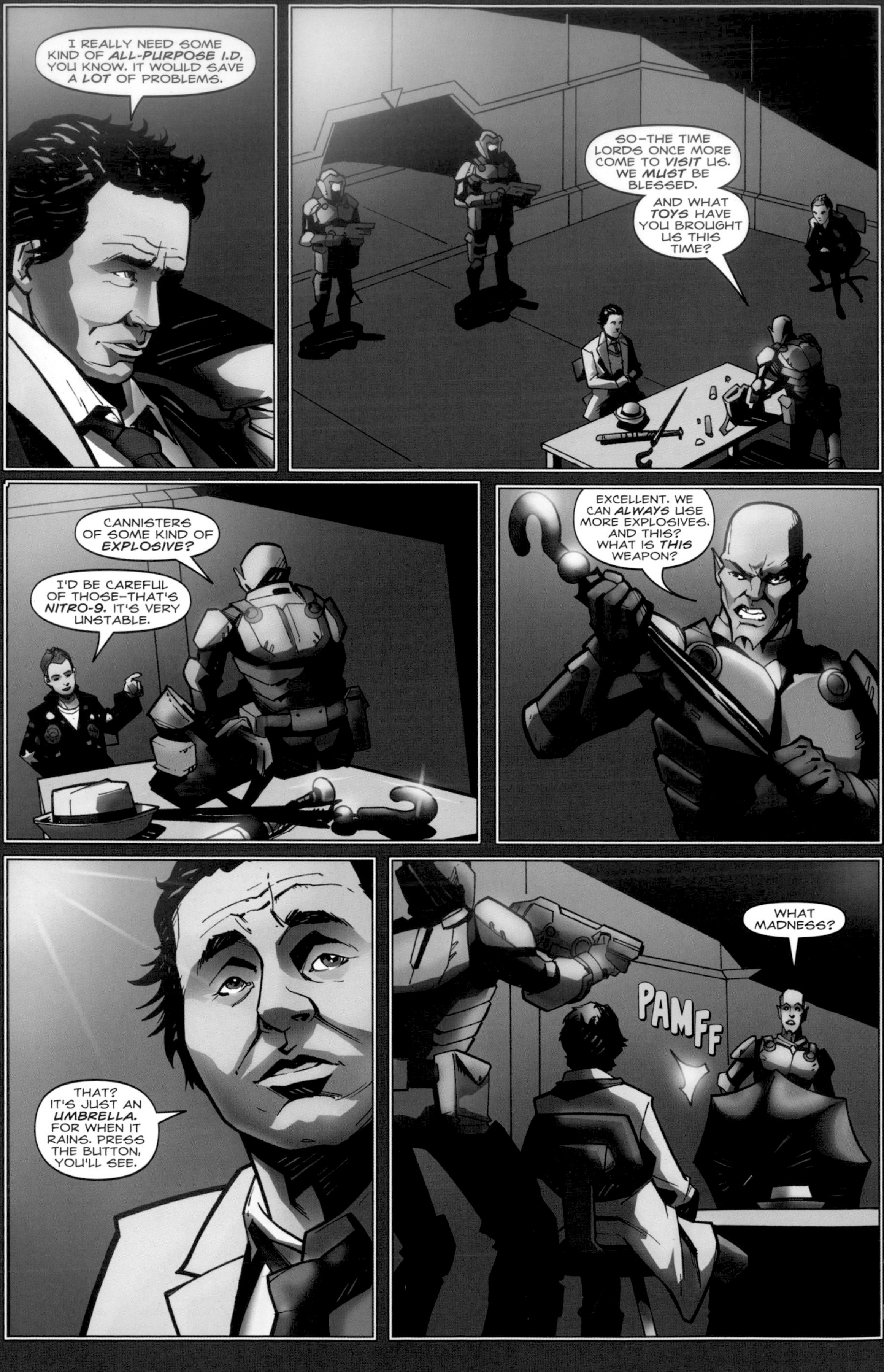
I REALLY NEED SOME KIND OF ALL-PURPOSE I.D, YOU KNOW. IT WOULD SAVE A LOT OF PROBLEMS.
SO–THE TIME LORDS ONCE MORE COME TO VISIT US. WE MUST BE BLESSED.
AND WHAT TOYS HAVE YOU BROUGHT US THIS TIME?
CANNISTERS OF SOME KIND OF EXPLOSIVE?
I'D BE CAREFUL OF THOSE–THAT'S NITRO-9. IT'S VERY UNSTABLE.
EXCELLENT. WE CAN ALWAYS USE MORE EXPLOSIVES. AND THIS? WHAT IS THIS WEAPON?
THAT? IT'S JUST AN UMBRELLA. FOR WHEN IT RAINS. PRESS THE BUTTON, YOU'LL SEE.
WHAT MADNESS?
PAMFF

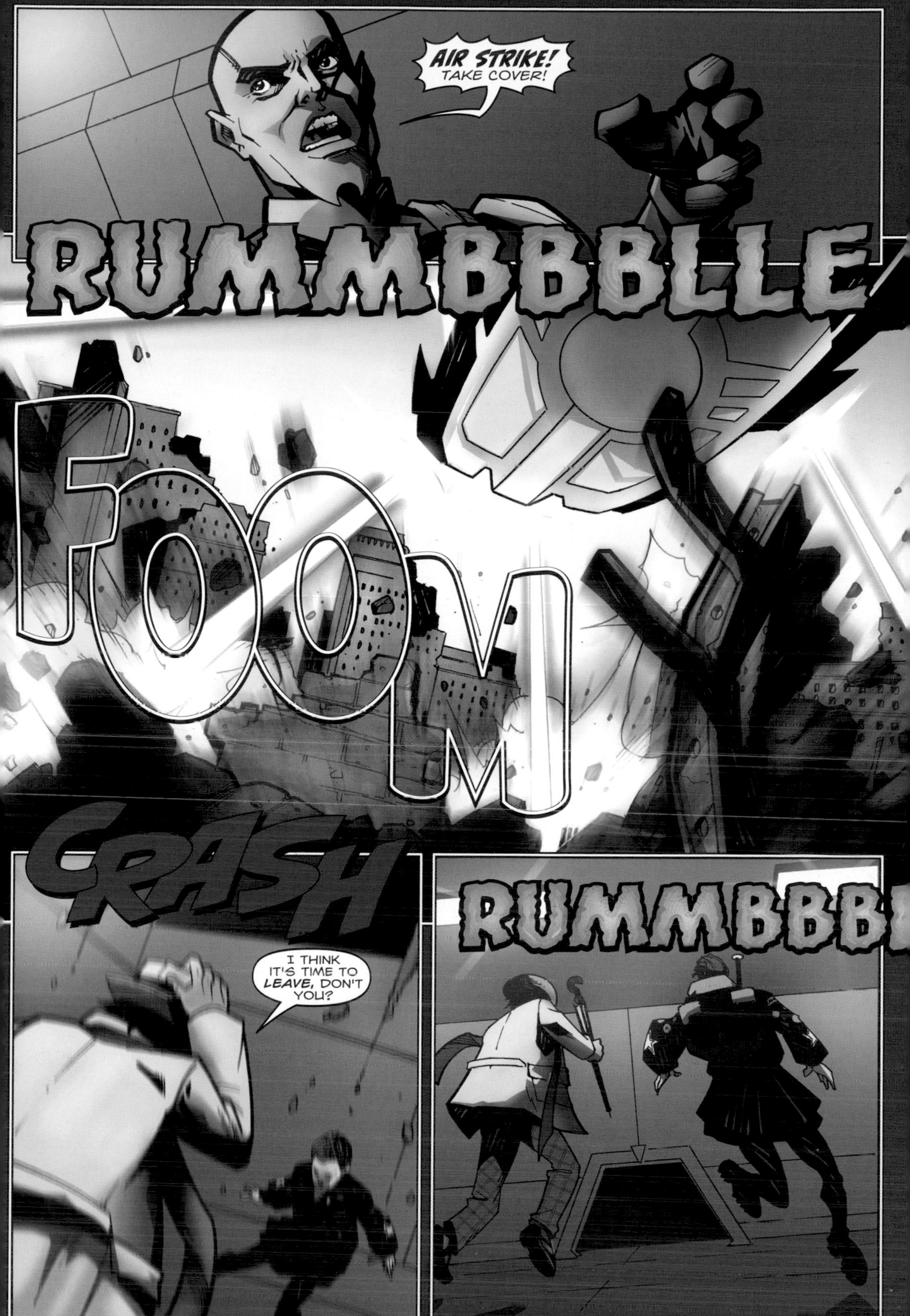
AIR STRIKE! TAKE COVER!
RUMMBBBLLE
FOOM
CRASH
I THINK IT'S TIME TO LEAVE, DON'T YOU?
RUMMBBB

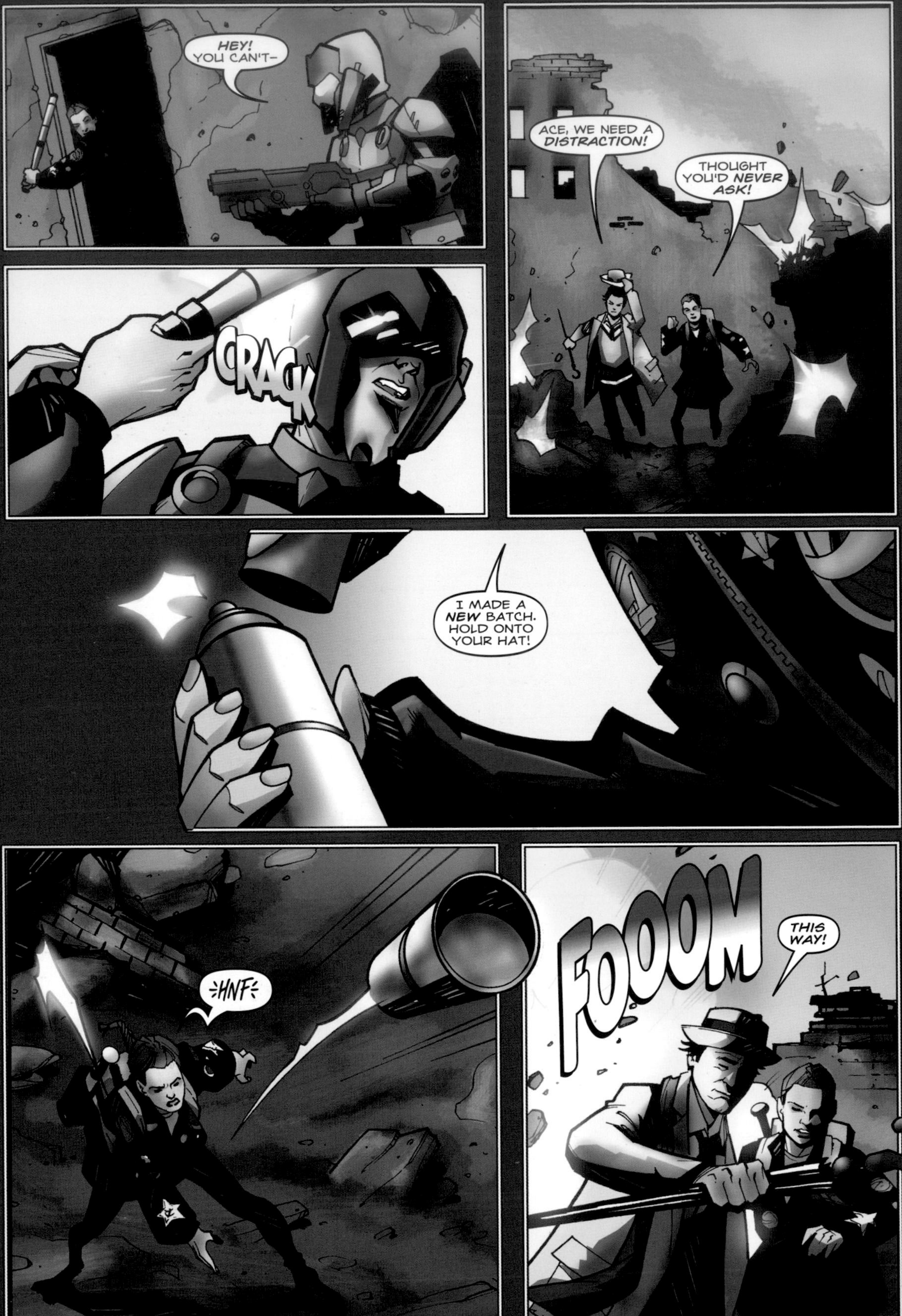
HEY! YOU CAN'T-
ACE, WE NEED A DISTRACTION!
THOUGHT YOU'D NEVER ASK!
CRACK
I MADE A NEW BATCH. HOLD ONTO YOUR HAT!
HNF
FOOOM
THIS WAY!

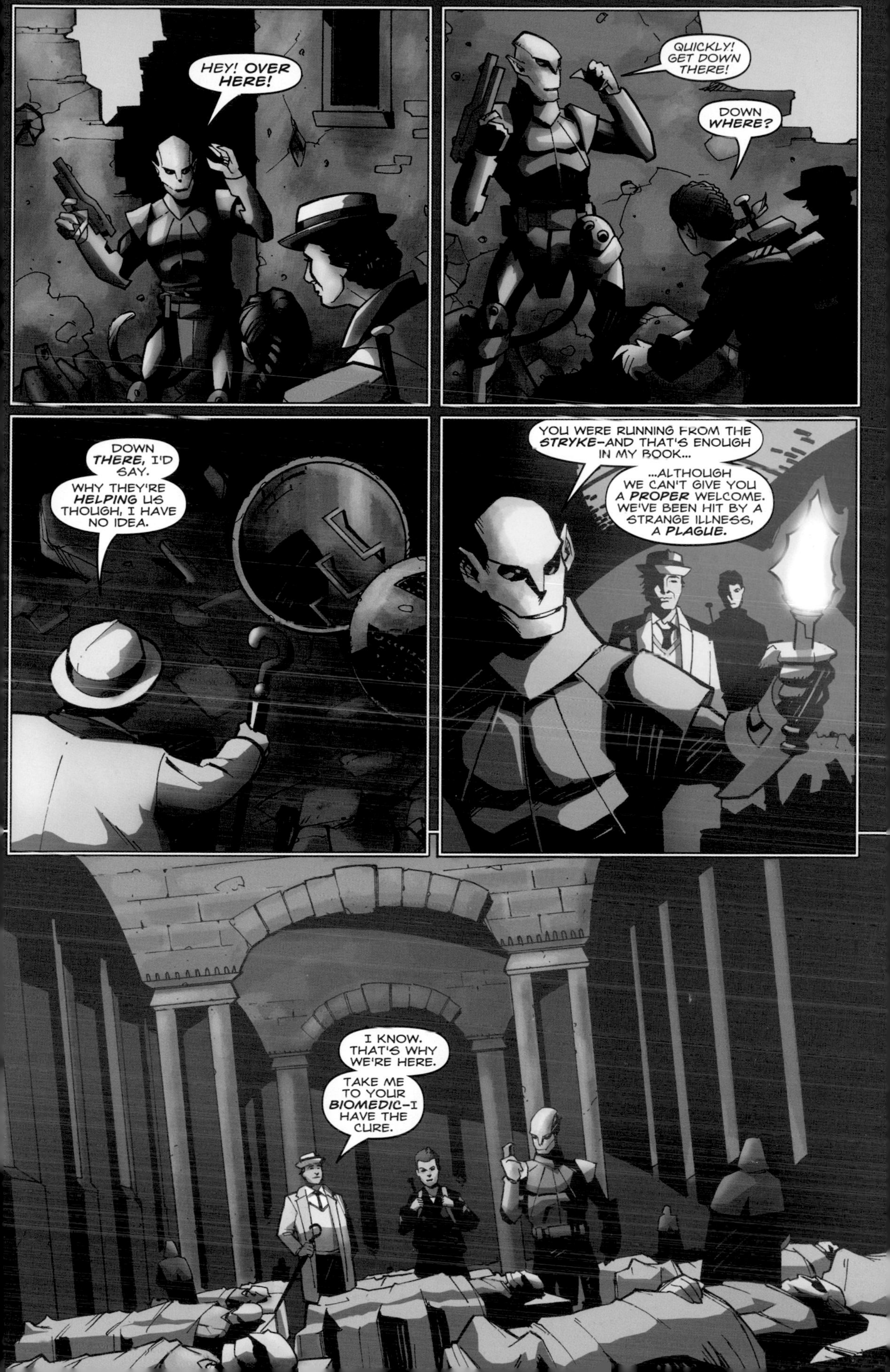
HEY! OVER HERE!
QUICKLY! GET DOWN THERE!
DOWN WHERE?
DOWN THERE, I'D SAY.
WHY THEY'RE HELPING US THOUGH, I HAVE NO IDEA.
YOU WERE RUNNING FROM THE STRYKE—AND THAT'S ENOUGH IN MY BOOK...
...ALTHOUGH WE CAN'T GIVE YOU A PROPER WELCOME. WE'VE BEEN HIT BY A STRANGE ILLNESS, A PLAGUE.
I KNOW. THAT'S WHY WE'RE HERE.
TAKE ME TO YOUR BIOMEDIC—I HAVE THE CURE.

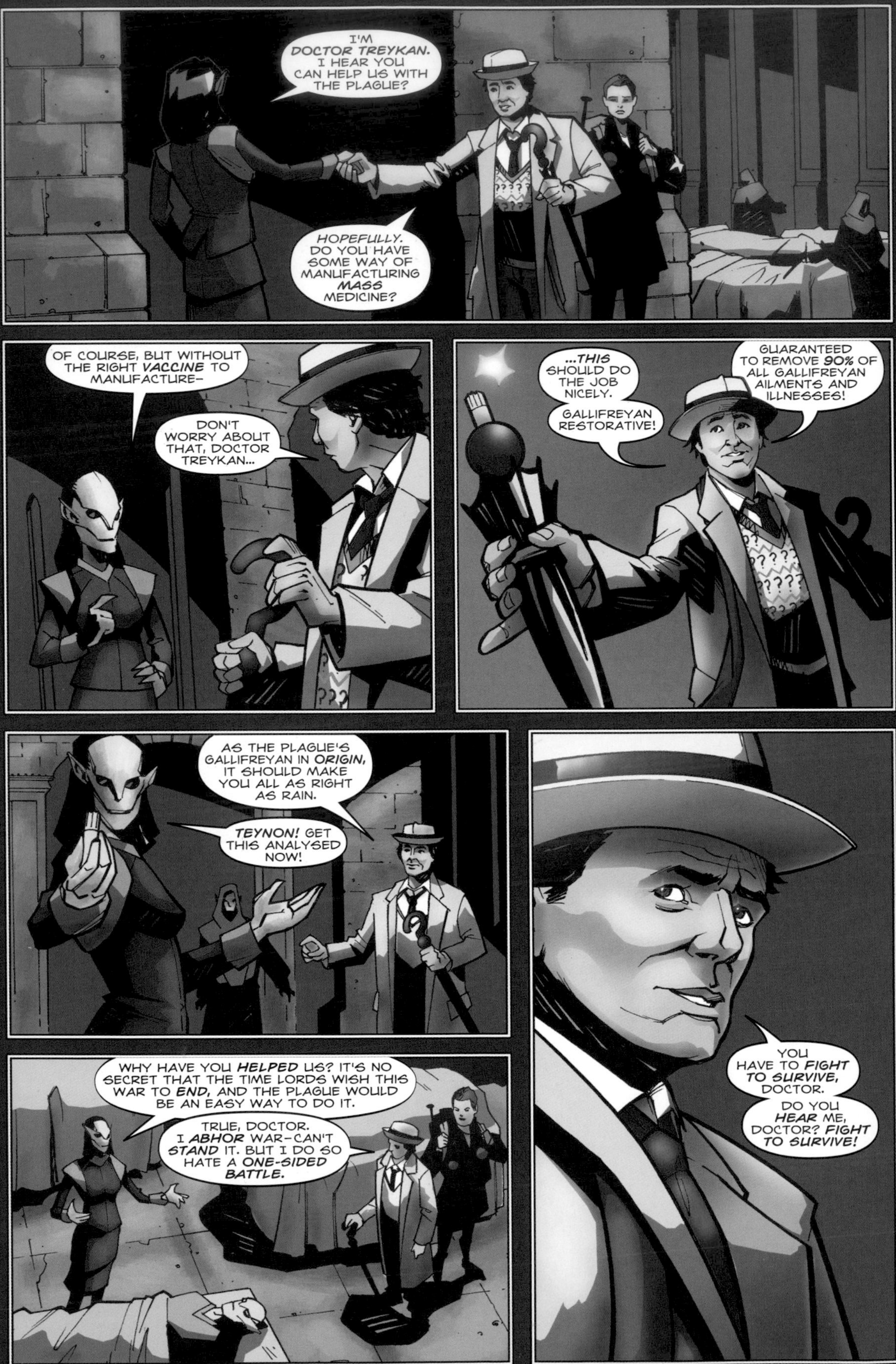
I'M DOCTOR TREYKAN. I HEAR YOU CAN HELP US WITH THE PLAGUE?
HOPEFULLY. DO YOU HAVE SOME WAY OF MANUFACTURING MASS MEDICINE?
OF COURSE, BUT WITHOUT THE RIGHT VACCINE TO MANUFACTURE–
DON'T WORRY ABOUT THAT, DOCTOR TREYKAN...
...THIS SHOULD DO THE JOB NICELY.
GALLIFREYAN RESTORATIVE!
GUARANTEED TO REMOVE 90% OF ALL GALLIFREYAN AILMENTS AND ILLNESSES!
AS THE PLAGUE'S GALLIFREYAN IN ORIGIN, IT SHOULD MAKE YOU ALL AS RIGHT AS RAIN.
TEYNON! GET THIS ANALYSED NOW!
WHY HAVE YOU HELPED US? IT'S NO SECRET THAT THE TIME LORDS WISH THIS WAR TO END, AND THE PLAGUE WOULD BE AN EASY WAY TO DO IT.
TRUE, DOCTOR. I ABHOR WAR–CAN'T STAND IT. BUT I DO SO HATE A ONE-SIDED BATTLE.
YOU HAVE TO FIGHT TO SURVIVE, DOCTOR.
DO YOU HEAR ME, DOCTOR? FIGHT TO SURVIVE!

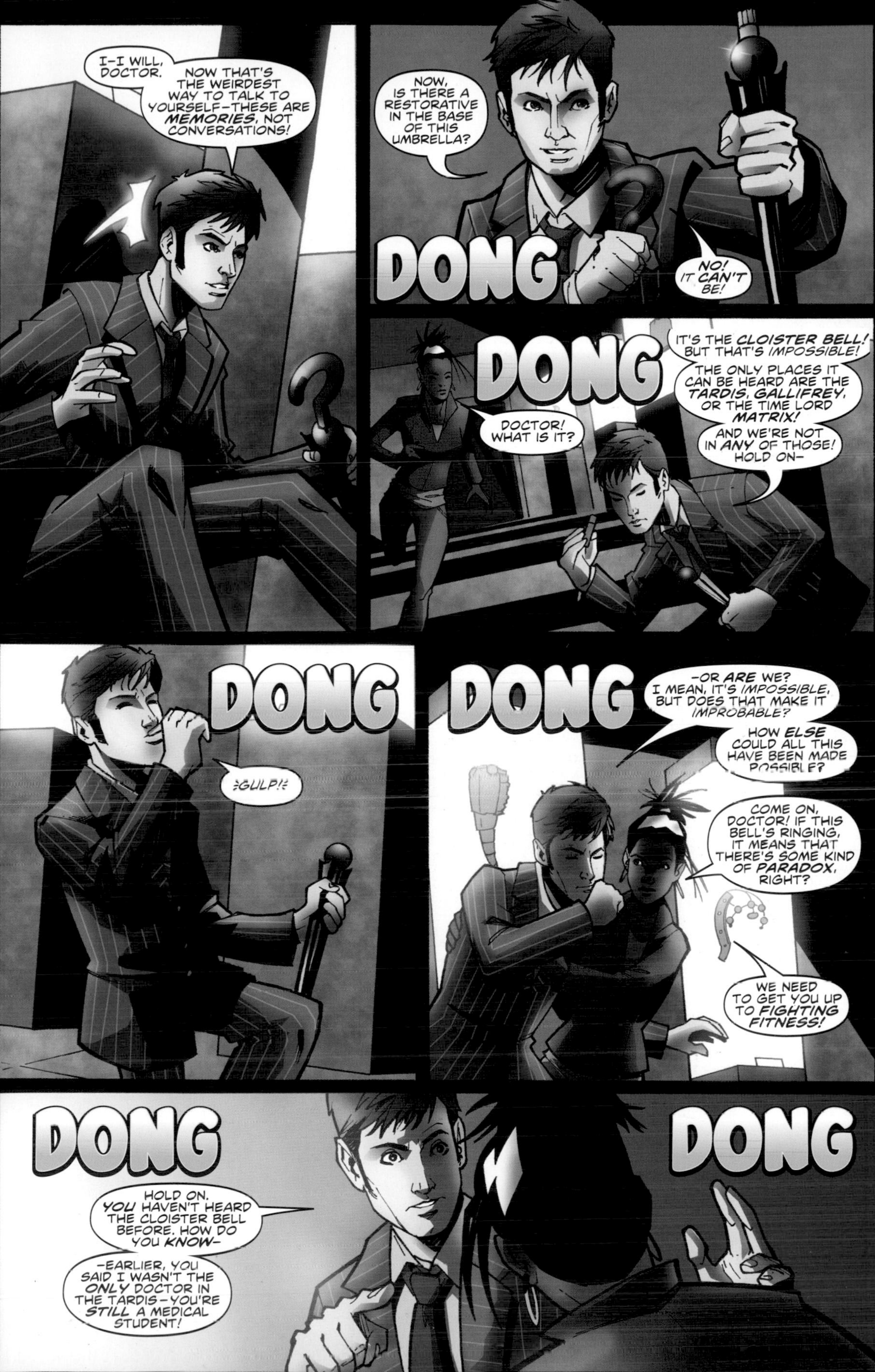

I—I WILL, DOCTOR.
NOW THAT'S THE WEIRDEST WAY TO TALK TO YOURSELF—THESE ARE *MEMORIES*, NOT CONVERSATIONS!
NOW, IS THERE A RESTORATIVE IN THE BASE OF THIS UMBRELLA?
DONG
NO! IT *CAN'T* BE!
DONG
DOCTOR! WHAT IS IT?
IT'S THE *CLOISTER BELL!* BUT THAT'S *IMPOSSIBLE!*
THE ONLY PLACES IT CAN BE HEARD ARE THE *TARDIS, GALLIFREY*, OR THE TIME LORD *MATRIX!*
AND WE'RE NOT IN *ANY* OF THOSE! HOLD ON—
DONG
GULP!
DONG
—OR *ARE* WE? I MEAN, IT'S *IMPOSSIBLE*, BUT DOES THAT MAKE IT *IMPROBABLE*?
HOW *ELSE* COULD ALL THIS HAVE BEEN MADE POSSIBLE?
COME ON, DOCTOR! IF THIS BELL'S RINGING, IT MEANS THAT THERE'S SOME KIND OF *PARADOX*, RIGHT?
WE NEED TO GET YOU UP TO *FIGHTING FITNESS!*
DONG
DONG
HOLD ON. *YOU* HAVEN'T HEARD THE CLOISTER BELL BEFORE. HOW DO YOU *KNOW*—
—EARLIER, YOU SAID I WASN'T THE *ONLY* DOCTOR IN THE TARDIS—YOU'RE *STILL* A MEDICAL STUDENT!

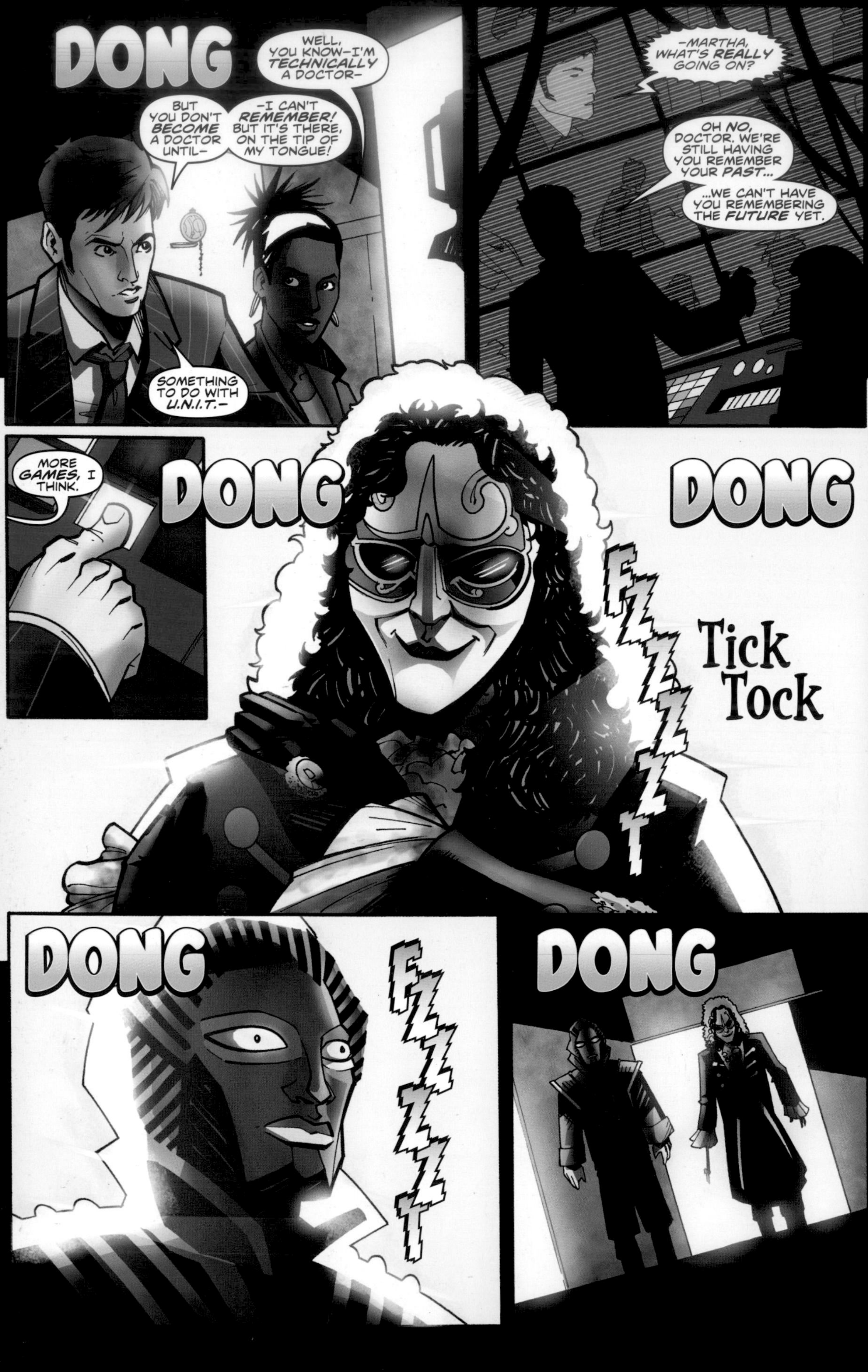
DONG
WELL, YOU KNOW—I'M TECHNICALLY A DOCTOR—
BUT YOU DON'T BECOME A DOCTOR UNTIL—
—I CAN'T REMEMBER! BUT IT'S THERE, ON THE TIP OF MY TONGUE!
SOMETHING TO DO WITH U.N.I.T.—
—MARTHA, WHAT'S REALLY GOING ON?
OH NO, DOCTOR. WE'RE STILL HAVING YOU REMEMBER YOUR PAST...
...WE CAN'T HAVE YOU REMEMBERING THE FUTURE YET.
MORE GAMES, I THINK.
DONG
DONG
FZZZZZT
Tick Tock
DONG
FZZZZZT
DONG

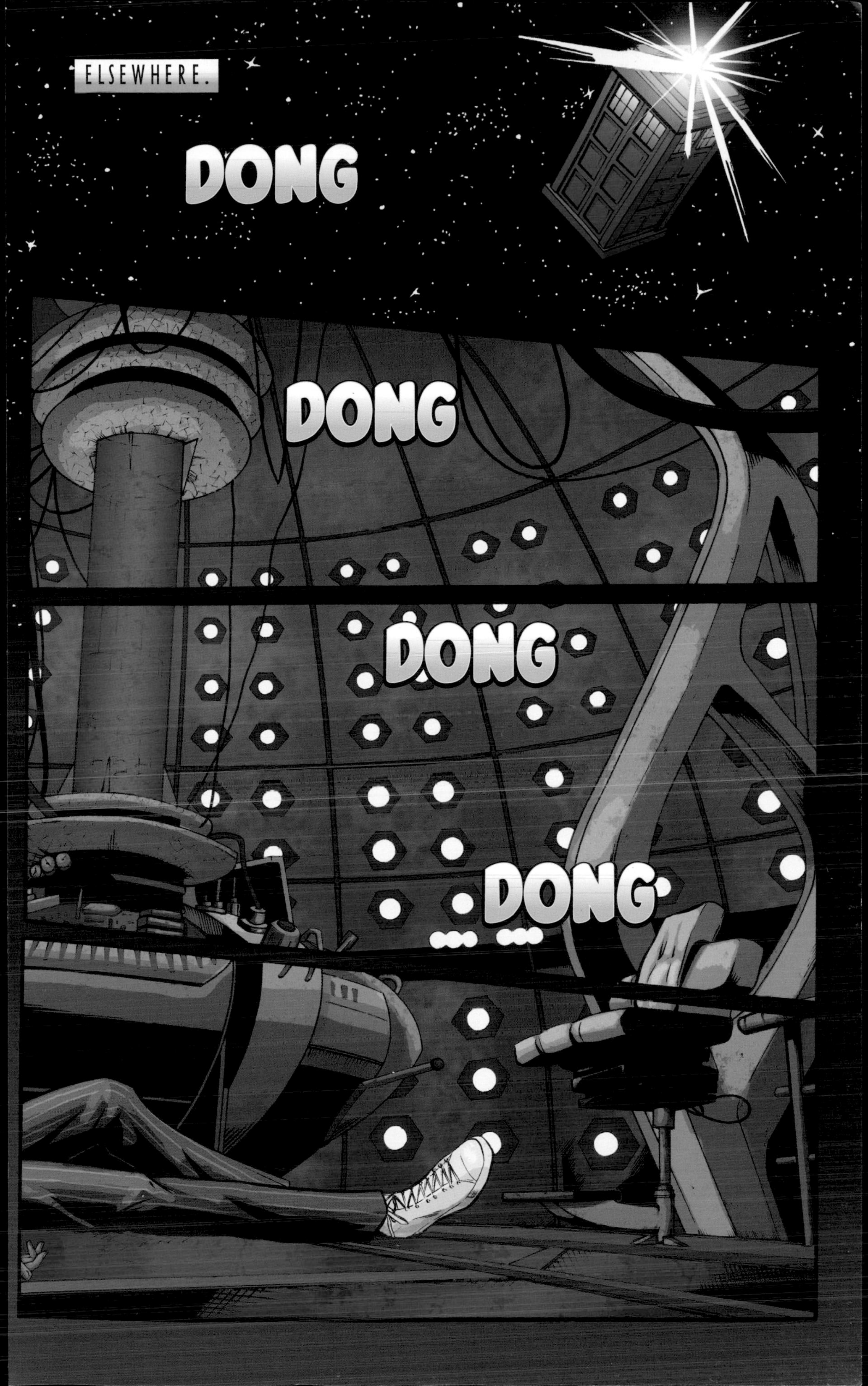
ELSEWHERE.
DONG
DONG
DONG
DONG

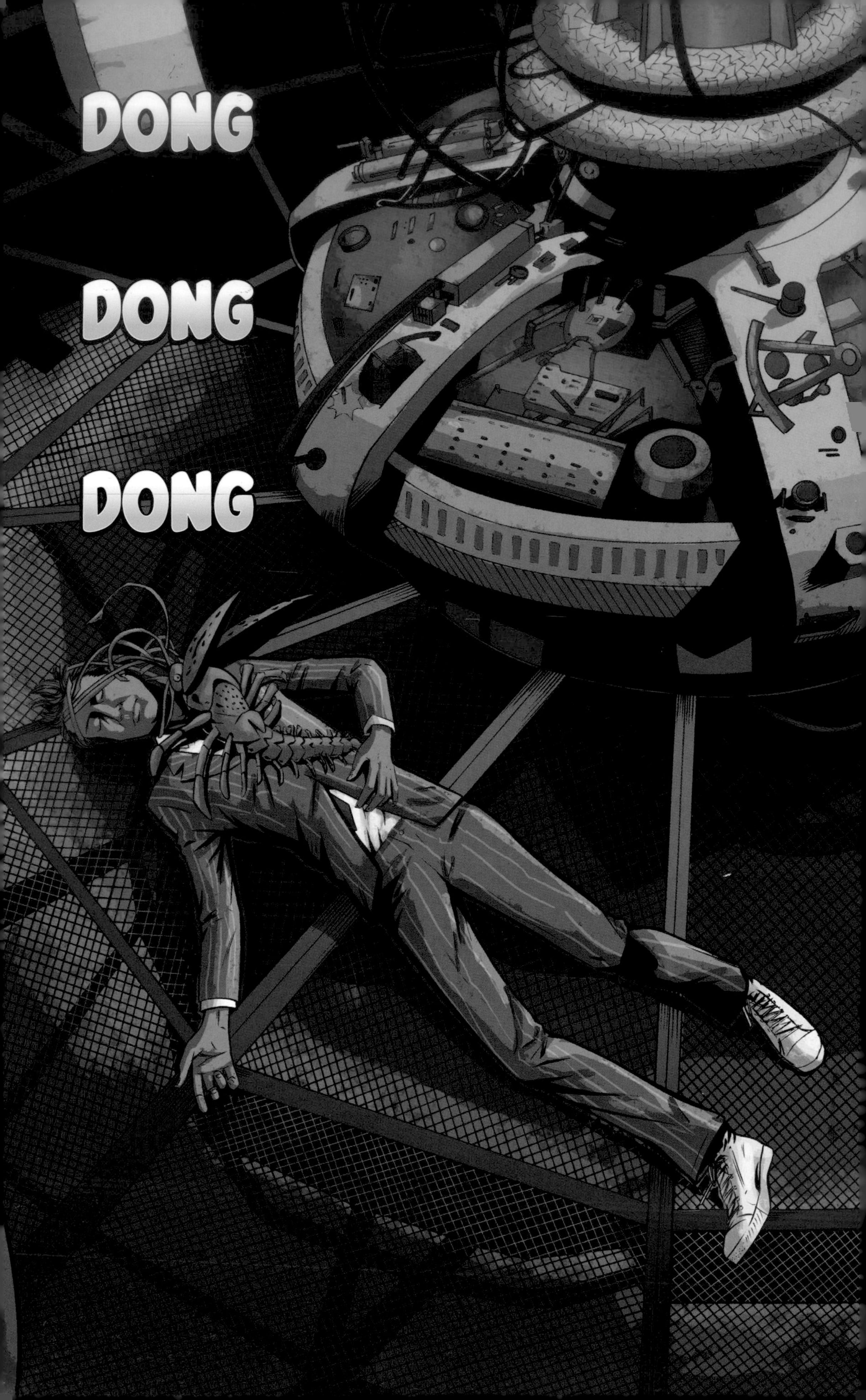
DONG
DONG
DONG

CHAPTER • FIVE
REVELATION

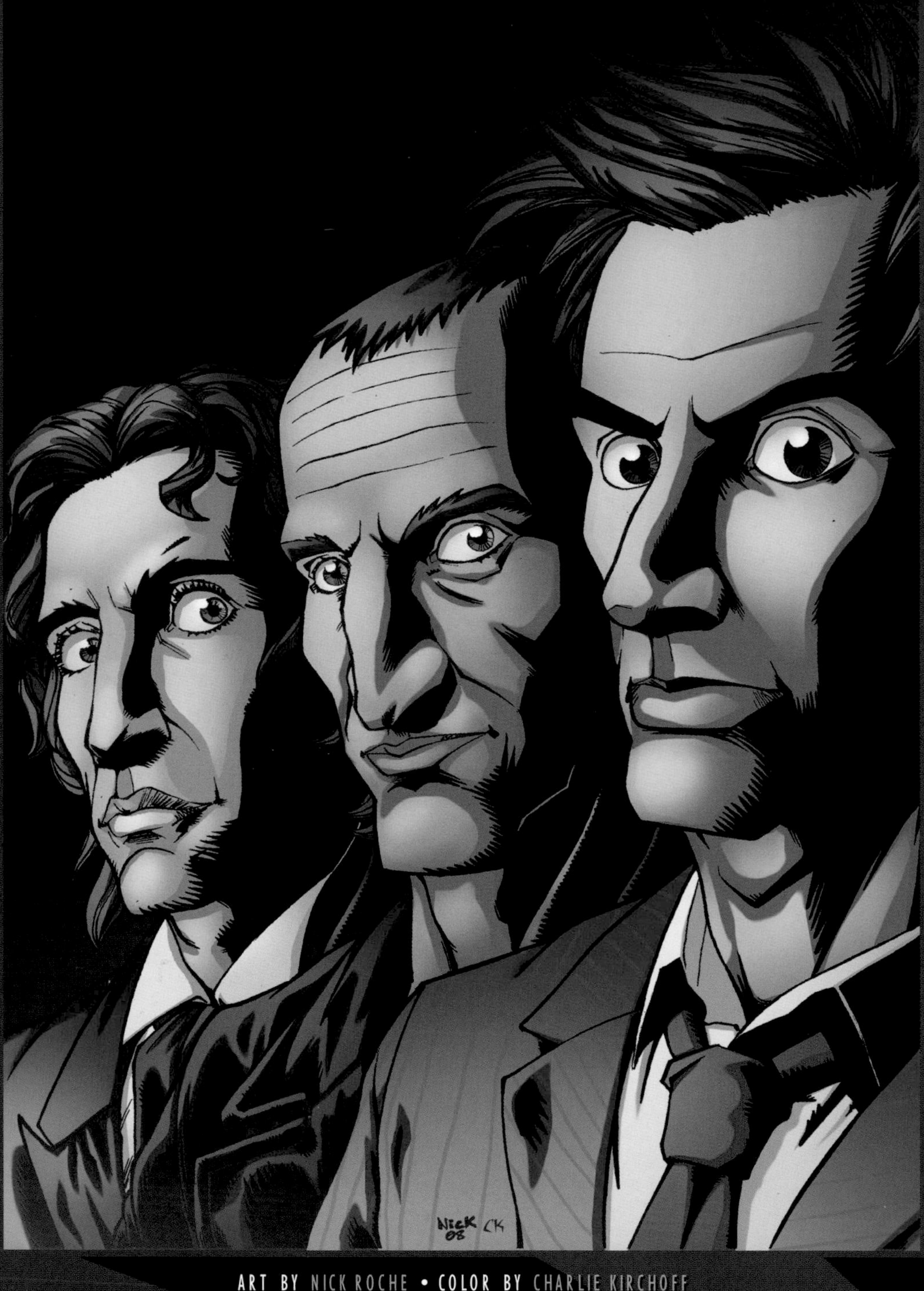
NICK 08 CK

ART BY NICK ROCHE • COLOR BY CHARLIE KIRCHOFF

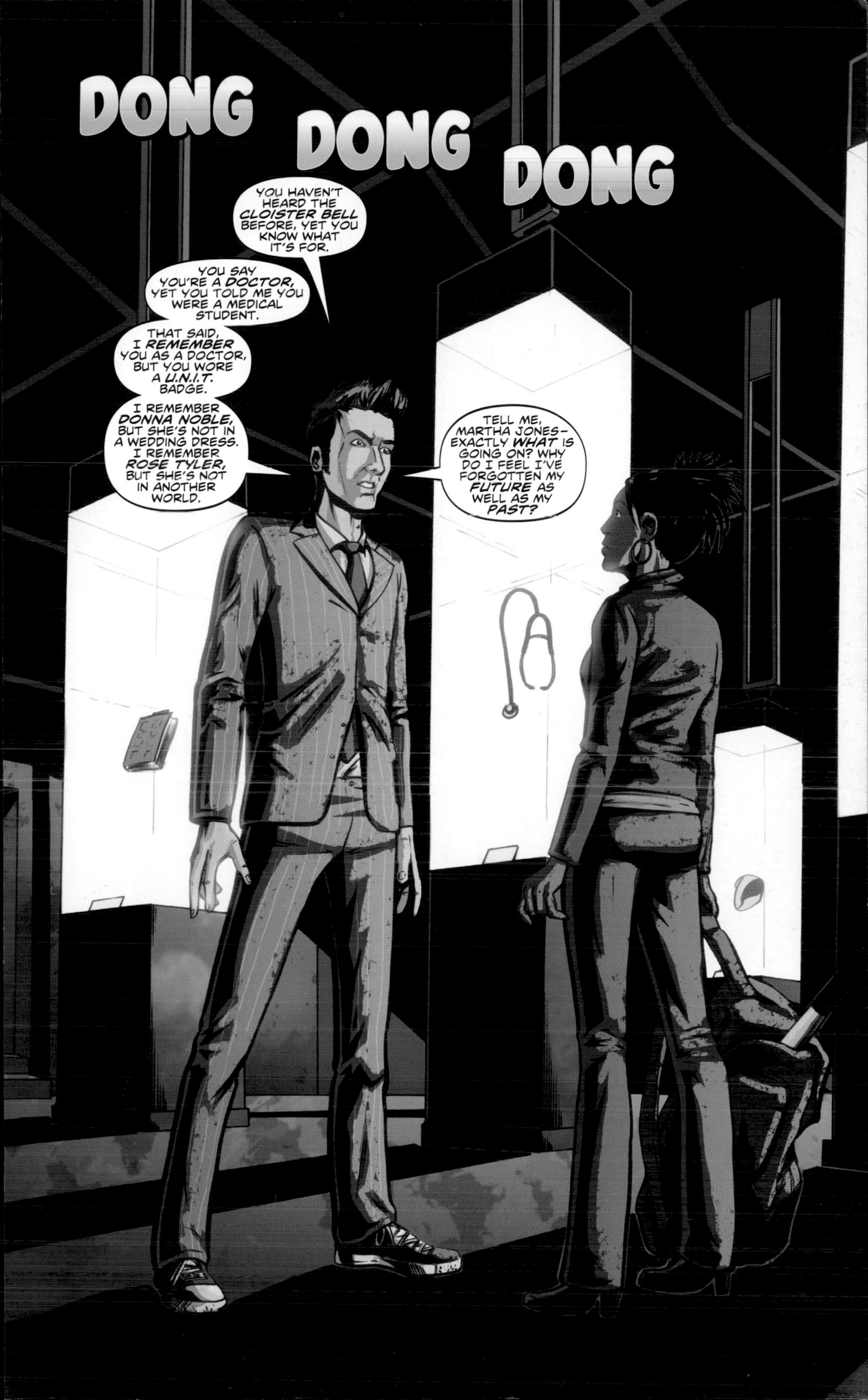
DONG DONG DONG
YOU HAVEN'T HEARD THE CLOISTER BELL BEFORE, YET YOU KNOW WHAT IT'S FOR.
YOU SAY YOU'RE A DOCTOR, YET YOU TOLD ME YOU WERE A MEDICAL STUDENT.
THAT SAID, I REMEMBER YOU AS A DOCTOR, BUT YOU WORE A U.N.I.T. BADGE.
I REMEMBER DONNA NOBLE, BUT SHE'S NOT IN A WEDDING DRESS. I REMEMBER ROSE TYLER, BUT SHE'S NOT IN ANOTHER WORLD.
TELL ME, MARTHA JONES- EXACTLY WHAT IS GOING ON? WHY DO I FEEL I'VE FORGOTTEN MY FUTURE AS WELL AS MY PAST?

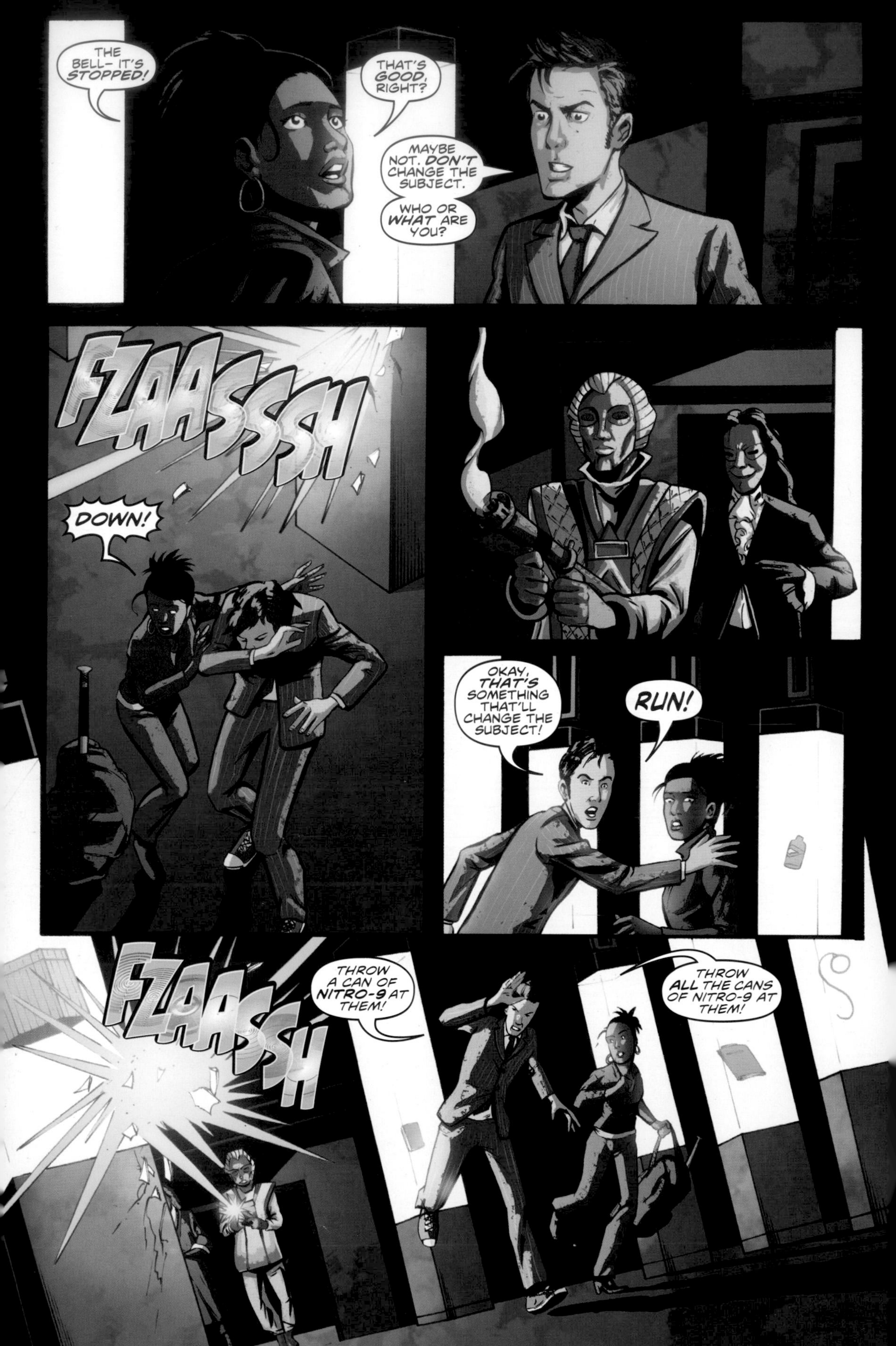
THE BELL– IT'S STOPPED!
THAT'S GOOD, RIGHT?
MAYBE NOT. DON'T CHANGE THE SUBJECT.
WHO OR WHAT ARE YOU?
FZAASSSH
DOWN!
OKAY, THAT'S SOMETHING THAT'LL CHANGE THE SUBJECT!
RUN!
FZAASSH
THROW A CAN OF NITRO-9 AT THEM!
THROW ALL THE CANS OF NITRO-9 AT THEM!

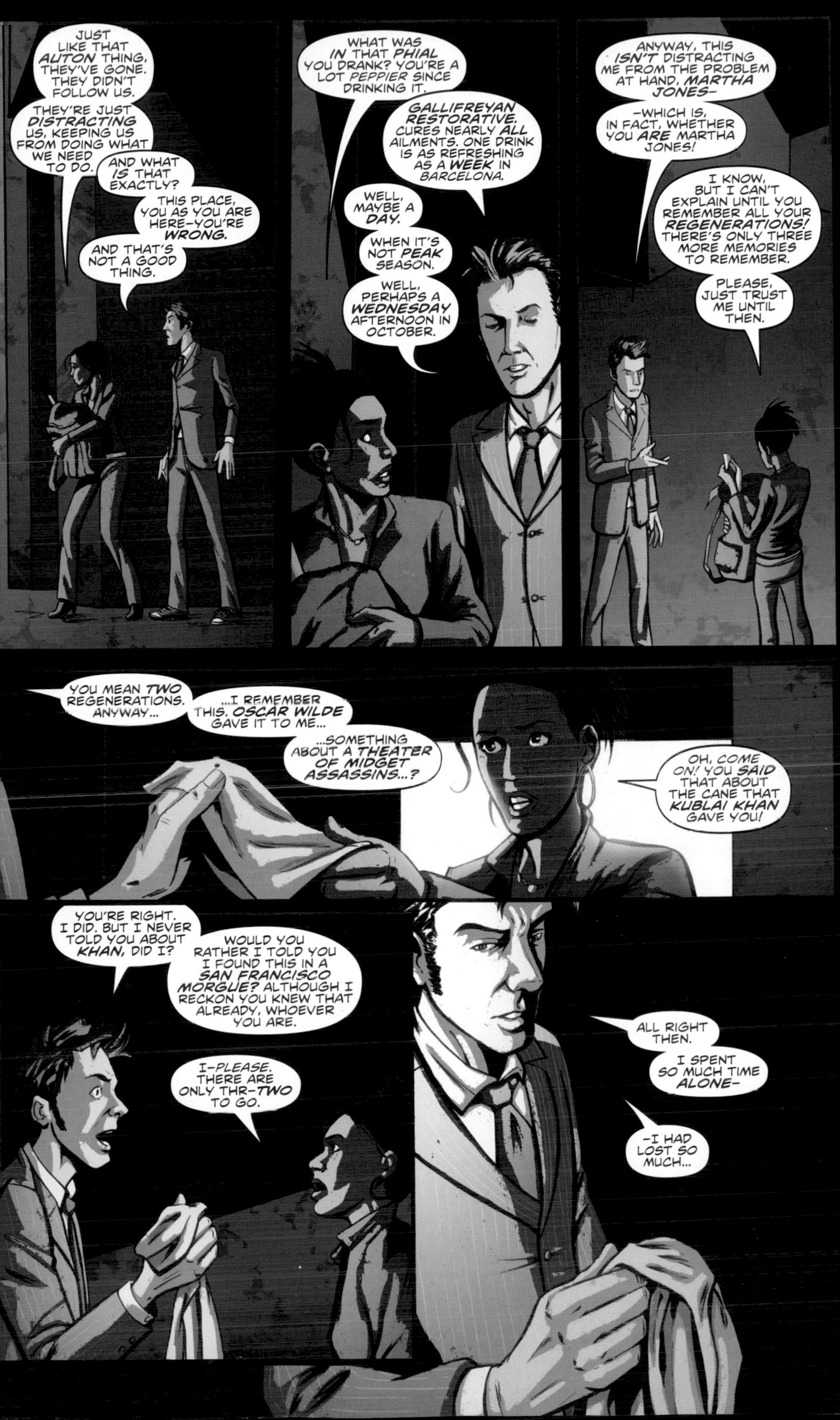
JUST LIKE THAT AUTON THING, THEY'VE GONE. THEY DIDN'T FOLLOW US.
THEY'RE JUST DISTRACTING US, KEEPING US FROM DOING WHAT WE NEED TO DO.
AND WHAT IS THAT EXACTLY?
THIS PLACE, YOU AS YOU ARE HERE—YOU'RE WRONG.
AND THAT'S NOT A GOOD THING.
WHAT WAS IN THAT PHIAL YOU DRANK? YOU'RE A LOT PEPPIER SINCE DRINKING IT.
GALLIFREYAN RESTORATIVE. CURES NEARLY ALL AILMENTS. ONE DRINK IS AS REFRESHING AS A WEEK IN BARCELONA.
WELL, MAYBE A DAY.
WHEN IT'S NOT PEAK SEASON.
WELL, PERHAPS A WEDNESDAY AFTERNOON IN OCTOBER.
ANYWAY, THIS ISN'T DISTRACTING ME FROM THE PROBLEM AT HAND, MARTHA JONES—
—WHICH IS, IN FACT, WHETHER YOU ARE MARTHA JONES!
I KNOW, BUT I CAN'T EXPLAIN UNTIL YOU REMEMBER ALL YOUR REGENERATIONS! THERE'S ONLY THREE MORE MEMORIES TO REMEMBER.
PLEASE, JUST TRUST ME UNTIL THEN.
YOU MEAN TWO REGENERATIONS. ANYWAY...
...I REMEMBER THIS. OSCAR WILDE GAVE IT TO ME...
...SOMETHING ABOUT A THEATER OF MIDGET ASSASSINS...?
OH, COME ON! YOU SAID THAT ABOUT THE CANE THAT KUBLAI KHAN GAVE YOU!
YOU'RE RIGHT. I DID. BUT I NEVER TOLD YOU ABOUT KHAN, DID I?
WOULD YOU RATHER I TOLD YOU I FOUND THIS IN A SAN FRANCISCO MORGUE? ALTHOUGH I RECKON YOU KNEW THAT ALREADY, WHOEVER YOU ARE.
I—PLEASE. THERE ARE ONLY THR—TWO TO GO.
ALL RIGHT THEN.
I SPENT SO MUCH TIME ALONE—
—I HAD LOST SO MUCH...

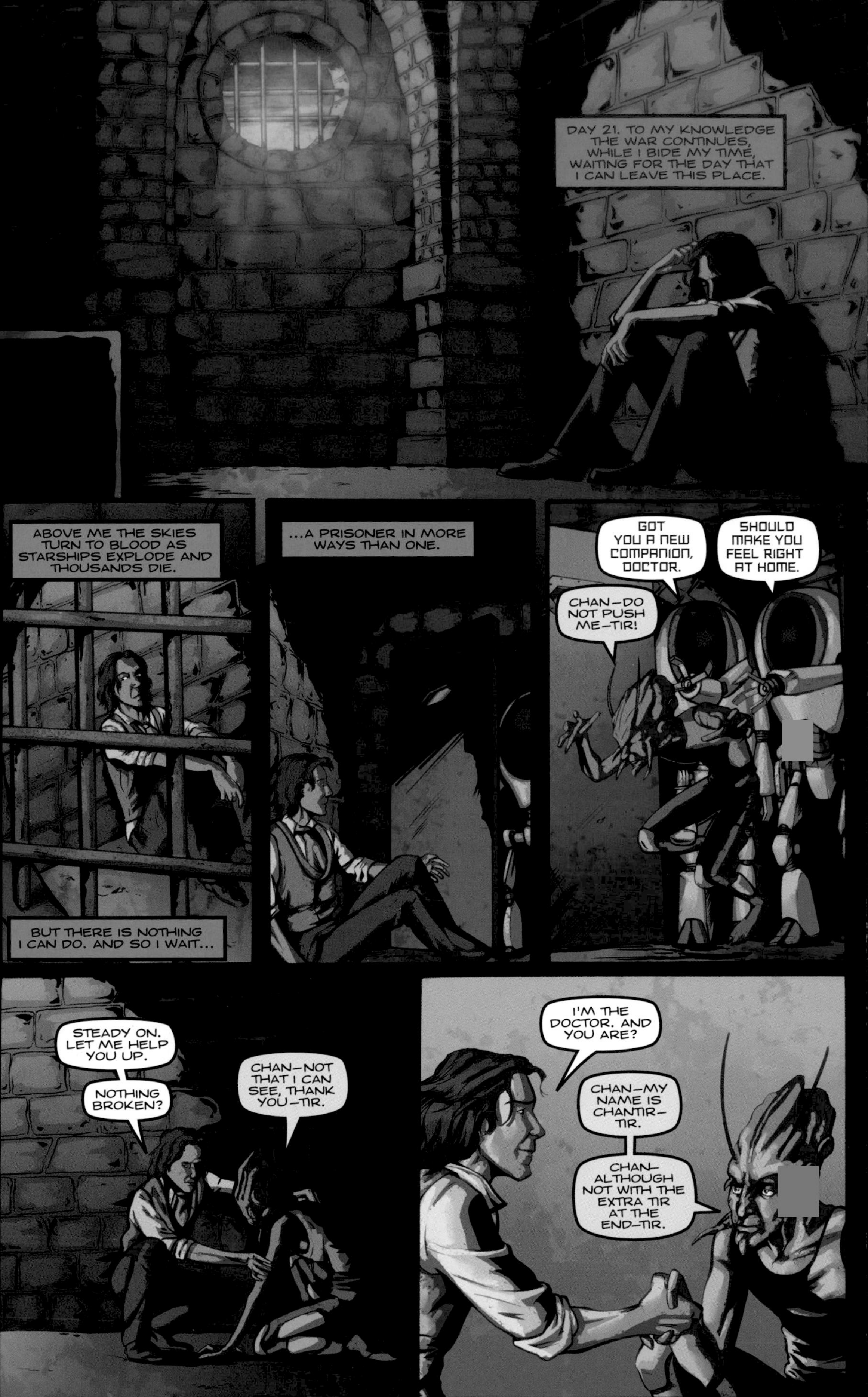
DAY 21. TO MY KNOWLEDGE THE WAR CONTINUES, WHILE I BIDE MY TIME, WAITING FOR THE DAY THAT I CAN LEAVE THIS PLACE.
ABOVE ME THE SKIES TURN TO BLOOD AS STARSHIPS EXPLODE AND THOUSANDS DIE.
BUT THERE IS NOTHING I CAN DO. AND SO I WAIT...
...A PRISONER IN MORE WAYS THAN ONE.
GOT YOU A NEW COMPANION, DOCTOR.
SHOULD MAKE YOU FEEL RIGHT AT HOME.
CHAN—DO NOT PUSH ME—TIR!
STEADY ON. LET ME HELP YOU UP.
NOTHING BROKEN?
CHAN—NOT THAT I CAN SEE, THANK YOU—TIR.
I'M THE DOCTOR. AND YOU ARE?
CHAN—MY NAME IS CHANTIR-TIR.
CHAN—ALTHOUGH NOT WITH THE EXTRA TIR AT THE END—TIR.

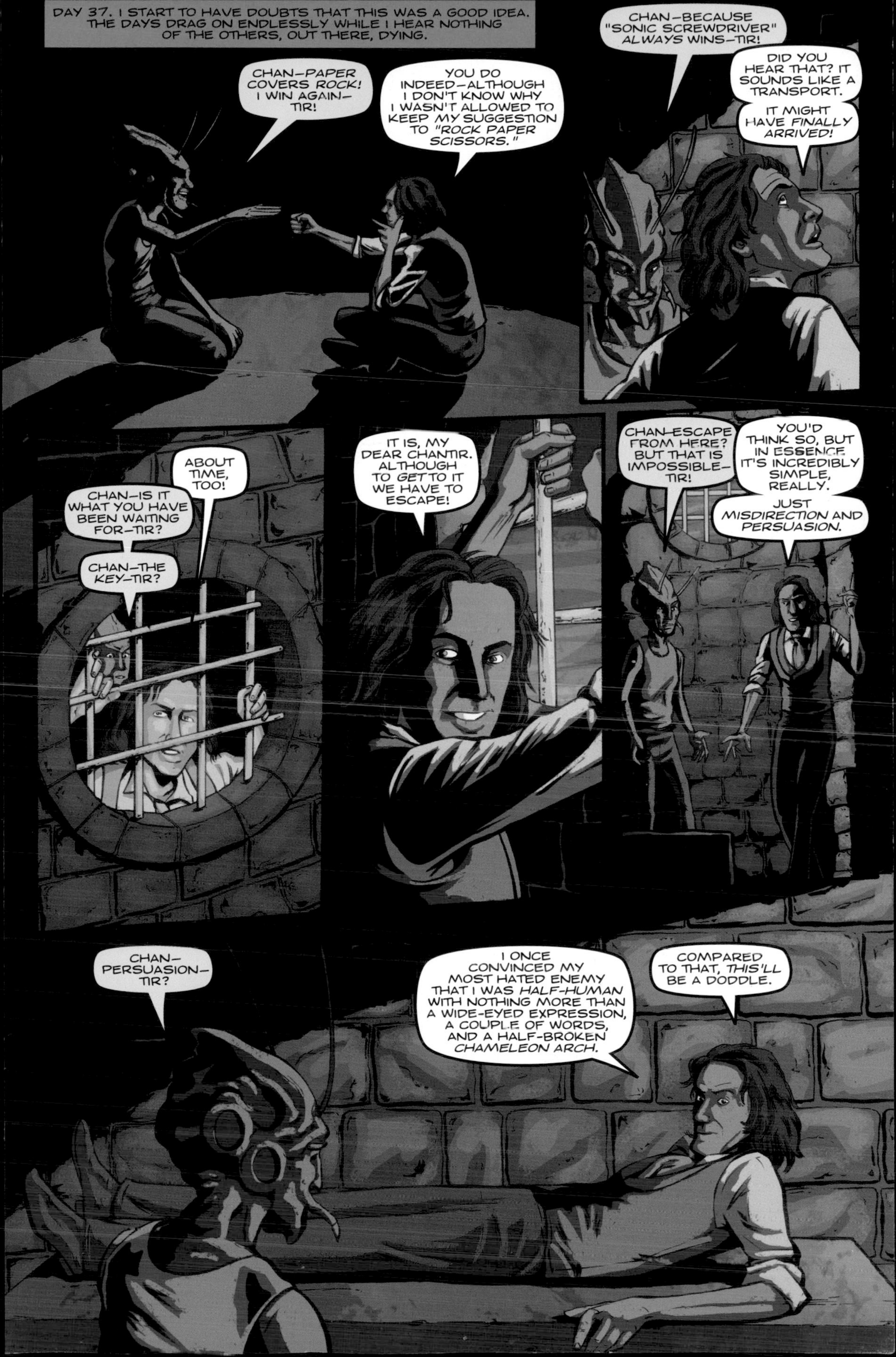

DAY 37. I START TO HAVE DOUBTS THAT THIS WAS A GOOD IDEA. THE DAYS DRAG ON ENDLESSLY WHILE I HEAR NOTHING OF THE OTHERS, OUT THERE, DYING.
CHAN—PAPER COVERS ROCK! I WIN AGAIN—TIR!
YOU DO INDEED—ALTHOUGH I DON'T KNOW WHY I WASN'T ALLOWED TO KEEP MY SUGGESTION TO "ROCK PAPER SCISSORS."
CHAN—BECAUSE "SONIC SCREWDRIVER" ALWAYS WINS—TIR!
DID YOU HEAR THAT? IT SOUNDS LIKE A TRANSPORT.
IT MIGHT HAVE FINALLY ARRIVED!
CHAN—IS IT WHAT YOU HAVE BEEN WAITING FOR—TIR?
ABOUT TIME, TOO!
CHAN—THE KEY—TIR?
IT IS, MY DEAR CHANTIR. ALTHOUGH TO GET TO IT WE HAVE TO ESCAPE!
CHAN—ESCAPE FROM HERE? BUT THAT IS IMPOSSIBLE—TIR!
YOU'D THINK SO, BUT IN ESSENCE IT'S INCREDIBLY SIMPLE, REALLY.
JUST MISDIRECTION AND PERSUASION.
CHAN—PERSUASION—TIR?
I ONCE CONVINCED MY MOST HATED ENEMY THAT I WAS HALF-HUMAN WITH NOTHING MORE THAN A WIDE-EYED EXPRESSION, A COUPLE OF WORDS, AND A HALF-BROKEN CHAMELEON ARCH.
COMPARED TO THAT, THIS'LL BE A DODDLE.

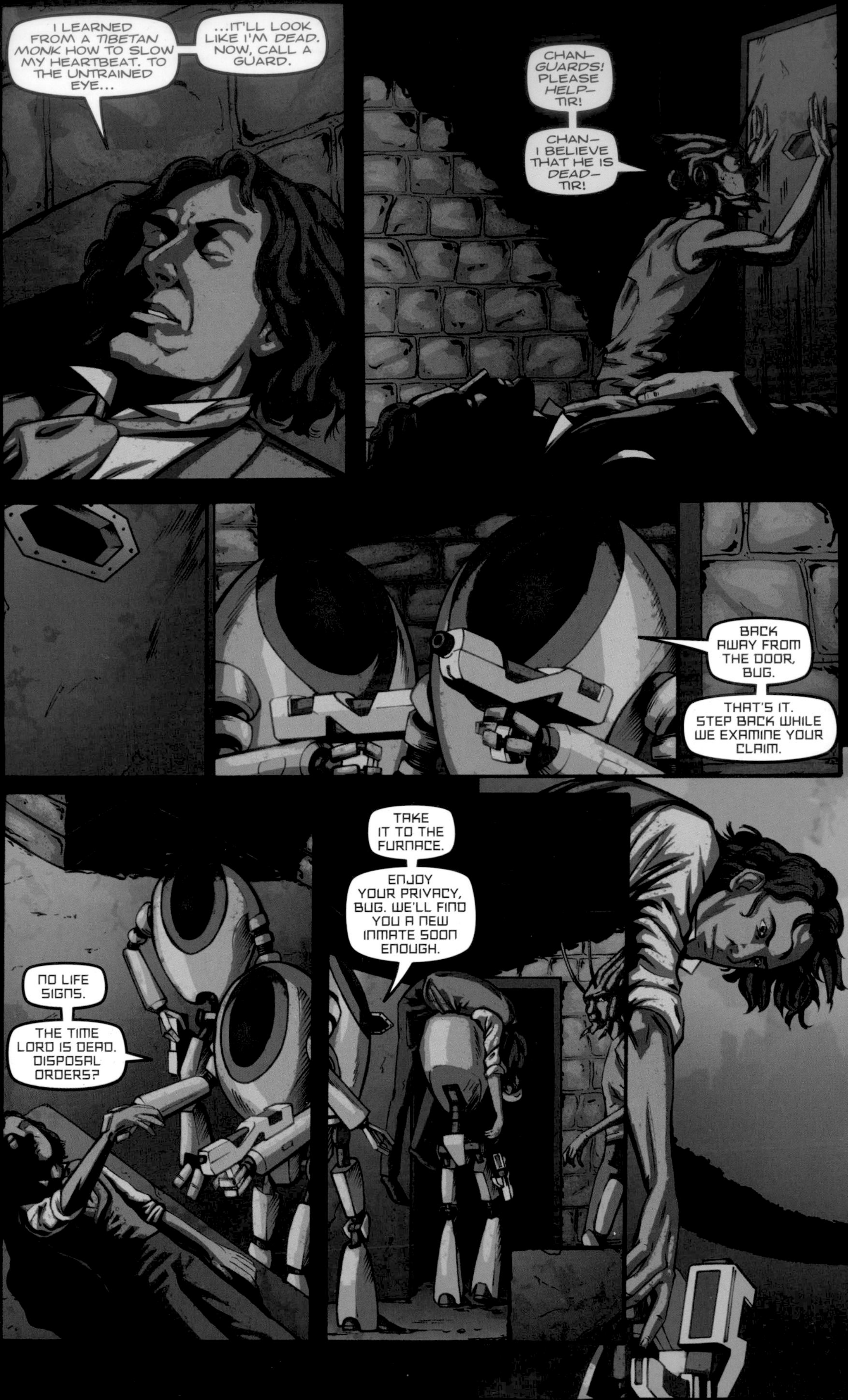
I LEARNED FROM A TIBETAN MONK HOW TO SLOW MY HEARTBEAT. TO THE UNTRAINED EYE...
...IT'LL LOOK LIKE I'M DEAD. NOW, CALL A GUARD.
CHAN-GUARDS! PLEASE HELP-TIR!
CHAN-I BELIEVE THAT HE IS DEAD-TIR!
BACK AWAY FROM THE DOOR, BUG.
THAT'S IT. STEP BACK WHILE WE EXAMINE YOUR CLAIM.
NO LIFE SIGNS.
THE TIME LORD IS DEAD. DISPOSAL ORDERS?
TAKE IT TO THE FURNACE.
ENJOY YOUR PRIVACY, BUG. WE'LL FIND YOU A NEW INMATE SOON ENOUGH.

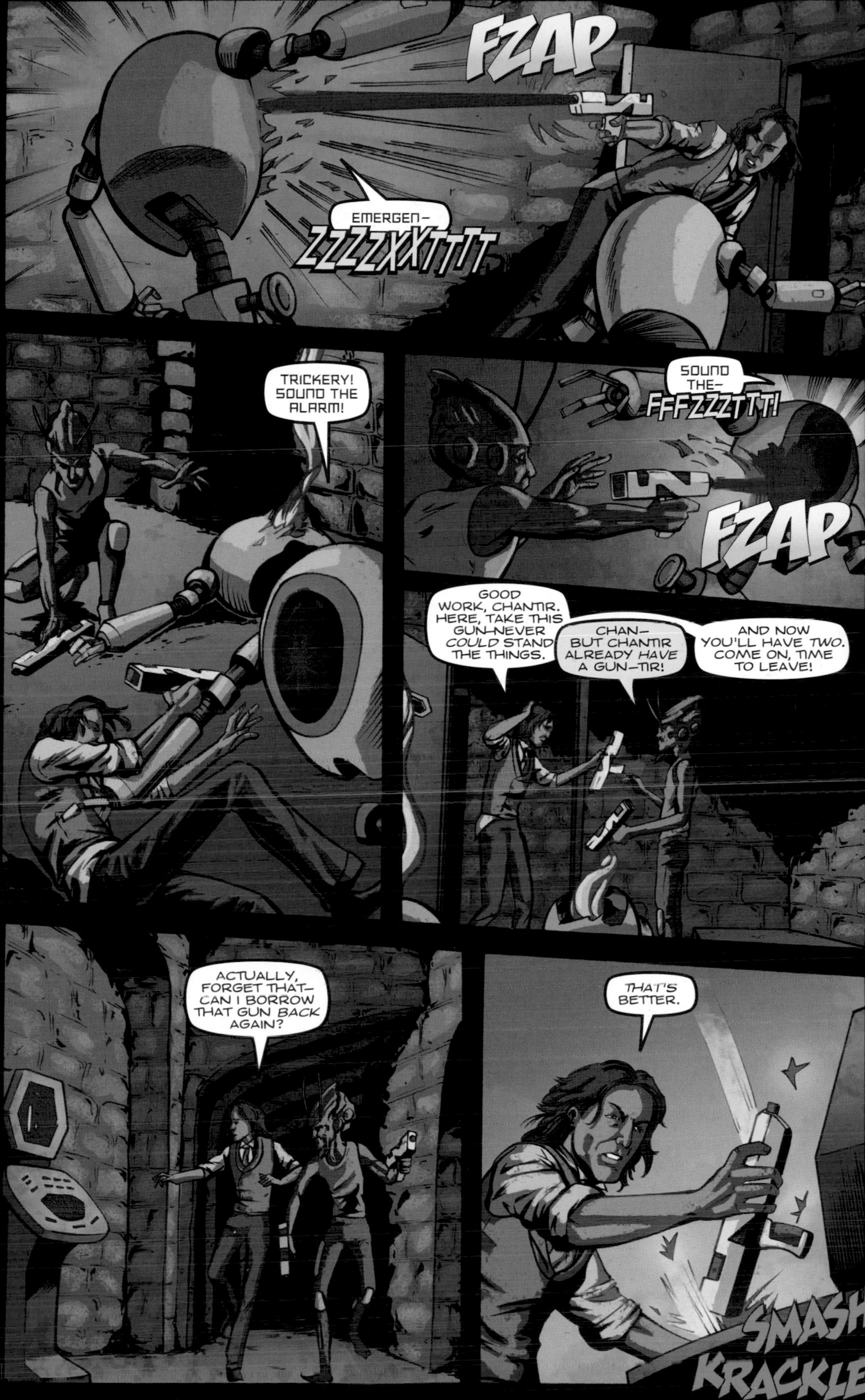
FZAP
EMERGEN–
ZZZZXXTTTT
TRICKERY! SOUND THE ALARM!
SOUND THE–
FFFZZZTTT!
FZAP
GOOD WORK, CHANTIR. HERE, TAKE THIS GUN–NEVER *COULD* STAND THE THINGS.
CHAN– BUT CHANTIR ALREADY *HAVE* A GUN–TIR!
AND NOW YOU'LL HAVE *TWO*. COME ON, TIME TO LEAVE!
ACTUALLY, FORGET THAT– CAN I BORROW THAT GUN *BACK* AGAIN?
THAT'S BETTER.
SMASH
KRACKLE

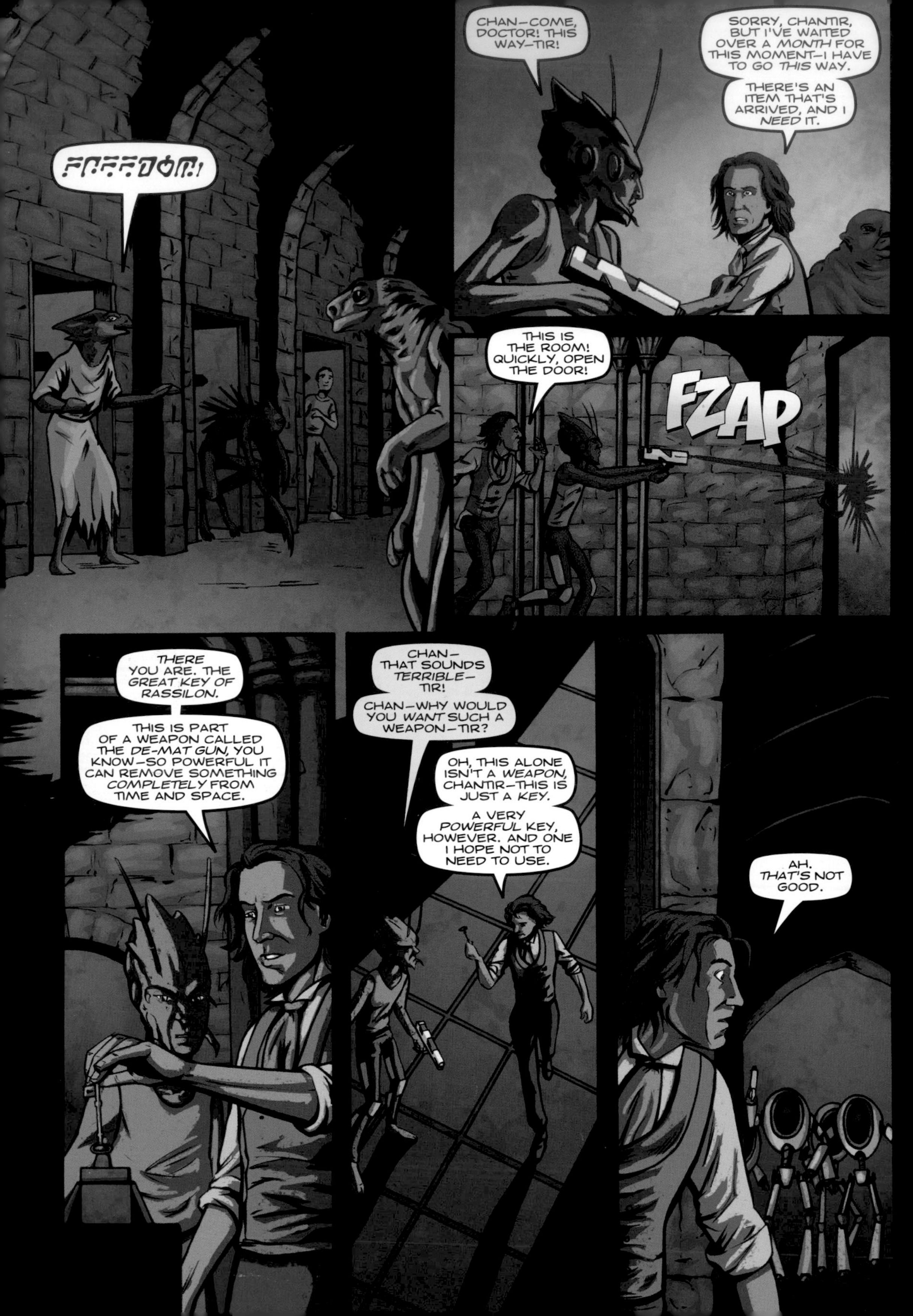
FREEDOM!
CHAN—COME, DOCTOR! THIS WAY—TIR!
SORRY, CHANTIR, BUT I'VE WAITED OVER A *MONTH* FOR THIS MOMENT—I HAVE TO GO *THIS* WAY.
THERE'S AN ITEM THAT'S ARRIVED, AND I *NEED* IT.
THIS IS THE ROOM! QUICKLY, OPEN THE DOOR!
FZAP
THERE YOU ARE. THE *GREAT KEY* OF RASSILON.
THIS IS PART OF A WEAPON CALLED THE *DE-MAT GUN*, YOU KNOW—SO POWERFUL IT CAN REMOVE SOMETHING *COMPLETELY* FROM TIME AND SPACE.
CHAN—THAT SOUNDS *TERRIBLE*—TIR!
CHAN—WHY WOULD YOU *WANT* SUCH A WEAPON—TIR?
OH, THIS ALONE ISN'T A *WEAPON*, CHANTIR—THIS IS JUST A *KEY*.
A VERY *POWERFUL* KEY, HOWEVER. AND ONE I HOPE NOT TO NEED TO USE.
AH. *THAT'S* NOT GOOD.

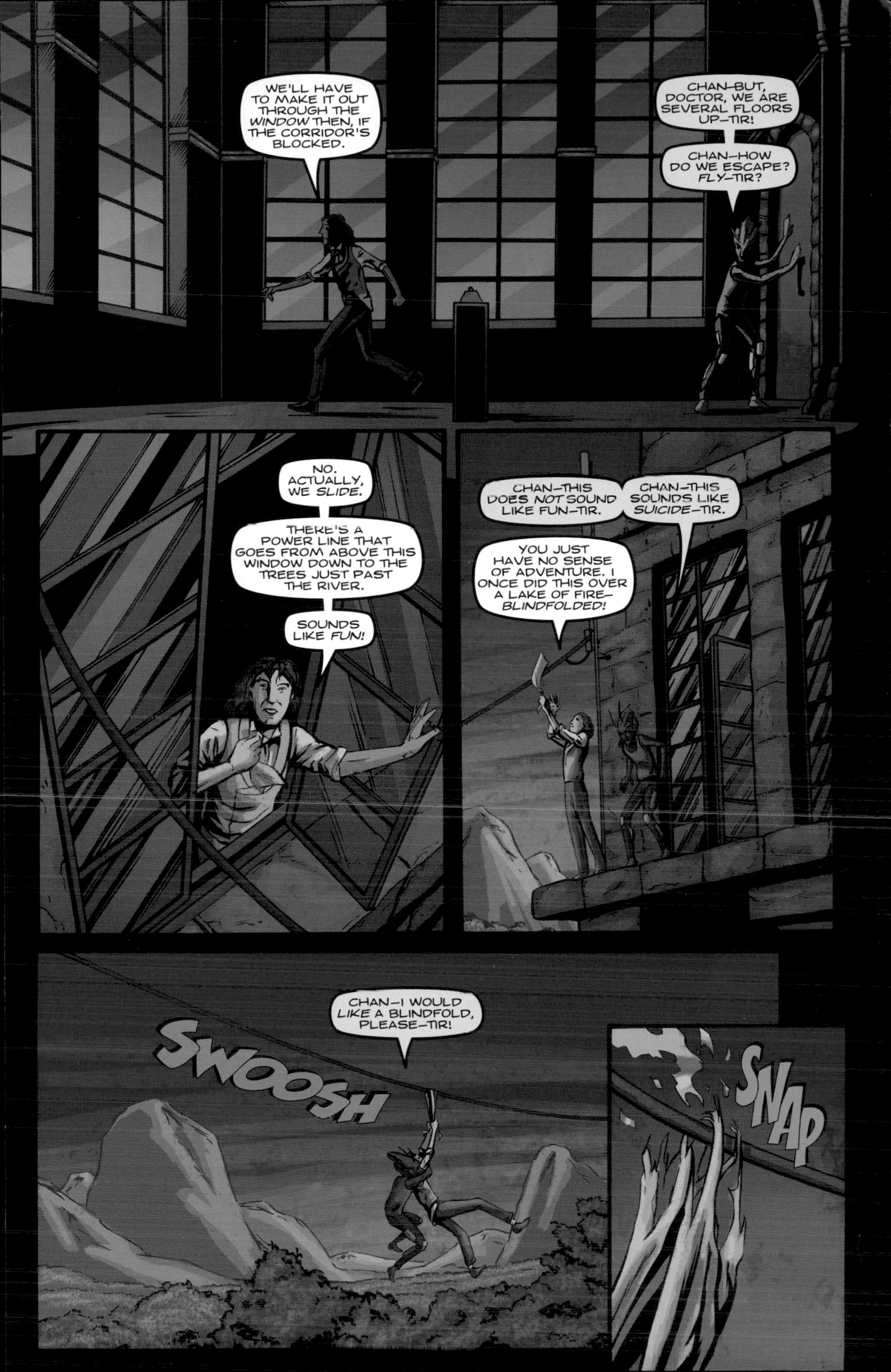
WE'LL HAVE TO MAKE IT OUT THROUGH THE *WINDOW* THEN, IF THE CORRIDOR'S BLOCKED.
CHAN–BUT, DOCTOR, WE ARE SEVERAL FLOORS UP–TIR!
CHAN–HOW DO WE ESCAPE? *FLY*–TIR?
NO. ACTUALLY, WE *SLIDE*.
THERE'S A POWER LINE THAT GOES FROM ABOVE THIS WINDOW DOWN TO THE TREES JUST PAST THE RIVER.
SOUNDS LIKE *FUN*!
CHAN–THIS DOES *NOT* SOUND LIKE FUN–TIR.
CHAN–THIS SOUNDS LIKE *SUICIDE*–TIR.
YOU JUST HAVE NO SENSE OF ADVENTURE. I ONCE DID THIS OVER A LAKE OF FIRE– *BLINDFOLDED*!
CHAN–I WOULD LIKE A BLINDFOLD, PLEASE–TIR!
SWOOSH
SNAP

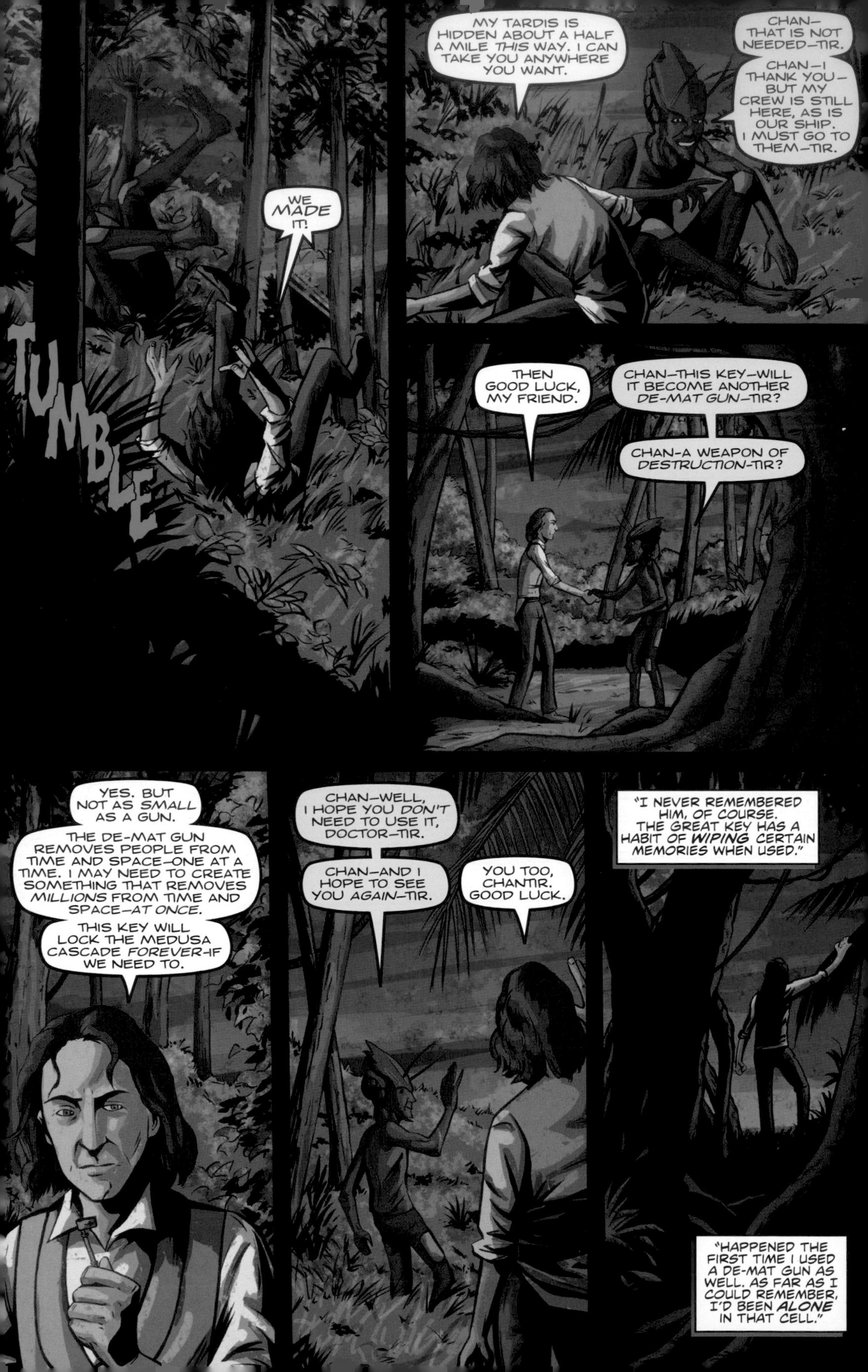
TUMBLE
WE MADE IT!
MY TARDIS IS HIDDEN ABOUT A HALF A MILE THIS WAY. I CAN TAKE YOU ANYWHERE YOU WANT.
CHAN– THAT IS NOT NEEDED–TIR.
CHAN–I THANK YOU– BUT MY CREW IS STILL HERE, AS IS OUR SHIP. I MUST GO TO THEM–TIR.
THEN GOOD LUCK, MY FRIEND.
CHAN–THIS KEY–WILL IT BECOME ANOTHER DE-MAT GUN–TIR?
CHAN–A WEAPON OF DESTRUCTION–TIR?
YES. BUT NOT AS SMALL AS A GUN.
THE DE-MAT GUN REMOVES PEOPLE FROM TIME AND SPACE–ONE AT A TIME. I MAY NEED TO CREATE SOMETHING THAT REMOVES MILLIONS FROM TIME AND SPACE–AT ONCE.
THIS KEY WILL LOCK THE MEDUSA CASCADE FOREVER–IF WE NEED TO.
CHAN–WELL, I HOPE YOU DON'T NEED TO USE IT, DOCTOR–TIR.
CHAN–AND I HOPE TO SEE YOU AGAIN–TIR.
YOU TOO, CHANTIR. GOOD LUCK.
"I NEVER REMEMBERED HIM, OF COURSE. THE GREAT KEY HAS A HABIT OF WIPING CERTAIN MEMORIES WHEN USED."
"HAPPENED THE FIRST TIME I USED A DE-MAT GUN AS WELL. AS FAR AS I COULD REMEMBER, I'D BEEN ALONE IN THAT CELL."

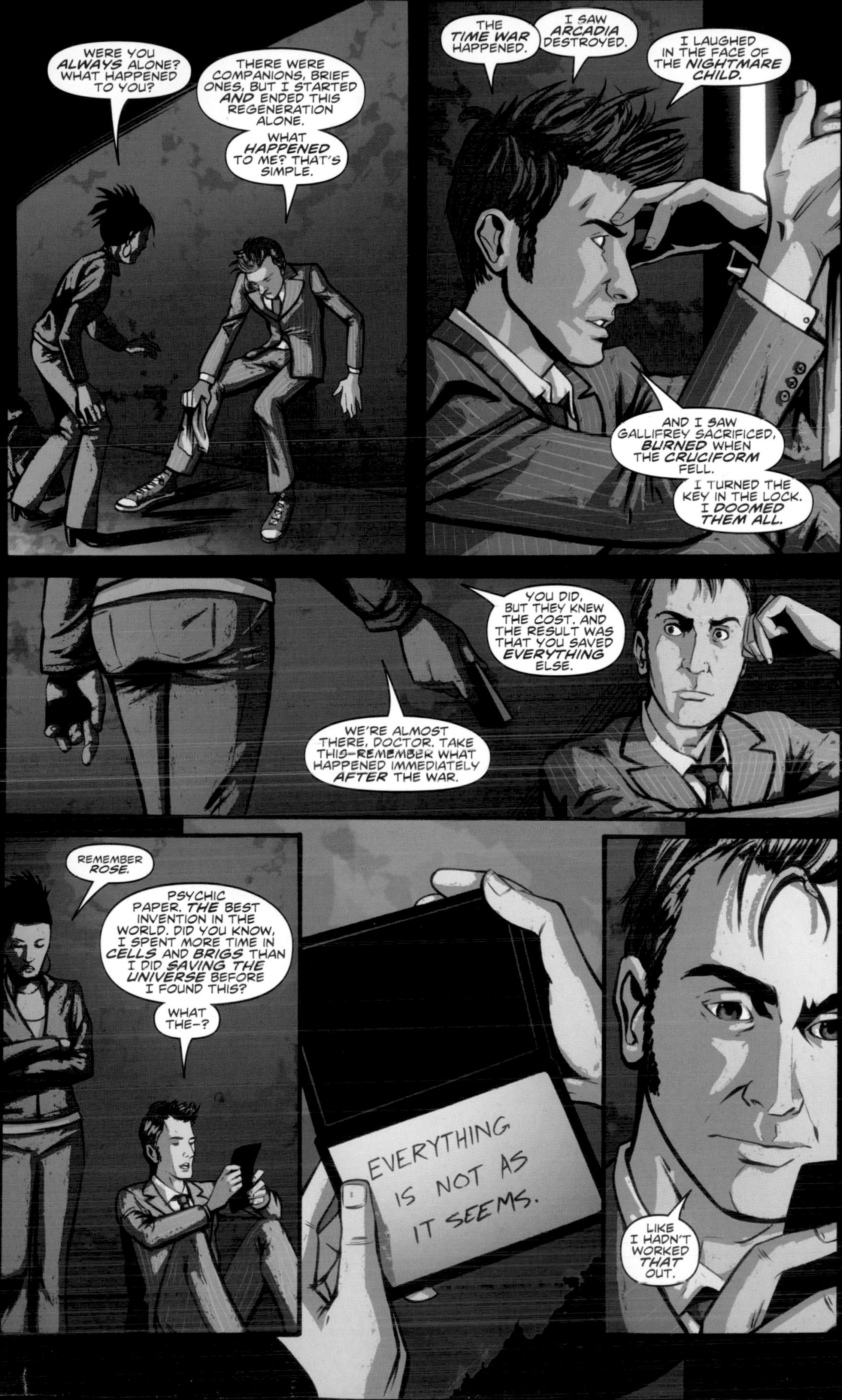
WERE YOU ALWAYS ALONE? WHAT HAPPENED TO YOU?
THERE WERE COMPANIONS, BRIEF ONES, BUT I STARTED AND ENDED THIS REGENERATION ALONE.
WHAT HAPPENED TO ME? THAT'S SIMPLE.
THE TIME WAR HAPPENED.
I SAW ARCADIA DESTROYED.
I LAUGHED IN THE FACE OF THE NIGHTMARE CHILD.
AND I SAW GALLIFREY SACRIFICED, BURNED WHEN THE CRUCIFORM FELL.
I TURNED THE KEY IN THE LOCK. I DOOMED THEM ALL.
YOU DID, BUT THEY KNEW THE COST. AND THE RESULT WAS THAT YOU SAVED EVERYTHING ELSE.
WE'RE ALMOST THERE, DOCTOR. TAKE THIS—REMEMBER WHAT HAPPENED IMMEDIATELY AFTER THE WAR.
REMEMBER ROSE.
PSYCHIC PAPER. THE BEST INVENTION IN THE WORLD. DID YOU KNOW, I SPENT MORE TIME IN CELLS AND BRIGS THAN I DID SAVING THE UNIVERSE BEFORE I FOUND THIS?
WHAT THE-?
EVERYTHING IS NOT AS IT SEEMS.
LIKE I HADN'T WORKED THAT OUT.

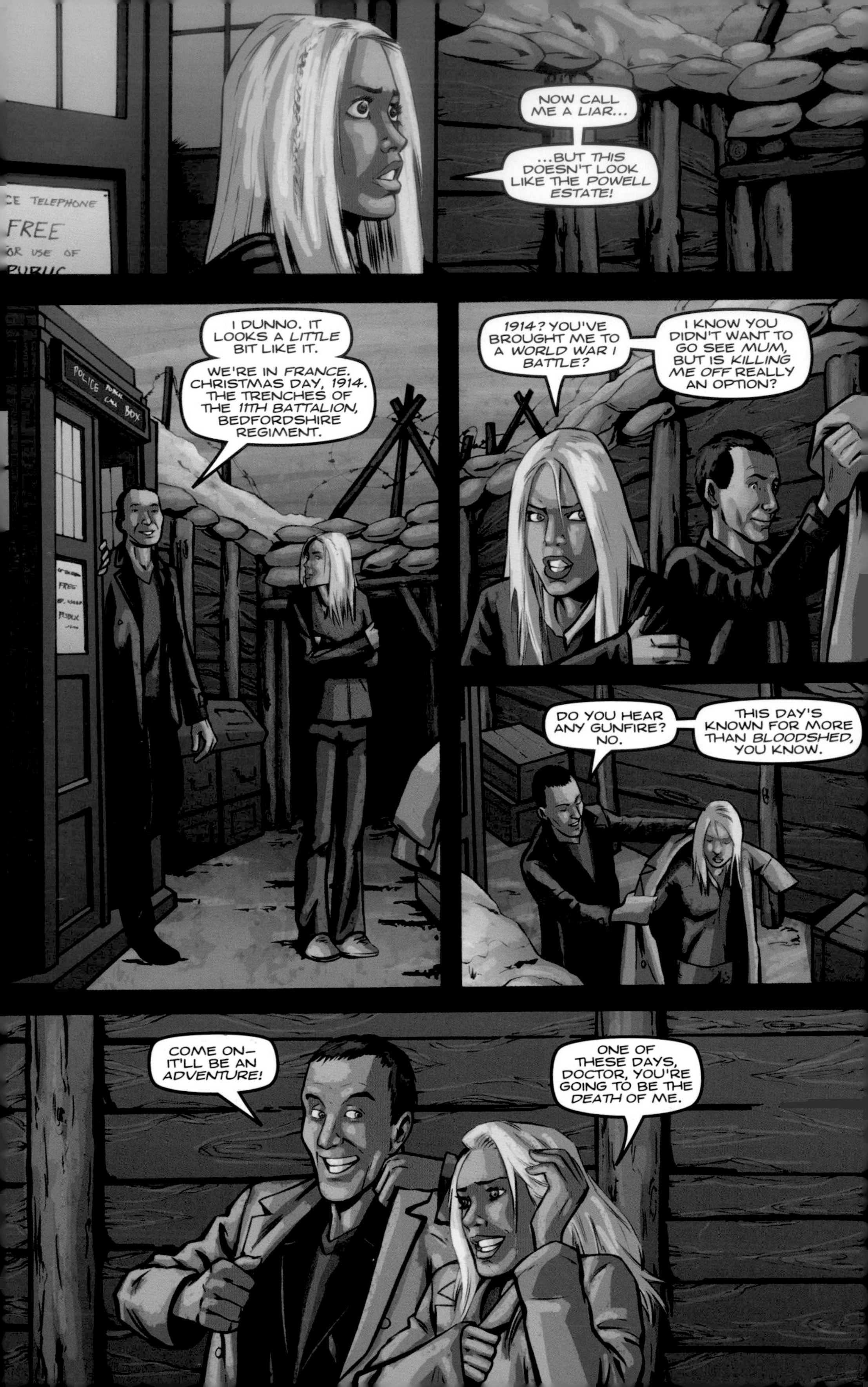

CE TELEPHONE
FREE
OR USE OF
NOW CALL ME A LIAR...
...BUT THIS DOESN'T LOOK LIKE THE POWELL ESTATE!
POLICE PUBLIC CALL BOX
I DUNNO. IT LOOKS A LITTLE BIT LIKE IT.
WE'RE IN FRANCE. CHRISTMAS DAY, 1914. THE TRENCHES OF THE 11TH BATTALION, BEDFORDSHIRE REGIMENT.
1914? YOU'VE BROUGHT ME TO A WORLD WAR I BATTLE?
I KNOW YOU DIDN'T WANT TO GO SEE MUM, BUT IS KILLING ME OFF REALLY AN OPTION?
DO YOU HEAR ANY GUNFIRE? NO.
THIS DAY'S KNOWN FOR MORE THAN BLOODSHED, YOU KNOW.
COME ON— IT'LL BE AN ADVENTURE!
ONE OF THESE DAYS, DOCTOR, YOU'RE GOING TO BE THE DEATH OF ME.

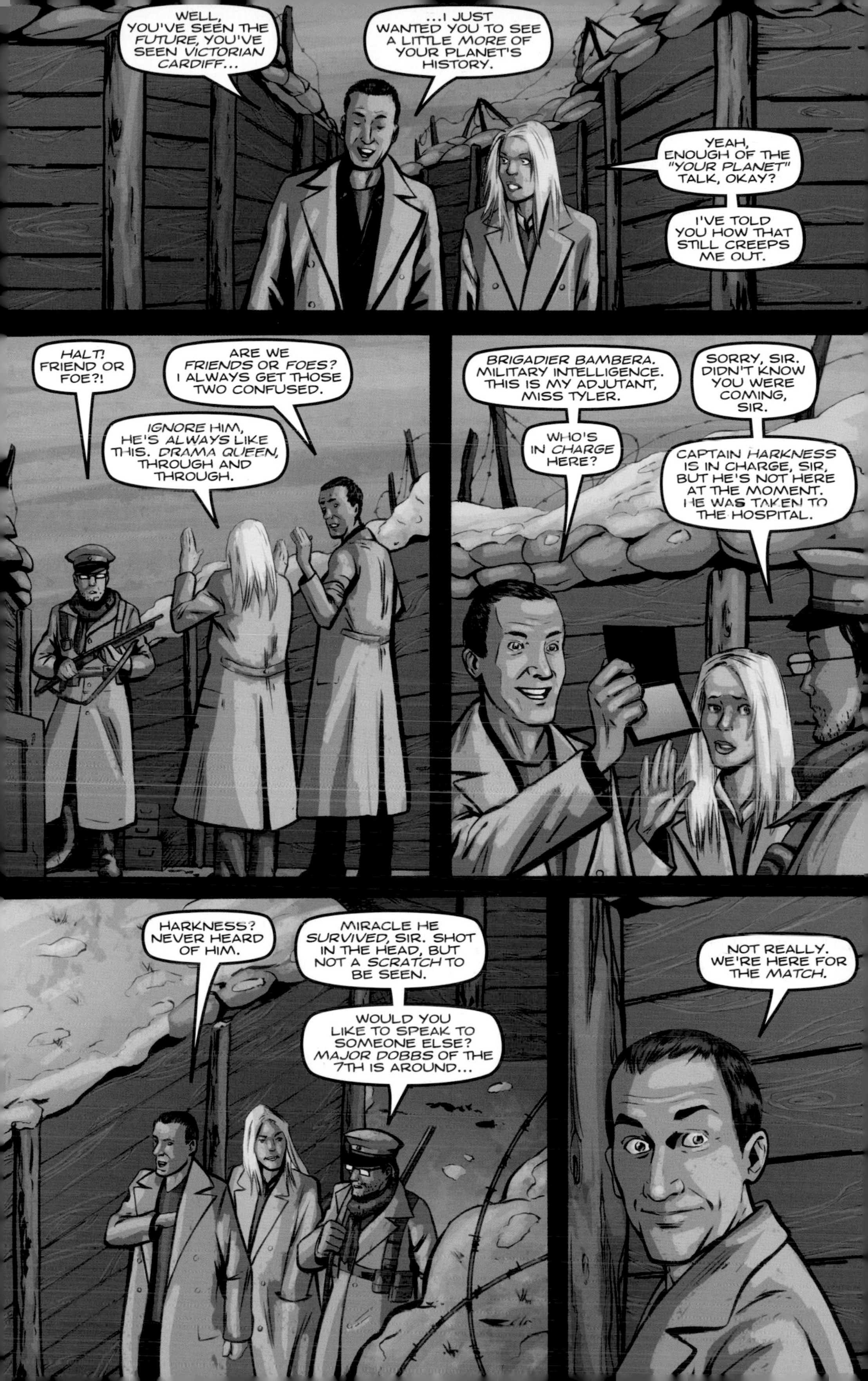
WELL, YOU'VE SEEN THE FUTURE, YOU'VE SEEN VICTORIAN CARDIFF...
...I JUST WANTED YOU TO SEE A LITTLE MORE OF YOUR PLANET'S HISTORY.
YEAH, ENOUGH OF THE "YOUR PLANET" TALK, OKAY?
I'VE TOLD YOU HOW THAT STILL CREEPS ME OUT.
HALT! FRIEND OR FOE?!
ARE WE FRIENDS OR FOES? I ALWAYS GET THOSE TWO CONFUSED.
IGNORE HIM, HE'S ALWAYS LIKE THIS. DRAMA QUEEN, THROUGH AND THROUGH.
BRIGADIER BAMBERA. MILITARY INTELLIGENCE. THIS IS MY ADJUTANT, MISS TYLER.
WHO'S IN CHARGE HERE?
SORRY, SIR. DIDN'T KNOW YOU WERE COMING, SIR.
CAPTAIN HARKNESS IS IN CHARGE, SIR, BUT HE'S NOT HERE AT THE MOMENT. HE WAS TAKEN TO THE HOSPITAL.
HARKNESS? NEVER HEARD OF HIM.
MIRACLE HE SURVIVED, SIR. SHOT IN THE HEAD, BUT NOT A SCRATCH TO BE SEEN.
WOULD YOU LIKE TO SPEAK TO SOMEONE ELSE? MAJOR DOBBS OF THE 7TH IS AROUND...
NOT REALLY. WE'RE HERE FOR THE MATCH.

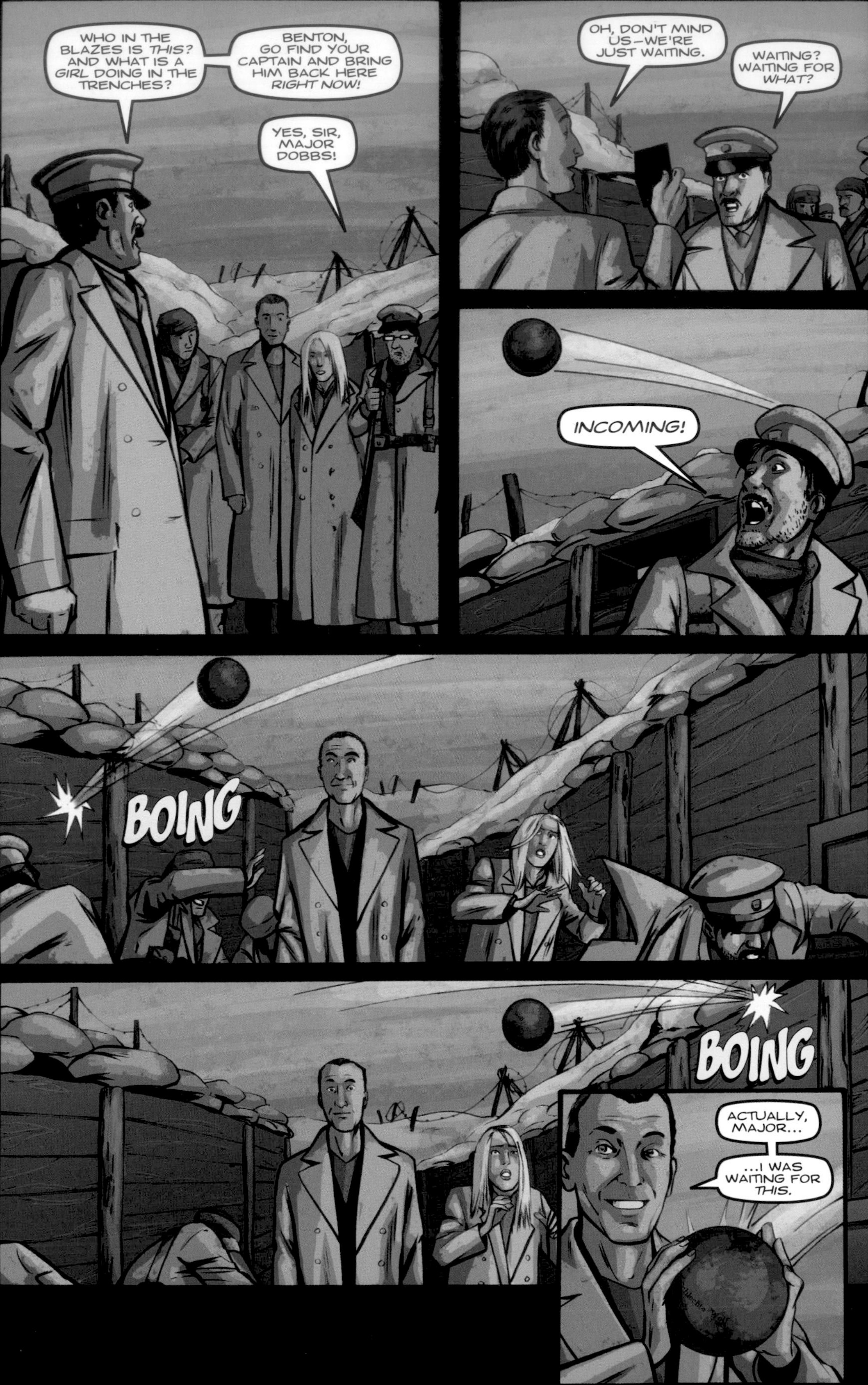
WHO IN THE BLAZES IS *THIS*? AND WHAT IS A *GIRL* DOING IN THE TRENCHES?
BENTON, GO FIND YOUR CAPTAIN AND BRING HIM BACK HERE *RIGHT NOW!*
YES, SIR, MAJOR DOBBS!
OH, DON'T MIND US—WE'RE JUST WAITING.
WAITING? WAITING FOR *WHAT?*
INCOMING!
BOING
BOING
ACTUALLY, MAJOR...
...I WAS WAITING FOR *THIS.*

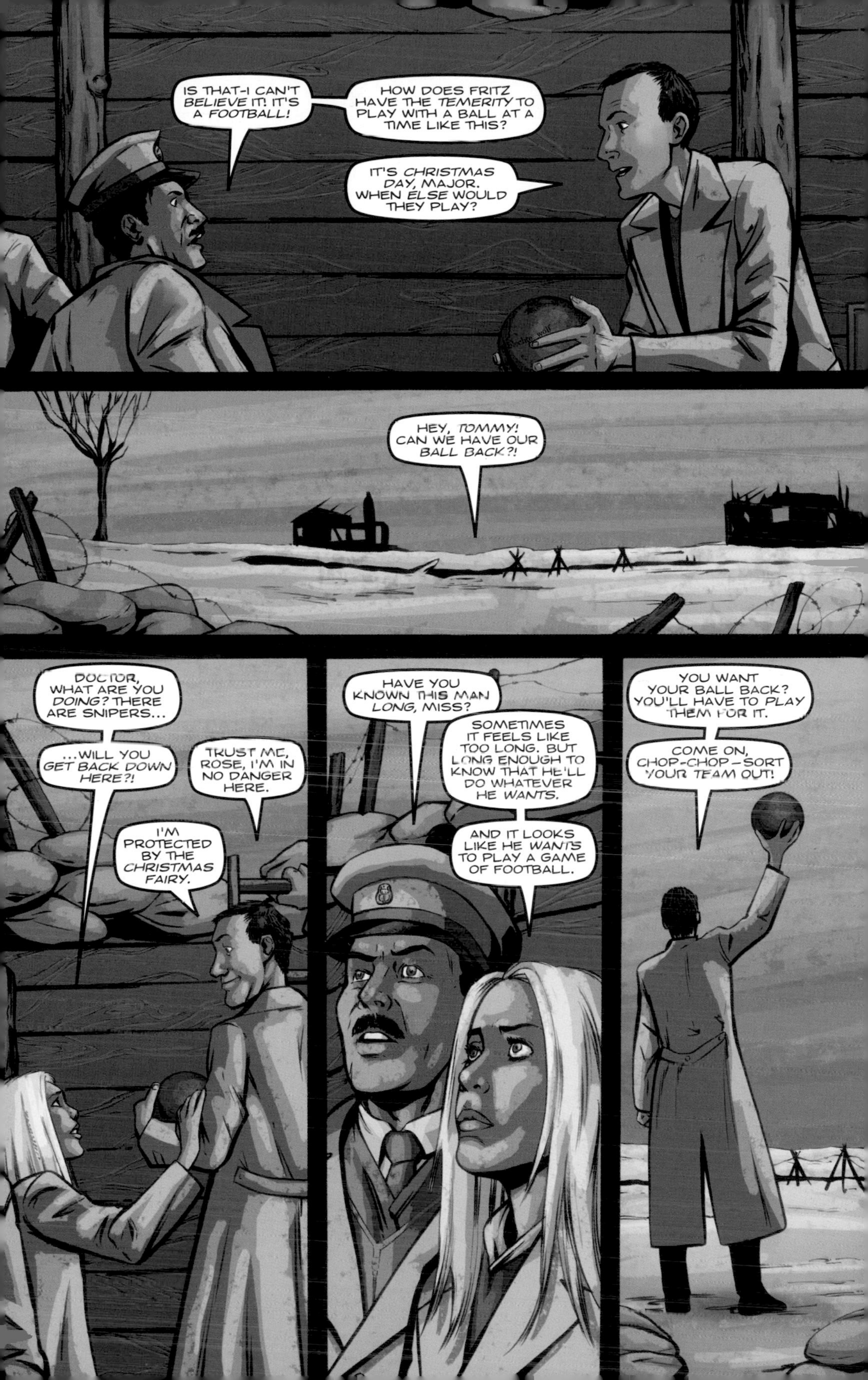
IS THAT-I CAN'T BELIEVE IT! IT'S A FOOTBALL!
HOW DOES FRITZ HAVE THE TEMERITY TO PLAY WITH A BALL AT A TIME LIKE THIS?
IT'S CHRISTMAS DAY, MAJOR. WHEN ELSE WOULD THEY PLAY?
HEY, TOMMY! CAN WE HAVE OUR BALL BACK?!
DOCTOR, WHAT ARE YOU DOING? THERE ARE SNIPERS...
...WILL YOU GET BACK DOWN HERE?!
TRUST ME, ROSE, I'M IN NO DANGER HERE.
I'M PROTECTED BY THE CHRISTMAS FAIRY.
HAVE YOU KNOWN THIS MAN LONG, MISS?
SOMETIMES IT FEELS LIKE TOO LONG. BUT LONG ENOUGH TO KNOW THAT HE'LL DO WHATEVER HE WANTS.
AND IT LOOKS LIKE HE WANTS TO PLAY A GAME OF FOOTBALL.
YOU WANT YOUR BALL BACK? YOU'LL HAVE TO PLAY THEM FOR IT.
COME ON, CHOP-CHOP-SORT YOUR TEAM OUT!

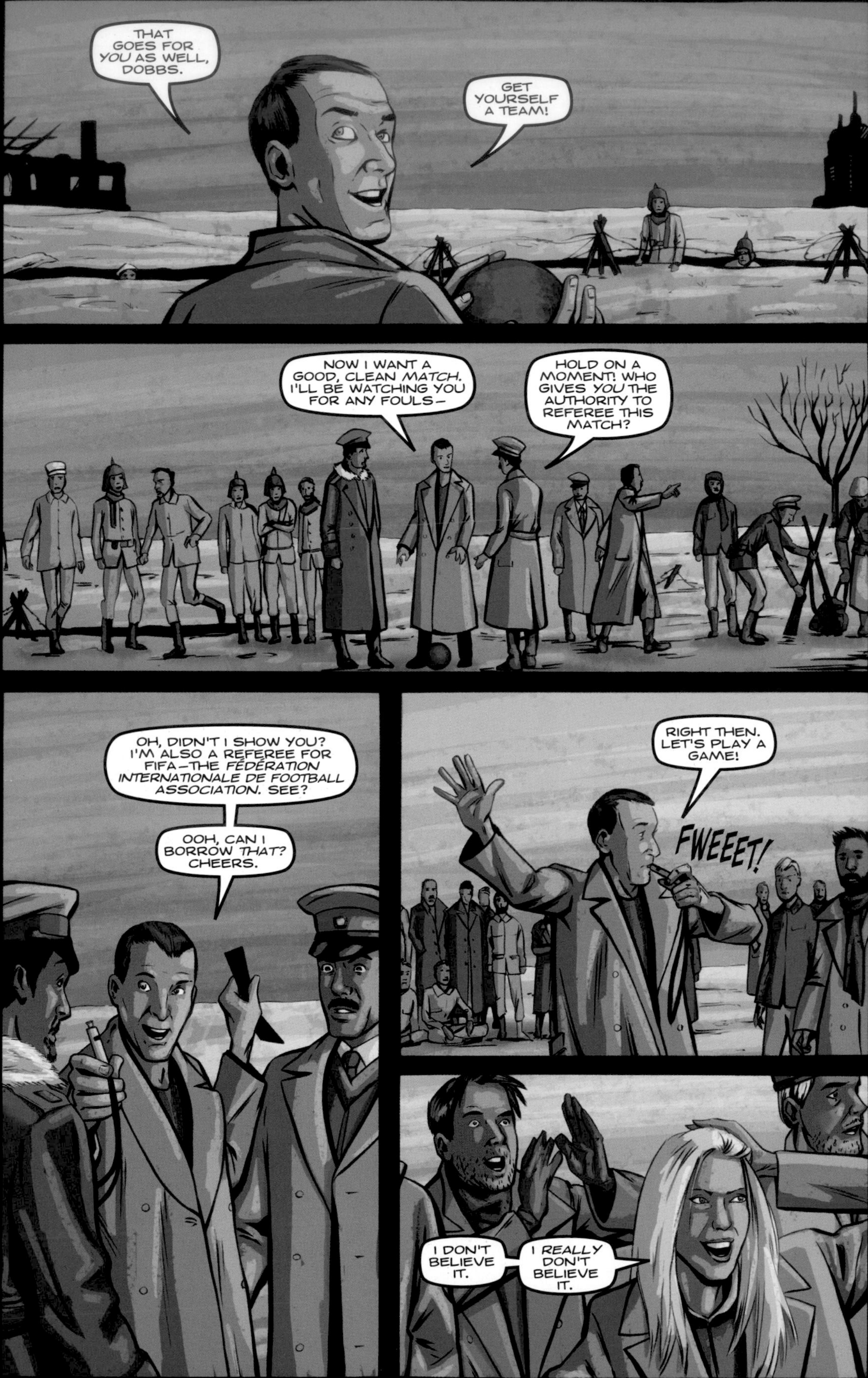
THAT GOES FOR *YOU* AS WELL, DOBBS.
GET YOURSELF A TEAM!
NOW I WANT A GOOD, CLEAN *MATCH*. I'LL BE WATCHING YOU FOR ANY FOULS—
HOLD ON A MOMENT! WHO GIVES *YOU* THE AUTHORITY TO REFEREE THIS MATCH?
OH, DIDN'T I SHOW YOU? I'M ALSO A REFEREE FOR FIFA—THE *FÉDÉRATION INTERNATIONALE DE FOOTBALL ASSOCIATION*. SEE?
OOH, CAN I BORROW *THAT*? CHEERS.
RIGHT THEN. LET'S PLAY A GAME!
FWEEET!
I DON'T BELIEVE IT.
I *REALLY* DON'T BELIEVE IT.

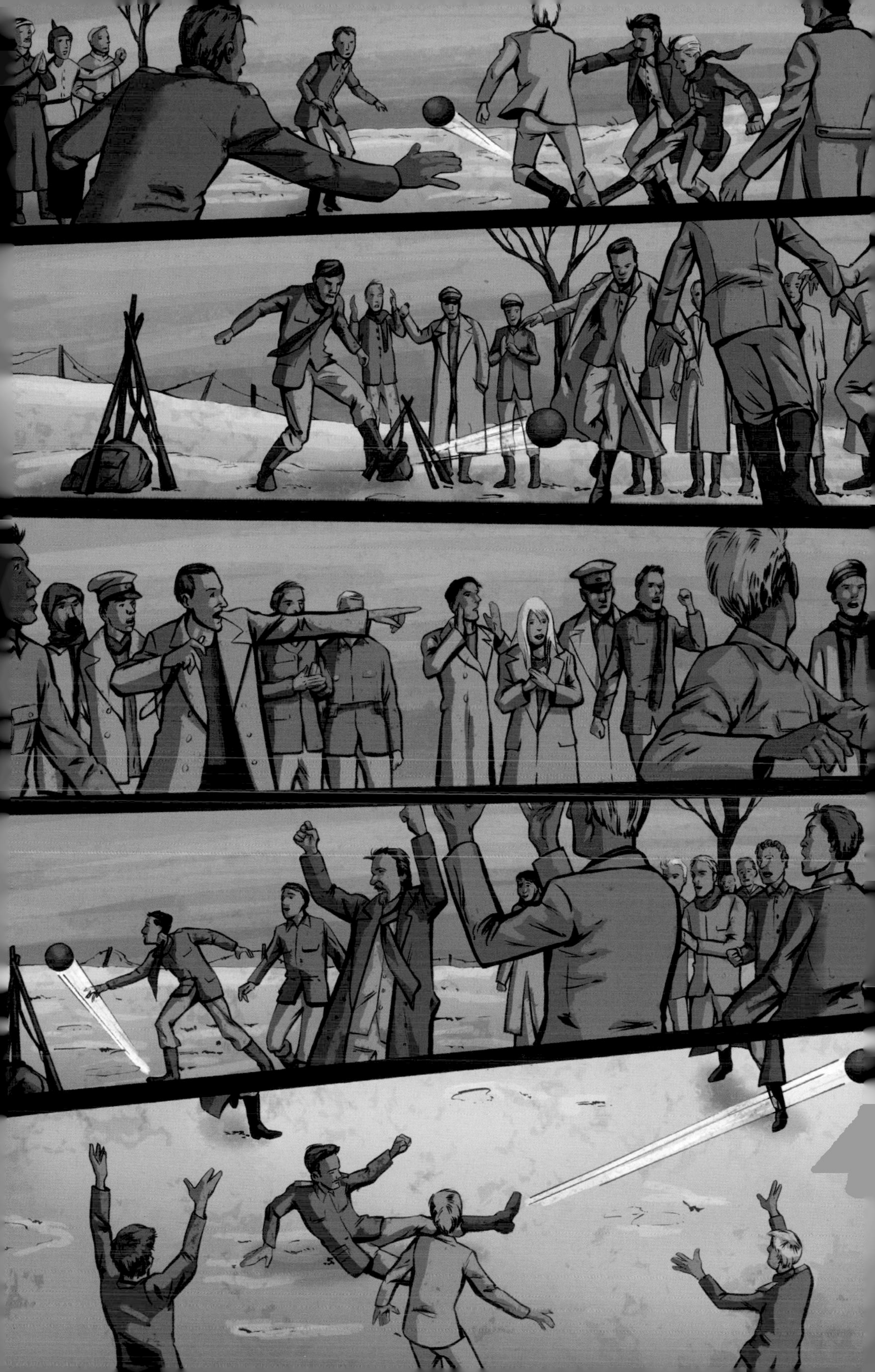

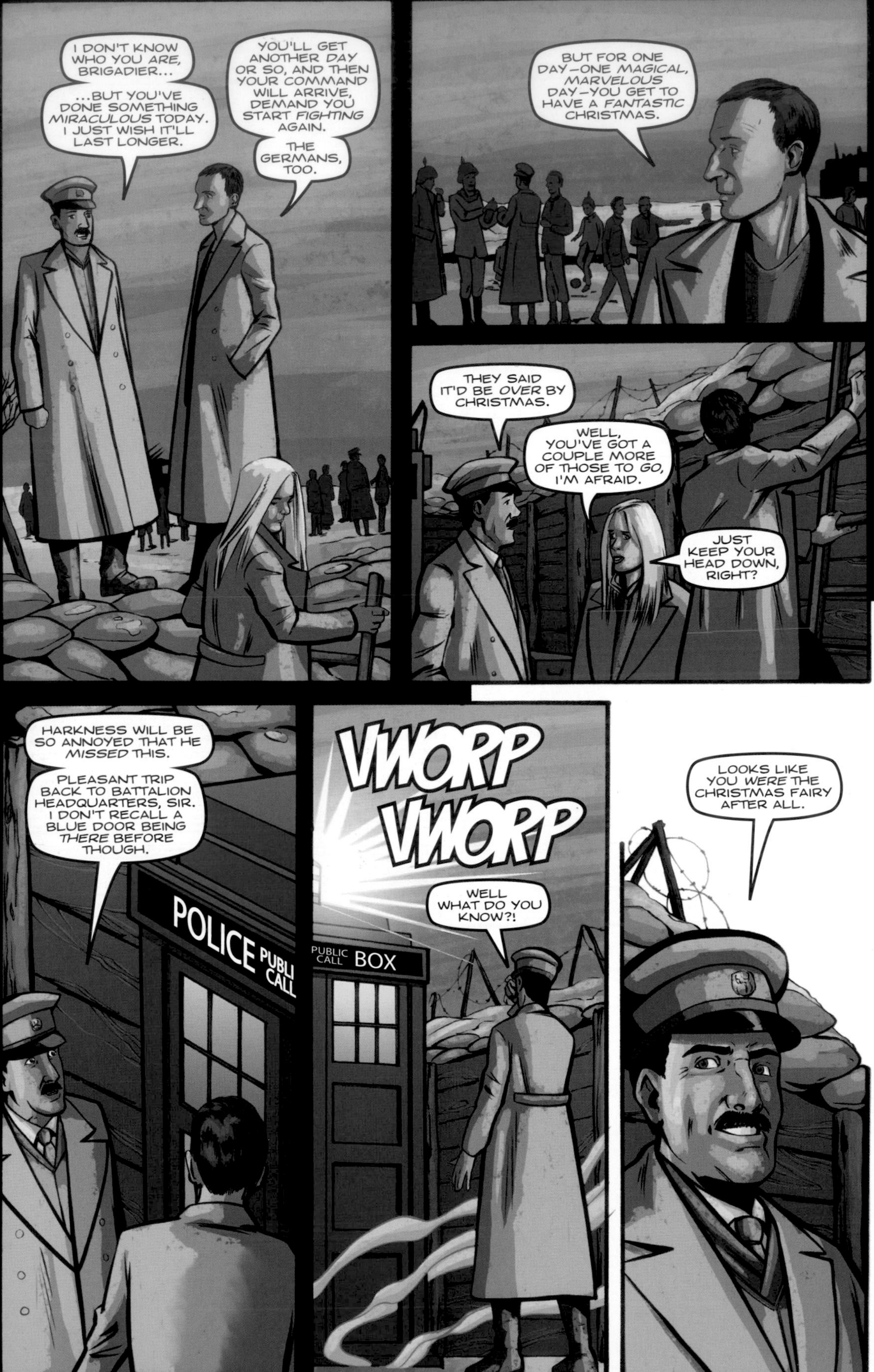
I DON'T KNOW WHO YOU ARE, BRIGADIER...
...BUT YOU'VE DONE SOMETHING *MIRACULOUS* TODAY. I JUST WISH IT'LL LAST LONGER.
YOU'LL GET ANOTHER *DAY* OR SO, AND THEN YOUR COMMAND WILL ARRIVE, DEMAND YOU START *FIGHTING* AGAIN.
THE GERMANS, TOO.
BUT FOR ONE DAY—ONE *MAGICAL, MARVELOUS* DAY—YOU GET TO HAVE A *FANTASTIC* CHRISTMAS.
THEY SAID IT'D BE *OVER* BY CHRISTMAS.
WELL, YOU'VE GOT A COUPLE MORE OF THOSE TO GO, I'M AFRAID.
JUST KEEP YOUR HEAD DOWN, RIGHT?
HARKNESS WILL BE SO ANNOYED THAT HE *MISSED* THIS.
PLEASANT TRIP BACK TO BATTALION HEADQUARTERS, SIR. I DON'T RECALL A BLUE DOOR BEING *THERE* BEFORE THOUGH.
POLICE PUBLIC CALL
VWORP VWORP
WELL WHAT DO YOU KNOW?!
PUBLIC CALL BOX
LOOKS LIKE YOU *WERE* THE CHRISTMAS FAIRY AFTER ALL.

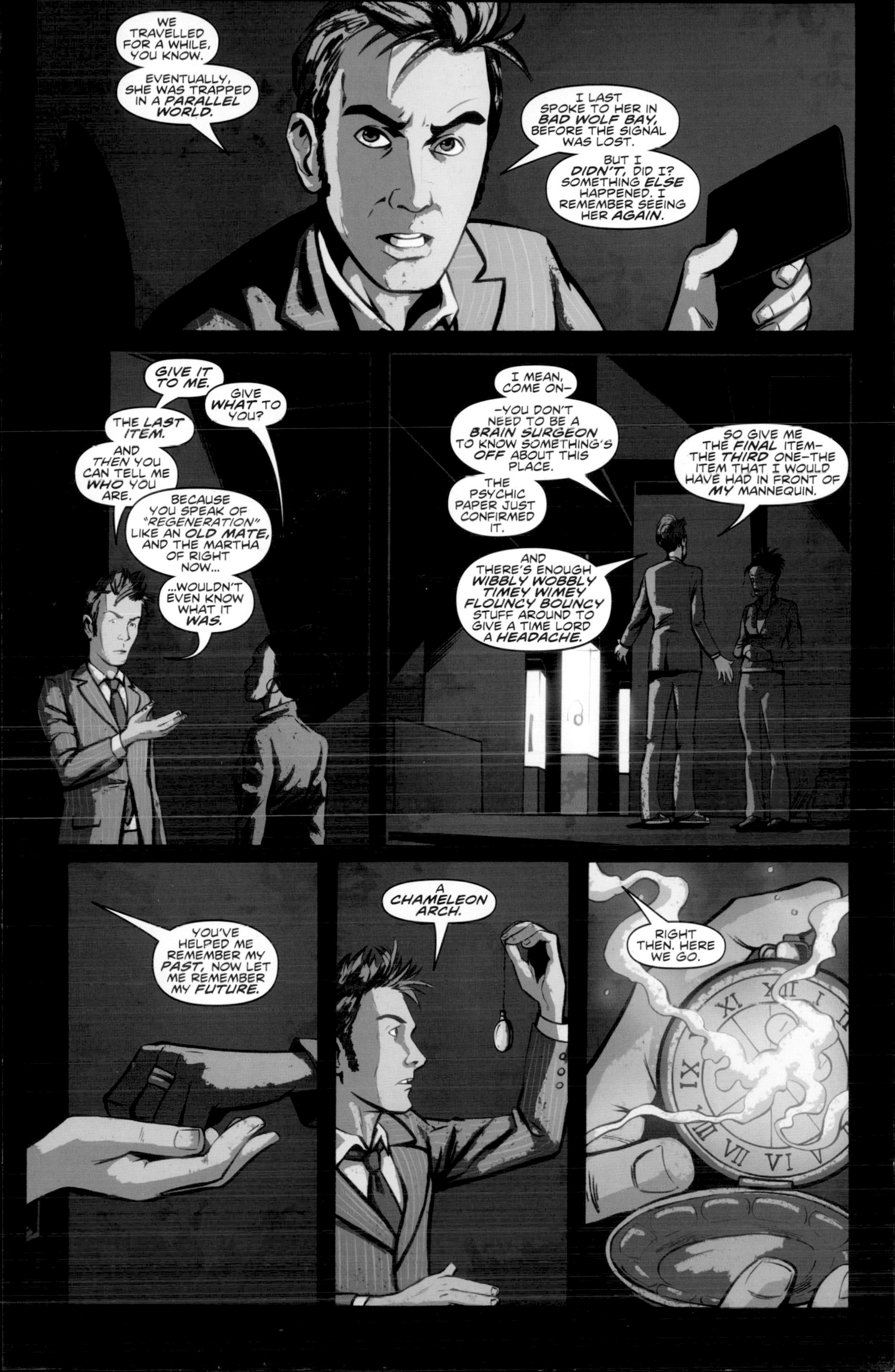
WE TRAVELLED FOR A WHILE, YOU KNOW.
EVENTUALLY, SHE WAS TRAPPED IN A *PARALLEL WORLD.*
I LAST SPOKE TO HER IN *BAD WOLF BAY,* BEFORE THE SIGNAL WAS LOST.
BUT I *DIDN'T,* DID I? SOMETHING *ELSE* HAPPENED. I REMEMBER SEEING HER *AGAIN.*
GIVE IT TO ME.
GIVE *WHAT* TO YOU?
THE *LAST ITEM.*
AND *THEN* YOU CAN TELL ME *WHO* YOU ARE.
BECAUSE YOU SPEAK OF *"REGENERATION"* LIKE AN *OLD MATE,* AND THE MARTHA OF RIGHT NOW...
...WOULDN'T EVEN KNOW WHAT IT *WAS.*
I MEAN, COME ON–
–YOU DON'T NEED TO BE A *BRAIN SURGEON* TO KNOW SOMETHING'S *OFF* ABOUT THIS PLACE.
THE PSYCHIC PAPER JUST CONFIRMED IT.
AND THERE'S ENOUGH *WIBBLY WOBBLY TIMEY WIMEY FLOUNCY BOUNCY* STUFF AROUND TO GIVE A TIME LORD A *HEADACHE.*
SO GIVE ME THE *FINAL* ITEM– THE *THIRD* ONE–THE ITEM THAT I WOULD HAVE HAD IN FRONT OF *MY* MANNEQUIN.
YOU'VE HELPED ME REMEMBER MY *PAST,* NOW LET ME REMEMBER MY *FUTURE.*
A *CHAMELEON ARCH.*
RIGHT THEN. HERE WE GO.

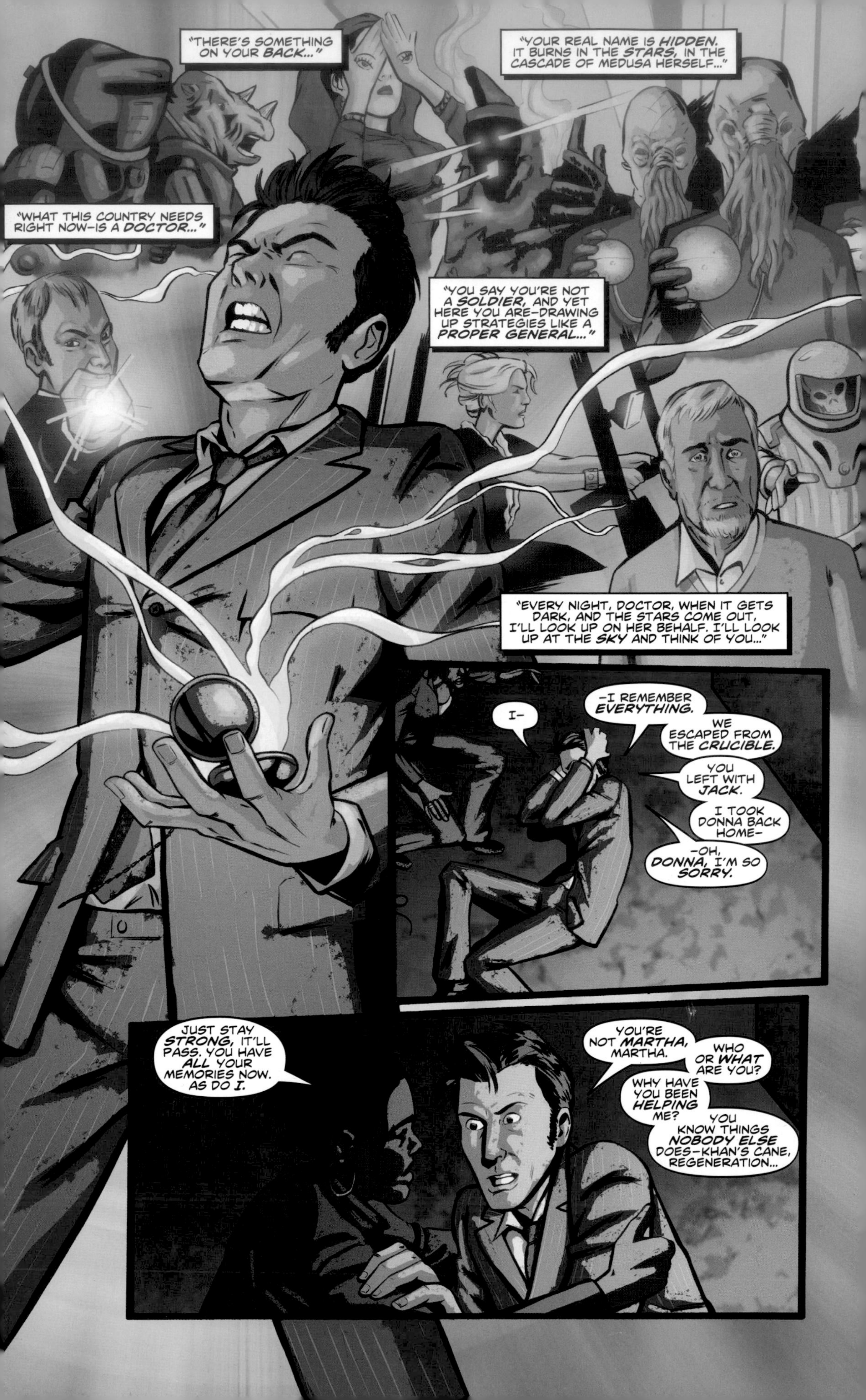
"THERE'S SOMETHING ON YOUR BACK..."
"YOUR REAL NAME IS HIDDEN. IT BURNS IN THE STARS, IN THE CASCADE OF MEDUSA HERSELF..."
"WHAT THIS COUNTRY NEEDS RIGHT NOW—IS A DOCTOR..."
"YOU SAY YOU'RE NOT A SOLDIER, AND YET HERE YOU ARE—DRAWING UP STRATEGIES LIKE A PROPER GENERAL..."
"EVERY NIGHT, DOCTOR, WHEN IT GETS DARK, AND THE STARS COME OUT, I'LL LOOK UP ON HER BEHALF. I'LL LOOK UP AT THE SKY AND THINK OF YOU..."
I—
—I REMEMBER EVERYTHING.
WE ESCAPED FROM THE CRUCIBLE.
YOU LEFT WITH JACK.
I TOOK DONNA BACK HOME—
—OH, DONNA, I'M SO SORRY.
JUST STAY STRONG, IT'LL PASS. YOU HAVE ALL YOUR MEMORIES NOW. AS DO I.
YOU'RE NOT MARTHA, MARTHA.
WHO OR WHAT ARE YOU?
WHY HAVE YOU BEEN HELPING ME?
YOU KNOW THINGS NOBODY ELSE DOES—KHAN'S CANE, REGENERATION...

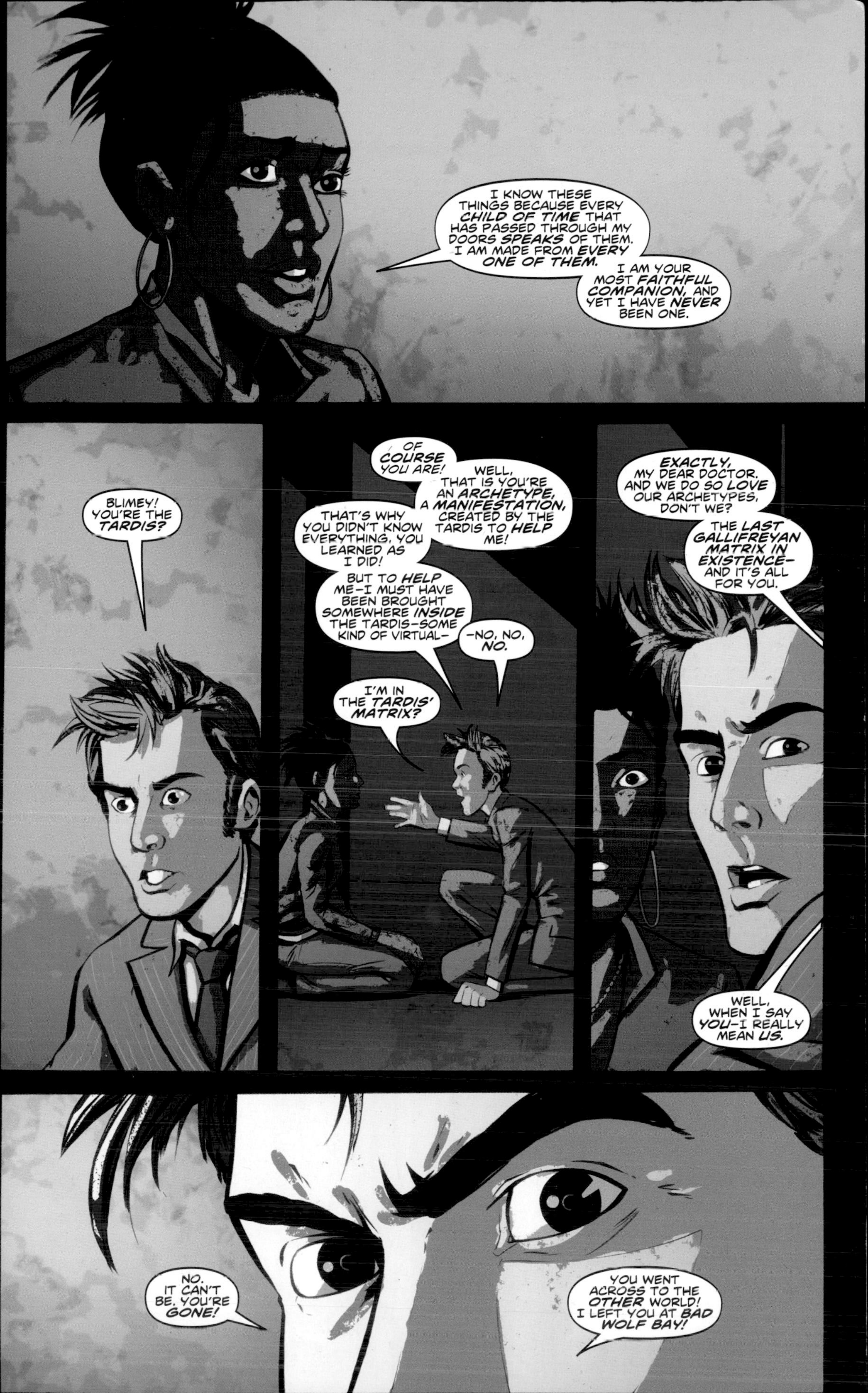
I KNOW THESE THINGS BECAUSE EVERY CHILD OF TIME THAT HAS PASSED THROUGH MY DOORS SPEAKS OF THEM. I AM MADE FROM EVERY ONE OF THEM.
I AM YOUR MOST FAITHFUL COMPANION, AND YET I HAVE NEVER BEEN ONE.
BLIMEY! YOU'RE THE TARDIS?
OF COURSE YOU ARE!
WELL, THAT IS YOU'RE AN ARCHETYPE, A MANIFESTATION, CREATED BY THE TARDIS TO HELP ME!
THAT'S WHY YOU DIDN'T KNOW EVERYTHING. YOU LEARNED AS I DID!
BUT TO HELP ME—I MUST HAVE BEEN BROUGHT SOMEWHERE INSIDE THE TARDIS—SOME KIND OF VIRTUAL—
—NO, NO, NO.
I'M IN THE TARDIS' MATRIX?
EXACTLY, MY DEAR DOCTOR. AND WE DO SO LOVE OUR ARCHETYPES, DON'T WE?
THE LAST GALLIFREYAN MATRIX IN EXISTENCE—AND IT'S ALL FOR YOU.
WELL, WHEN I SAY YOU—I REALLY MEAN US.
NO. IT CAN'T BE. YOU'RE GONE!
YOU WENT ACROSS TO THE OTHER WORLD! I LEFT YOU AT BAD WOLF BAY!

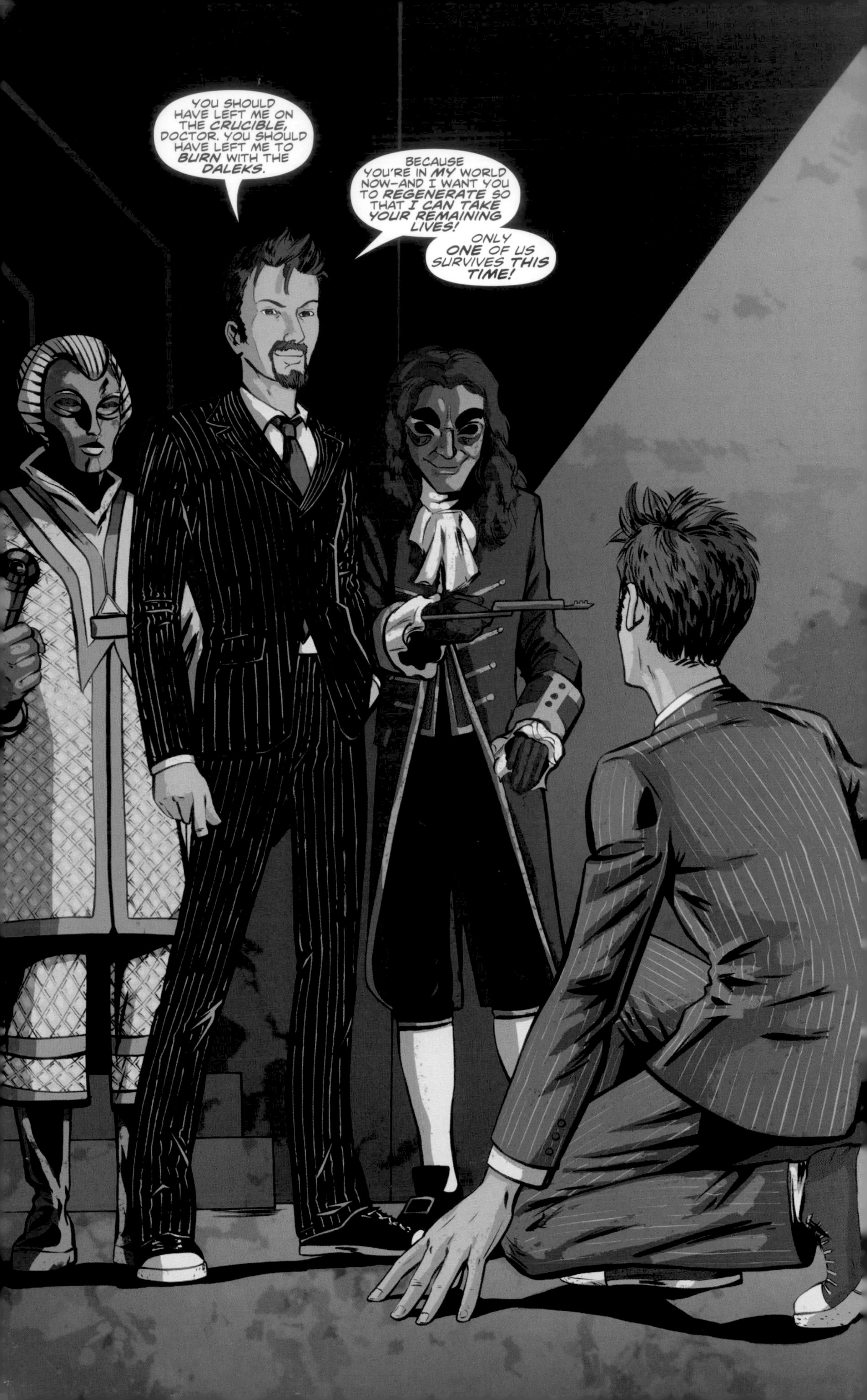
YOU SHOULD HAVE LEFT ME ON THE CRUCIBLE, DOCTOR. YOU SHOULD HAVE LEFT ME TO BURN WITH THE DALEKS.
BECAUSE YOU'RE IN MY WORLD NOW—AND I WANT YOU TO REGENERATE SO THAT I CAN TAKE YOUR REMAINING LIVES!
ONLY ONE OF US SURVIVES THIS TIME!

CHAPTER · SIX
REUNION

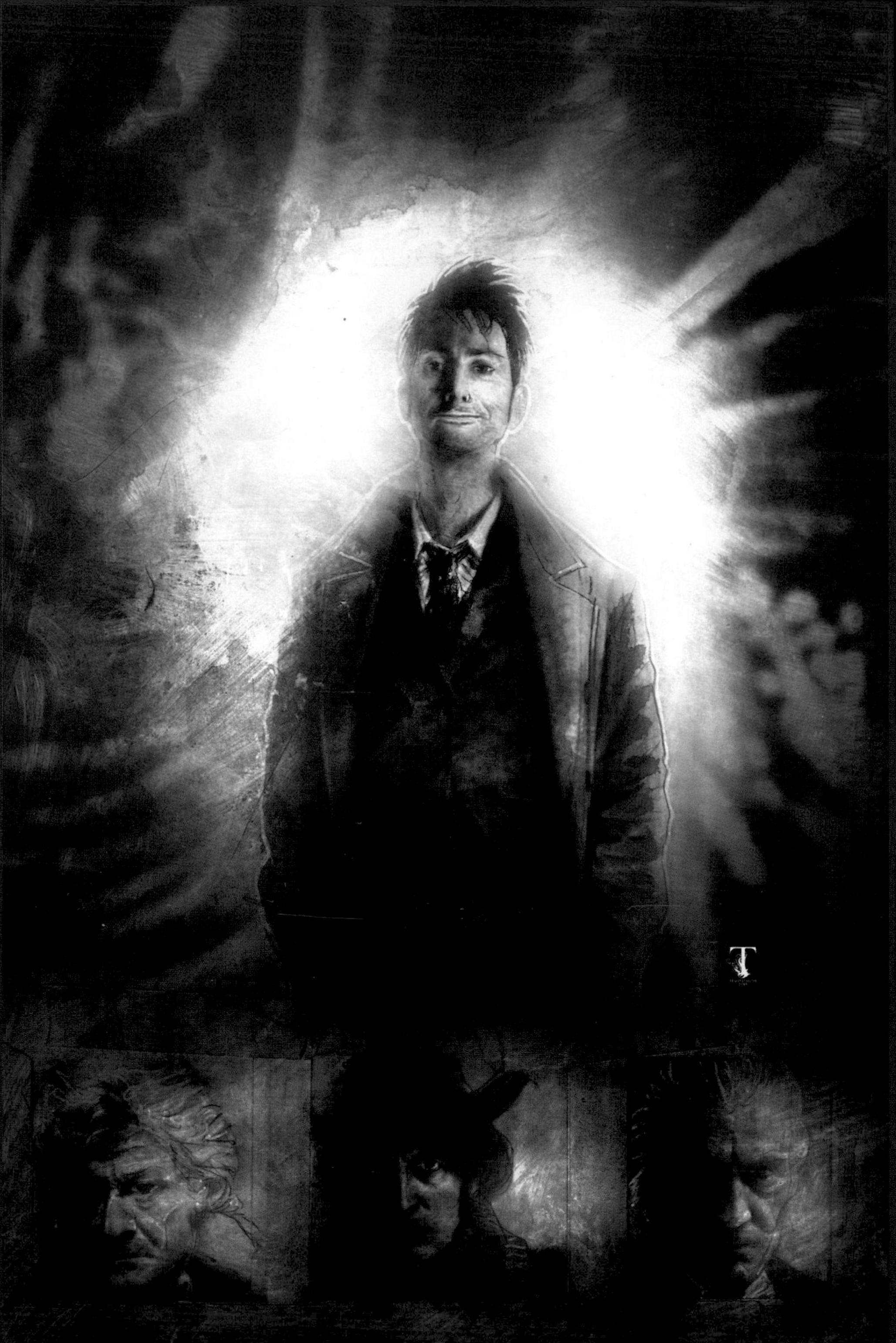

ART BY BEN TEMPLESMITH

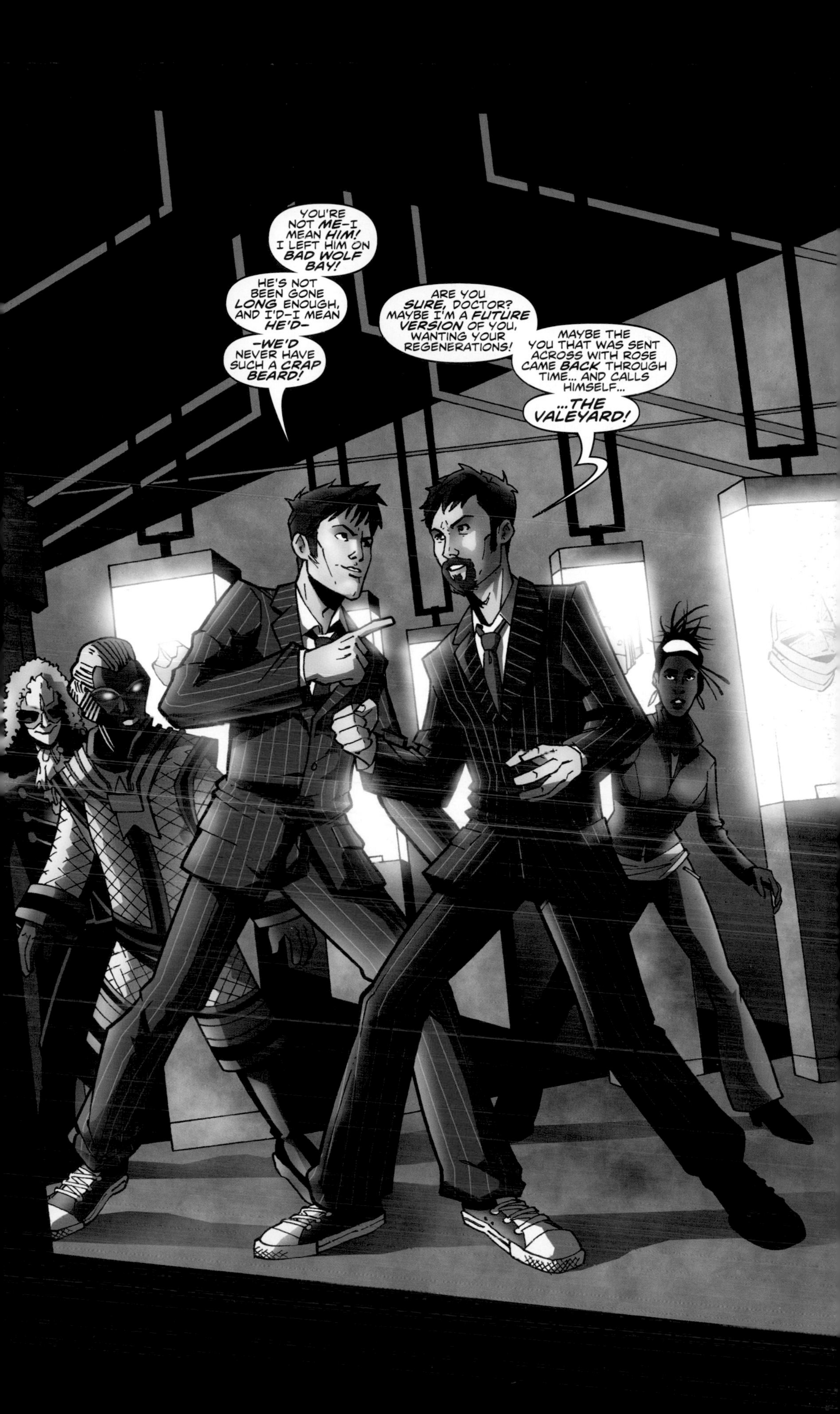
YOU'RE NOT ME–I MEAN HIM! I LEFT HIM ON BAD WOLF BAY!
HE'S NOT BEEN GONE LONG ENOUGH, AND I'D–I MEAN HE'D–
–WE'D NEVER HAVE SUCH A CRAP BEARD!
ARE YOU SURE, DOCTOR? MAYBE I'M A FUTURE VERSION OF YOU, WANTING YOUR REGENERATIONS!
MAYBE THE YOU THAT WAS SENT ACROSS WITH ROSE CAME BACK THROUGH TIME... AND CALLS HIMSELF...
...THE VALEYARD!

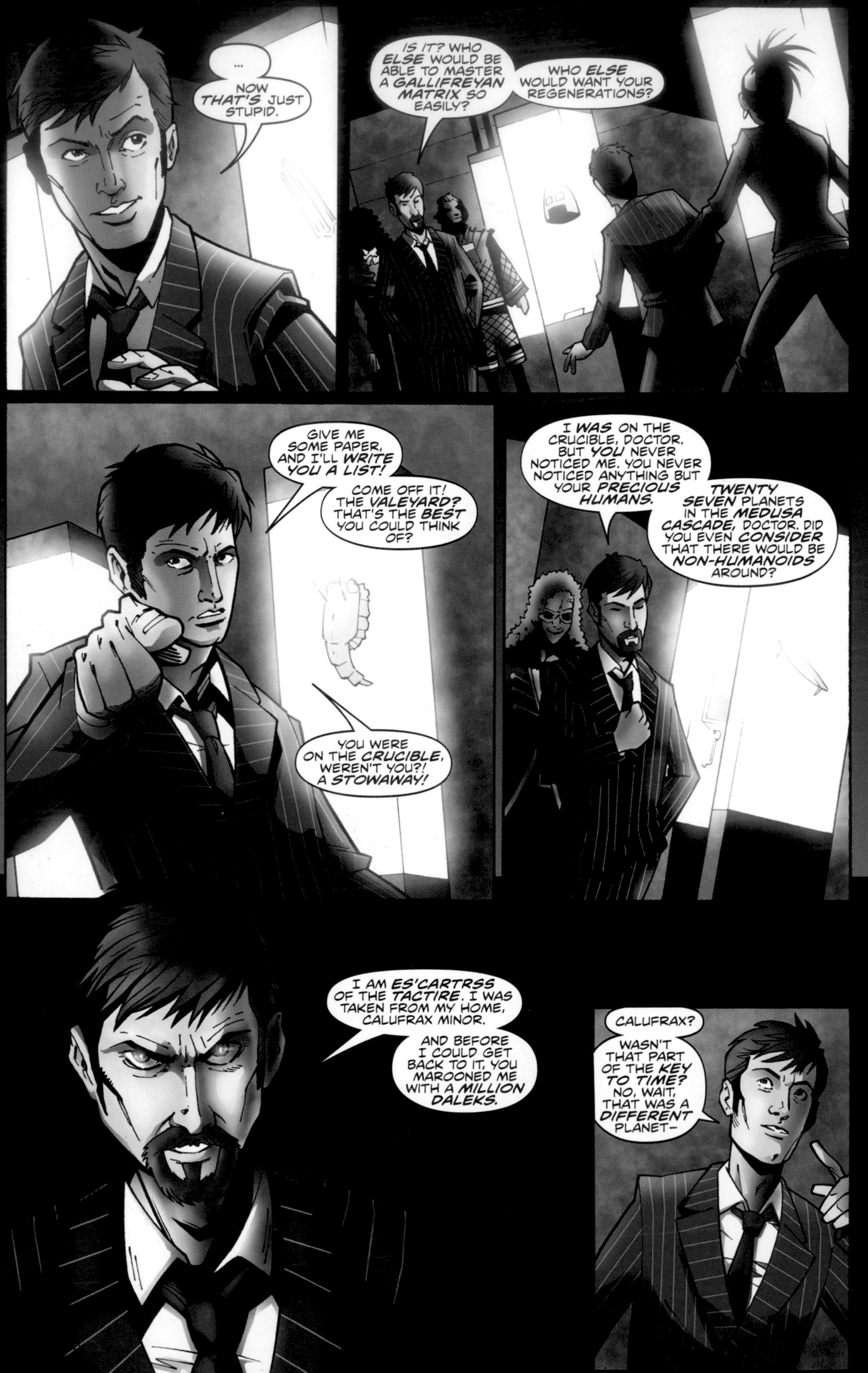
...
NOW THAT'S JUST STUPID.
IS IT? WHO ELSE WOULD BE ABLE TO MASTER A GALLIFREYAN MATRIX SO EASILY?
WHO ELSE WOULD WANT YOUR REGENERATIONS?
GIVE ME SOME PAPER, AND I'LL WRITE YOU A LIST!
COME OFF IT! THE VALEYARD? THAT'S THE BEST YOU COULD THINK OF?
YOU WERE ON THE CRUCIBLE, WEREN'T YOU?! A STOWAWAY!
I WAS ON THE CRUCIBLE, DOCTOR. BUT YOU NEVER NOTICED ME. YOU NEVER NOTICED ANYTHING BUT YOUR PRECIOUS HUMANS.
TWENTY SEVEN PLANETS IN THE MEDUSA CASCADE, DOCTOR. DID YOU EVEN CONSIDER THAT THERE WOULD BE NON-HUMANOIDS AROUND?
I AM ES'CARTRSS OF THE TACTIRE. I WAS TAKEN FROM MY HOME, CALUFRAX MINOR.
AND BEFORE I COULD GET BACK TO IT, YOU MAROONED ME WITH A MILLION DALEKS.
CALUFRAX?
WASN'T THAT PART OF THE KEY TO TIME? NO, WAIT, THAT WAS A DIFFERENT PLANET–

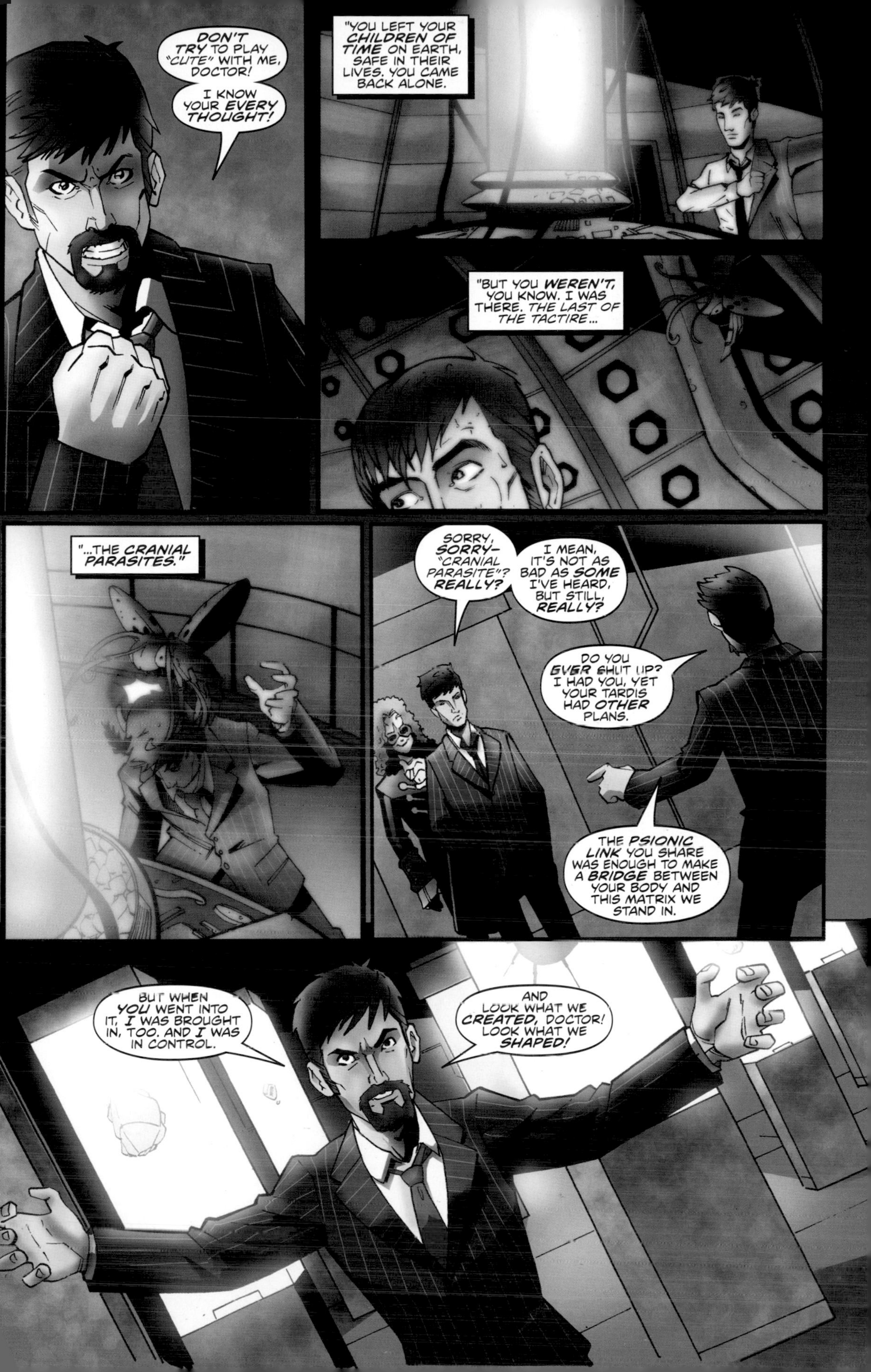
DON'T TRY TO PLAY "CUTE" WITH ME, DOCTOR!
I KNOW YOUR EVERY THOUGHT!
"YOU LEFT YOUR CHILDREN OF TIME ON EARTH, SAFE IN THEIR LIVES. YOU CAME BACK ALONE.
"BUT YOU WEREN'T, YOU KNOW. I WAS THERE. THE LAST OF THE TACTIRE...
"...THE CRANIAL PARASITES."
SORRY, SORRY-- "CRANIAL PARASITE"? REALLY?
I MEAN, IT'S NOT AS BAD AS SOME I'VE HEARD, BUT STILL, REALLY?
DO YOU EVER SHUT UP? I HAD YOU, YET YOUR TARDIS HAD OTHER PLANS.
THE PSIONIC LINK YOU SHARE WAS ENOUGH TO MAKE A BRIDGE BETWEEN YOUR BODY AND THIS MATRIX WE STAND IN.
BUT WHEN YOU WENT INTO IT, I WAS BROUGHT IN, TOO. AND I WAS IN CONTROL.
AND LOOK WHAT WE CREATED, DOCTOR! LOOK WHAT WE SHAPED!

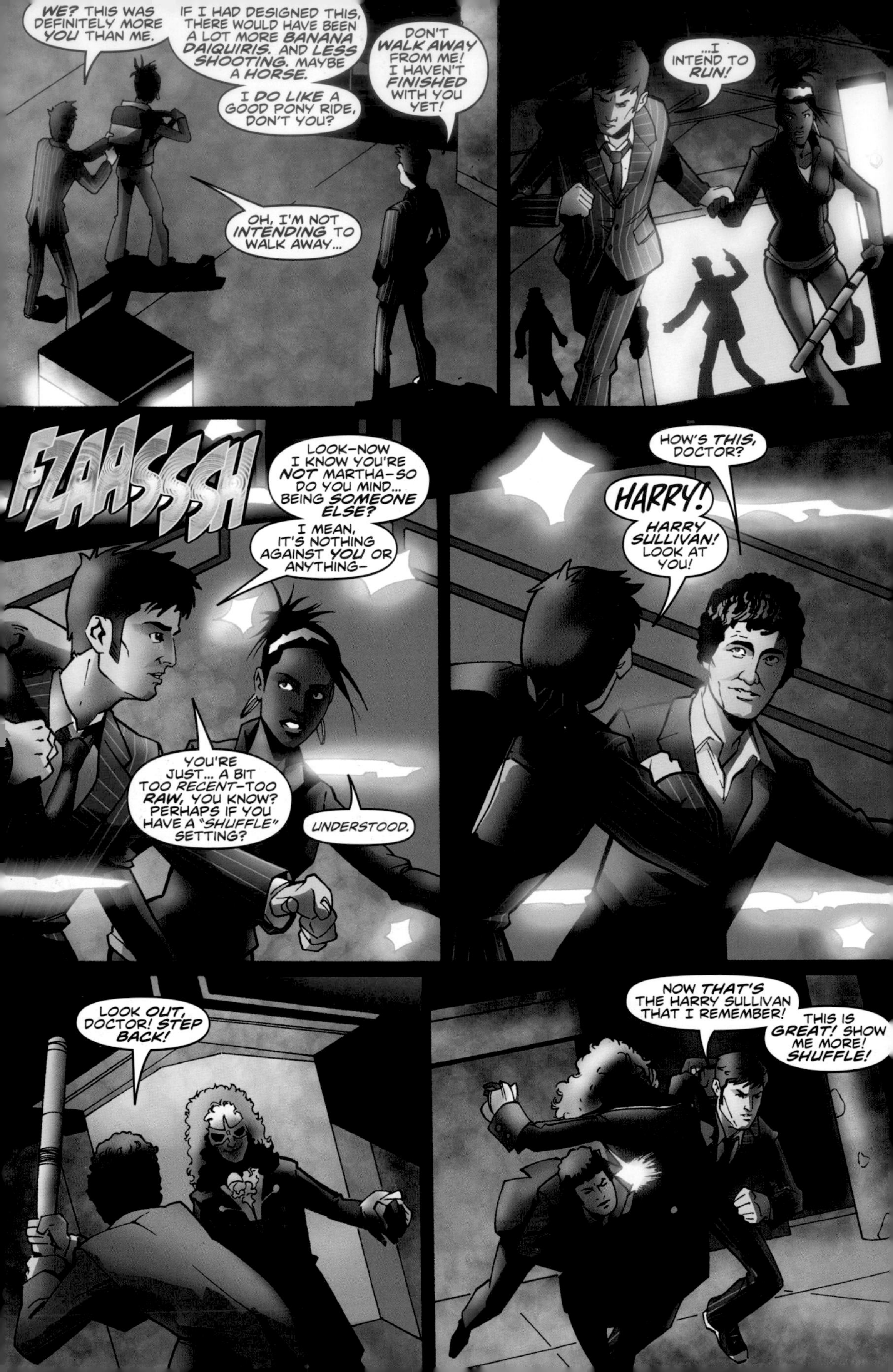
WE? THIS WAS DEFINITELY MORE YOU THAN ME.
IF I HAD DESIGNED THIS, THERE WOULD HAVE BEEN A LOT MORE BANANA DAIQUIRIS. AND LESS SHOOTING. MAYBE A HORSE.
I DO LIKE A GOOD PONY RIDE, DON'T YOU?
DON'T WALK AWAY FROM ME! I HAVEN'T FINISHED WITH YOU YET!
OH, I'M NOT INTENDING TO WALK AWAY...
...I INTEND TO RUN!
FZAASSSH
LOOK–NOW I KNOW YOU'RE NOT MARTHA–SO DO YOU MIND... BEING SOMEONE ELSE?
I MEAN, IT'S NOTHING AGAINST YOU OR ANYTHING–
YOU'RE JUST... A BIT TOO RECENT–TOO RAW, YOU KNOW? PERHAPS IF YOU HAVE A "SHUFFLE" SETTING?
UNDERSTOOD.
HOW'S THIS, DOCTOR?
HARRY!
HARRY SULLIVAN! LOOK AT YOU!
LOOK OUT, DOCTOR! STEP BACK!
NOW THAT'S THE HARRY SULLIVAN THAT I REMEMBER!
THIS IS GREAT! SHOW ME MORE! SHUFFLE!

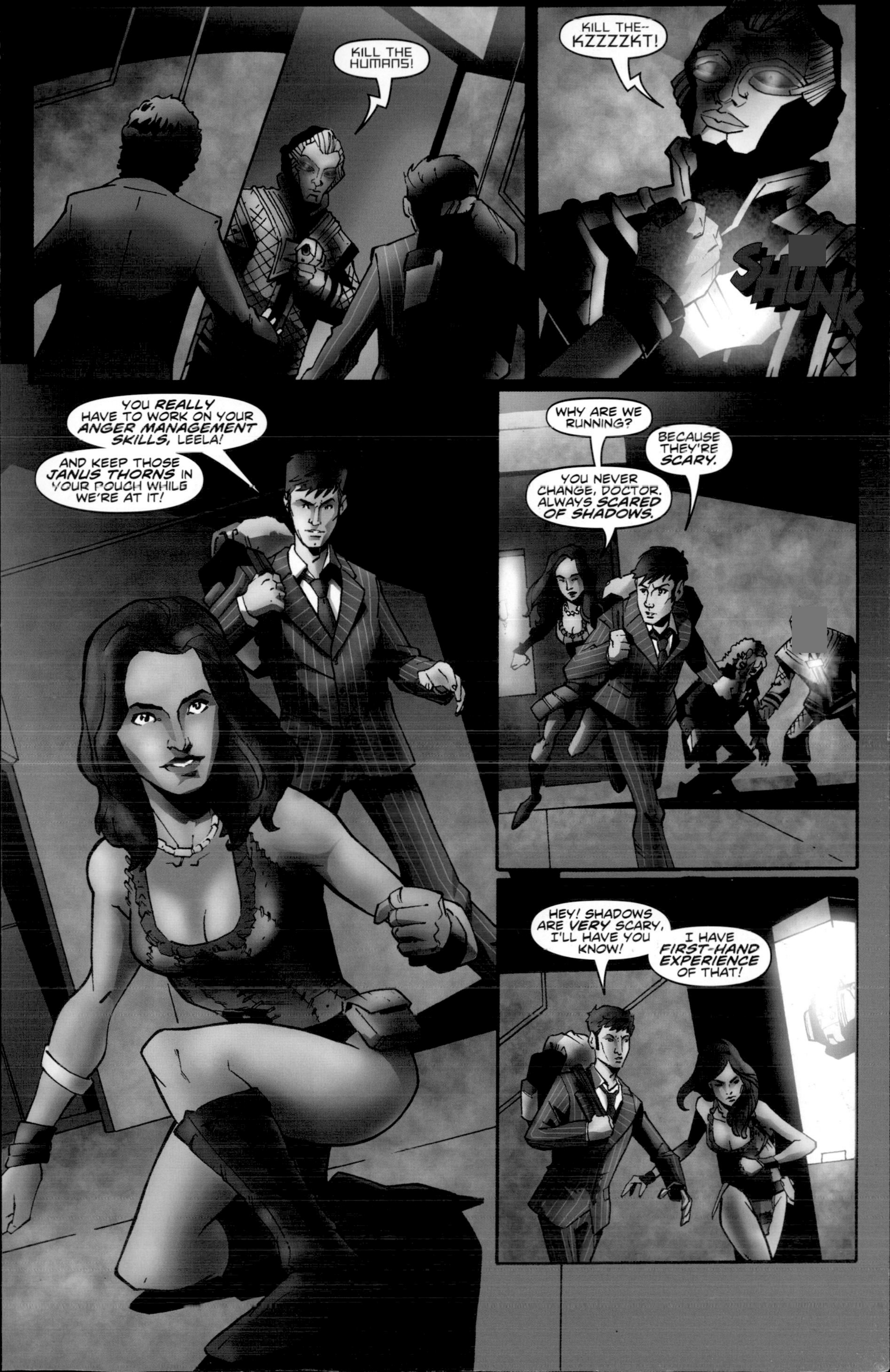
KILL THE HUMANS!
KILL THE-- KZZZZKT!
SHUNK
YOU REALLY HAVE TO WORK ON YOUR ANGER MANAGEMENT SKILLS, LEELA!
AND KEEP THOSE JANUS THORNS IN YOUR POUCH WHILE WE'RE AT IT!
WHY ARE WE RUNNING?
BECAUSE THEY'RE SCARY.
YOU NEVER CHANGE, DOCTOR. ALWAYS SCARED OF SHADOWS.
HEY! SHADOWS ARE VERY SCARY, I'LL HAVE YOU KNOW!
I HAVE FIRST-HAND EXPERIENCE OF THAT!

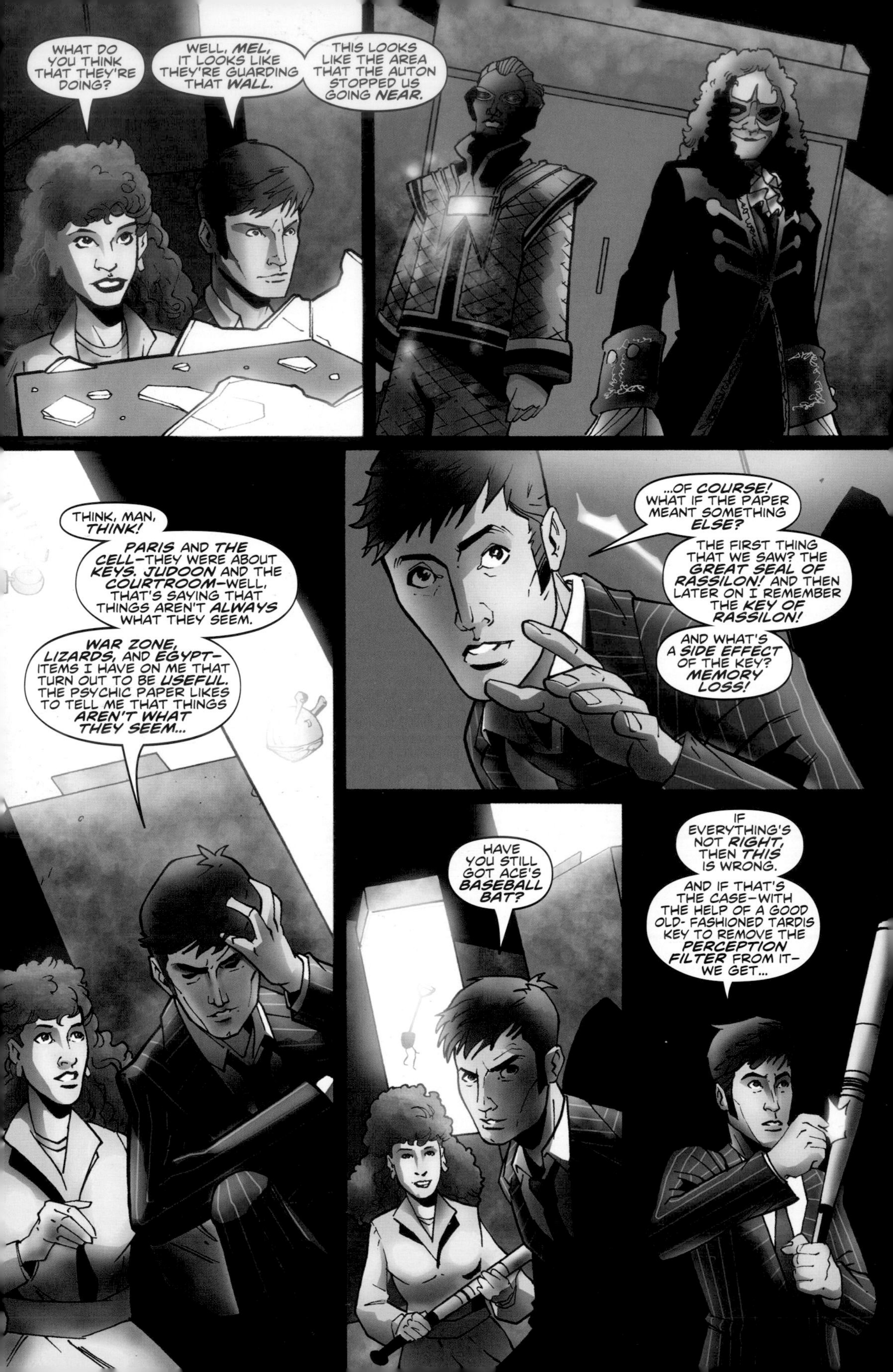
WHAT DO YOU THINK THAT THEY'RE DOING?
WELL, MEL, IT LOOKS LIKE THEY'RE GUARDING THAT WALL.
THIS LOOKS LIKE THE AREA THAT THE AUTON STOPPED US GOING NEAR.
THINK, MAN, THINK!
PARIS AND THE CELL—THEY WERE ABOUT KEYS. JUDOON AND THE COURTROOM—WELL, THAT'S SAYING THAT THINGS AREN'T ALWAYS WHAT THEY SEEM.
WAR ZONE, LIZARDS, AND EGYPT—ITEMS I HAVE ON ME THAT TURN OUT TO BE USEFUL. THE PSYCHIC PAPER LIKES TO TELL ME THAT THINGS AREN'T WHAT THEY SEEM...
...OF COURSE! WHAT IF THE PAPER MEANT SOMETHING ELSE?
THE FIRST THING THAT WE SAW? THE GREAT SEAL OF RASSILON! AND THEN LATER ON I REMEMBER THE KEY OF RASSILON!
AND WHAT'S A SIDE EFFECT OF THE KEY? MEMORY LOSS!
HAVE YOU STILL GOT ACE'S BASEBALL BAT?
IF EVERYTHING'S NOT RIGHT, THEN THIS IS WRONG.
AND IF THAT'S THE CASE—WITH THE HELP OF A GOOD OLD- FASHIONED TARDIS KEY TO REMOVE THE PERCEPTION FILTER FROM IT—WE GET...

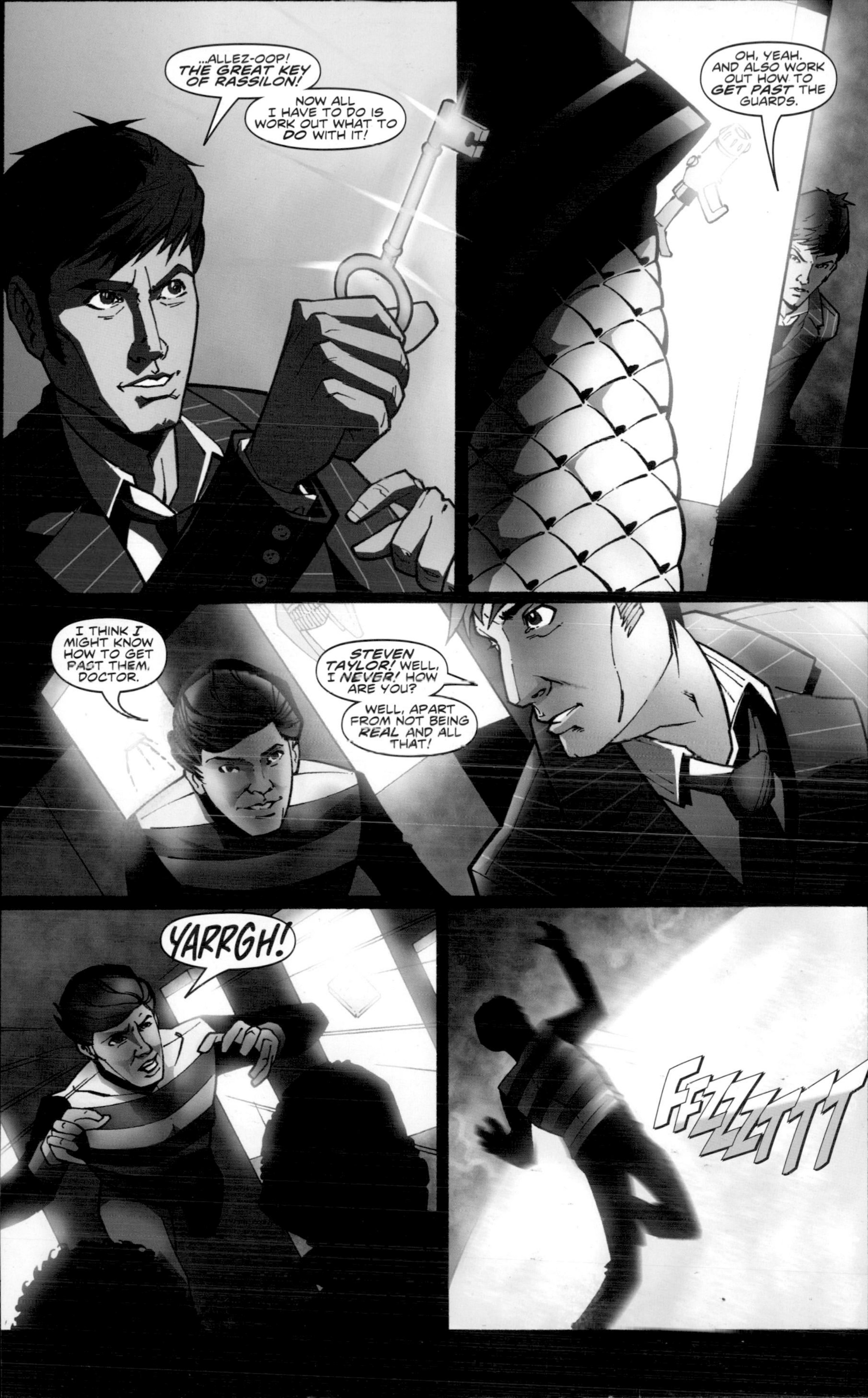
...ALLEZ-OOP! THE GREAT KEY OF RASSILON!
NOW ALL I HAVE TO DO IS WORK OUT WHAT TO DO WITH IT!
OH, YEAH. AND ALSO WORK OUT HOW TO GET PAST THE GUARDS.
I THINK I MIGHT KNOW HOW TO GET PAST THEM, DOCTOR.
STEVEN TAYLOR! WELL, I NEVER! HOW ARE YOU?
WELL, APART FROM NOT BEING REAL AND ALL THAT!
YARRGH!
FFZZZTTTT

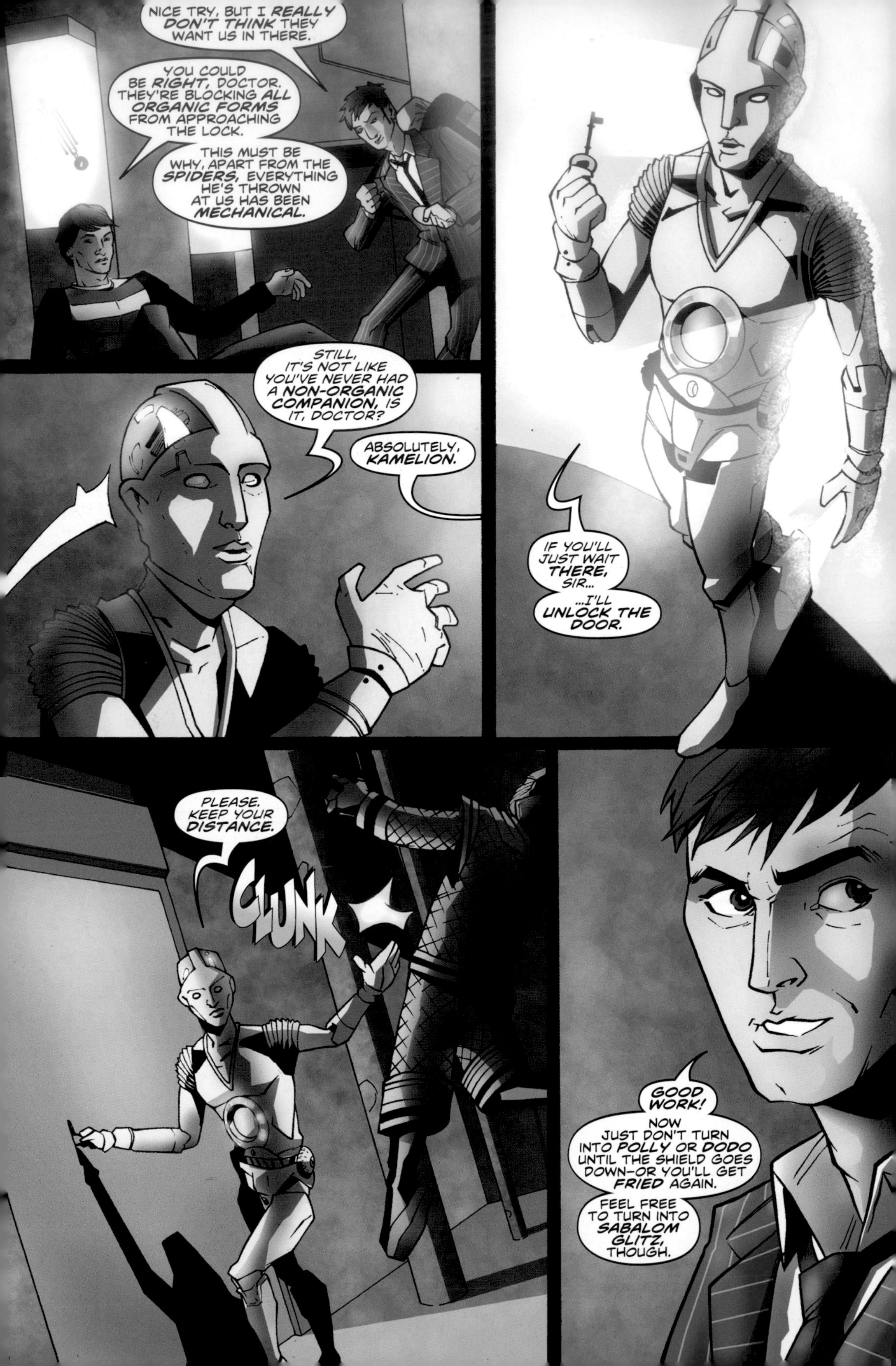
NICE TRY, BUT I REALLY DON'T THINK THEY WANT US IN THERE.
YOU COULD BE RIGHT, DOCTOR. THEY'RE BLOCKING ALL ORGANIC FORMS FROM APPROACHING THE LOCK.
THIS MUST BE WHY, APART FROM THE SPIDERS, EVERYTHING HE'S THROWN AT US HAS BEEN MECHANICAL.
STILL, IT'S NOT LIKE YOU'VE NEVER HAD A NON-ORGANIC COMPANION, IS IT, DOCTOR?
ABSOLUTELY, KAMELION.
IF YOU'LL JUST WAIT THERE, SIR...
...I'LL UNLOCK THE DOOR.
PLEASE. KEEP YOUR DISTANCE.
CLUNK
GOOD WORK!
NOW JUST DON'T TURN INTO POLLY OR DODO UNTIL THE SHIELD GOES DOWN—OR YOU'LL GET FRIED AGAIN.
FEEL FREE TO TURN INTO SABALOM GLITZ, THOUGH.

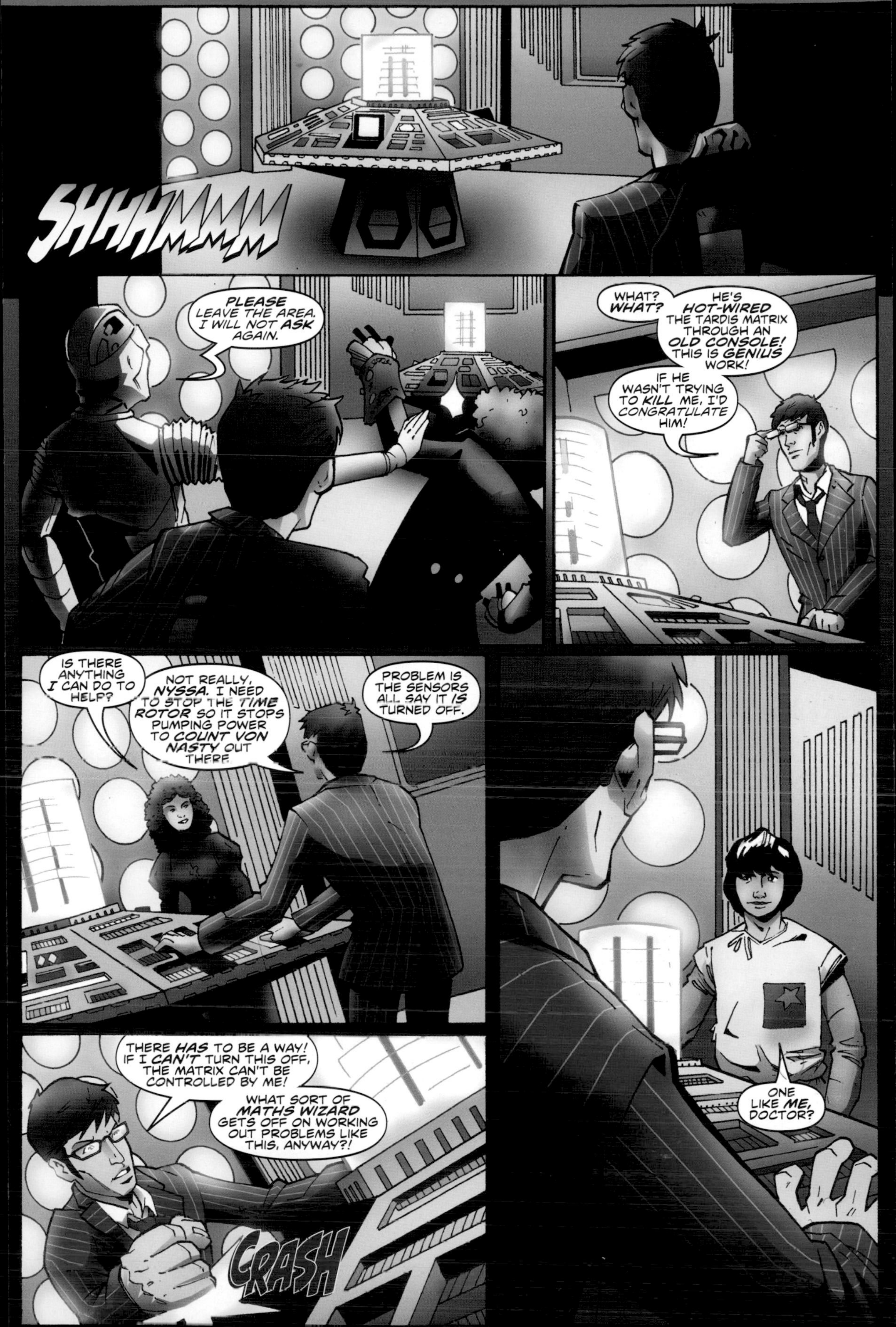
SHHHMMMM
PLEASE LEAVE THE AREA. I WILL NOT ASK AGAIN.
WHAT? WHAT?
HE'S HOT-WIRED THE TARDIS MATRIX THROUGH AN OLD CONSOLE! THIS IS GENIUS WORK!
IF HE WASN'T TRYING TO KILL ME, I'D CONGRATULATE HIM!
IS THERE ANYTHING I CAN DO TO HELP?
NOT REALLY, NYSSA. I NEED TO STOP THE TIME ROTOR SO IT STOPS PUMPING POWER TO COUNT VON NASTY OUT THERE.
PROBLEM IS THE SENSORS ALL SAY IT IS TURNED OFF.
THERE HAS TO BE A WAY! IF I CAN'T TURN THIS OFF, THE MATRIX CAN'T BE CONTROLLED BY ME!
WHAT SORT OF MATHS WIZARD GETS OFF ON WORKING OUT PROBLEMS LIKE THIS, ANYWAY?!
CRASH
ONE LIKE ME, DOCTOR?

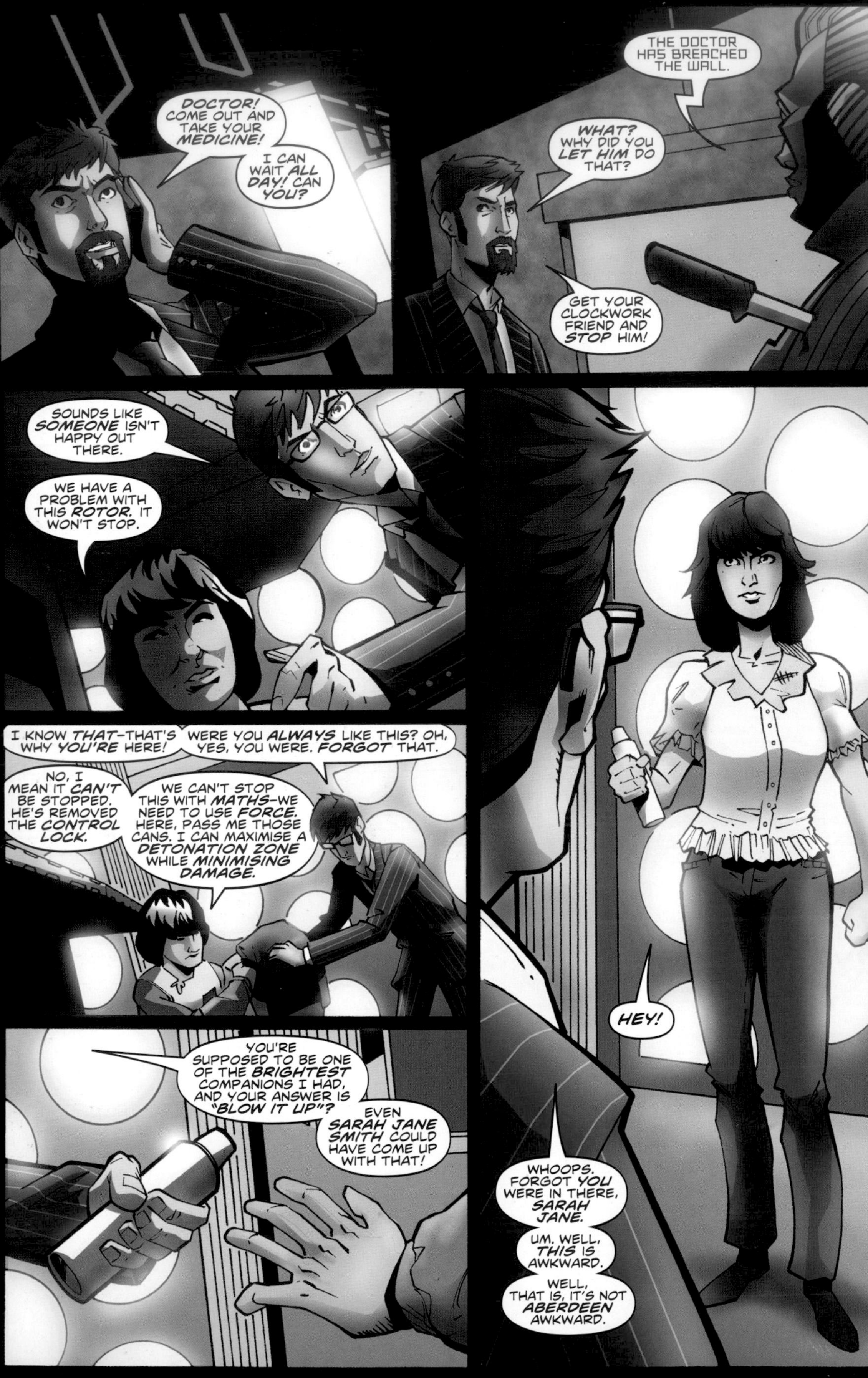
DOCTOR! COME OUT AND TAKE YOUR MEDICINE!
I CAN WAIT ALL DAY! CAN YOU?
THE DOCTOR HAS BREACHED THE WALL.
WHAT? WHY DID YOU LET HIM DO THAT?
GET YOUR CLOCKWORK FRIEND AND STOP HIM!
SOUNDS LIKE SOMEONE ISN'T HAPPY OUT THERE.
WE HAVE A PROBLEM WITH THIS ROTOR. IT WON'T STOP.
I KNOW THAT–THAT'S WHY YOU'RE HERE!
NO, I MEAN IT CAN'T BE STOPPED. HE'S REMOVED THE CONTROL LOCK.
WERE YOU ALWAYS LIKE THIS? OH, YES, YOU WERE. FORGOT THAT.
WE CAN'T STOP THIS WITH MATHS–WE NEED TO USE FORCE. HERE, PASS ME THOSE CANS. I CAN MAXIMISE A DETONATION ZONE WHILE MINIMISING DAMAGE.
YOU'RE SUPPOSED TO BE ONE OF THE BRIGHTEST COMPANIONS I HAD, AND YOUR ANSWER IS "BLOW IT UP"?
EVEN SARAH JANE SMITH COULD HAVE COME UP WITH THAT!
HEY!
WHOOPS. FORGOT YOU WERE IN THERE, SARAH JANE.
UM. WELL, THIS IS AWKWARD.
WELL, THAT IS, IT'S NOT ABERDEEN AWKWARD.

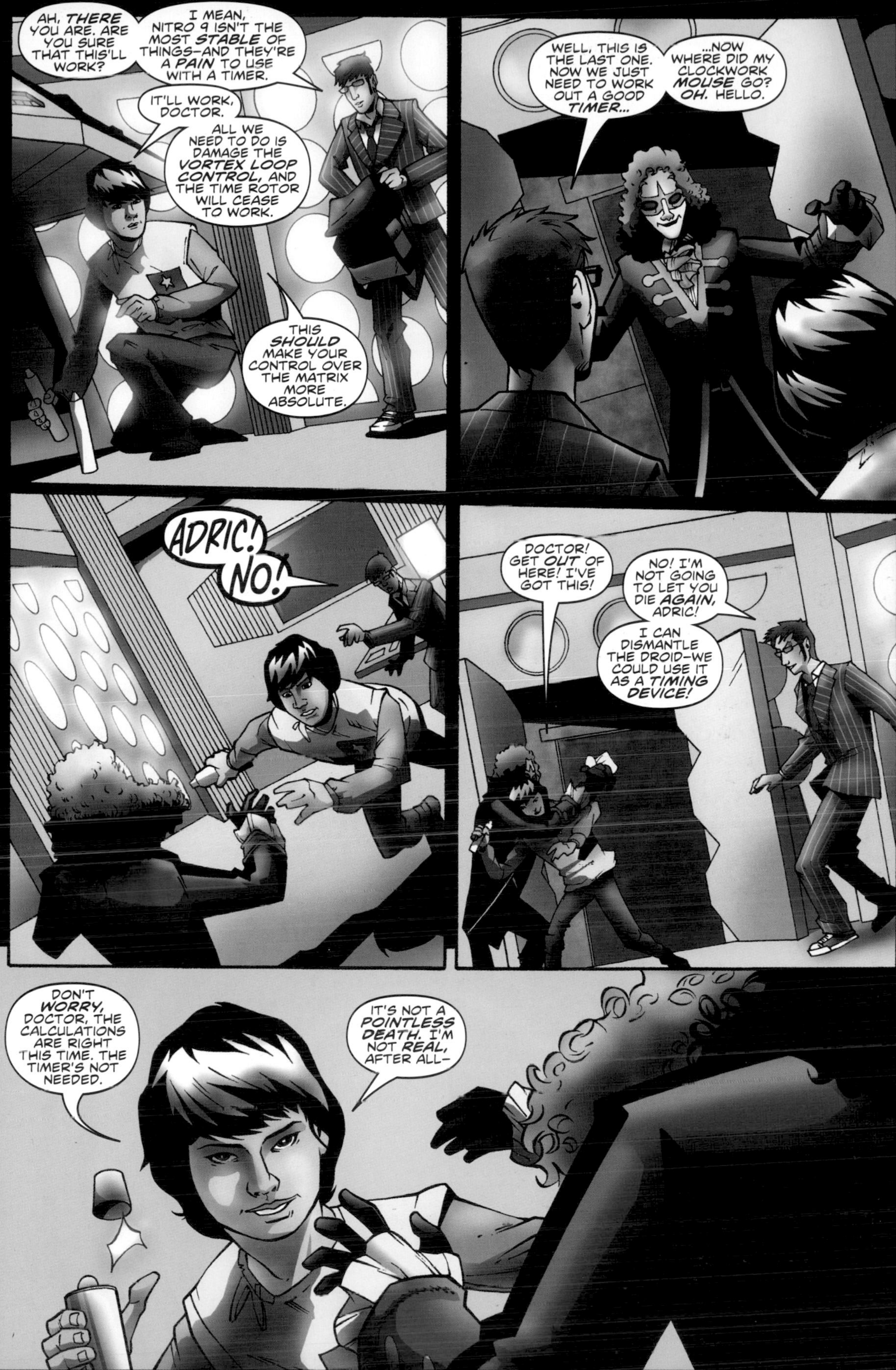
AH, THERE YOU ARE. ARE YOU SURE THAT THIS'LL WORK?
I MEAN, NITRO 9 ISN'T THE MOST STABLE OF THINGS—AND THEY'RE A PAIN TO USE WITH A TIMER.
IT'LL WORK, DOCTOR.
ALL WE NEED TO DO IS DAMAGE THE VORTEX LOOP CONTROL, AND THE TIME ROTOR WILL CEASE TO WORK.
THIS SHOULD MAKE YOUR CONTROL OVER THE MATRIX MORE ABSOLUTE.
WELL, THIS IS THE LAST ONE. NOW WE JUST NEED TO WORK OUT A GOOD TIMER...
...NOW WHERE DID MY CLOCKWORK MOUSE GO? OH. HELLO.
ADRIC! NO!
DOCTOR! GET OUT OF HERE! I'VE GOT THIS!
NO! I'M NOT GOING TO LET YOU DIE AGAIN, ADRIC!
I CAN DISMANTLE THE DROID—WE COULD USE IT AS A TIMING DEVICE!
DON'T WORRY, DOCTOR, THE CALCULATIONS ARE RIGHT THIS TIME. THE TIMER'S NOT NEEDED.
IT'S NOT A POINTLESS DEATH. I'M NOT REAL, AFTER ALL—

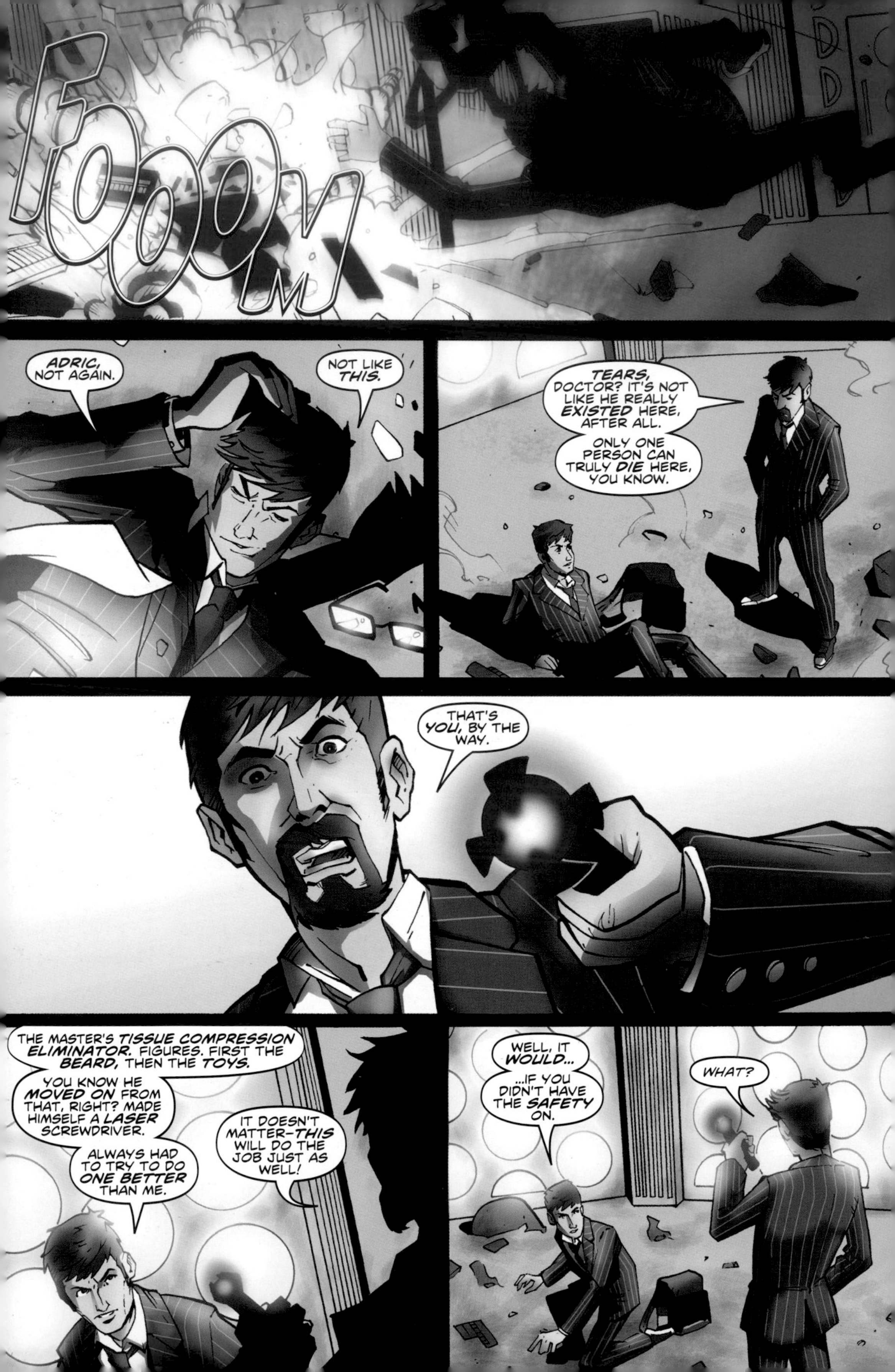
BOOOOM
ADRIC, NOT AGAIN.
NOT LIKE THIS.
TEARS, DOCTOR? IT'S NOT LIKE HE REALLY EXISTED HERE, AFTER ALL.
ONLY ONE PERSON CAN TRULY DIE HERE, YOU KNOW.
THAT'S YOU, BY THE WAY.
THE MASTER'S TISSUE COMPRESSION ELIMINATOR. FIGURES. FIRST THE BEARD, THEN THE TOYS.
YOU KNOW HE MOVED ON FROM THAT, RIGHT? MADE HIMSELF A LASER SCREWDRIVER.
ALWAYS HAD TO TRY TO DO ONE BETTER THAN ME.
IT DOESN'T MATTER–THIS WILL DO THE JOB JUST AS WELL!
WELL, IT WOULD...
...IF YOU DIDN'T HAVE THE SAFETY ON.
WHAT?

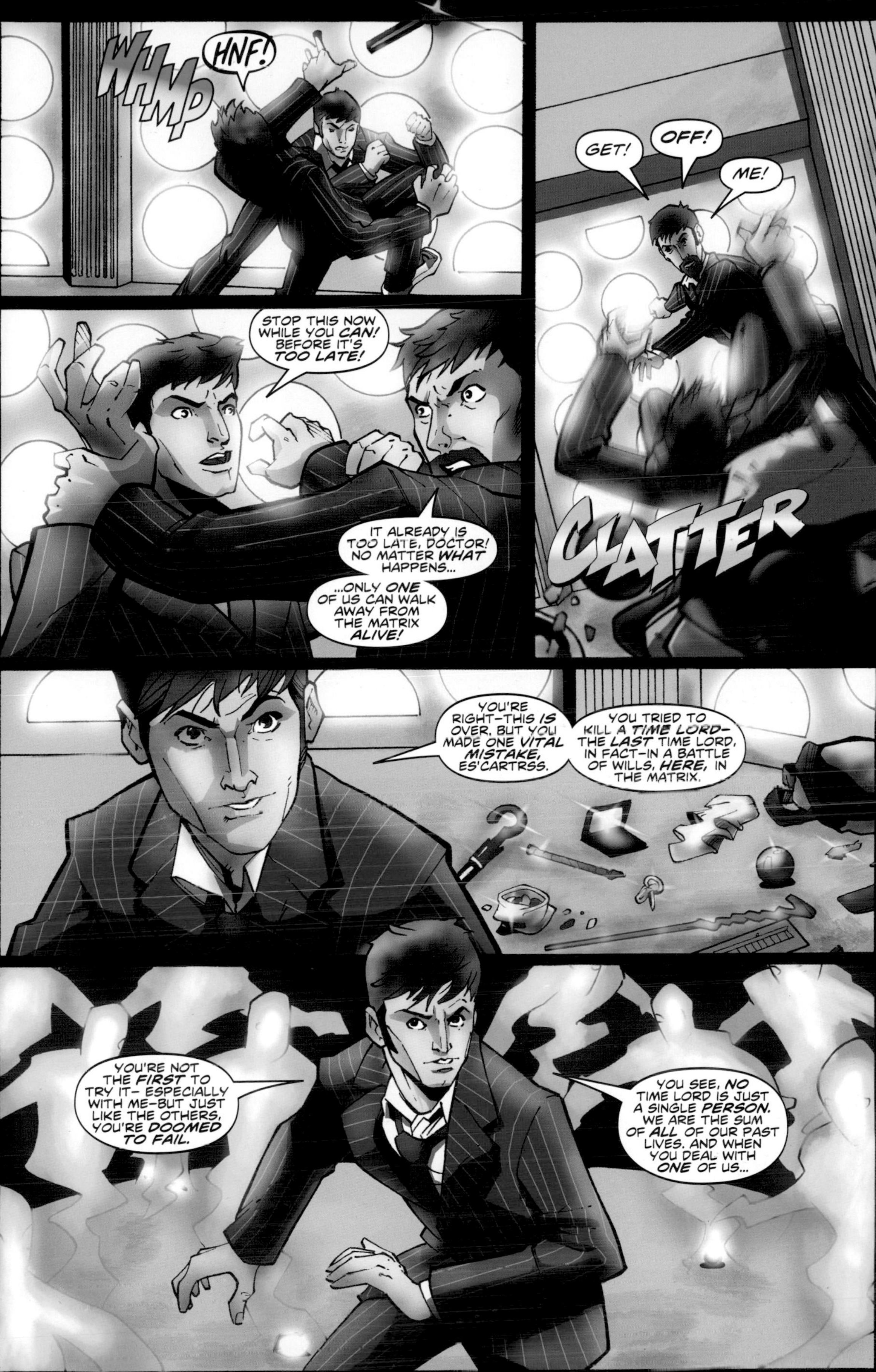
WHMP
HNF!
GET!
OFF!
ME!
STOP THIS NOW WHILE YOU CAN! BEFORE IT'S TOO LATE!
IT ALREADY IS TOO LATE, DOCTOR! NO MATTER WHAT HAPPENS...
...ONLY ONE OF US CAN WALK AWAY FROM THE MATRIX ALIVE!
CLATTER
YOU'RE RIGHT–THIS IS OVER, BUT YOU MADE ONE VITAL MISTAKE, ES'CARTRSS.
YOU TRIED TO KILL A TIME LORD– THE LAST TIME LORD, IN FACT–IN A BATTLE OF WILLS, HERE, IN THE MATRIX.
YOU'RE NOT THE FIRST TO TRY IT– ESPECIALLY WITH ME–BUT JUST LIKE THE OTHERS, YOU'RE DOOMED TO FAIL.
YOU SEE, NO TIME LORD IS JUST A SINGLE PERSON. WE ARE THE SUM OF ALL OF OUR PAST LIVES. AND WHEN YOU DEAL WITH ONE OF US...

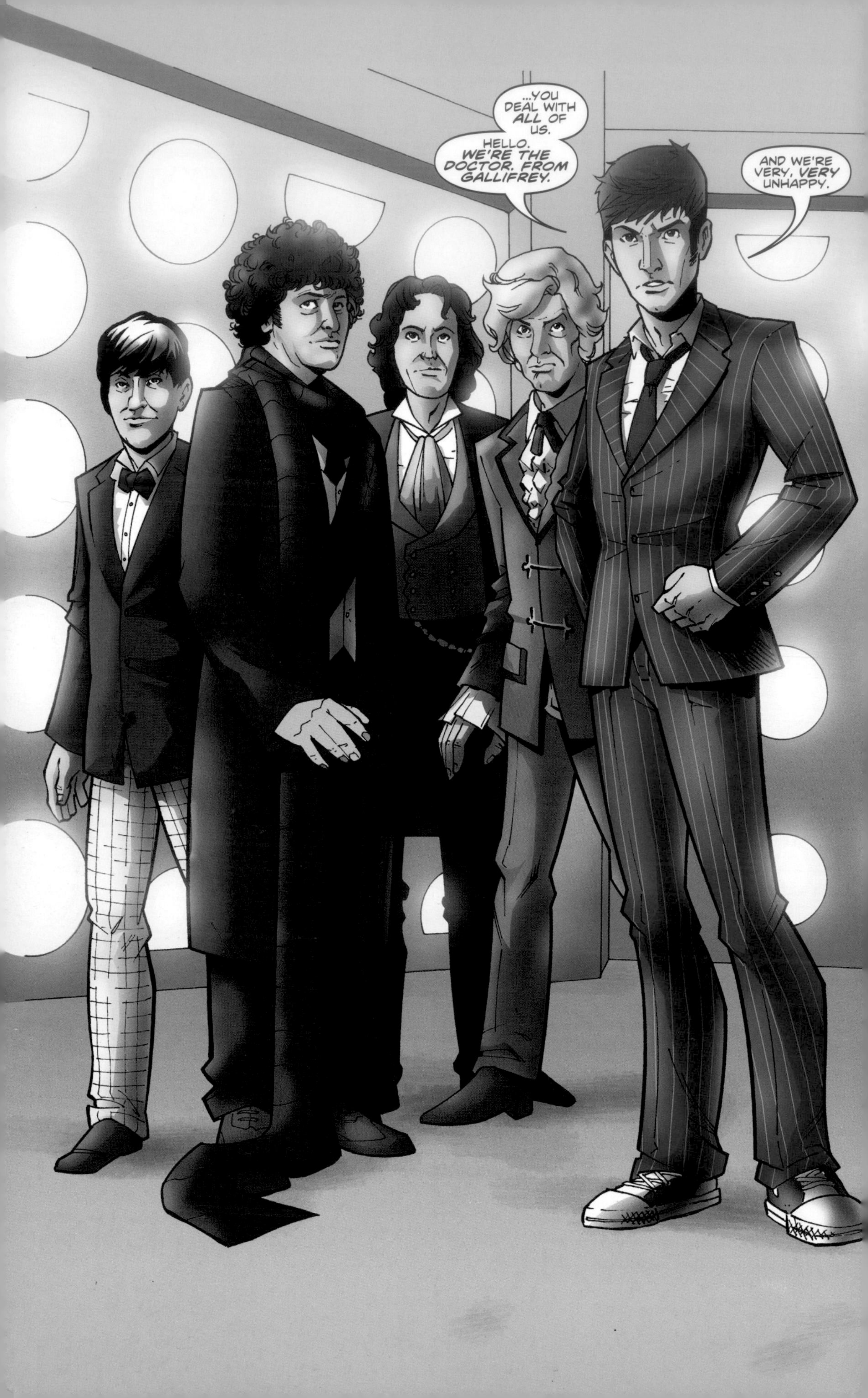
HELLO. WE'RE THE DOCTOR. FROM GALLIFREY.
...YOU DEAL WITH ALL OF US.
AND WE'RE VERY, VERY UNHAPPY.

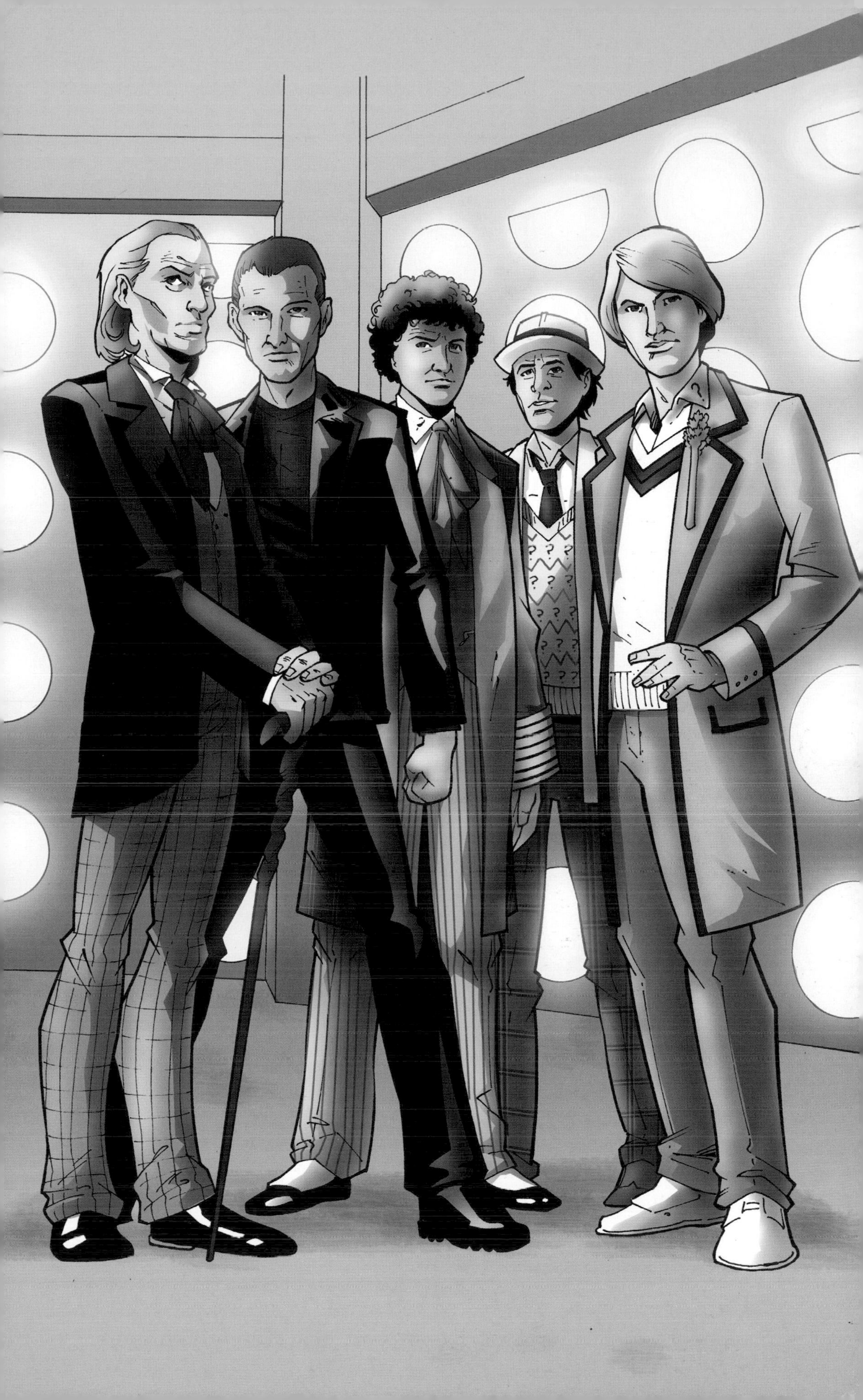

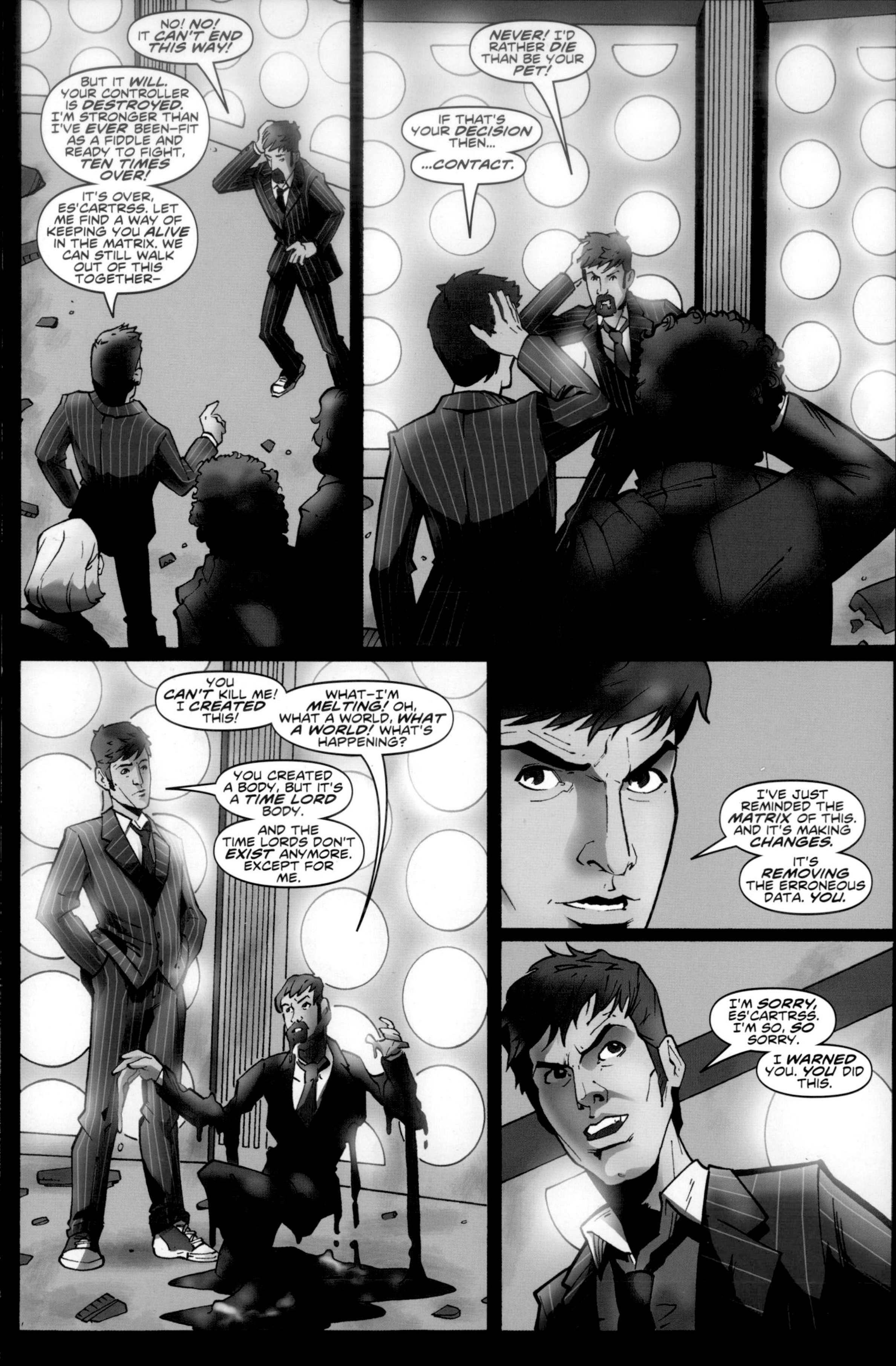
NO! NO! IT CAN'T END THIS WAY!
BUT IT WILL. YOUR CONTROLLER IS DESTROYED. I'M STRONGER THAN I'VE EVER BEEN—FIT AS A FIDDLE AND READY TO FIGHT, TEN TIMES OVER!
IT'S OVER, ES'CARTRSS. LET ME FIND A WAY OF KEEPING YOU ALIVE IN THE MATRIX. WE CAN STILL WALK OUT OF THIS TOGETHER–
NEVER! I'D RATHER DIE THAN BE YOUR PET!
IF THAT'S YOUR DECISION THEN...
...CONTACT.
YOU CAN'T KILL ME! I CREATED THIS!
WHAT–I'M MELTING! OH, WHAT A WORLD, WHAT A WORLD! WHAT'S HAPPENING?
YOU CREATED A BODY, BUT IT'S A TIME LORD BODY.
AND THE TIME LORDS DON'T EXIST ANYMORE. EXCEPT FOR ME.
I'VE JUST REMINDED THE MATRIX OF THIS. AND IT'S MAKING CHANGES.
IT'S REMOVING THE ERRONEOUS DATA. YOU.
I'M SORRY, ES'CARTRSS. I'M SO, SO SORRY.
I WARNED YOU. YOU DID THIS.

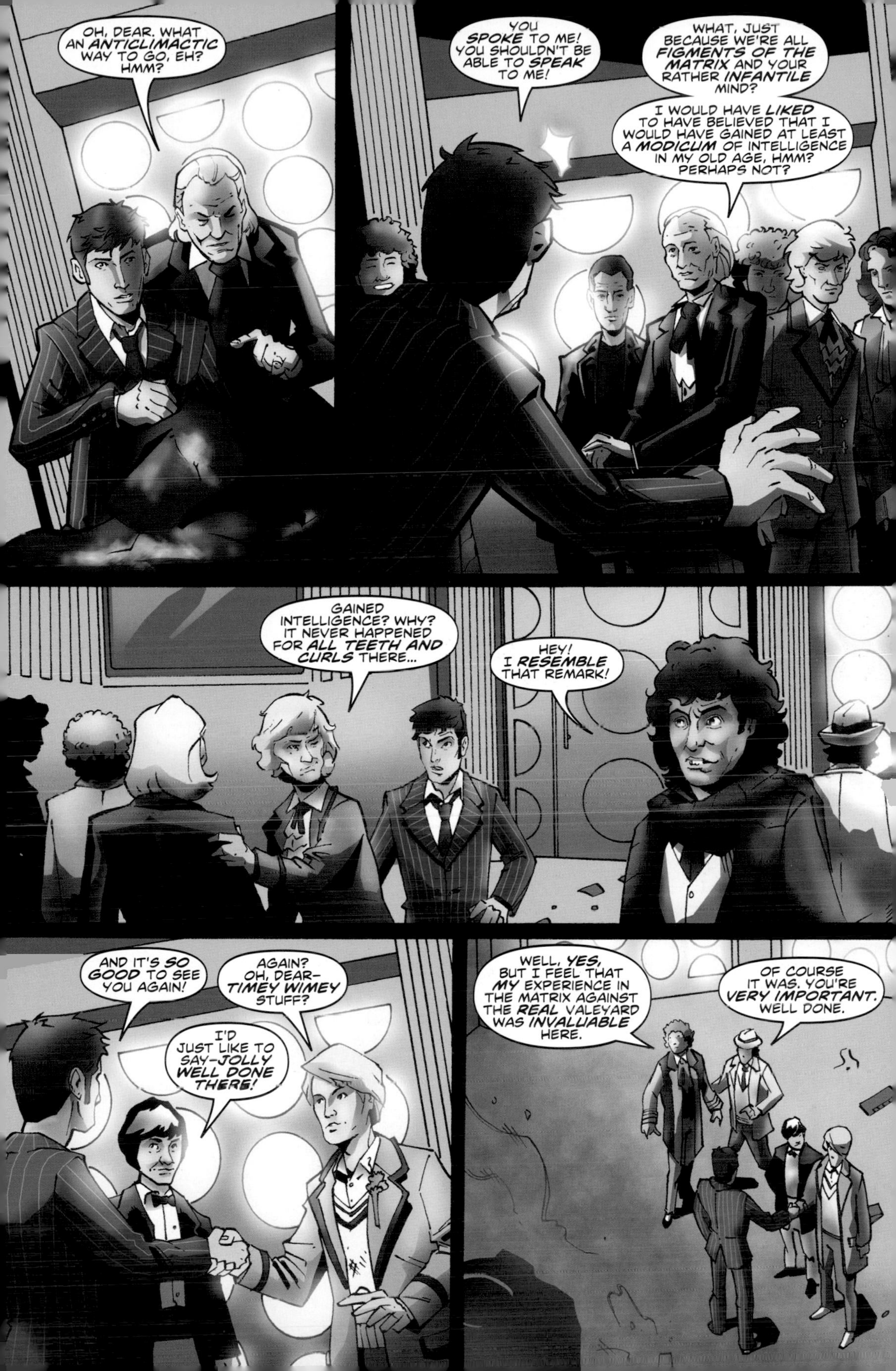

OH, DEAR. WHAT AN ANTICLIMACTIC WAY TO GO, EH? HMM?
YOU SPOKE TO ME! YOU SHOULDN'T BE ABLE TO SPEAK TO ME!
WHAT, JUST BECAUSE WE'RE ALL FIGMENTS OF THE MATRIX AND YOUR RATHER INFANTILE MIND?
I WOULD HAVE LIKED TO HAVE BELIEVED THAT I WOULD HAVE GAINED AT LEAST A MODICUM OF INTELLIGENCE IN MY OLD AGE, HMM? PERHAPS NOT?
GAINED INTELLIGENCE? WHY? IT NEVER HAPPENED FOR ALL TEETH AND CURLS THERE...
HEY! I RESEMBLE THAT REMARK!
AND IT'S SO GOOD TO SEE YOU AGAIN!
AGAIN? OH, DEAR- TIMEY WIMEY STUFF?
I'D JUST LIKE TO SAY-JOLLY WELL DONE THERE!
WELL, YES, BUT I FEEL THAT MY EXPERIENCE IN THE MATRIX AGAINST THE REAL VALEYARD WAS INVALUABLE HERE.
OF COURSE IT WAS. YOU'RE VERY IMPORTANT. WELL DONE.

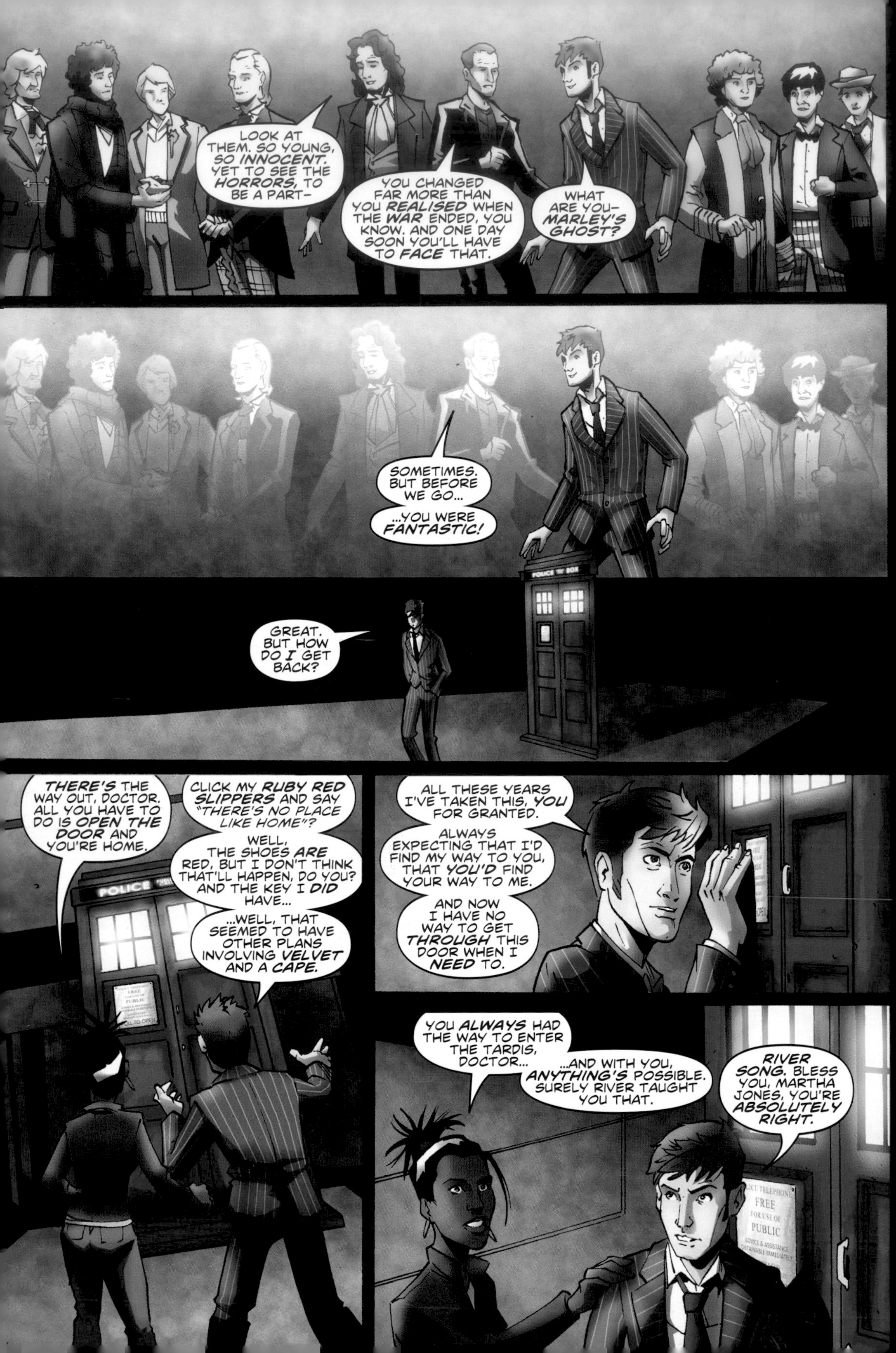
LOOK AT THEM. SO YOUNG, SO INNOCENT. YET TO SEE THE HORRORS, TO BE A PART-
YOU CHANGED FAR MORE THAN YOU REALISED WHEN THE WAR ENDED, YOU KNOW. AND ONE DAY SOON YOU'LL HAVE TO FACE THAT.
WHAT ARE YOU- MARLEY'S GHOST?
SOMETIMES. BUT BEFORE WE GO...
...YOU WERE FANTASTIC!
GREAT. BUT HOW DO I GET BACK?
THERE'S THE WAY OUT, DOCTOR. ALL YOU HAVE TO DO IS OPEN THE DOOR AND YOU'RE HOME.
CLICK MY RUBY RED SLIPPERS AND SAY "THERE'S NO PLACE LIKE HOME"?
WELL, THE SHOES ARE RED, BUT I DON'T THINK THAT'LL HAPPEN, DO YOU? AND THE KEY I DID HAVE...
...WELL, THAT SEEMED TO HAVE OTHER PLANS INVOLVING VELVET AND A CAPE.
ALL THESE YEARS I'VE TAKEN THIS, YOU FOR GRANTED.
ALWAYS EXPECTING THAT I'D FIND MY WAY TO YOU, THAT YOU'D FIND YOUR WAY TO ME.
AND NOW I HAVE NO WAY TO GET THROUGH THIS DOOR WHEN I NEED TO.
YOU ALWAYS HAD THE WAY TO ENTER THE TARDIS, DOCTOR...
...AND WITH YOU, ANYTHING'S POSSIBLE. SURELY RIVER TAUGHT YOU THAT.
RIVER SONG. BLESS YOU, MARTHA JONES, YOU'RE ABSOLUTELY RIGHT.

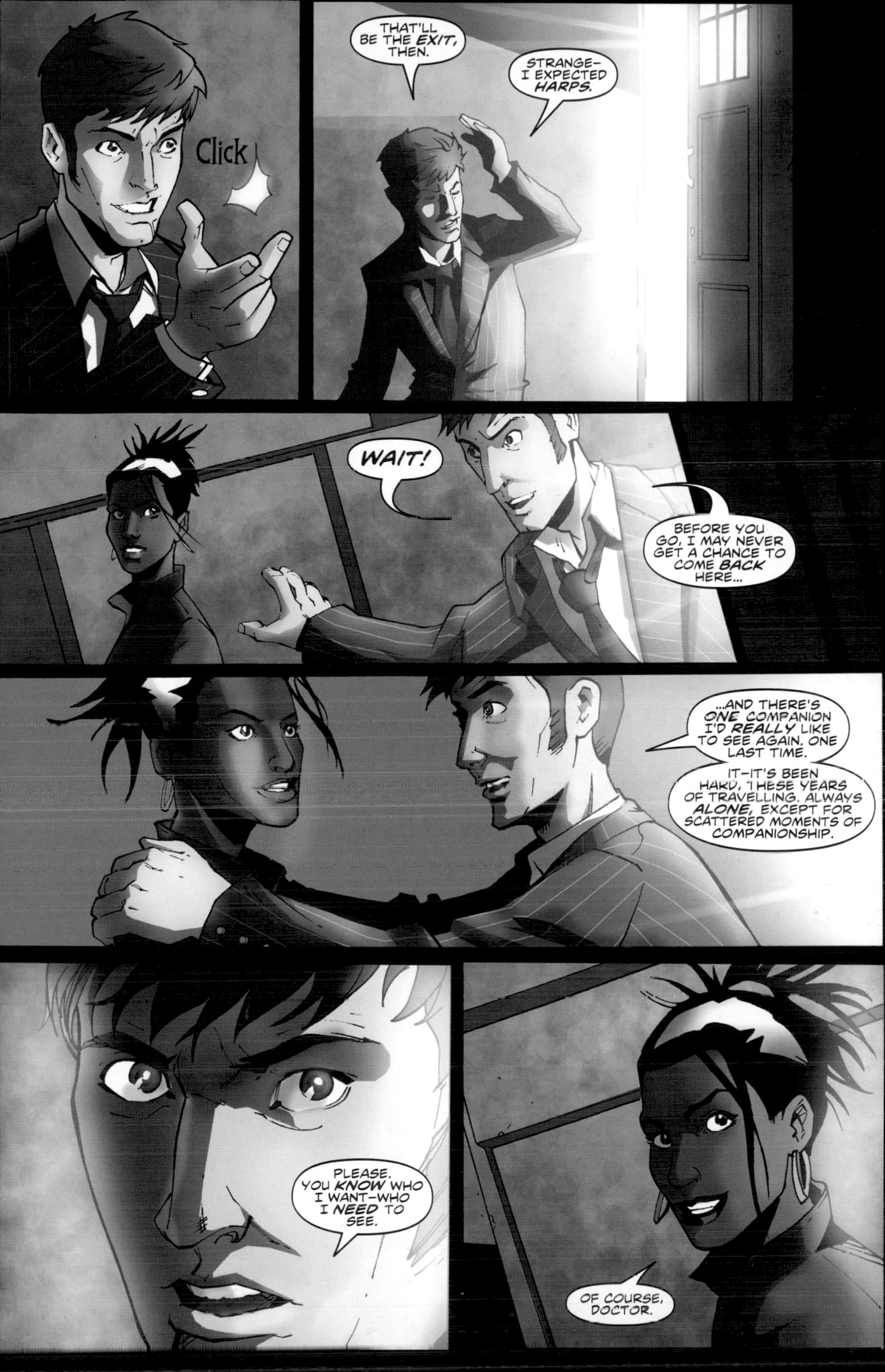
Click
THAT'LL BE THE EXIT, THEN.
STRANGE– I EXPECTED HARPS.
WAIT!
BEFORE YOU GO, I MAY NEVER GET A CHANCE TO COME BACK HERE...
...AND THERE'S ONE COMPANION I'D REALLY LIKE TO SEE AGAIN. ONE LAST TIME.
IT–IT'S BEEN HARD, THESE YEARS OF TRAVELLING. ALWAYS ALONE, EXCEPT FOR SCATTERED MOMENTS OF COMPANIONSHIP.
PLEASE. YOU KNOW WHO I WANT–WHO I NEED TO SEE.
OF COURSE, DOCTOR.

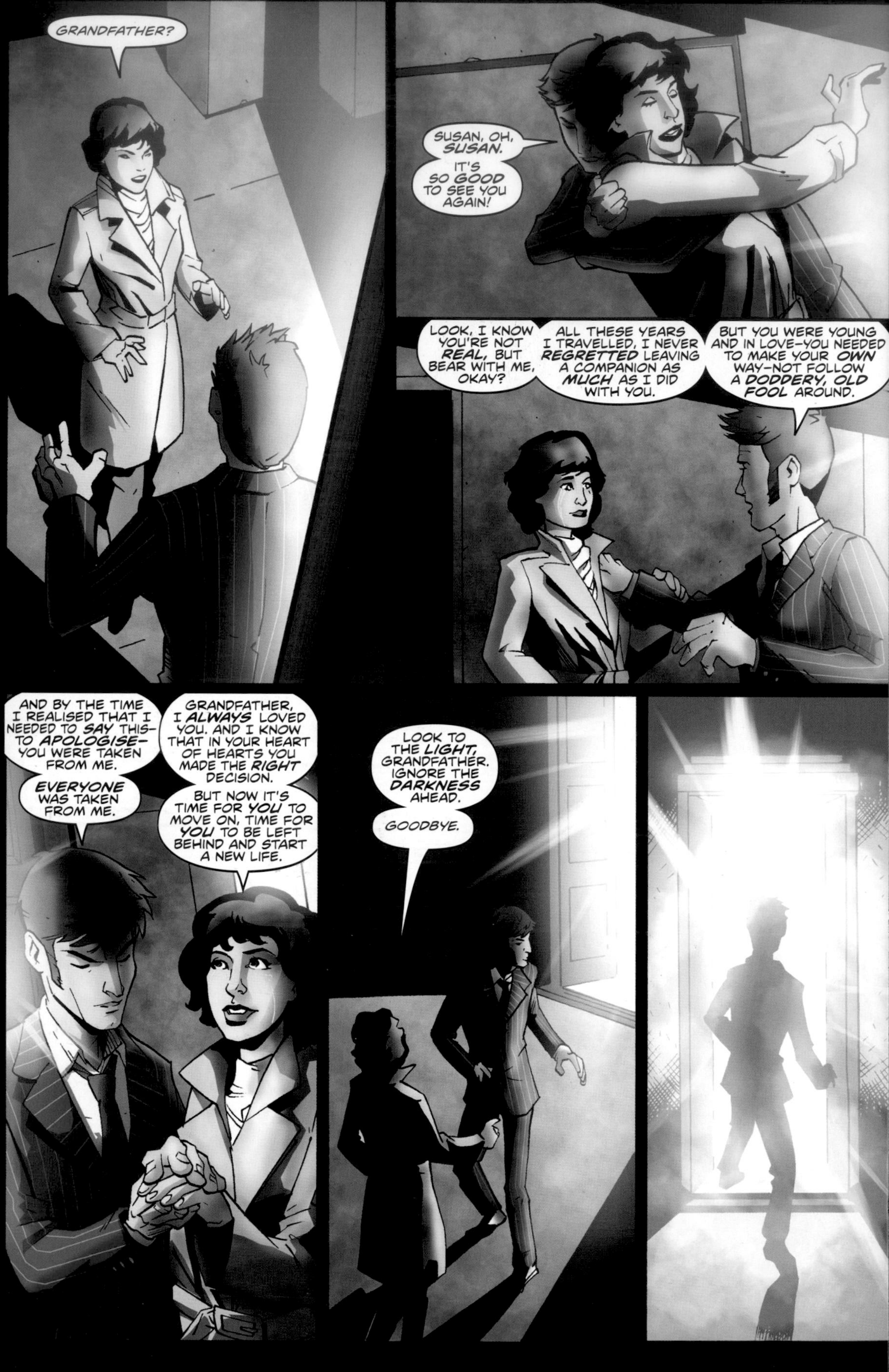
GRANDFATHER?
SUSAN, OH, SUSAN. IT'S SO GOOD TO SEE YOU AGAIN!
LOOK, I KNOW YOU'RE NOT REAL, BUT BEAR WITH ME, OKAY?
ALL THESE YEARS I TRAVELLED, I NEVER REGRETTED LEAVING A COMPANION AS MUCH AS I DID WITH YOU.
BUT YOU WERE YOUNG AND IN LOVE–YOU NEEDED TO MAKE YOUR OWN WAY–NOT FOLLOW A DODDERY, OLD FOOL AROUND.
AND BY THE TIME I REALISED THAT I NEEDED TO SAY THIS–TO APOLOGISE–YOU WERE TAKEN FROM ME.
EVERYONE WAS TAKEN FROM ME.
GRANDFATHER, I ALWAYS LOVED YOU. AND I KNOW THAT IN YOUR HEART OF HEARTS YOU MADE THE RIGHT DECISION.
BUT NOW IT'S TIME FOR YOU TO MOVE ON, TIME FOR YOU TO BE LEFT BEHIND AND START A NEW LIFE.
LOOK TO THE LIGHT, GRANDFATHER. IGNORE THE DARKNESS AHEAD.
GOODBYE.

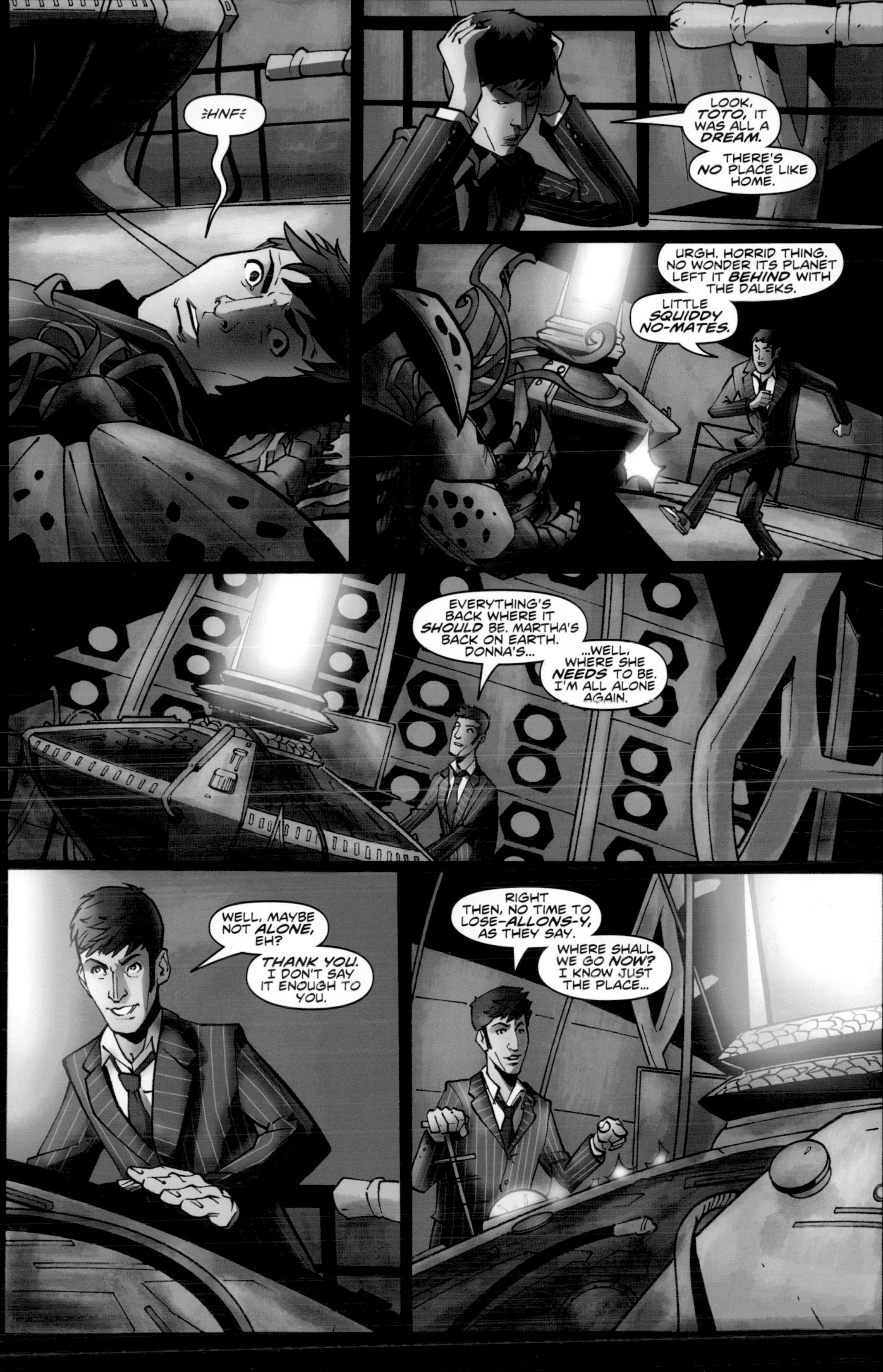
HNF
LOOK, TOTO, IT WAS ALL A DREAM.
THERE'S NO PLACE LIKE HOME.
URGH. HORRID THING. NO WONDER ITS PLANET LEFT IT BEHIND WITH THE DALEKS.
LITTLE SQUIDDY NO-MATES.
EVERYTHING'S BACK WHERE IT SHOULD BE. MARTHA'S BACK ON EARTH. DONNA'S...
...WELL, WHERE SHE NEEDS TO BE. I'M ALL ALONE AGAIN.
WELL, MAYBE NOT ALONE, EH?
THANK YOU. I DON'T SAY IT ENOUGH TO YOU.
RIGHT THEN, NO TIME TO LOSE–ALLONS-Y, AS THEY SAY.
WHERE SHALL WE GO NOW? I KNOW JUST THE PLACE...

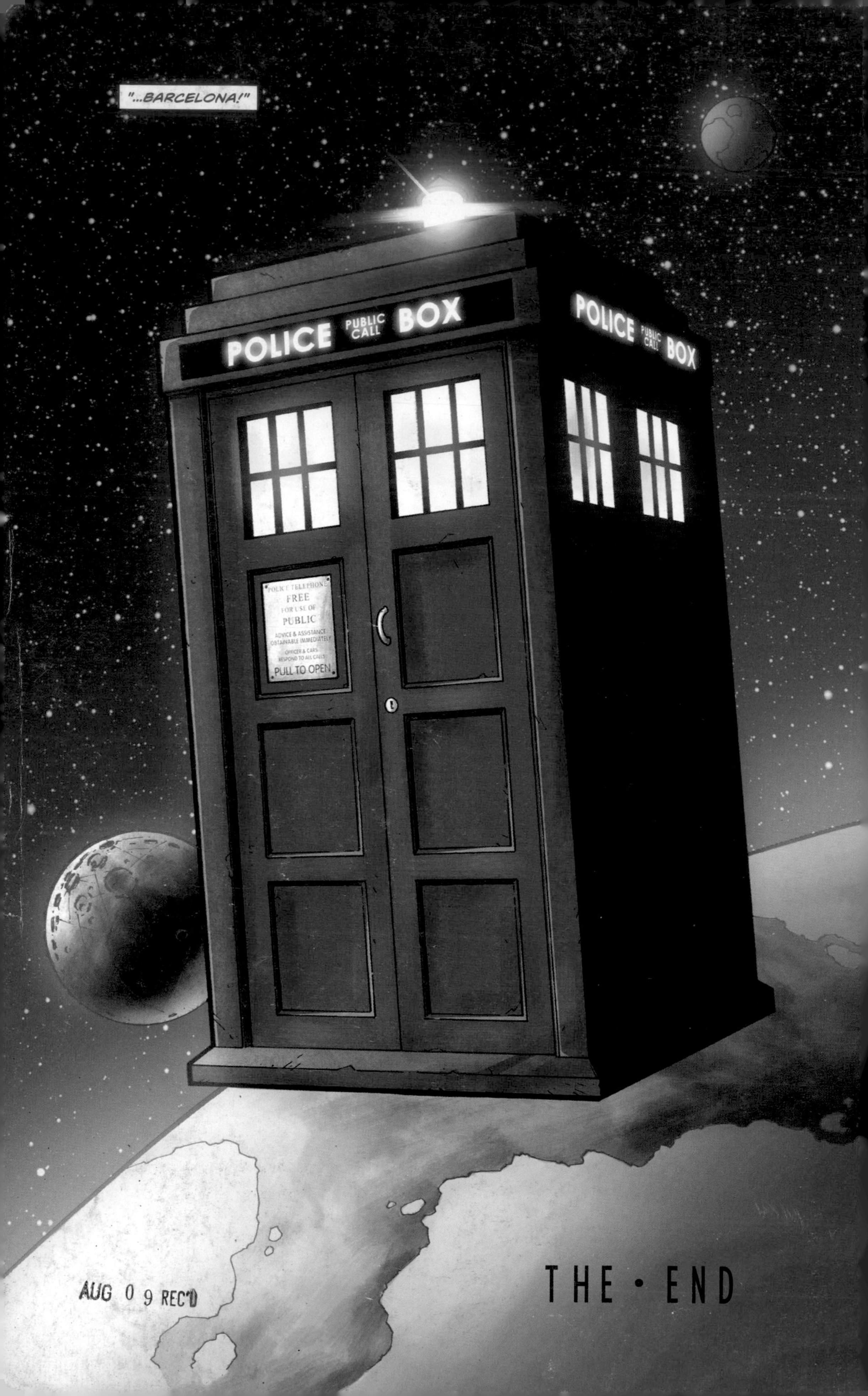
"...BARCELONA!"
POLICE PUBLIC CALL BOX
POLICE PUBLIC CALL BOX
POLICE TELEPHONE
FREE
FOR USE OF
PUBLIC
ADVICE & ASSISTANCE OBTAINABLE IMMEDIATELY
OFFICER & CARS RESPOND TO ALL CALLS
PULL TO OPEN
THE • END